British Romanticism and Denmark

Edinburgh Critical Studies in Romanticism
Series Editors: Ian Duncan and Penny Fielding

Available Titles
A Feminine Enlightenment: British Women Writers and the Philosophy of Progress, 1759–1820
JoEllen DeLucia

Reinventing Liberty: Nation, Commerce and the Historical Novel from Walpole to Scott
Fiona Price

The Politics of Romanticism: The Social Contract and Literature
Zoe Beenstock

Radical Romantics: Prophets, Pirates, and the Space Beyond Nation
Talissa J. Ford

Literature and Medicine in the Nineteenth-Century Periodical Press: Blackwood's Edinburgh Magazine, *1817–1858*
Megan Coyer

Discovering the Footsteps of Time: Geological Travel Writing in Scotland, 1700–1820
Tom Furniss

The Dissolution of Character in Late Romanticism
Jonas Cope

Commemorating Peterloo: Violence, Resilience, and Claim-making during the Romantic Era
Michael Demson and Regina Hewitt

Dialectics of Improvement: Scottish Romanticism, 1786–1831
Gerard Lee McKeever

Literary Manuscript Culture in Romantic Britain
Michelle Levy

Scottish Romanticism and Collective Memory in the British Atlantic
Kenneth McNeil

Romantic Periodicals in the Twenty-First Century: Eleven Case Studies from Blackwood's Edinburgh Magazine
Nicholas Mason and Tom Mole

Godwin and the Book: Imagining Media, 1783–1836
J. Louise McCray

Thomas De Quincey: Romanticism in Translation
Brecht de Groote

Romantic Environmental Sensibility: Nature, Class and Empire
Ve-Yin Tee

Romantic Pasts: History, Fiction and Feeling in Britain and Ireland, 1790–1850
Porscha Fermanis

British Romanticism and Denmark
Cian Duffy

Forthcoming Titles
Romantic Networks in Europe: Transnational Encounters, 1786-1850
Carmen Casaliggi

Romanticism and Consciousness
Richard Sha and Joel Faflak

Death, Blackwood's Edinburgh Magazine and Authoring Romantic Scotland
Sarah Sharp

The Lady's Magazine (1770-1832) and the Making of Literary History
Jennie Batchelor

Mary Wollstonecraft: Cosmopolitan
Laura Kirkley

Seeking Justice: Literature, Law and Equity during the Age of Revolutions
Michael Demson and Regina Hewitt

Remediating the 1820s
Jon Mee and Matthew Sangster

Visit our website at: www.edinburghuniversitypress.com/series/ECSR

British Romanticism and Denmark

Cian Duffy

EDINBURGH
University Press

Edinburgh University Press is one of the leading university presses in the UK. We publish academic books and journals in our selected subject areas across the humanities and social sciences, combining cutting-edge scholarship with high editorial and production values to produce academic works of lasting importance. For more information visit our website: edinburghuniversitypress.com

© Cian Duffy, 2022, 2024

Edinburgh University Press Ltd
The Tun – Holyrood Road
12(2f) Jackson's Entry
Edinburgh EH8 8PJ

First published in hardback by Edinburgh University Press 2022

Typeset in 10.5/13 Adobe Sabon by
IDSUK (DataConnection) Ltd

A CIP record for this book is available from the British Library

ISBN 978 1 4744 9822 7 (hardback)
ISBN 978 1 4744 9823 4(paperback)
ISBN 978 1 4744 9824 1 (webready PDF)
ISBN 978 1 4744 9825 8 (epub)

The right of Cian Duffy to be identified as the author of this work has been asserted in accordance with the Copyright, Designs and Patents Act 1988, and the Copyright and Related Rights Regulations 2003 (SI No. 2498).

Contents

Acknowledgements	vii
Selected Chronology	viii
Introduction: 'The country of our ancestors'	1
1. 'One of the finest capitals of Europe': Some British Romantic Views of Copenhagen	25
2. 'The dwelling-place of a mighty people': Travellers beyond Copenhagen	61
3. 'A mine yet to be explored': Romanticism and Anglo-Danish Literary Exchanges	92
4. 'The brothers of Englishmen': British Reflections on the Danish National Character	127
5. 'No trifling kingdom': Anglo-Danish Politics beyond the Revolutionary and Napoleonic Wars	159
Coda: The 'German' Oehlenschläger	181
Appendices	186
Notes	192
Bibliography	233
Index	242

'Der er et Yndigt Land'
                Adam Oehlenschläger, 'Fædrelands-sang' (1819)

Acknowledgements

Parts of Chapters 2 and 4 were first published on the webpages of the Nordic Association for Romantic Studies (NARS), The Wordsworth Trust and European Romanticisms in Association (ERA, Rêve) and are reproduced here with kind permission. Material from various chapters was first aired at conferences in Bamberg, Brno, Edge Hill and Tromsø. Thanks to organisers Pascal Fischer, Christoph Houswitschka, Gioia Angeletti, Mike Bradshaw, Andy McInnes and Cassandra Falke for the opportunity to speak. The help gleaned from discussion with colleagues at these events is too extensive to enumerate, but special thanks to Christoph Bode, Mark Bruhn, Fred Burwick, Peter Kitson, Nicola Watson and the late Rolf Lessenich for memorably productive responses. Thanks to Michelle Houston, Penny Fielding and Ian Duncan at Edinburgh University Press and to both my anonymous readers for thoughtful feedback. Finally, very special thanks are due to my Danish colleagues and friends in the Nordic Association for Romantic Studies (NARS). Their rich knowledge of Danish Romanticism, and their warm welcome when I arrived in Denmark, contributed more to this book than I could ever possibly identify. Thanks to Karina Lykke Grand, Lone Kølle Martinsen, Lis Møller, Gertrud Oelsner, Robert Rix and Anna Sandberg. Thanks to my parents, Luan and Mary. And thanks to Lisbet, for introducing me to the 'broad beeches' and the 'blue sea belts' of *gamle Danmark*.

Selected Chronology
Britain and Denmark in the long eighteenth century

1694 Publication of Robert Molesworth's *Account of Denmark, as it was in the Year 1692* and Jodocus Crull's *Denmark Vindicated: Being an Answer to a late Treatise called, An Account of Denmark*.

1766 Marriage of Caroline Matilda of Great Britain to Christian VII of Denmark; she is crowned queen of Denmark on 1 May 1767.

1770 Rumours of an affair between Caroline Matilda and Johann Friedrich Struensee, the physician of Christian VII and de facto ruler of the country during the king's illness.

1770 Publication of Thomas Percy's *Northern Antiquities: or, Description of the Manners, Customs, Religion and Laws of the Ancient Danes, and other Northern Nations*, an expanded translation of an earlier work, in French, by Paul Henri Mallet, professor of belles lettres at Copenhagen University.

1772 Caroline Matilda, Struensee and some of his close associates are arrested on charges of plotting to overthrow the monarchy (January); she is imprisoned in Kronborg Castle, at Elsinore (January–March); trial and execution of Struensee (February–April); dissolution of Caroline Matilda's marriage to Christian VII (April); she removes to Celle Castle in the Electorate of Hanover, but must leave her children in Denmark.

1775 Death of Caroline Matilda (10 May); publication of Nathaniel Wraxall's *Cursory Remarks made in a Tour through some of the Northern Parts of Europe*, which is highly critical of Denmark.

1784 Publication of William Coxe's *Travels into Poland, Russia, Sweden and Denmark*.

1796 Publication of Mary Wollstonecraft's *Letters Written during a Short Residence in Sweden, Norway, and Denmark*.

1798 Samuel Taylor Coleridge, in Germany with William and Dorothy Wordsworth, makes a list of contemporary Danish authors in his notebooks (September–October).

1801 The Battle of Copenhagen (2 April). A British naval expeditionary force commanded by Hyde Parker and Horatio Nelson attacks Copenhagen with the aim of disbanding the League of Armed Neutrality (between Denmark–Norway, Sweden and Russia), which has been ignoring the British blockade on French ports. After four hours of intense fighting, Nelson sends a dispatch to Frederik VI of Denmark, addressed 'To the Brothers of Englishmen; the Danes'. A ceasefire is declared and negotiations begin to end Danish participation in the League. British forces take temporary possession of Danish West and East India colonies.

1805 (26 August) The Danish Anglophile and travel writer Andreas Andersen Feldborg meets Lord Nelson in London; the two discuss Feldborg's account of the Battle of Copenhagen in his recently published *Tour in Zealand, in the year 1802* (1805).

1807 The Bombardment of Copenhagen (2–5 September). Concerned that Denmark might ally with Napoleonic France, or that Danish ships of the line could be seized by the French, Britain demands the transfer of the Danish fleet to British control. When Denmark refuses, Britain mounts a land and sea assault, during which Thomas De Quincey's brother, Richard, is taken prisoner. Britain shells Copenhagen using Congreve rockets, causing great destruction and loss of civilian life and forcing a Danish surrender. Denmark is subsequently allied with France, and Britain and Denmark remain at war until 1814. British forces once again take possession of Danish West and East India colonies. The bombardment is extremely controversial, both in Britain and across Europe, and elicits stinging responses from Lord Byron, Percy Bysshe Shelley and many others.

1807 The Danish actor Peter Foersom publishes, at Copenhagen, the first of his Danish translations of the plays of Shakespeare; publication continues until Foersom's death in 1817.

1813 Danish state bankruptcy, triggered by the economic fallout of the war with Britain.

1814   The Treaty of Kiel brings to an end the war between Britain and Denmark. Under the terms of the treaty, Denmark gains formal possession of Greenland but is forced to cede Norway to Swedish control.

1815   The Icelandic scholar Grimur Jónsson Thorkelin, a professor at Copenhagen University, publishes the first print edition of *Beowulf*, prepared from the original manuscript. An earlier version of Thorkelin's work was destroyed, shortly before publication, during the British bombardment of Copenhagen in 1807.

1815   Publication in London of *Poems from the Danish*, edited and translated by Andreas Andersen Feldborg and William Sidney Walker.

1817   The Danish Neoclassical sculptor Bertel Thorvaldsen makes a bust of Lord Byron, who sits for it in Thorvaldsen's studio at Rome. Knud Lyne Rahbek publishes at Copenhagen the first Danish translations of Byron's poetry.

1819   Publication in *The Westmorland Gazette* of Thomas De Quincey's essays arguing for the Danish origins of the dialect spoken in the English Lake District.

1821   *Blackwood's Edinburgh Magazine* begins its 'Horae Danicae' series of articles on contemporary Danish drama; four instalments are published in 1821–2.

1822   De Quincey begins to translate into English Ludvig Holberg's *Niels Klim*, possibly in connection with *Blackwood's* 'Horae Danicae'; De Quincey uses Jens Baggesen's Danish translation rather than Holberg's Latin original as his source.

1824   Publication of Andreas Andersen Feldborg's *Denmark Delineated*.

1826   Publication of George Borrow's *Romantic Ballads, Translated from the Danish*.

1829   The Danish pastor and writer Nikolaj Frederik Severin Grundtvig, whose work played a substantial role in the shaping of modern Denmark and Danish culture in the mid-nineteenth century, makes the first of four visits to England

Introduction: 'the country of our ancestors'

In October 1788, the Scottish traveller Andrew Swinton (1746–1817) sailed in 'dreary weather' around Skagens Odde, the 'low land forming the north point of Jutland'.[1] This, Swinton writes, is 'the Country of our Ancestors', 'the ancient Cimbrica Chersonesus, from which issued that hive of people called the Angles, who conquered England, and gave their name to our country'.[2] Swinton's history and geography are a little out. Almost twenty years earlier, in *Northern Antiquities* (1770), the English antiquarian Thomas Percy (1729–1811) affirmed the theory of Paul Henri Mallet (1730–1807), professor of belles lettres at Copenhagen University, that the 'Danes' who had settled England in the fifth century CE comprised 'a considerable number of Jutes', from northern Jutland, as well as Angles, from the southern part of the peninsula.[3] Historical and geographical vagaries notwithstanding, then, when Swinton described Denmark as 'the country of our ancestors' he was, broadly speaking, correct according to the knowledge of his time. 'Although this people were not yet known by the name of Danes,' Percy had written, 'it is evident, that at least two thirds of the conquerors of Great Britain came from Denmark.'[4] What might be less apparent to a reader today, however, is the extent to which Swinton, in describing Jutland as 'the country of our ancestors', was participating in a burgeoning and multifaceted discourse about Britain and Denmark which gathered force in the latter decades of the eighteenth century. That discourse, which operated across a wide range of different areas of enquiry and genres of cultural productivity, is my subject in this book.

British antiquarian interest in classical Scandinavian culture during the late eighteenth and early nineteenth centuries has, by now, been well documented in both anglophone and Nordic scholarship, although important work in that area continues to be done.[5] The contribution of this so-called 'Antiquarian Revival' to the emergence of new, 'Romantic' themes and modes in British and Danish poetry is also, by now, relatively familiar to scholars of those two national literatures. As Hildor Arnold Barton observes, 'Nordic antiquity exercised a powerful enchantment' for late eighteenth-century readers and writers saturated by Classical themes and Neoclassical forms.[6] British writing about *contemporary* Denmark, however, constitutes a substantial, significant and hitherto largely neglected component of the cultural history of Britain during the late eighteenth and early nineteenth centuries. That it should be so substantial is hardly surprising. The two countries had a tempestuous political relationship during these years, comprising not only the ill-fated marriage of Caroline Matilda (1751–75), sister of George III (1738–1820), to Christian VII of Denmark (1749–1808), but also two British naval assaults on Copenhagen during the Napoleonic Wars, in April 1801 and September 1807 – conflicts which spilled over into Danish territorial possessions in the West and East Indies and which saw Denmark declare a state bankruptcy in 1813. Horatio Nelson (1758–1805), second in command of British forces in April 1801, considered that engagement second only to the Battle of the Nile (1798) in difficulty and strategic significance; Thomas De Quincey (1785–1859), the 'English Opium-Eater', began to learn Danish and to translate Danish literature after his brother, Richard, was taken prisoner of war in 1807. Trade between Britain and Denmark also became 'considerable', as William Rae Wilson (1772–1849) puts it in his *Travels*, in the period covered by *British Romanticism and Denmark*: Wilson estimates British imports from Denmark in 1822 at just over £110,000 and exports at almost £400,000.[7] The work of the celebrated Neoclassical sculptor Bertel Thorvaldsen (1770–1844), whom *Blackwood's Magazine* called 'the Phidias of Denmark', was as well known and sought after in Britain as it was in other countries in Europe – and of course Thorvaldsen produced two enduring material images of British Romanticism still familiar today: his busts of George Gordon, Lord Byron (1788–1824) and Walter Scott (1771–1832).[8]

Driven by the engines of antiquarianism, cultural exchange and contemporary politics, then, British writing about contemporary Denmark flourished between the 1770s and 1820s. Hence the extended account of Copenhagen given in what is today one of the best-known works of British Romantic-period travel writing, Mary Wollstonecraft's (1759–97) *Letters Written during a Short Residence in Sweden, Norway, and Denmark* (1796), was, at the time of its publication, merely one among many such engagements, across many modes, genres and media, from periodicals to panoramas. In recovering and examining British Romantic-period engagements with Denmark, then, *British Romanticism and*

Denmark addresses a vibrant but today relatively unfamiliar aspect of the cultural history of Britain in the late eighteenth and early nineteenth centuries. In doing so, the book also sheds new light on the development of Romanticism and Romantic nationalism in both Britain and Denmark. Although Anglo-Danish relations in these years were marked by political intrigue and armed conflict, British cultural engagements with Denmark tend often to explore not division but, conversely, to insist upon a sense of common 'Northern' values rooted in the classical Scandinavian past. The despatch sent by Nelson to Frederik V of Denmark (1768–1839) at the height of the Battle of Copenhagen in April 1801 – addressed 'to the Brothers of Englishmen; the Danes' – is only the best-known of the many contemporary appeals to this idea of a shared 'Northern' culture which could be marshalled in opposition to the Revolutionary, French 'South'.[9] Cultural geographies based on regional rather than national identities find expression, of course, in a number of high-profile Romantic-period works from around Europe, and most notably, perhaps, in Germaine de Staël's (1776–1817) *De la littérature considérée dans ses rapports avec les institutions sociales* (1799) and *De l'Allemagne* (1813), to which I return later in this introduction. But the particular prevalence of appeals to regional identity in British writing about Denmark, and in at least some Danish writing about Britain, certainly complicates, as I will argue here, received scholarly accounts of the relationship between Romanticism and nationalism in those two countries. A larger aim of *British Romanticism and Denmark*, then, is to suggest that cultural exchange between Britain and Denmark in the late eighteenth and early nineteenth centuries can help us also to refine our understanding of how individual national Romanticisms interacted within and across national borders at the very moment in the history of Europe when those borders were first beginning to be fixed in their modern forms.

Writing in 2004, the Danish critic and historian Peter Mortensen felt it necessary to begin his study of *British Romanticism and Continental Influences* with the reminder that 'the emergence of British Romanticism coincided with a dramatically increased awareness of Continental literature, both on the parts of popular audiences and critical observers'.[10] But the 'enticing' questions posed by this relationship 'are not the kind', Mortensen suggests, 'that Anglo-American critics of Romanticism have traditionally been inclined' to address.[11] Whether or not this was actually the case in 2004, it is certainly true that the last decade has seen, in anglophone scholarship, a widespread resurgence of interest in the study of 'Romanticism' as a European phenomenon, that is to say, in what

René Wellek long ago called 'the unity of European Romanticism', as well as a number of attempts to document how various national Romanticisms from around Europe interacted.[12] 'Continental perspectives', as Diego Saglia puts it in his introduction to *European Literatures in Britain, 1815–1832*, 'are once again at the centre of critical attention.'[13] Part of this work, as Saglia notes, has involved the publication of anthologies whose purpose is to make Romantic-period texts and contexts from across Europe available, in translation, to anglophone readers. Stephen Prickett's thousand-page *European Romanticism: A Reader*, for instance, provides 'historical introductions' to fourteen European national Romanticisms, with essays also on American Romanticism and on the impact of European Romanticisms in Japan, as well as sample texts from across these traditions, grouped into eight thematic sections including 'Art and Aesthetics', 'The Self' and 'Language and Interpretation'. Paul Hamilton's equally monumental *Oxford Handbook of European Romanticism* offers thematic and author-focused essays, grouped under 'Languages' and 'Discourses', covering nine different European national Romanticisms, and addresses themes from natural philosophy to perceptions and representations of Britain in other national literatures. To these studies will soon be added the forthcoming *Cambridge History of European Romantic Literature*, edited by Patrick Vincent, with critical essays on genres, themes and national contexts. Other scholars have taken a more material approach, focusing on specific Romantic-period cultural texts and artefacts. Theodore Ziolkowski's *Stages of European Romanticism*, for example, discusses and compares selected works of art in different media from across Europe in the decades between 1798, the year of *Lyrical Ballads* and Ludwig van Beethoven's (1770–1827) *Sonata Pathétique*, and 1848, which saw the publication of Alexandre Dumas's (1824–95) *La Dame aux camélias* and the first performance of Giuseppe Verdi's (1813–1901) opera *Il Corsaro*, based on Byron's celebrated poem *The Corsair* (1814). While I write – in Copenhagen, still partly locked-down during the COVID-19 pandemic in April 2021 – the most recent instance of this kind of artefactual focus is the *Rêve Virtual Exhibition* hosted by ERA (European Romanticisms in Association), 'showcasing and sharing Romantic texts, objects, and places through collaborations between academic researchers, museums, galleries and other cultural groupings'.[14]

Individually and collectively, these projects bear witness to the remarkable conceptual, formal, medial, geographical and chronological diversity of the cultural texts that we now call 'Romantic'. But they also highlight the myriad problems to which this same diversity gives rise.

Both Hamilton and Prickett, for instance, structure the introductions to their respective anthologies around the enumeration of the various objections which might be made to the very notion of the 'European Romanticism' which they seek to describe for the reader, a notion which has been 'systematically contested', as Hamilton warns in his opening sentence, since the debate between Lovejoy and Wellek in the first half of the twentieth century about the coherence or divergence of national Romanticism(s).[15] Some of these problems are methodological, and 'inevitable', as Prickett recognises, when compiling any anthology.[16] There is, for example, the question of how to decide *which* texts to present as equally and simultaneously representative of both a specific national tradition and a broader, European Romanticism, as well as the attendant difficulty (in some cases at least) of deciding which *parts* of those texts to excerpt for the reader. Then there is the problem of how best to describe or to map the ways in which those individual cultural texts interacted both within and across national borders. One can, for example, adopt the broadly comparative approach taken by Ziolkowski and, at least implicitly, by Hamilton. Alternatively, one can attempt to discover and to document specific material and genetic histories of contact and influence as in, for example, some of the essays in my collection *Romantic Norths: Anglo-Nordic Exchanges, 1770–1842*.[17] Or, rather than focusing on individual cases or types of case, one can, following the approach used by Saglia in *European Literatures in Britain*, attend to wider, 'overarching mechanisms' to describe 'literary internationalism', using 'selected instances of intercultural contact, translation and importation' to 'illuminate different forms of interaction between British and foreign traditions'.[18]

Regardless of the approach chosen, language, as both Hamilton and Prickett emphasise, remains a key factor and potential stumbling-block. On the one hand, any attempt to construct a genetic history of influence during the Romantic period depends, precisely, upon the ability to demonstrate not only the possibility of material access but also of linguistic access, that is to say, that author X could actually have read book Y. On the other hand, those who seek to present European Romantic literature to modern anglophone readers are cast back on the necessity of translation – 'difficult' at the best of times, as Prickett says, but more than usually so when it involves the decoupling of Romantic-period cultural texts from the very national languages whose history and modality those texts often make an explicit formal and thematic concern.[19] Romanticism – as one of the Romantic period's finest translators, Percy Bysshe Shelley (1792–1822), makes clear – is intensely aware of what Shelley calls the 'vanity', in the dual senses of egotism and pointlessness, 'of translation'.[20] 'It were as wise', Shelley says:

> to cast a violet into a crucible that you might discover the formal principle of its color and odour, as seek to transfuse from one language into another the creations of a poet. The plant must spring again from its seed or it will bear no flower – and this is the burthen of the curse of Babel.[21]

Alongside these practical, methodological difficulties involved in the attempt to assemble and present a coherent European Romanticism to a twenty-first-century reader, there are also considerable difficulties involved in the very concept of Romanticism as a European phenomenon. These difficulties, which we might call epistemological, centre on the problem of determining the referent of the term 'European Romanticism'. Silvia Bordoni suggests that we can understand that term to refer to a quantifiable project in the cultural life of the period: 'a consciously constructed network of intellectual and cultural interactions, closely related to, but also independent from, specific national literatures'.[22] Such specificity is hard to establish in practice, however; nor does it seem altogether satisfactory to limit 'European Romanticism' to an identifiable network of intentional contacts and interactions, even if one could identify them all. Rather, used in either a national or international context, we can perhaps understand the term 'Romanticism' – as opposed to the terms 'Romantic' or 'Romantic-period' – to signal the outcome of the complex interaction between cultural texts and historical events in late eighteenth- and early nineteenth-century Europe. What we mean by 'European Romanticism', in other words, is the phenomenon resulting from the interaction of those cultural texts which we call 'Romantic' with the historical events of what we call 'the Romantic period'. Thus defined, 'European Romanticism' seems a term either hopelessly inclusive or else – as the celebrated traveller William Coxe (1748–1828) says of the druids in his *Travels into Poland, Russia, Sweden and Denmark* (1784) – a term under which 'we are too apt to shelter our ignorance'.[23] Despite such difficulties, however, it seems not only perfectly in keeping with common sense but also highly desirable for various reasons – and more so, perhaps, than ever in these days of Brexit and pandemics – to be able to talk about Romanticism as a European phenomenon, to be able to talk about, that is to say, a 'European Romanticism' that we can all recognise when we see it, to adapt Kenneth Clarke's well-known response to Notre-Dame in his BBC television series *Civilization* (1969). 'Romanticism', as Aidan Day long ago put it, 'was a European phenomenon.'[24]

In his essay on 'Europe' in Nicholas Roe's collection *Romanticism: An Oxford Guide* (2005), Christoph Bode some time ago suggested, with characteristic perspicacity, that we might resolve many of the difficulties arising from the 'similarities and discrepancies' of Romantic-period cultural texts with origins in different national traditions simply by remembering that the term 'Romanticism' does not refer to any concrete historical phenomenon but is, rather, 'a *construct* (a concept we have developed because we have reason to believe it is useful as a *tool*)'.[25] The 'similarities and discrepancies' of Romantic-period cultural texts 'need not worry us', Bode continues, 'if we reconceptualize European Romanticism as a *set of responses*, highly differentiated and at times downright contradictory, to a historically-specific *challenge*: the challenge of the ever-accelerating modernization of European society'.[26] What Bode calls 'family likenesses' between cultural texts from different national Romanticisms are, then, inevitable because those texts have 'common roots in that they form diverging responses to the same set of cultural challenges'.[27] Hence it is not necessary, Bode concludes, to attempt to pinpoint genetic histories of contact or influence when discussing how or why 'individual European writers came up with surprisingly similar solutions to the political, poetical, and philosophical problems that defined the era'.[28]

Various inflections of the relationship to which Bode points here – that is to say, of the connection between 'the modernization of European society' and the 'problems that defined' the Romantic period – have been tracked and documented by scholars and there is general consensus now that 'Romanticism', as Hamilton puts it, 'was implicated in the creation of modern Europe'.[29] Particular attention has been paid, in this respect, to the connection between Romanticism and nationalism: to the idea that nationalism (at least in its modern form) is fundamentally a 'Romantic' phenomenon and that many nation states (in Europe at least) can trace their modern form back to the historical events of the Romantic period. As I argue in my introduction to *Romantic Norths*, academic studies of Romantic nationalism, such as Joep Leersen's seminal *National Thought in Europe*, have often tended to present it as premised primarily upon interiority, that is to say upon the definition of national and cultural identity through the demarcation of difference from other nations and cultures. Hence, according to Leerssen, 'Romantic nationalism' considers:

> nations as natural human categories, each defined in its individual identity by a transcendent essence, each self-perpetuating that identity transgenerationally through history, each deserving of its own self-determination. Each nation has a natural or moral right to be incorporated in its own state, while conversely every state should incorporate the natural, organic solidarity of its proper constituent nation.[30]

In Leerssen's analysis, the Revolutionary and Napoleonic Wars were the main triggers for the emergence of this kind of Romantic nationalism, thus understood 'as the articulation and instrumentalization of collective self-images, derived from an opposition against different, other nations'.[31]

Many influential academic histories of individual national Romanticisms have made similar arguments about the role of interiority and difference in the articulation of national identity during the Romantic period. Indeed, on this view of things, Romanticism is what makes nationalism national, and nationalism is what makes Romanticism 'Romantic'. Romantic nationalism succeeds the historical moment described by Colin Kidd in which (in the British context at least) 'identities were not exclusively determined by ethnicity, nor were ethnic identities crudely confined by national categories'.[32] Hence, Linda Colley's *Britons*, for instance, traces to the eighteenth century and Romantic period what Colley calls the 'forging' of a new sense of Britishness, visible in various genres and modes of cultural productivity, and defined through the assertion of difference from France, Italy and other European nations.[33] More recently, Mortensen, in *British Romanticism and Continental Influences*, points to what he sees as the pivotal role of what he calls a 'discourse of Romantic Europhobia' which 'construed European literature as an overwhelming menace to Britain's moral and political health'.[34] Citing, among other examples, William Wordsworth's (1770–1850) well-known condemnation of 'sickly and stupid German tragedies' in the 1802 Preface to *Lyrical Ballads*, Mortensen argues that 'one should not underestimate the extent to which some of the most prominent [British] Romantic writers construed their own public reputations in explicit opposition to [. . .] foreign writers' and 'confronted and exploited this menacing otherness in their own writings'.[35] And, in a Scandinavian context, histories of the Swedish 'Age of Liberty' [Frihetstiden] and the Danish 'Golden Age' [Guldalder] routinely link those great flowerings of national cultural productivity to a diminished international status and loss of territory and a consequent turning inwards towards national histories and motifs.[36]

Of late, however, scholars have begun increasingly to question the adequacy of describing Romanticism in national terms or of speaking of distinct, national Romanticisms. Stephen Prickett, for example, following a path first laid out by works like Katie Trumpener's *Bardic Nationalism* and Murray Pittock's *Scottish and Irish Romanticism*, has recently pointed again to 'the problem of Nationalism *within* the United Kingdom', asking how one might negotiate the relationship between English, Welsh, Scottish and Irish Romanticisms, and the idea of an overarching *British* Romanticism.[37] Saglia, in the same vein, stresses the need to understand 'literature in the British Isles' during the Romantic period as 'a reticulation of competing and intersecting national traditions'.³⁸ Similar interrogations of the description of Romanticism in national(ist) terms are visible in recent studies of the relationship between British and European writing during the late eighteenth and early nineteenth centuries. Indeed, even Peter Mortensen grants that for all its ostensible 'Europhobia', British Romantic-period writing often 'assimilates' European cultural texts, with the effect that 'Continental pre-Romanticism [. . .] is never simply conquered or subordinated' but 'survives and is carried forward, in spectral secondary traces'.³⁹ Most recently, Diego Saglia, whose work focuses on the two decades following the end of the Napoleonic Wars, 'tests the still influential notion of an intrinsically insular British cultural sphere', in a period which, he says, marked 'a significant turning point in the history of the international connections of English and British literature'.⁴⁰ Using a paradigm of 'cultural translation' with its roots in the work of Bourdieu and Foucault, Saglia maps 'how foreign works and ideas made their way into Britain, how they were discussed, circulated, recycled, and reworked, and in which material and ideological contexts these forms of reception developed'.⁴¹

As many of these scholars note, there are, of course, precedents for such interrogations of the national bases of Romanticism to be found in the Romantic period itself, in cultural texts from many different national traditions. Such precedents might be said to exhibit two primary, albeit very often overlapping positions. First, we have those Romantic-period works which assert a teleological, cosmopolitan understanding of 'literature' as a mode of cultural productivity which develops across national and cultural boundaries, the best-known instance of which is certainly Johann Wolfgang von Goethe's (1749–1832) concept of *Weltliteratur* [world literature]. In a specifically British context, we might think, here, of the assessment by Thomas De Quincey in his essay on 'Jean Paul Friedrich Richter' in the *London Magazine* for December 1821, of how the 'youth and vigour' of contemporary German literature could rejuvenate a flagging English letters.⁴² De Quincey – whose familiarity with Danish literature and speculations about the Danish origins of the Westmorland dialect I discuss in Chapter 3 – is certainly writing back, here, against (among other things) the condemnation of 'sickly and stupid German tragedies' by William Wordsworth in his 'Preface' to *Lyrical Ballads*. But the terms of De Quincey's rebuttal are instructive. Noting 'that the Golden Pippin is now almost, if not quite, extinct in England [. . .] for want of some exotic, but congenial, inoculation', De Quincey goes on to affirm that 'so it is with literatures of whatsoever land; unless crossed by some other of different breed, they all tend to superannuation'.⁴³

De Quincey points quite precisely, here, to the idea that individual national literatures develop and advance through 'exotic, but congenial, inoculation' by other national literatures, using a botanical analogy to confirm that the 'youth and vigour' of any one national literature can only be sustained when writers 'engraft' influences from others. In such an analysis, then, the distinctiveness of any individual national literature becomes increasingly difficult to identify, just as De Quincey (as we shall see in Chapter 3) would argue that the supposedly native English dialect spoken in Westmorland and valorised by Wordsworth as the 'language really used by men' was in fact a hybrid of Danish.[44]

Alongside texts like De Quincey's, which call into question the idea of distinctly *national* literatures, we have other Romantic-period cultural texts which argue for the existence of regional cultures which transcend contemporary national, political and geographical boundaries. As noted, the best-known examples of such paradigms for regional cultures can be found in the work of Germaine de Staël. In the 'General Observations' with which she opens *De l'Allemagne*, which was translated twice into English in the year of its publication, for example, de Staël insists that 'the origin of the principal nations of Europe may be traced to three great distinct families: the Latin, the German, and the Sclavonic'.[45] Of more immediate relevance to my purposes here, however, is the discussion 'Of the Literature of the North' which de Staël included in her earlier *De la littérature considerée dans ses rapports avec les institutions sociales*, which was translated into English in 1812 as *The Influence of Literature Upon Society*.

De Staël begins her account 'Of the Literature of the North' by asserting the existence of regional literatures which transcend national borders. 'There appear to be two distinct kinds of literature still extant', she says:

> one derived from the east, the other from the north; the origin of the first may be traced to Homer, that of the last to Ossian. The Greeks, the Latins, the Italians, the Spanish, and the French of the century of Louis XIV, belong to that style of literature which I shall call Eastern. The works of the English and German, with some of the Danish and Swedish writings, may be classed as the literature of the North.[46]

A twenty-first-century reader might find much that is puzzling, perhaps even disconcerting, in the cultural lineages and boundaries which de Staël proposes here, and not least in her assumptions about Ossian and Homer.[47] Be that as it may, what I want particularly to notice is that de Staël groups England, Germany and the Nordic countries together as representative of a common 'Northern' literature which, in her analysis, is diametrically opposed to another literature which she calls 'Eastern', although it is geographically southern and formally Classical and Neoclassical. For de Staël, this 'Northern' literature is essentially vernacular rather than cosmopolitan, albeit being still a literature which crosses national boundaries. 'The English as well as the Germans', she writes:

> have without doubt often imitated the ancients [i.e. Classical Greek and Roman authors], and drawn very useful lessons from that fruitful study; but their original beauties carry a sort of resemblance, a certain poetic grandeur, of which Ossian is the most splendid example.[48]

In order to explain this cultural 'resemblance' across such a wide territorial range, de Staël points to 'the climate' as 'one of the principal causes of the difference between the images that pleased in the North and those which were admired in the East' (notwithstanding the fact that the 'climate' is in reality quite diverse both within and across the nations which de Staël combines as 'Northern').[49] Anticipating De Quincey's botanical analogy about the 'strength and vigour' of German literature, de Staël attributes 'the vivid imagination of the people of the North' directly to the struggle to transcend 'the boundaries of a world whose confines they inhabited', 'where the prospects of nature had almost unbounded influence over them; but it affected them as it appeared in their climate, always dark and gloomy'.[50] In this harsh environment, de Staël concludes, 'independence was the sole happiness of the Northern nations' and hence 'Northern poetry', to a much greater degree than 'the Eastern', is the product of 'the minds of a free people'.[51] 'Long before the theory of constitutions', she writes:

> and the advantages of a representative government were known in England, the warlike spirit which shone with so much enthusiasm in the Erse and Scandinavian poetry, inspired man with a prodigious idea of his own strength and the power of his will.[52]

The problematic racial-cultural assumptions which inform de Staël's thinking here, and, in particular, the distinction which she draws between the free-spirited inhabitants of 'the North' and those of 'the East', whom, she says, 'were much more easily subdued to slavery', are, of course, not untypical of eighteenth-century and Romantic-period debates about national and racial character, to which I return in Chapter 4.[53] Whatever issues we might find with the specific form that it takes, or with the manner in which it is expressed, though, de Staël's paradigm of regional, vernacular cultural identities which transcend modern national borders is certainly capable of providing us with a new way of mapping the relationship between individual national Romanticisms and the idea of an overarching European Romanticism to which those traditions contribute. For the more immediate purposes of *British Romanticism and Denmark*, however, de Staël's assertion of a 'Northern' culture which transcends national boundaries is highly revealing – because British late eighteenth-century and Romantic-period writing about modern Denmark is often characterised precisely by the attempt to articulate and to interrogate the notion of a shared Anglo-Danish culture rooted in the natural freedoms of the classical Scandinavian past. Hence, by recovering and examining British Romantic-period writing about Denmark, this book not only illuminates a neglected aspect of the relationship between nationalism and Romanticism in the cultural history of late eighteenth- and early nineteenth-century Britain. Rather, *British Romanticism and Denmark* also contributes to the ongoing scholarly investigation of European Romanticism by revealing a largely unstudied 'regional' Romanticism which transcended national and political borders in a period of armed conflict between the two countries involved.

Academic studies of the relationship between British Romanticism and other European national Romanticisms have not, in the main, had a great deal to say about the Nordic countries but have tended to focus, rather, on Central European and Mediterranean traditions. Saglia's discussion of *European Literatures in Britain, 1815–1832*, for instance, is concerned only with French, German, Italian and Spanish literatures (breaking notably and instructively across Germaine de Staël's northern–eastern dichotomy), while Michael Ferber's *Companion to European Romanticism* (2005) makes no mention of the Scandinavian countries at all. This tendency is, of course, neither surprising nor especially problematic on its own terms. After all, as I argue in my introduction to *Romantic Norths*, such histories have most often, and for good reasons, looked 'south and east for influences – following a pathway of adaptation or appropriation encoded in terms like "Augustan", "neoclassical", "Gothic", "Oriental", and of course "Romantic" itself'.[54] Otherwise, scholarly studies of British interest in Scandinavia in the late eighteenth and early nineteenth centuries have concentrated for the most part, as noted, on the Antiquarian Revival, or else on engagements with the High North and the Arctic, as in Angela Byrne's *Geographies of the Romantic North* and Robert Rix's forthcoming study of British Romantic-period responses to Greenland.

The essays in my collection *Romantic Norths* sought to redress this comparative lack of attention by retrieving and examining the 'thriving and diverse' modes of cultural exchange between Britain and Scandinavia during the late eighteenth century and Romantic period.[55] As I noted in my introduction to *Romantic Norths*, however, our efforts there drew considerably on the earlier work of those scholars (many of them based in the Nordic countries) who have, over the last decades, attended to various aspects of the cultural relationships between Britain and Scandinavia, and, in particular, to the emergence and valorisation of the idea of 'the North' in British and Nordic national Romanticisms. In *Northbound*, for example, Karen Klitgaard Povlsen identifies the late eighteenth and early nineteenth century as 'a central period' for the emergence of modern conceptions of 'the North', while Robert Rix, in his introduction to a special Nordic-themed issue of *European Romantic Review*, highlights the role played by 'the transnational flow of influences between the Nordic countries and beyond' in 'the central concerns' of national Romanticisms in Scandinavia.[56]

Such scholarship has borne ample testimony, in other words, to the validity of Peter Fjågesund's call for 'a macro-cultural perspective on a region that is not normally treated as a distinct unit', but also to the various tensions involved in the construction of 'the North', at the time, as an imagined geospatial unit, both within the Nordic countries and beyond them.[57] As Hendriette Kliemann-Geisinger observes, 'throughout time the North has symbolized different regions with shifting extensions, the particular definition depending on the context and the viewpoint, the intention and the interests of the observer'.[58] 'The North', in other words, is not a stable configuration during the period covered by *British Romanticism and Denmark*: ideas both about *what* 'the North' represented and *where* 'the North' could be found were highly variable and frequently contested at the time. In their collection *The Cultural Construction of Norden*, for example, Øystein Sørensen and Bo Stråth chart the emergence within nineteenth-century Scandinavia of a relatively coherent idea of the *Sonderweg*, or *special path*, taken by emergent nationalisms in Denmark, Norway and Sweden: 'a particular inflection of the Enlightenment', readily distinguishable 'in comparison with the rest' of Europe, 'which provoked not revolution but just enlightenment', which 'had the peasant as its foremost symbol', which was rooted in 'rural' and agricultural rather than 'urban' spheres, and which gave birth to the modern, social-democratic Nordic model.[59] Outside Scandinavia, however, the emergence of a new, 'Romantic' configuration of 'the North' as a transnational, geospatial region, often imaginatively overdetermined, is usually traced back to de Staël's *Of Germany* in particular, and to the work of others in her circle at Coppet more generally, and the forging of the idea of a Northern European culture, with Germany at its centre, comprising the Scandinavian countries, Iceland, Greenland, Britain, the Netherlands and even Switzerland. This 'Romantic' construction of 'the North', as Fjågesund and others have observed, formed a 'contentious and dialectic bond' with 'the South', 'which is broadly understood as Mediterranean', and played a key role in the 'cultural development' of Europe both during the Romantic period and since, manifesting, for example, in a rejection of (Neo)classicism in British and Scandinavian cultural texts during the late eighteenth and early nineteenth centuries.[60] It also had a number of discernible impacts on the emergence of nationalism in Romantic-period Britain: Hildor Arnold Barton, Mark Davies, Peter Fjågesund and Ruth Symes, for example, have all written about the representation of Britain and the Nordic countries in British eighteenth-century and Romantic-period travel writing, and all emphasise how descriptions of 'the North' played an important role in British 'self-perception' and the 'growth of a national British identity', as Fjågesund and Symes put it.[61] Penny Fielding, in a similar vein, examines how Romantic-period representations of Scotland partook of 'modes and structures that produced a geography of the north for British subjects and also enveloped the nation in wider European and global geographies'.[62] Such representations, Fielding shows, facilitated a process by which 'Britain emerges as a northern nation' as part of a cultural shift 'from the Classical south to a growing interest in the origins of British culture in primitive, northern European tribes'.[63]

Absent from this substantial body of scholarship on constructions of 'the North' and their influence on the emergence of Romanticism and Romantic nationalisms in Britain and the Nordic countries, however, has been any real attention to British eighteenth-century and Romantic-period engagements with contemporary Denmark and contemporary Danish culture. This omission is all those more striking when we remember the fractious political relations between the two countries during the period covered by *British Romanticism and Denmark* and the widespread and varied engagement with Denmark in British cultural texts from that time. A recurrent focus of *British Romanticism and Denmark*, then, is the tension, often visible in British responses to Denmark, between, on the one hand, the desire to document the realities of that country's culture and politics, and, on the other hand, the need to locate Denmark within the shifting, ideological and often highly imaginative investment in the nascent 'Romantic' idea of 'the North'. That tension is clearly visible, for example, in many of the responses to what is certainly the seminal British response to Denmark in the long eighteenth century: Robert Molesworth's (1656–1725) *Account of Denmark, as it was in the Year 1692* (1694), which reached multiple posthumous editions by the 1790s.

Molesworth, an Irish Williamite and Whig, was the English ambassador to Denmark from 1689 to 1692. His *Account*, which was first published anonymously, is less concerned with topographical description than with the social, political and economic condition of Denmark, which had established an absolute monarchy under Frederik III (1609–70) in 1660 and which was therefore, in theory at least, one of the most authoritarian states in Europe. Molesworth, it is fair to say, is unwaveringly damning in his appraisal, and it is no wonder that he chose to omit his name from the first edition of his *Account*, even though his posting as ambassador had ended. I return throughout *British Romanticism and Denmark*, and in Chapter 5 in particular, to various strands of Molesworth's arguments and subsequent responses to them, so for now an overview should suffice. In brief, Molesworth represents the Danish political system as a 'disease' from which the entire country suffers.[64] The common labourers and peasants, he says, 'are all as absolute slaves as the negroes are in Barbadoes, but with this difference, that their fare is not so good'.[65] Even the aristocracy 'prefer gilded slavery to coarse domestic liberty'.[66] Danes are apparently 'mean-spirited [and] inclined to gross cheating, and to suspect that others have a design to cheat them', and are 'much addicted to drinking' and, apparently, 'extremely addicted to gardening' (!).[67] The Danish language 'is very ungrateful, and not unlike the Irish in its whining complaining tone'.[68] There are 'only two seasons of the year, winter and summer', so 'you immediately leap from extremity of heat to extremity of cold', and Copenhagen, the capital, is in summer 'constantly troubled with the plague of flies'.[69] Molesworth, we must assume, had a splendid time during his tenure as ambassador!

On a more serious note, however, three central strands of Molesworth's *Account* are of major interest to *British Romanticism and Denmark*. First is the extent to which Molesworth consistently represents the Danish political system as government 'after the Turkish manner': the Danes, he argues, suffer 'most of the Mischiefs of a Turkish Government in an infinitely worse climate'.[70] Molesworth's Denmark, in other words, despite its geographical position, is an Oriental 'Other', exemplary of the kind and the consequences of despotic rule routinely associated by English writers at the time with the Ottoman Empire, which was still a major political contestant, in the seventeenth century, of England and other European states. Second is Molesworth's insistence that modern Danish polity contrasts markedly with 'how great the rights of the people were' under what he calls 'the antient form of government in this kingdom': a much more liberal 'form' which, he says, 'continued with very little interruption' until the establishment of the absolute monarchy in 1660.[71] This 'antient form', Molesworth argues, 'was the same which the Goths and Vandals established in most, if not all, parts of Europe [. . .] and which in England is retained to this day for the most part'.[72] And its decline Molesworth attributes unhesitatingly to the influence of the French: Denmark, he laments, 'has often had the misfortune to be governed by French counsels'.[73] Third is Molesworth's tendency to use Denmark as an object lesson for England and the kind of polity which England should avoid at all costs, visible in his observation that England still retains a more progressive form of government with its roots in the classical Scandinavian past. His *Account* is replete from the outset with suggestions that 'an Englishman should be shewn the misery of the enslaved parts of the world, to make him in love with the happiness of his own country' – and Denmark serves him as a case in point.[74]

From Molesworth's *Account*, then, emerges an image of modern Denmark as a despotic, Oriental state which, despite a shared culture in the past, has now suffered a decline and fall into the political and social 'Other' of England.[75] This image has surprising longevity in a wide range of cultural texts from the period covered by *British Romanticism and Denmark*. Mary Wollstonecraft's condemnation, in her *Letters Written during a Short Residence*, of the 'men' in Copenhagen whom she felt were 'domestic tyrants' ('fathers, brothers, or husbands', 'men of business') is very much in that vein.[76] Indeed, as we shall see in Chapter 5, as late as 1824, the Danish traveller, editor and Anglophile Andreas Andersen Feldborg (1782–1838) – a largely forgotten figure about whose work I have much to say in *British Romanticism and Denmark* – still felt the need to argue, in his compendium *Denmark Delineated*, that Molesworth's strictures were 'no longer extensively applicable' to his country.[77]

Longevity notwithstanding, however, Molesworth's *Account* was controversial and contested from the outset. Indeed, only a few months after *An Account* was published, the German-born writer Jodocus Crull (1660–1713) offered a detailed, point-by-point refutation in *Denmark Vindicated* (1694), arguing that Molesworth's book was neither 'true' nor 'impartial', but rather a deliberate attempt to 'misrepresent the State' and full of 'extravagancies and groundless assertions'.[78] Particularly problematic in Crull's opinion is what he calls 'the gross and unaccountable Comparison' which Molesworth 'made betwixt the Northern parts of the World and the Turkish Government'.[79] So outlandish, indeed, did Crull find Molesworth's *Account* to be that he suspects (taking a hint from Molesworth himself) that the real intention of the work cannot have been to give an accurate account of Denmark but rather to give an object lesson in the kind of polity which England should avoid, 'that the Author did not intend to give us a just account [. . .] but under a Romantick Cover of Arbitrary Power, to represent Tyranny in its worst shape to the English Nation'.[80]

The first significant *eighteenth-century* rebuttal of Molesworth's *Account*, made by Joseph Marshall (dates unknown) in his *Travels*

(1772), observes politely that, while Molesworth's 'book has been transcribed over and over again by every author that has written any thing concerning Denmark', Molesworth's information is, to say the least, out of date:

> almost every circumstance to be gathered from that writer, is changed essentially since his time; insomuch, that although his book is a very able performance, yet it is little more than an old almanack for turning to, to gain information of the present times.[81]

A key tranche of Marshall's argument, which he supports by a lengthy (and quite possibly fictional) account of a discussion with a Danish aristocrat on whose Jutland estate he says he stayed for some days, is that, although Denmark is in fact an absolute monarchy and may well have been despotic in Molesworth's day, the present government is, in practice, actively benevolent and improving. 'I do not apprehend', Marshall insists, 'that there is a kingdom in Europe in which greater changes have been made.'[82] 'The throne of Denmark', he assures the reader, has, of late years, been filled with three or four very able princes, who have shewn, in every department of the state, such a spirited conduct, with so much attention to the welfare of their subjects', although he does wonder what the condition of the people would be 'under a weak or a wicked Prince, or even under a negligent one'.[83] As currently governed, then, Marshall sees Denmark not so much as an object lesson for England in the ills of despotism, but rather as a country which actually reminds him of England: he describes, for instance, a countryside 'cultivated, with great numbers of farm houses and cottages, the inhabitants of which seemed as easy, chearful, and happy, as if they had been resident in England'.[84]

In Marshall's writing back against Molesworth's *Account*, then, we can discern some of the key features of the British eighteenth-century and Romantic-period discourse about Denmark which I recover and examine in *British Romanticism and Denmark*. As we shall see in Chapter 5, Marshall's cautious but clear distinction between the theory and practice of absolutist rule in Denmark (which remained an absolute monarchy until 1848) finds many analogues in later writing across different modes and genres. What we can also see exemplified in Marshall's *Travels*, however, is the beginning of a shift away from the representation of Denmark as an Oriental 'Other' and towards an image of Denmark as 'intimately allied to England, in ancient blood and language', as the botanist and poet William Herbert (1778–1847) put it in December 1803, when dedicating his *Select Icelandic Poetry*

(1804) to Carsten Anker (1747–1824), the director of the Danish Asia Company at Copenhagen.[85] This new understanding of Denmark and England as 'allied' by a common, 'Northern' culture with its roots in the classical Scandinavian past is my subject in *British Romanticism and Denmark*: its history, its cultural significance, and its implications for our understanding of the relationship between Romanticism and Romantic nationalism in the two countries.

British Romanticism and Denmark starts in Copenhagen, from where I write. As the capital of Denmark and a major international port, Copenhagen was an important destination in its own right for British eighteenth-century and Romantic-period travellers, but it was also a key transit-point on the route to and from Norway and Sweden. 'The beaten track', as Barton says, 'consisted generally of the triangle connecting Copenhagen, Christiania [Oslo], and Stockholm.'[86] Hence, almost all British travellers who went to Scandinavia have at least something to say about Copenhagen, which came to be widely regarded as 'the best built city of the north', as Coxe put it in his *Travels*.[87] As I show in Chapter 1, British writing about the city in many respects functions as a barometer of changing attitudes to Denmark. While earlier travellers see everywhere signs of despotism and neglect, towards the end of the eighteenth century and in the early nineteenth century, British visitors increasingly emphasise the architectural, cultural and social richness of the city – except, of course, for Mary Wollstonecraft, who (as we shall see) seems to go out of her way to dislike the place. British writing about Copenhagen also sheds interesting light on the emergence of 'Romantic' constructions of 'the North' and the concomitant Romanticising of Denmark in the British imagination: the city, which is more or less on the same latitude as Edinburgh, is often talked about as if it were in the Arctic, at least by those who had not actually been there.

Copenhagen, of course, became a particular focus point of British writing about Denmark in the wake of the two British attacks on the city, in April 1801 and September 1807. The latter, in which newly developed incendiary Congreve rockets were used against the city, proved particularly controversial both in Britain and internationally, with Byron, for example, citing it as an instance of 'perfidious Albion' in *The Curse of Minerva* (1813):

> Look to the Baltic – blazing from afar,
> Your old Ally yet mourns perfidious war.
> Not to such deeds did Pallas lend her aid,
> Or break the compact which herself had made;[88]

Byron's characterisation of Denmark as an 'old Ally' which Britain has now betrayed typifies how British attitudes to Denmark had shifted in the late eighteenth century from the perception of the country as an Oriental other towards a sense of common culture. As I show in Chapter 1, the first British attack on Copenhagen, in April 1801, played (paradoxically enough) a key role in the cementing of that new idea of Northern 'brothers' with a common and real enemy in the French. Following the Danish defeat in 1807, Britain aided her 'old Ally' to an extent by establishing the neutrality of Iceland and the Faroe Islands, both technically Danish territories, which made it possible for trade with Denmark to continue, even if the expenses and privations of the war forced Denmark (as noted) to declare state bankruptcy in 1813. And 'perfidy' surfaced again following the defeat of Napoleon (1769–1805) with the signing of the Treaty of Kiel (1814), which brought the war between Britain and Denmark to an end: under the terms of the treaty, Denmark was given formal possession of Greenland, but forced to cede Norway, which had great cultural and economic importance, to Sweden. Murray's *Hand-Book for Travellers in Denmark, Norway, Sweden, and Russia* (1829) looked back on the treaty, from the safe distance of fifteen years, as 'a death blow to the prosperity of Denmark, and a transaction but little respectable to England'.[89] 'When Norway, bound to the Danish Crown by a close connection of centuries, and the strong affection of a free people for the king they personally loved, was at once torn away', the *Hand-Book* continues, 'and without equivalent as without pretext, handed over to the Swedes, the national spirit of the Danes received a shock from which it is little likely to recover.'[90]

In Chapter 1 we also meet for the first time a key figure in *British Romanticism and Denmark*: Andreas Andersen Feldborg. The Danish *saloniste* Karen Margrethe ('Kamma') Rahbek (1775–1829) rather unkindly described Feldborg, who was born in Copenhagen in 1782, as someone who 'was – or tried to be – a success in Denmark by being English and in England by being Danish'.[91] In point of fact, Feldborg was rather well connected in both countries and spent a considerable portion of the first two decades of the nineteenth century in Britain, where most of his works were published. He twice had an audience with Nelson and Emma Hamilton (1765–1815) in London; he corresponded with Robert Southey (1774–1843) in 1814 about the possibility of a Danish translation of his *Life of Nelson* (1813); and he was an intimate of the *Blackwood's Edinburgh Magazine* circle in Scotland in the 1820s. 'Who is there in Edinburgh or Copenhagen that knows not Feldberg the Dane?', asked the anonymous reviewer of Feldborg's *Denmark Delineated* in *Blackwood's* in September 1821, who was almost certainly (as

I show in Chapter 3) either Robert Pearse Gillies (1788–1858) or John Gibson Lockhart (1794–1854).[92] Feldborg conceived himself, explicitly, as a kind of unofficial cultural-liaison between Denmark and Britain and set out, across a substantial body of travel writing, historical biography and an edition of contemporary Danish poetry in translation, to emphasise and to shore up the common cultural ground between the two countries.

Chapter 2 looks at the work of those British travellers who describe in some detail not just their experiences of Copenhagen but also of other parts of Denmark, often in the context of overland journeys from Germany through Jutland and Funen to the capital. Academic studies of British eighteenth-century and Romantic-period travel writing about Scandinavia have tended to focus on Norway and Sweden, giving the impression that Denmark was a country through which travellers passed as quickly as they could on their way to or from somewhere else, or alternatively sailed around, like Swinton, with whose view of Jutland this introduction began. Such studies have often also, like Barton, concluded that 'Denmark and the Danes fared less well' in British travel writing and 'tended in general to suffer in comparison' with their Nordic neighbours, in respect of a whole range of areas from physical appearance to political-economy.[93] British travel in Scandinavia became popular during the Revolutionary and Napoleonic Wars, which 'closed the gates of the south', as John Carr (1782–1832) puts it in *A Northern Summer* (1805), and this emphasis in academic studies has been driven by the assumption that British Romantic-period travellers to Scandinavia came 'increasingly' in search of 'natural wonders', to use Barton's phrase, which could take the place of the Alps and the Italian volcanoes – and instances of the natural sublime are undoubtedly less frequent in Denmark than in Sweden or Norway.[94] But that is simply not the case. Conversely, as I show in Chapter 2, the late eighteenth and early nineteenth centuries saw a proliferation of extended accounts of travel in Denmark, often by writers famous in their day like William Coxe and Edward Daniel Clarke (1769–1822), whose names are still familiar to scholars today, as well as by others, also well known in their day but now forgotten, like Carr and Feldborg, who published his widely read *Tour of Zealand* in 1805. Carr's *Northern Summer*, as we shall see, saw the publication of two long-forgotten early works by William Hayley (1745–1820) and Leigh Hunt (1784–1859). Chapter 2 of *British Romanticism and Denmark* focuses on three key areas of British travel writing about Denmark beyond Copenhagen in which we can see, most visibly, the articulation of the idea of a common, Northern cultural identity shared by the two countries and rooted in the Classical Scandinavian past: descriptions of prehistoric monuments in Denmark, which would later play a key role in Danish Romantic nationalism; descriptions of Helsingør [Elsinore], famous in Britain on account of its association with Shakespeare; and Feldborg's travelogue *A Dane's Excursions in Britain* (1809).

I have already noted Thomas De Quincey's interest in Danish literature. Chapter 3 of *British Romanticism and Denmark* sets that interest in the context of the wider British response to what the anonymous author of the 'Notices of Danish Literature' (which ran in *The New Monthly Magazine* for 1 July 1819) called 'a mine yet unexplored by the literati of Great Britain'.[95] British interest in classical Scandinavian literature has, as I have already shown in this introduction, been well documented by British and Nordic scholars working on eighteenth-century antiquarianism, philology and related areas of enquiry. But hardly any scholarly attention at all has been paid to British interest, during the late eighteenth and early nineteenth centuries, in contemporary Danish literature, that is to say, in what the author of the 'Notices' calls 'the recent poetry of that country'.[96] Writing in 1819, the author of the 'Notices' is not quite correct to say that this 'literature' is 'yet unexplored'. In 1820–1, as we shall see, Robert Pearse Gillies ran four instalments of 'Horae Danicae' in *Blackwood's Magazine*, alongside the now more familiar 'Horae Germanicae', in which he introduced readers to contemporary Danish drama, covering three works by Adam Oehlenschläger (1779–1850), Denmark's pre-eminent contemporary writer, and one by Bernhard Severin Ingemann (1789–1862). Most of the contemporary Danish poems included by George Borrow (1803-81) in his *Romantic Ballads, Translated from the Danish* (1826) are either themselves versions of classical Scandinavian texts or have 'Norse' themes, but Borrow does include some with present-day motifs and concerns in the 'miscellanies', by Oehlenschläger and Johannes Evald (1743–81). Well before the 1820s, however, there was considerable interest from British writers in Danish Romantic-period literature, and this interest was further augmented by the publication, in 1815, of the anthology *Poems from the Danish* by Feldborg and the English writer and critic William Sidney Walker (1795–1846). Chapter 3 of *British Romanticism and Denmark* explores the various ways in which contemporary literature formed a vehicle of cultural exchange between the two countries, examining not only the reception of Danish Romantic-period literature in Britain but also the transmission of British literature to Denmark during the 'Romantic' period. A particular focal point in this latter respect will be British responses to the reception of Shakespeare in Denmark and the first translations of Shakespeare into Danish, a process which, as Kristian Smidt has argued, was closely 'allied with the growth of the romantic movement' in Denmark.[97]

Discussions of 'national character' form an important strand of Enlightenment philosophy in a variety of European national contexts and pave the way, in many respects, for the emergence of Romantic nationalism with its valorisation of the vernacular and the formative links between peoples and places. Chapter 4 of *British Romanticism and Denmark* surveys the (surprisingly) extensive body of British writing about the Danish national character, taking its point of departure in the droll dialogue on the subject between a group of nuns in Matthew Gregory Lewis's (1775–1818) notorious novel *The Monk* (1796). The increasing articulation in late eighteenth- and early nineteenth-century British writing of the idea of a common 'Northern' culture shared by Britain and Denmark was premised not just upon the sense of shared values inherited from the classical Scandinavian past but also upon claims for an ethnic and racial relationship. We have already seen Swinton's appeal to this claim in his *Travels*, and it becomes ubiquitous after the turn of the century. In his account of the Battle of Copenhagen in his *Life of Nelson*, for instance, Southey, discussing Nelson's aforementioned despatch to Frederik VI, interprets Nelson's use of the word 'brothers' in both a cultural and a racial sense. 'The Danes were an honourable foe,' Southey writes: 'they were of English mould as well as English blood; and now that the battle had ceased, [Nelson] regarded them rather as brethren than as enemies.'[98] One might well argue, given the history of the Danish conquest of England, that Southey has the order of priority inverted here, but his point is clear enough: the bonds linking the English and the Danish are formed of 'blood' as well as culture ('mould').

Following a survey of the major currents of eighteenth-century philosophical enquiry into national character and the influence of that enquiry on the emergence of Romantic nationalism, Chapter 4 of *British Romanticism and Denmark* turns to the specifics of British writing about the Danish national character – a body of writing which, as I argue, was often (and inevitably) as much concerned with defining the British as the Danish character. Denmark has, in recent years, routinely been ranked among the 'happiest' countries in the world and on a number of occasions as *the* happiest. As we shall see, this seemingly very modern idea has a notable prehistory in the late eighteenth century and early nineteenth centuries, in both British and Danish writing, and is, of course, also visible in the apocryphal 'second part' of the *Candide* (1759) of Voltaire (1694–78), published in 1760, in which the protagonists choose to live in Copenhagen: not El Dorado, but a place 'where everything was not bad'.[99] British eighteenth-century and Romantic-period writing about the Danish national character tended, as I show in Chapter 4, to proceed on the basis of comparisons and contrasts between the Danes and other European nations, outlining perceived similarities and differences. A particular and recurrent trope within this comparative discourse was the attempt to determine whether or not it was possible to discern a distinctly 'Northern' character which transcended contemporary national borders, elements of which Britons and Danes had in common. A further recurrent concern of British writing about the Danish national character was the attempt to evaluate the relationship between ancient and modern Danes, a concern which is also visible, for example, in much British Romantic-period writing about modern Greece. British accounts of the Danish national character often tend to present modern Britons, rather than modern Danes, as the true inheritors of classical Scandinavian traits, and this is one of the ways in which British writing about the Danish national character becomes, in effect, a discourse about *Britishness*, albeit one based on perceptions of similarity rather than difference across national borders. Chapter 4 ends with a coda in which I examine the account given by Andreas Andersen Feldborg, in *Denmark Delineated*, of some time he spent in Copenhagen in May 1822 with the celebrated Italian explorer and Egyptologist Giovanni Battista Belzoni (1778–1823), whom Feldborg calls in as a kind of expert witness to testify against those British travel writers still critical of modern Danish polity and cultural life.

The final chapter of *British Romanticism and Denmark* returns to territory about which I have already had a good deal to say in this introduction: British eighteenth-century and Romantic-period writing about Danish politics, domestic and foreign. In Chapter 5, however, my focus is on British responses to those aspects of Danish political life and foreign policy which were not directly connected to the Revolutionary and Napoleonic Wars, politics, we might say, beyond the circumstances surrounding the two British attacks on Copenhagen, in 1801 and 1807. With this focus in mind, Chapter 5 has three areas of interest: the development of British assessments of the nature and impact of absolutist rule in Denmark; British responses to the marriage and divorce of Caroline Matilda to Christian VII; and British writing about the Danish West and East Indies, as well as Denmark's early move to abolish the trade in slaves. Writing in his *Travels* in 1772, Joseph Marshall describes Denmark as 'no trifling kingdom, though not considerable when compared with some others in Europe'.[100] It is certainly the case that in each of the aspects of Danish political life which I examine in Chapter 5 we can see a gradual but steady decline, in various ways, of Denmark's international status and influence – and one could certainly argue that the articulation, in British writing, of the idea of a common 'Northern' culture which Denmark and Britain share develops, in inverse relationship, with that decline in status.

Such a narrative would be consistent, for the most part, with received histories of the development of Romanticism and Romantic nationalism in Denmark, which, as I noted earlier, have understood those developments, exactly, as flowerings of domestic culture prompted by diminished international presence. But, on the other hand, to state so complex a relationship between two cultures in so simple a formula risks, also, reproducing uncritically those very narratives about national Romanticisms in Britain and Denmark, and about European Romanticism, which *British Romanticism and Denmark* intends to challenge. There is an expression, in Danish, which holds that a successful relationship is achieved by living together, but still separately: *at leve sammen, men alligevel hver for sig*. The task facing the historian of European Romanticism today consists, precisely, in the difficulty of mapping the interaction between different national traditions while never losing sight of the differences between them, differences which those texts are often at pains to emphasise. Nor are these difficulties the unique preserve of historians and critics in our day. Conversely, in order to illustrate the extent to which British Romantic-period writers were themselves aware of the strengths and limitations involved in the paradigm of regional literatures which crossed political and linguistic borders, I turn in closing, in a brief coda, to an 1820 essay by the English theologian Julius Charles Hare (1795–1855) which sets out to argue the ostensibly very difficult case that Adam Oehlenschläger, whom Hare calls 'the great poet of Denmark', can meaningfully be considered representative of 'recent German drama'.[101]

Chapter 1

'One of the finest capitals of Europe': Some British Romantic Views of Copenhagen

In the second volume of his *Life of Nelson* (1813), Robert Southey (1774–1843) describes Copenhagen as 'the best city of the north, one of the finest capitals of Europe; visible, with its stately spires, far off'.[1] There had been some dissenting voices, of course, notably including Mary Wollstonecraft's (1759–97) gloomy account of Copenhagen in her *Letters Written during a Short Residence in Sweden, Norway, and Denmark* (1796), the book which Robert Southey told his brother made him 'fall in love with a cold climate & frost & snow, with a Northern moonlight'.[2] For the most part, however, in his account of Copenhagen, Southey was merely repeating what had been a commonplace of British travel writing about the Nordic countries for at least the previous thirty years. In his *Travels into Poland, Russia, Sweden, and Denmark* (1785), for example, the celebrated traveller William Coxe (1748–1829) had affirmed that 'Copenhagen is the best-built city of the north', and most of those who came after him had agreed.[3] Forty years later, this consensus remained: Richard Jones (dates unknown) in his highly detailed compendium *Copenhagen and its Environs* (1829), designed as a handbook for British tourists, confirms that Copenhagen is not only 'one of the most ancient and powerful Cities of Europe' but also 'one of the handsomest'.[4] And yet, despite the extent to which the Danish capital became ostensibly familiar to British travellers in the late eighteenth and early nineteenth centuries, Copenhagen often also remains in the literature of the period very much an *imaginary* space, the representation of which was inextricably bound up with wider 'Romantic' attitudes to 'the North'. Such tensions are plainly visible, for example, in the three stanzas which the nineteen-year-old Percy Bysshe Shelley (1792–1822) sent to his friend Thomas Jefferson Hogg (1792–1862) on 11 January 1811, and which he later worked up into a 'Fragment of a Poem; the original idea of which was suggested by the cowardly and infamous bombardment of Copenhagen'. As the British shell the city in this reimagining of the events of 2–5 September 1807:

> The ice-mountains echo, the Baltic, the Ocean
>   Where Cold sits enthroned on his solium of snow;
> E'en Spitzbergen perceives the terrific commotion,
>   The roar floats on the whirlwinds of sleet as they blow —
> Blood tinges the streams as half frozen they flow,
> The meteors of War horrid flame through the air,
> They mix their bright gleam with the red Polar glare.[5]

This is certainly not Shelley's finest poetry, but the lines are remarkable for the extent to which the Copenhagen that they imagine is a distinctly *Arctic* space, altogether *unlike* the actual geographical setting for the British attack on the city, in good weather, in September 1807.

This first chapter of *British Romanticism and Denmark* examines the representation of Copenhagen in British writing across a range of genres in the late eighteenth and early nineteenth centuries. It shows how the city serves as a focal point for various contemporary discourses surrounding 'the North' and that representations of it are, consequently, often marked by the tension between actual and imagined versions of the city which is visible in Shelley's stanzas. The chapter focuses, in particular, on literary responses to the two British attacks on Copenhagen – in April 1801 and September 1807 – which effectively redrew the map of Napoleonic Europe and which had a transformative effect not only on British representations of the Danish capital but also on the wider construction of cultural links between Britain and Denmark which had been ongoing since the 'Antiquarian Revival' of the mid-eighteenth century.

'A stranger may spend his time not unpleasantly': British Travellers in Copenhagen

'I have now been here near a week, and begin to find that a stranger may spend his time not unpleasantly'. Thus, with somewhat faint praise, does Nathaniel Wraxall (1751–1831) open his account of the Danish capital in a letter dated there 25 April 1774 and published the following year in his *Tour through Some of the Northern Parts of Europe*.[6] Wraxall, a former employee of the British East India Company, who had served in Gujarat and Baruch, passed through Copenhagen on his way to Russia. As a *tourist* in Copenhagen, Wraxall felt himself to be something of a novelty: 'so few persons visit this metropolis or kingdom from motives of curiosity', he writes, 'that they are quite surprised when I assure them that I have no sort of business here, and am only employed in the search of knowledge.'[7] And indeed this 'surprise' was to become, for Wraxall, a source of minor inconvenience: arrived in Copenhagen just two years after the dénouement of the affair between Caroline Matilda (1751–75) and Johann Friedrich Struensee (1737–72), which I discuss in Chapter 5, his 'absence of an avowed motive' for being in the city apart from 'curiosity' meant that 'so little an individual as myself, so humble and unknown a traveller as I am, is not only publickly talked of, but even suspected as a spy, because I come from England'.[8]

In view of this response from the locals, it is perhaps not surprising that Wraxall's account of Copenhagen is more concerned with the social and the political than with the built environment. He notes that the inhabitants 'have a great turn for politics' and an especial interest 'in those of the English nation'.[9] He also notes with some surprise, and somewhat surprisingly, 'that there is no face of industry or business here; and Copenhagen, though one of the finest ports in the world, can boast of little commerce'.[10] He complains about the weather, noting the absence, even in late April, of 'any marks of that sweet season, which the Italians so justly denominate the *gioventu del anno*, but which is pretty much unknown to Danish poets'.[11] And he remarks – perhaps in consequence of having fallen in love almost immediately upon his arrival in the city with a 'fair Norwegian' – that he has 'not seen above three or four very handsome or very elegant women in Copenhagen. Perhaps I may be too premature in my determination, but I do not think them, in general, to be compared for loveliness with our own women.'[12] So far, in a way, so conventional: Wraxall was neither the first nor the last travel writer to conclude that things were better at home!

Those sites which Wraxall does describe, however, would subsequently become the staples of a visit to Copenhagen. These include the 'very singular' Round Tower (Rundetaarn) built in 1642 by Christian IV of Denmark (1577–1643) as an observatory, up which it was possible to drive a chariot; Rosenborg Castle and its gardens, 'one of the chief diversions of the city'; and the Royal Museum at Christiansborg Palace, which included among its 'greatest and most valuable curiosities, the chair in which Tycho Brahe [1546–1601] was used to sit, when he made his astronomical observations at Uraniborg'.[13] Wraxall's response to the royal residences, in particular, is instructive both in the extent to which it seeks to differentiate between Danish and English royalty and in the manner of the distinction which it makes. The decoration of Christian IV's chamber at Rosenborg, for example, Wraxall felt to be, on account of its erotic imagery, more appropriate for a 'mussulman' than a 'Lutheran' monarch, while the 'prodigious size' of Christiansborg prompted him to reflect that, 'if I was inclined to find fault with it, I should say, it is too splendid and too magnificent for a king of Denmark; on the same principle, as foreigners constantly remark, that the palaces in England are far beneath the dignity and greatness of the British empire.'[14] Wraxall had earlier remarked, on a similar note, that the Danish army was 'much too large for this little kingdom'.[15]

Wraxall compares the Danish monarchy, in other words, with the supposed opulence and extravagance of 'Oriental' or 'Southern' states – ostensibly familiar to him from his service with the East India Company – and contrasts it unflatteringly with the dignified restraint of the English. And, indeed, Wraxall confirms exactly this same stereotypical attitude to the Northern and the Southern when he reviews 'the portraits of all the reigning monarchs of Europe' on show at Christiansborg.[16] 'I could not but smile at the different manner in which they have been pleased to habit themselves', he says, before contrasting the 'modest portrait' of Frederick II of Prussia with the 'ridiculous ostentation' of Charles III of Spain.[17]

Wraxall's account of Copenhagen as representative of an 'Oriental' Danish polity, of a Denmark which is the 'Other' of England and Prussia, is not uncommon in early appraisals of political conditions in the country. For instance, while Robert Molesworth's (1656–1725) critique of Danish absolutism in *An Account of Denmark* (1693) had connected it with a barbarian North in contradistinction from an arcadian South, the anonymous author of *Observations on the Present State of Denmark, Russia, and Switzerland* (1784) notes with irony, in his discussion of 'the severe exactions of public labour', 'and yet a Dane would be shocked at the despotism of a Turkish bashaw'.[18] It is exactly these attitudes which would come to change so entirely during the late eighteenth and early nineteenth centuries, when the cultural significance of Denmark began for British writers to be realigned away from perceptions of difference and towards perceptions of a common, Northern identity rooted in the Scandinavian past rather than in the Classical culture of the South or the 'Oriental' culture of the Ottoman Empire. And the city of Copenhagen became a key focal point in that realignment.

Observations on the Present State of Denmark 'has little to say' about the Danish capital.[19] Having remarked in that now familiar, Orientalist vein that 'every approach towards opulence or grandeur marks the abode of the king, or his favourites', on the 'external and internal magnificence' of Christiansborg Palace, on the impressive harbour and fortifications, and on the 'several good paintings' and 'mostly polemical theologians, and magnificent editions of the fathers' in the Royal Museum, our anonymous author feels that they have 'fulfilled the duty of a journalist', barring a final, passing mention of the Round Tower.[20] But 'the motives of curiosity' which Wraxall felt so distinguished his presence in Copenhagen were soon to become de rigueur for British travellers to the city: by the end of the eighteenth century, Copenhagen was no longer visited primarily for trade or as the main gateway to 'the North' but was well on its way to being established as a mainstream tourist destination in its own right, the kind of destination for which Jones's *Copenhagen and its Environs* was not only an appropriate but also an increasingly necessary resource.

The beginnings of what we might then consider British *tourism* in Copenhagen can arguably be traced to the account of the city given by William Coxe in the first edition of his *Travels into Poland, Russia, Sweden, and Denmark*. Coxe provides a detailed, fold-out map of Copenhagen marking the principal sites of what he, as we have seen, describes as 'the best built city of the north'. Coxe's first visit, made in April 1779, 'was very short, and principally during passion-week, which the natives observe with great strictness', and so he did not have 'many opportunities of experiencing the hospitality of the Danish nobility'.[21] But Coxe's account in *Travels* (1784) contains none of the unflattering comparisons made by Wraxall and *Observations*. Conversely, Coxe has only praise for the 'well-paved' streets, 'splendid' buildings and 'extremely beautiful new part of the town', which he pays the compliment of being 'scarcely inferior to Bath'.[22]

In marked contrast to Wraxall, Coxe also finds that 'the busy spirit of commerce is visible in Copenhagen' and this is a significant observation to the extent that it signals Coxe's altogether more positive assessment of the Danish establishment and its influence on the city and his departure from the 'Orientalist' comparisons of earlier accounts.[23] Hence, while Coxe suggests that Copenhagen 'owes its principal beauty to a dreadful fire in 1728, that destroyed five churches and sixty-seven streets, which have since been rebuilt in the modern style', he is also keen to stress the role of successive monarchs in improving not only the royal residences but also the entire city.[24] Coxe's positive assessment of Danish polity is most in evidence, however, when he comes to reflect upon its role in promoting the arts and the sciences. He remarks in particular on the foundation and support by successive monarchs of Copenhagen University and the Royal Academy of Sciences 'for the encouragement and diffusion of general learning'.[25] The former, he notes, 'has a very considerable fund; the professors have liberal salaries; and many students are instructed gratis'.[26] The latter, 'in consequence of the royal favour', began 'searching into, and explaining the history and antiquity of their country [. . .] natural history, physicks, and mathematicks', with some fifteen volumes of transactions extant at the time of Coxe's visit.[27]

Of especial interest to Coxe, and to our story here, was the role played by these royal institutions in preserving and making available the classical culture of Scandinavia. 'In general the Danish literati have particularly turned their researches upon the history and antiquities of the North,' Coxe observes, 'on which subjects many curious works have been already printed, and more are still preparing for the publick inspection.'[28] Among these, the studies of classical 'Icelandick' texts, he continues, 'deserve particular notice; as they tend to throw considerable light upon the antiquities, history, and mythology of the northern nations; Iceland being in the remote ages, while Sweden, Denmark, and Norway, were in a state of perpetual warfare, the sole refuge and repository of Northern literature.'[29]

Coxe's historiography of classical Scandinavia is a bit off here, but what he points to is, of course, the beginnings at Copenhagen of the Antiquarian Revival which would have, as I noted in my introduction, such a profound impact upon the development of English literature and upon Britain's developing sense of itself as a 'Northern nation' during the years of the Revolutionary and Napoleonic Wars. Hence Coxe, like many after him, identifies Copenhagen as the 'repository' of the artefacts of that shared, 'Northern' cultural inheritance, an inheritance which would come to include, by the second decade of the nineteenth century, the first complete translations of *Beowulf*, made at the Danish capital. Coxe's Copenhagen, then, is far from the 'Oriental' other visited by Wraxall and the author of *Observations*.

Nor is Coxe's praise for Danish scholars and their royal patrons confined solely to antiquarian researches: 'they have by no means been deficient', he assures the reader, 'in the study of nature'.[30] As a primary example here Coxe cites the *Flora Danica* being compiled by the German-Danish botanist Georg-Christian Oeder (1728–91), 'through the liberality of his monarch', Frederik V of Denmark (1723–66): a 'magnificent and accurate' compendium, 'carried on at the king's expence', intended ultimately to contain:

> figures [i.e., illustrations] of all the indigenous plants of Denmark, Norway, those of the duchies of Sleswick and Holstein, and of many from Iceland; a tract of country extending more than 16 degrees, between the 54th degree of latitude and the North Cape.[31]

Coxe also notes that 'the kings of Denmark have occasionally deputed, and still continue to send, at their expence, men of learning through their own territories, and into various parts of the world, for the purpose of extending the bounds of knowledge'.³² Such expeditions were primarily focused on 'the antient history of the North', but Coxe observes that the one 'which reflects the highest honour upon the crown of Denmark, and holds up an example to be imitated by other sovereigns, was begun in 1761, under the auspices of Frederick V'.³³ This 'curious and interesting journey' was the Danish Arabia Expedition led by Carsten Niebuhr (1733–1815) in 1761–7, which I discuss in Chapter 5.³⁴

Coxe's Copenhagen is thus not only a beautiful city but also a cultural and scientific capital, thriving under enlightened royal patronage and far from the decadent, 'Oriental' polity condemned by Wraxall and the author of *Observations*. Indeed, Copenhagen emerges from Coxe's *Travels* as in many respects a kind of model state and analogue of England, and hence – again, in contrast to Wraxall's unflattering Oriental comparisons – the many complimentary parallels which Coxe draws, between Copenhagen and England and between the cultural life of Britain and Denmark.

Coxe's *Travels*, which went through a number of subsequent editions, set the tone for most subsequent, late eighteenth-century British accounts of Copenhagen, such as those given by Matthew Consett (1757–1831) and William Thomson (1746–1817), with whose *Travels* I began this book. Consett made a brief stay in the Danish capital in the autumn of 1786 on his return from an expedition to Lapland with Henry Liddell (1749–91), the grandfather of the famous historian and lexicographer. The brevity of Consett's account matches the brevity of his stay (of just a few days), but his actual and idiomatic debts to Coxe's way of seeing the city seem obvious. Consett notes that 'Copenhagen is a handsome well-built town', that 'Commerce flourishes here exceedingly', and that the city 'is intersected by canals, so that merchandize can be brought to the doors of the warehouses', a detail also noted by Coxe, in almost identical phrasing.³⁵ 'Most of the structures', Consett observes praisingly, have a 'magnificent appearance', especially Christiansborg Palace, which has 'a distinguishing royalty which strikes the stranger's eye'.³⁶ Like Coxe before him, Consett also praises the influence of Danish polity on the cultural life of Copenhagen. The city is safe ('you may walk the streets at all hours of the night or day, without any molestation'); 'there is a very good and well endowed University, as well as an Academy of Sciences', and 'a Museum containing many curiosities both of nature and art'.³⁷ And also like Coxe before him, Consett notes in particular that 'literature flourishes' under the influence of Frederik V, who is 'much and deservedly respected by his people':

> No small part of his private Fortune is dedicated to the promotion of learning and the Encouragement of learned men. This is a singular Instance in

the History of Nations; and there is great reason to hope that the beautiful appearance of this rising Sun will be succeeded by a full blaze of meridian Splendor.[38]

Hence, although Consett notes the ponderousness of Danish civil law and the 'Severity' of Danish criminal law, and laments that 'the Nobility, though they resigned their power to the Crown, still exercise great authority over the Peasantry whom they keep in a state of vassalage', his account of Copenhagen contains none of the Orientalist critiques made by Wraxall and *Observations*.[39] Conversely, flattering comparisons with England abound in his description of the city, as they had done in Coxe's: the 'Women' at Copenhagen, for example, 'are fair, well made, and not unlike the English', while 'the Soldiers in general are well chosen men; the Officers exceedingly polite and well bred; their uniforms resemble those of the English, which is also the case in their discipline'.[40] This, in short, is a Copenhagen which is the same, not different.

In October 1788, William Thomson set off on what he describes in the first letter of his *Travels into Norway, Denmark, and Russia* (1792) as 'my third expedition to the north', granting, in a phrase which Robert Southey might have recalled in his assessment of Wollstonecraft's *Short Residence*, and which demonstrates an emerging 'Romantic' attitude to 'the North', that 'it is a strange whim to get in love with deserts, with ice and with snow'.[41] Thomson opens his preface to *Travels* by suggesting that his familiarity with 'the North' is still comparatively unusual, although this should certainly be read as part of the sales pitch for his book: 'the northern parts of Europe are seldom visited by English travellers', he says, 'nor have any of these, within the space of fifteen years, two Gentleman only excepted, published their travels'.[42] These 'two gentleman', of course, are Wraxall and Coxe, the former of whom Thomson damns with some impressively faint praise: 'it is impossible either to disregard the admirable alacrity of this Gentleman's movements', he writes, 'or to suppose that he had it in his power to draw many of his reflections from actual observation.'[43] Coxe, by contrast, 'travelled at a pace somewhat slower, and much more solemn', and has, in consequence, 'given us many accurate and useful details'.[44] This is an instructive contrast, and not least because Thomson will go on to single out Wraxall's account of Denmark, in particular – which Thomson, we remember, describes as 'the country of our ancestors' – as not only inaccurate but also 'unjust' and ideologically motivated.[45] 'Mr. Wraxhal [*sic*]', Thomson concludes, 'determined to abuse Denmark at a time when there was a misunderstanding between the Danish Court and that of London, has rejected every authority in favour of the Danish dominions, both in prose and verse.'[46]

In his critique of Wraxall's account of Denmark, then, Thomson registers precisely that shift which I am describing here from a sense of difference and 'misunderstanding' towards a perception of shared cultural inheritance, from a Denmark which is represented as *other* to a Denmark which is seen as 'the country of our ancestors', and from a Danish polity which is condemned as 'Oriental' to a view of the Danish establishment as enlightened and benevolent, as an analogue of the English.

In view of all this, Thomson's account of the Danish capital is revealing. Despite his quips about Wraxall's 'alacrity', Thomson has almost nothing to say about Copenhagen: he was only passing through, of course, in October 1788, on his way further north, and his *Travels* is in general far more concerned with historical and sociocultural observation than with loco-descriptive accounts, whether of capital cities or of those 'deserts' of 'ice' and 'snow' for which he had acquired that 'whim'. What little he does say, however, reveals precisely the extent to which Copenhagen was becoming at the end of the eighteenth century a contested space in the British imagination. Thomson's brief account of Copenhagen is actually one of the few moments in his *Travels* to exhibit the kind of picturesque discourse that was becoming a commonplace of 'Romantic' travel writing and is, as I have said, in marked contrast to the prevailing tone of his book. Thomson describes not the details of the city itself, not the actual city, but only the view from afar, 'of the spires of Copenhagen', as he sails down the Øresund, between Sweden and Denmark.[47] 'The site of Copenhagen is so low', he continues, 'that it seems, even at a small distance, to be built in the water: yet the appearance is truly noble.'[48]

For Thomson, then, the Danish capital is a kind of northern Venice and – like that city – remains in *Travels* very much an imagined space, despite Thomson's reminding the reader that he has been there before and evidently knows the area well: 'This capital of Denmark', he concludes, 'is formed by Nature to be the mistress of the Baltic.'[49] The epithet is oxymoronic – a city, 'formed by Nature' – but the comparison between the two cities, as they appear from the sea, is accurate enough. The rhetorical purpose of the epithet also seems clear: to remediate 'the North' to unfamiliar readers through a pre-existent, familiar discourse about another beautiful city, 'mistress' of another sea – and a central topos in much of British travel writing and Gothic fiction. What is most striking about the passage, however, is the extent to which it tends to remove Copenhagen from the historical, political and geographical specificity which dominates Thomson's *Travels* and to relocate the city within a 'Romantic' discourse of the exotic and, ironically, of the South. In short, Thomson's *Travels*, a book which is openly concerned to provide an accurate account of 'the North', offers its readers an almost entirely imaginary version of the Danish capital.

Writing under his own name, in his *Letters from Scandinavia*, published four years after his *Travels*, Thomson focuses a little more closely on Copenhagen. His account of the city echoes that given in *Travels* to the extent that he remarks how 'the northern cities make the finest show at some distance. Their gilded spires give an idea of much grandeur and magnificence, but they do not bear so narrow an inspection as our own cities.'[50] But beyond this slight caveat, and the observation that 'the Danes delight in what is shewy', Thomson's closer acquaintance with the Danish capital prompts nothing but praise.[51] He notes, with admiration, and again in contrast to Wraxall, that 'Copenhagen must carry on a great extent of commerce. The canals in every street are filled with shipping; and you see a vessel opposite to almost every house.'[52] 'This mixture of houses and vessels', he observes, 'has a strange but noble appearance.'[53] He is also full of praise for the Royal Museum, the 'particulars' of which it would be, he says 'endless to enumerate'.[54] And moreover, Thomson, like Coxe and others after him, sees this museum as evidence of a progressive Danish polity: 'such collections do honour to a nation', he writes, 'and to human nature, in thus bringing under our eye works which could not be seen by so many in any other situation.'[55] This, again, is a Copenhagen which is the analogue rather than the antithesis of London.

That more subjective, and we might say 'Romantic', reimagining of Copenhagen which we saw in Thomson's *Travels*, however – which is so markedly different from the prevailing discourse of both that earlier work and of his *Letters* – was soon to become a more pronounced feature of British responses to the Danish capital. It is vividly on show, for example, in the description of Copenhagen given by the today best-known British traveller to visit the city during the eighteenth century: Mary Wollstonecraft. Wollstonecraft arrived in Copenhagen in September 1795 at the end of her 'short residence' in Scandinavia, a few months after the fire of 5–7 July which had devastated much of the city and rendered homeless a substantial portion of the population. Like most other British travellers of the period, Wollstonecraft approached Copenhagen from the north, on the road from Helsingør (Elsinore), and 'the view of the city, as we drew near', she admits, 'was rather grand, but, without any striking feature to interest the imagination, except the trees which shade the foot-paths'.[56]

This mixture of somewhat grudging admiration, general dissatisfaction, and attention to natural beauty, very much sets the tone of Wollstonecraft's description of the city. It is, indeed, the prevailing tone of her *Letters Written during a Short Residence*. As Christoph Bode has argued, Wollstonecraft's depressed state of mind during her stay in Scandinavia – brought on by the collapse of her relationship with her former lover Gilbert Imlay (1754–28), the father of her two-year-old daughter, Fanny (1794–1816), with whom she was travelling – seems to have made it all but impossible for her to 'open up' to the scenes she encountered or to move beyond her own 'emotional and cultural predispositions'.[57] Moreover, as Bode also notes, drawing on the discoveries made by Per Nyström and Gunnar Molden, the real reason for Wollstonecraft's journey to Scandinavia – to discover the fate of a ship carrying silver which Imlay had been trying to smuggle from France – is systematically suppressed from *Short Residence*.[58] In this sense, then, Wollstonecraft's account of Copenhagen – and of Scandinavia in general – is doubly filtered, by her state of mind and by her need for secrecy. Hence the seeming emotional immediacy of her account, which was so admired by contemporary readers, including Southey and Wollstonecraft's future husband, William Godwin (1756–1836) – who wrote in his *Memoirs* that 'if ever there was a book calculated to make a man in love with its author, this appears to me to be the book' – is thus to a considerable extent performed, 'calculated' to use Godwin's phrase.[59]

Wollstonecraft's state of mind in the Danish capital is amply illustrated by the sole surviving private letter which she wrote from there, to Imlay, on 6 September 1795. She notes that she is 'weary of travelling' and yet feels that she has 'no home', that she has thought again of suicide on her travels, and that she feels that she has encountered, in her life, mostly hearts of 'stone'.[60] Of the city itself, she says only: 'I see here nothing but ruins, and only converse with people immersed in trade and sensuality', presumably the type, in her mind, of Imlay himself.[61] Less an objective or factual account, then, the description of Copenhagen given by Wollstonecraft in her *Short Residence* is very much mediated through the contemporary discourses of sentimental travel, of the picturesque and, above all, of ruin-sentiment.[62] Her account, in other words, shifts the prevailing representation of the Danish capital away from the perception generated by her immediate predecessors of an enlightened polity in many respects the analogue of England and towards a more subjective, 'Romantic' reimagining centred on the tropes of decline and of ruin, infrastructural and political alike.[63]

This transition is apparent from the outset of Wollstonecraft's account of Copenhagen. As she drew close to the city, she – as yet ignorant of the fire – saw 'a number of tents' which she took at first for evidence of 'the rage for encampments'.[64] She 'soon discovered', however, that 'they were the asylum of many of the poor families who had been driven out of their habitations by the late fire'.[65] Evidently low on the emotional reserves needed to enter fully into the sufferings of others, however, Wollstonecraft reflects rather on the extent to which the visible 'misery' of present 'devastation' hindered any attempt to see the ruined city in picturesque terms:

> There was little in the appearance of fallen bricks and stacks of chimneys to allure the imagination into soothing melancholy reveries; nothing to attract the eye of taste, but much to afflict the benevolent heart [. . .] I therefore desired the driver to hasten to the hotel.[66]

The following morning, 'walking around the town', Wollstonecraft grew 'weary of observing the ravages'.[67] She grants that she has 'seen it in a very disadvantageous light', but still can hardly credit the 'rapture' with which Danes, 'even those who had seen Paris and London', describe Copenhagen: 'the utmost that can, or could ever, I believe, have been said in its praise', she concludes, 'might be comprised in a few words.'[68] Those 'few words', for Wollstonecraft, are that 'the streets are open, and many of the houses large', but she 'saw nothing to rouse the idea of elegance or grandeur', except for the royal residence at Amalienborg.[69] And, in a curious echo of Wraxall's strictures on Danish indolence, she notes that 'considering Copenhagen as the capital of Denmark and Norway, I was surprised not to see so much industry or taste as in Christiania [Oslo]', although she later grants that 'the canals, which intersect the streets' are 'convenient and wholesome'.[70] Recounting an anecdote concerning how a dog was 'made a counsellor of state' by Christian VII of Denmark (1749–1808), Wollstonecraft also echoes Wraxall's critique of the excesses of the Danish monarchy: she suggests that the burning of the palace at Christiansborg 'was, in fact, a fortunate circumstance, as it afforded a pretext for reducing the establishment of the household, which was far too great for the revenues of the crown'.[71] The current regent, Frederik VI (1768–1839), she felt, 'runs into the opposite extreme; and the formality, if not the parsimony, of the court, seems to extend to all the other branches of society'.[72] '[N]othing can give a more forcible idea of the dullness which eats away all activity of mind', Wollstonecraft concludes, 'than the insipid routine of a court, without magnificence or elegance.'[73] The Danish government, like the Danish capital, it seems, could not win in Wollstonecraft's view: either it was too ostentatious or not ostentatious enough!

The 'childish incidents' of a play – not one word of which, of course, could she understand – Wollstonecraft takes as 'sufficient to shew the state of the dramatic art in Denmark, and the gross taste of the audience'.[74] 'The public library', she says, 'consists of a collection much larger than I expected to see; and it is well arranged.'[75] She 'could not form a judgement' of the 'value of the Icelandic manuscripts' – a repository constituting the primary record of classical Scandinavian myth – but says that 'the alphabet of some of them amused me'.[76] She found 'some good pictures in the royal museum', but they 'were mixed indiscriminately with the bad ones, in order to assort the frames'.[77] She thought 'the specimens of natural history, and curiosities of art, were likewise huddled together without that scientific order which alone renders them useful', although at least she allows that 'this may partly have been occasioned by the hasty manner in which they were removed from the palace, when in flames'.[78] Undoubtedly the most striking example of Wollstonecraft's conflicted attitude to the influence of Danish polity on public life in the city comes, however, when she observes that:

> One of the best streets in Copenhagen is almost filled with hospitals, erected by the government; and, I am assured, as well regulated as institutions of this kind are in any country; but whether hospitals or workhouses, are any where superintended with sufficient humanity, I have frequently had reason to doubt.[79]

Wollstonecraft seems absolutely determined to find grounds for critique: even such an evident attempt at progressive government policy is met only with scepticism. An instructive contrast might be made, on this particular point, with the observations made by John Carr (1772–1832) on these same institutions during his visit to Copenhagen in 1804, which he found 'all very humane foundations and well maintained', noting further that 'to an Englishman such establishments [. . .] are proudly familiar to his eye'.[80]

By way of mitigating all this negative description, Wollstonecraft at least admits that she 'may be a little partial, and view everything with the jaundiced eye of melancholy – for I am sad – and have cause'.[81] Given this state of mind, then, it is perhaps not surprising that ruin-sentiment constitutes such an important trope in her description of Copenhagen. The site which most earns her admiration is the 'deserted' palace of Rosenborg, the former summer residence of Christian IV. Here, she was charmed by 'a gloomy kind of grandeur throughout':

> Every object carried me back to past times, and impressed the manners of the age forcibly on my mind [. . .] The vacuum left by departed greatness was every where observable [. . .] It seemed a vast tomb, full of the shadowy phantoms of those who had played or toiled their hour out [. . .] Could they be no more – to whom my imagination thus gave life? Could the thoughts, of which there remained so many vestiges, have vanished quite away? And

these beings, composed of such noble materials of thinking and feeling, have they only melted into the elements to keep in motion the grand mass of life? It cannot be![82]

In contrast to the immediate 'misery' and 'devastation' by which Wollstonecraft was confronted on her arrival in Copenhagen, then, the 'deserted' Rosenborg is appreciated by her precisely because there is nothing to disturb her private, sentimental meditation on the transience of life.

The only other aspects of the city to which Wollstonecraft had any kind of positive response share this trait: the gardens at Hirsholm and 'the view of the sea' from Kastellet, although the latter suffered considerably when contrasted with her 'fresh memory' of 'the various bold and picturesque shores' which she had recently seen in Norway.[83] Here, then, we have the crux of Wollstonecraft's assessment of the Danish capital. The city is at its most appealing to her when civil society does not get in the way of subjective reflection, when the urban space approaches most closely to a *natural* space. There is an evident tension, in other words, in Wollstonecraft's account, between the actual, historical Copenhagen of 1795, and the ability of the traveller to use the city as a space for reflection. In Wollstonecraft's *Short Residence*, we see, then, the culmination of an eighteenth-century engagement with the Danish capital which leads from a critique of 'Oriental' absolutism, through praise for an enlightened polity, to a wish to inscribe the city within a nascent, 'Romantic' reimagining of 'the North' as a natural rather than a civil space, and declined from a glorious past. Indeed, the detailed and on-the-whole quite complimentary 'Sketch of the City of Copenhagen and of the Manners of the Inhabitants' which was published in *The German Museum* for February 1801, five years after Wollstonecraft's *Short Residence*, shows just how much her strictures on Danish polity, in particular, already belonged to a previous generation.

'Brothers of Englishmen': The Battle of Copenhagen (1801)

For some five hours on 2 April 1801, British and Danish ships fought a close battle in Copenhagen Roads, just east of the city. The political circumstances leading to the outbreak of hostilities were complex and deeply implicated in the wider network of the French Revolutionary Wars.[84] The British intention, having tried and failed to resolve the matter through negotiation, was to break by force the Second League of Armed Neutrality, an alliance of Denmark–Norway, Sweden, Russia and Prussia which had been openly flouting the British blockade on French ports. The British fleet was commanded by Admiral Hyde Parker (1739–1807), with Horatio Nelson (1758–1805) as second in command. The Danish ships, floating batteries, and land-based guns were commanded by Steen Andersen Bille (1751–1833) and Johan Olfert Fischer (1747–1829). In total, around three thousand men were killed or injured, with approximately four hundred more casualties on the Danish side, before a ceasefire was declared and negotiations began for a Danish surrender. Although less familiar today than the Battles of the Nile (1798) or Trafalgar (1805), the events of 2 April 1801 were seen at the time as a substantial and significant moment in the course of the war with France. Many sources quoted Nelson's remark that Copenhagen had been his most difficult engagement to date, and public interest in Britain was sufficient for Robert (1739–1806) and Henry Aston Barker (1774–1856) to exhibit a panorama of the subject in their Leicester Square premises, after Henry had made drawings on site.[85]

Although nominally a defeat for Denmark – indeed to an extent perhaps *because* a defeat – the Battle of Copenhagen played a key role in the emergence of Danish Romantic nationalism. The heroism with which the Danes fought, which was lauded publicly and repeatedly by Nelson, became a recurrent trope in Danish painting and literature, as, for example, in the celebrated painting by Christian Mølsted (1862–1930), made a century after the battle, of the seventeen-year-old Peter Willemoes (1783–1808) commanding Fleet Battery 9 at the heart of the engagement. My focus here, however, is on the impact of the battle on Anglo-Danish relations and, in particular, on the extent to which the aftermath of the battle, which might have seemed the moment for traumatic collapse in relations between the two countries, paradoxically became the occasion, in both Britain and Denmark, for the articulation of exactly that sense of common, 'Northern' cultural identity which is the subject of this book. The Battle of Copenhagen was, in other words, a key nexus in the development of Romanticisms and Romantic nationalisms in the two countries.

This rebirth of a sense of community out of conflict can already be seen while the guns were still firing in Copenhagen Roads on 2 April 1801. At around 3pm, Nelson sent a despatch to Frederik VI of Denmark, observing that he 'has directions to spare Denmark when no longer resisted, but, if the firing is continued on the part of Denmark, Lord Nelson will be obliged to set on Fire all the floating Batteries he has taken, – without having the power of saving the brave Danes who have defended them'.[86] Military historians have debated the purpose of this communique, and it has been variously interpreted as an act of benevolence to an heroic opponent, as a ruse de guerre, and, most recently, as a prudent response to the fact that damaged British ships of the line were coming in range of land-based Danish artillery and that the course of the battle might therefore quickly turn to Danish advantage. What is of interest to me here, however, is the salutation with which Nelson addressed this despatch: 'to the Brothers of Englishmen; the Danes'.[87] This resonant phrase quickly became the leitmotif of British responses to the battle: the heroism and humanity displayed by both sides confirmed that the Danes and the English, far from being natural opponents and cultural contestants, were, in fact, culturally, and in some accounts even racially, 'brothers' – and that the true foe of both, the true 'Other', was Revolutionary France.

This leitmotif – which set Northern 'brothers' against the revolutionary and atheistical South – is plainly visible in Thomas Campbell's (1777–1844) response to events at Copenhagen in his poem 'The Battle of the Baltic' (1801). Born in Glasgow, Campbell, the son of a tobacco merchant who had been more or less ruined by the collapse of his business during the American War of Independence, had family connections with the Scottish Common Sense philosopher Thomas Reid (1710–96) and was later involved in the foundation of London University (now UCL). In 1800–1, he was travelling in Germany, where he met the poet Gottlieb Friedrich Klopstock (1724–1803), but he returned to Scotland following the Anglo-Danish conflict.

'The Battle of the Baltic' is Campbell's follow-up to 'Ye Mariners of England', which he composed in March 1801 when hostilities were first declared (and revised in 1805, following Nelson's death) – and the two poems later earned him a small government pension in recognition of their patriotism. Composed in ballad form (eight octaves with a trimeter envoi), the poem opens with an invocation to 'Nelson and the North' and the 'glorious day's renown, / When to battle fierce came forth / All the might of Denmark's crown'.[88] Campbell then draws a series of contrasts, in British favour: between the Danish 'leviathans afloat' and 'the lofty British line'; between the British cry 'Hearts of oak' and the 'feeble cheer' in reply from 'the Dane'; and between the sustained British volleys ('Again! again! again!') and the Danish 'shots' which 'ceased'.[89] And then comes the decisive intervention from Nelson: not his ignoring of Parker's signal but his despatch to Frederik VI. 'Out spoke the victor then', Campbell writes, resolving the contrasts he has established between British and Danish into a sense of shared identity:

> As he hail'd them o'er the wave;
> Ye are brothers! ye are men!
> And we conquer but to save;
> So peace instead of death let us bring:

> But yield, proud foe, thy fleet,
> With the crews, at England's feet,
> And make submission meet
> To our king.[90]

The jingoistic tone is unmistakable here, but so is the resolution of the British–Danish contrasts which Campbell has established into a sense of British–Danish alliance: Nelson has come to 'save' Britain and Denmark from the true foe of both: the French. And in Campbell's poem, the Danes recognise and reciprocate:

> Then Denmark blest our chief,
> That he gave her wounds repose;
> And the sounds of joy and grief
> From her people wildly rose.[91]

As it moves towards a close, Campbell's poem then cements this new alliance by reflecting on the heroic dead of both sides in terms which invoke both *The Tempest* and *Hamlet*, reminding readers, in the latter case at least, of the close cultural links between Britain and Denmark:

> Let us think of them that sleep
> Full many a fathom deep,
> By thy wild and stormy steep,
> Elsinore.[92]

There is, of course, nothing particularly steep in the scenery around Helsingør and the battle was fought off Copenhagen, some fifty kilometres to the south: Campbell's point in invoking this Romantic image of the castle – where *Hamlet* is set, and where Caroline Matilda had lived after the collapse of her marriage – is to remind his readers of the lengthy, cultural history shared by Britain and Denmark.

As noted, the bravery and humanity with which the Danish fought on 1 April – publicly lauded by Nelson in the aftermath of the battle – became an important part of the Danish response to the defeat. Danish bravery, however, was also a key trope of British responses to the battle. Some six years later, for example, the London bookseller John Fairburn (1789–1840), in his *Authentic Account of the Bombardment of Copenhagen* (1807), recalled of 2 April 1801 that:

> This dreadful engagement, heard, seen, and felt, on the Danish shore, wound up the feelings of all ranks to the highest pitch of sensibility; but all individual hopes and fears seemed to be lost in a general blaze of patriotic ardour. From the Crown Prince, to the humblest citizen, one heroic mind

and purpose seemed to animate and unite the whole. Never did the Danish valour, even in the brightest periods of their history, shine out with more distinguished lustre.[93]

To an extent, of course, emphasising Danish 'valour' had the effect of emphasising the scale of the British victory. But a recognition of the bravery and humanity with which both sides fought very often also became, as I have suggested, the basis for claims – echoing Nelson's despatch – that the Danes and the English were 'brothers' with a common enemy in the French.

Exactly such a claim can be seen, for example, in *The Battle of Copenhagen* (1806) by the antiquarian and bookseller Thomas Rodd (1763–1822). Rodd's poem – composed as his tells us in his Preface 'soon after the battle' although 'it makes its appearance late', following the death of Nelson in January 1806 – opens with a dedicatory 'Sonnet, to the Spirit of the Immortal Nelson' before providing a detailed account of the run-up to, course and aftermath of 2 April, across three cantos.[94] It its early movements, Rodd's poem lays the blame for the Anglo-Danish conflict firmly at the door of the Paul I of Russia (1754–1801), the instigator of the Second League of Armed Neutrality, and his 'union' with Napoleonic France:

> The Northern Pow'rs, beneath his influence rouz'd,
> In evil hour a common cause espous'd;
> So deeply did they dread his strength in arms
> Might vex their weaker states with dire alarms.
> O hapless nations! hapless Denmark most!
> [...]
> Why for her naval rights, more dear than life,
> With Britain seek a needless cause of strife?[95]

Once battle has been joined, however, differences between the Danish and the English are progressively elided by Rodd's poem, to the point at which he uses the same metaphor to describe them both: the familiar English emblem of the lion. As 'loud the cannon roar'd / And from the decks a dreadful broadside pour'd', he writes, 'Denmark trembl'd to its deepest bases, / Tho' conscious valour fill'd its hardy race'.[96] And it is the display of this shared 'valour' which leads, as I have said, to Rodd's eventual elision of the difference between the two combatants, the Danish and the English:

> More dreadful now the raging contrast grows,
> And *every heart* stupendous valour shews.
> As when *two lions*, with terrific roar,
> In combat join of Afric's burning shore.[97]

'The sons of Denmark such resistance made', Rodd affirms, echoing Nelson's claim: 'As if stern war had been their only trade, / And ne'er the British Admiral saw a fray / Of stormy fury equal to this day'.[98]

And once the battle has ended, Rodd is keen to emphasise how this mutual 'valour' in combat becomes the foundation for a renewed sense of common, cultural identity. 'A royal banquet Denmark then prepar'd', Rodd writes of the opening of negotiations, 'That Nelson and his Captain Hardy shar'd':

> And mutual courage was the noble theme,
> Begetting mutual love and warm esteem.
> 'Are we not brethren of a race', they cried,
> 'Whose courage oft has been in battle try'd?
> Be shame and sorrow the reward of those,
> Whose artful machinations made us foes!'.[99]

To the phrase 'Are we not brethren of a race', Rodd adds a somewhat spurious footnote: 'The common appellation of Englishmen in Denmark'.[100] But the point he wishes to make is clear: far from causing the collapse of Anglo-Danish relations, the 'mutual courage' – *mutual* is the word Rodd uses again and again – displayed throughout the Battle of Copenhagen has re-established a sense of common cultural and racial identity between the English and the Danes and distinguishes them from the 'artful machinations' of their true 'foe'.

This tendency of contemporary British responses to represent the Battle of Copenhagen as the occasion for the rebirth of community out of conflict was widespread. Witness, by way of further example, the refrain of the anonymous poem published in *The Scots Magazine* in May 1801, which returned again to that key moment in the battle, 'On Lord Nelson's sending a flag of truce to Copenhagen in the midst of victory':

> The brave may bleed – the brave may yield;
> But Mercy binds the brave again!
> [. . .]
> Returning friendship warms the Dane,
> The brave may fight – the brave may yield,
> But Mercy binds the brave again!'[101]

Nor was it short-lived. Some twelve years after the battle, for example, Robert Southey, in his *Life of Nelson*, wrote of the admiral's reaction that 'The Danes were an honourable foe; they were of English mould as well as English blood; and now that the battle had ceased, he regarded them rather as brethren than as enemies.'[102] Neither was this response merely – as one might reasonably expect it to have been – the convenient propaganda of the victor and limited to the English side. Conversely, in Denmark, too, commentators tended to focus not only on the heroism of the Danish on 2 April 1801 as an occasion for Romantic nationalist pride, but also on the battle as the moment for a reorientation of Danish cultural policy away from the French and back towards an historical connection with the English. Almost paradoxically, the emergence of the Danish Romantic nationalist responses to the Battle of Copenhagen went hand in hand with the development of a sense of transnational community with their antagonist.

A prime example of this rhetorical strategy can be found in the work of the Danish traveller, man of letters and Anglophile Andreas Andersen Feldborg (1782–1838). Feldborg published the first of his three English-language travel books, *A Tour in Zealand*, in 1804, while he was visiting England. I discuss Feldborg's travel writing in detail in Chapter 3, but what concerns me here is the 'Historical Account of the Battle of Copenhagen' which Feldborg included with his *Tour* and, in redacted form, in his anthology *Poems from the Danish* (1815). In his 'Advertisement' to the 'Historical Account', Feldborg justifies its inclusion in the following, striking terms:

> As the Battle of Copenhagen, which has been so beneficial in its effects to Denmark, has not been hitherto impartially described, I have here endeavoured to relate it with truth; and in so doing I flatter myself with having performed no unacceptable service to both nations, which, by its issue, have been, reciprocally, raised in the estimation of each other.[103]

This claim, it is probably worth reminding the reader, is made in a book, the title of which identifies its author as *A Native of Denmark*. Feldborg's desire to position himself and his work as a kind of cultural embassy or mediation between Denmark and England is apparent in his hope to have 'performed no unacceptable service to both nations'. But what is most striking is Feldborg's claim that Denmark has benefited from the defeat of 2 April, implicitly by being removed from French influence and explicitly by the restoration and augmentation of relations with England.

In the final paragraph of his 'Historical Account', Feldborg confirms that the 'substantial benefits to Denmark' which the battle 'yielded' consisted in 'the speedy reestablishment of that harmony which has so long subsisted' between England and Denmark.[104] And in the revised version of this final paragraph, in the American edition of Feldborg's *Tour*, published in 1807, the point is made even more explicitly:

Thus the rough 2d of April, like the overwhelming inundation of the Nile, has left its benefits behind – benefits, which the uninterrupted calm of an eighty years peace, was unable to afford us. We have been taught confidence in each other; we have provided for the safety and security and honour of the kingdoms; and, if I may be allowed to pronounce from experience, we have gained the esteem and affection of the British nation.[105]

Feldborg's reference to the restorative annual flooding of the Nile – and, implicitly, to Nelson's 'overwhelming' defeat of the French at the Battle of the Nile in August 1798 – confirms this sense that out of conflict between England and Denmark has come a restored sense of cultural community, beneficial to both nations, providing 'confidence [. . .] safety and security and honour'.

That these sentiments played well in Feldborg's native Denmark is sufficiently evident from his 'Preface' to the second edition of his *Tour*, where he expresses not just his 'gratitude' for 'the indulgence of the British public', but also his being 'highly gratified' to learn that Laurids Engelstoft (1774–1851), Professor of History at Copenhagen University, had 'reviewed my book, and bestowed upon it the fiat of his commendation'.[106] And indeed, as Feldborg later revealed in his *A Dane's Excursions in Britain* (1809), his 'Historical Account' earned him on 26 August 1805 'the honour of an interview' with Nelson and Emma Hamilton (1765–1815), the former of whom Feldborg had first met in Pall Mall 'a few days after' his arrival in London in October 1802.[107] Nelson was complimentary, but also took the occasion to observe that Feldborg, on one (sadly unspecified) occasion in his 'Historical Account' did 'hold the pencil in a manner different from what an Englishman would have done'![108] In response to Nelson's question 'how the book has then been received in Denmark?', Feldborg takes the opportunity to note that he was not 'fully' aware, at the time of the interview, 'of the various criticisms and indulgent opinions which the people of Denmark and Norway had passed', and he quotes from Engelstoft's praising review:

> The author has established a solid claim on the gratitude of his countrymen; and both nations will, no doubt, bestow their approbation on a work which teaches the one to esteem the other, and places in its true point of view an event equally interesting to both.[109]

Once again, the leitmotif is the rebirth of Anglo-Danish cultural community, of 'mutual esteem', out of the conflict of 2 April 1801.

What Feldborg's 'Historical Account' also adds to the narrative of the battle as perceived in Britain, however, is a detailed description of the

Danish cultural response. He describes the pride of the people in the heroism displayed on the day; the dignity with which Nelson was received when he landed in the city, and his praise for the conduct of the Danish defenders; the burial of the dead, the monuments commissioned, and the medallions struck; the many subscriptions raised; and the numerous responses in painting, prose and verse, notably including those published by the prominent Danish man of letters Knud Lyne Rahbek (1760–1830) in his periodical *Den Danske Tilskuer* [The Danish Spectator]. In short, what Feldborg charts for the British readers of his 'Historical Account' is the first stirrings of Danish Romantic nationalism in the responses to 2 April 1801. In this sense, through the work of Feldborg and others, the battle brought to British attention not just the heroism of the Danes, but also the rich cultural life of the country and the extent of the common cultural ground between Britain and Denmark.

But alas, this renewed sense of the common cultural cause that was celebrated in British and Danish responses to the Battle of Copenhagen was not to endure: only six years later, British ships once again opened fire off Copenhagen – and this time on the city itself.

'One of the most remarkable events': The Bombardment of Copenhagen (1807)

For historians of British Romanticism, the phrase 'one of the most remarkable events of modern times' will immediately call to mind Edmund Burke's (1730–97) well-known characterisation of the French Revolution, in his *Reflections* (1790), as 'the most astonishing that has hitherto happened in the world'.[110] In this case, however, the phrase is used by F. L. Sommer (dates unknown; possibly a pseudonym) in his widely circulated *Description of Denmark; And a Narrative of the Siege, Bombardment, and Capture of Copenhagen* (1807), to describe the British bombardment of Copenhagen on 2–5 September 1807, using the recently developed incendiary weapon known as the Congreve Rocket.[111] The presumably intentional echo of Burke signals the significance that the bombardment was felt to have, and not only was Sommer's *Narrative* widely disseminated, but other accounts also deployed the same, or similar, phrasing: in his *Particulars of the Expedition to Copenhagen* (1808), for example, Septimus Crookes (dates unknown) describes it as 'one of the most striking events of modern times'.[112] Like the Battle of Copenhagen before it, the Bombardment of Copenhagen was viewed by contemporaries as another key milestone in the course of the war with France.[113] Indicatively, Arthur Wellesley (1769–1852), 1st Duke of Wellington, named the horse which he later rode at the Battle of Waterloo (1815), foaled in 1808, in honour of the engagement.

The historical and political context for the bombardment was in many respects similar to that which had occasioned the Battle of Copenhagen in 1801. Fearing that Napoleon would either persuade or compel now neutral Denmark–Norway to join the war against Britain and close the Baltic to British ships, the British government tried to negotiate the transfer of Denmark's navy, which had been partly rebuilt since 1801, to British control, and finally offered an ultimatum to surrender the ships or face an attack. When Denmark refused to comply, Britain sent an expeditionary force commanded by William Cathcart (1775–1843) and James Gambier (1756–1833) which attacked Copenhagen from land and sea, culminating in a three-day bombardment which forced a Danish surrender – and during which around 1,200 civilians were killed or injured and large parts of the city centre destroyed. After the departure of the British force, Denmark allied itself with France and remained at war with Britain until the Treaty of Kiel (1814) brought a formal end to hostilities.

Earlier in this chapter, I discussed Percy Bysshe Shelley's angry response to the bombardment, with its imagining of an Arctic Copenhagen, which was written some four years after the events it purports to describe. However, it is fair to say that the indignation expressed in Shelley's 'Fragment of a Poem' was also felt across much of Britain and Europe in the immediate aftermath of 2–5 September 1807, and on both sides of the political divide.[114] So controversial, indeed, was this brutal attack on a neutral and ostensibly friendly country – on a people whom, as we have seen, Nelson had hailed as 'brothers' – that George III of England was forced to issue an explanation on 25 September 1807:

> His Majesty owes to himself and to Europe a frank exposition of the motives which have dictated his late measures in the Baltic.
>
> His Majesty has delayed this exposition only in the hope of that more amicable arrangement with the Court of Denmark which it was his Majesty's first wish and endeavour to obtain, for which he was ready to make great efforts and sacrifices, and of which he never lost sight even in the moment of the most decisive hostility.
>
> Deeply as the disappointment of this hope has been felt by his Majesty, he has the consolation of reflecting that no exertion was left untried on his part to produce a different result. And, while he laments the cruel necessity which has obliged him to have recourse to acts of hostility against a nation with which it was his Majesty's most earnest desire to have established the relations of common interest and alliance, his Majesty feels confident that, in the eyes of Europe and of the world, the justification of his conduct will

be found in the commanding and indispensable duty, paramount to all others amongst the obligations of a sovereign, or providing, while there was yet time, for the immediate security of his people.[115]

This 'Declaration' was included, often with commentary, in a number of British accounts of the bombardment, and the political controversy rumbled on for many months. The British Houses of Lords and Commons debated the issue for the last time on 21 and 24 March 1808 respectively, during which the Whig opposition again asserted, as it had done throughout the winter of 1807 and the spring of 1808, the immorality of the action, while the Tory government continued to defend it on grounds of pragmatic necessity, as an instance of what came, after the analysis of the foreign secretary George Canning (1770–1827), to be called 'the new morality' of the Revolutionary and Napoleonic Wars.[116] James Gillray (1756–1815) made it the subject of a cartoon 'British Tars, towing the Danish fleet into harbour' (1807), in which a small boat crewed by Canning and two others attempt to secure the Danish ships while a sea-monster, with the heads of prominent members of the opposition, spouts water at them; Copenhagen burns in the background while Napoleon dances over a burning Europe.[117]

The controversy over the events of 2–5 September raged in the periodical reviews with an intensity no less than in the Houses of Commons and Lords. As David Erdman pointed out in an article of 1968, William Blake (1757–1827) made in 1807–8 a transcription in one of his notebooks of 'Lines Written on hearing the surrender of Copenhagen', by the Radical, Birmingham-based bookseller and poet James Bisset (c.1762–1832).[118] Bisset's 'Lines' open with the quite-Blakean assertion that 'The Glory of Albion is tarnish'd with Shame', before going on to lament how the country which had once defended 'the Seraph of Peace' had now 'puru'd her' to 'the gloom of the North' which it lit up with 'the meteor of Death', a clear reference to Congreve Rockets.[119] Erdman had not then identified the source from which Blake copied the poem: it was first published in *The Oracle* for 14 October 1807 and reprinted in *The Spirit of the Public Journals* for 1808 along with an anonymous tercet on the same theme entitled 'Denmark':

> When Denmark's ships, and Denmark's stores,
>   Arrive at old Britannia's shores,
> The Ministers, alas! will find
> That they have left a *stain behind*![120]

As Burton Pollin has shown, a satire of Robert Southey's anti-war poem 'After Blenheim' was published in the *Morning Chronicle* for 26 October 1808, immediately following the final parliamentary debates on the bombardment, under the title 'A Danish Tale', serving 'the double purpose of lampooning the dominant party for a specific campaign and reiterating the humanitarian horror of war'.[121]

My focus in the remainder of this chapter will be on British literary responses to the bombardment of Copenhagen and, in particular, on how those responses often express outrage by invoking exactly that trope of common cultural identity which emerged from the battle of 2 April 1801. In other words, if British (and Danish) responses to the Battle of Copenhagen in 1801 often saw it as an occasion on which mutual heroism led to mutual esteem and a sense of cultural community, then British literary responses to the bombardment of Copenhagen in 1807 – even those which are ostensibly patriotic, such as that by Samuel Taylor Coleridge (1772–1834) – often saw it, conversely, as an occasion on which Danish valour had exposed British dishonour, on which Britain had betrayed its Northern 'brothers'.[122] An anonymous poem in the *Morning Chronicle* for 15 February 1808 entitled 'Song on the New Affair of Copenhagen (not Lord Nelson's)' made this contrast between 1801 and 1807 forcefully apparent in its ironic opening lines:

> O tell us no more of old Nelson's renown,
> How in doughty fair battle he conquered the Dane,
> Since Canning's the boy who could batter a town,
> And filch a whole navy by legerdemain[123]

In a similar vein, Lord Byron (1788–1824), in 'The Curse of Minerva' (1811), written four years later, when listing British iniquities abroad, suggested 'Look to the Baltic – blazing from afar, / Your old Ally yet mourns perfidious war'.[124]

The life and work of at least one famous British Romantic-period writer was touched directly by the events of 2–5 September 1807. Thomas De Quincey's (1785–1859) brother Richard (b. 1789), known as 'Pink', was part of the crew of the *Prometheus*, one of the ships sent against Copenhagen, and he and some of his comrades were taken prisoner when they landed in Jutland, while en route, in an attempt to procure additional provisions. De Quincey attributes his learning of Danish to this incident, which was a source of considerable distress to his family at the time (see Chapter 3).[125] William Wordsworth (1770–1850), too, might have had some – granted, considerably less direct – connection to Anglo-Danish naval conflicts: in his poem 'The Sailor's Mother', composed in 1802 and published in *Poems, in Two Volumes* in April 1807, the mother of the title laments to the speaker that she 'had a Son, who many a day / Sailed on the seas, but he is dead; / In Denmark he was cast away'.[126]

For most in Britain, however, information about the bombardment of Copenhagen was of course gained second-hand, from the numerous accounts – some of them, at least, purporting to be eyewitness accounts – which soon after began to circulate. Prominent among these is the aforementioned *Description of Denmark; and a Narrative of the Siege, Bombardment, and Capture of Copenhagen*, by F. L. Sommer. This *Narrative* poses a number of puzzles for the literary historian. As the *Monthly Magazine* for November 1807 makes clear, the *Narrative* was first 'printed in English at Copenhagen' in that month, under the title *An Account of the Siege, Bombardment, and Capitulation of Copenhagen in the Year 1807*.[127] The following year, a second edition was printed in Colchester, by I. Marsden.[128] In this second edition, Sommer's *Account* is preceded by a fourteen-page *Description of Denmark*, almost certainly by a different hand, and most certainly written from an English rather than a Danish perspective. The *Account* was also frequently excerpted and sometimes printed entire in other British accounts, such as John Fairburn's *Authentic Account of the Bombardment of Copenhagen* (1808) or the anonymous *Authentic Account of the Siege of Copenhagen* published in London in 1807.[129] How the second, English edition, with its added *Description*, came about, however, is unknown, although it is tempting to suspect that Andreas Andersen Feldborg, who was in Britain in 1807–8, might have had some hand in it. Nor has any information survived about the original author.[130] Could 'F. L. Sommer' in fact have been another pseudonym of Feldborg, who, as we have seen, published his *Dane's Excursions in Britain* in 1809 – in which he remains pointedly silent about the bombardment – under the pseudonym J. A. Andersen? It is certainly plausible that Feldborg might have sent a text home for publication at Copenhagen, a text which – since it was written in English – was clearly intended for an international rather than a domestic audience.

Be that as it may, Sommer's *Account* was, as I have said, widely disseminated in Britain and highly influential in colouring British literary responses to the events of 2–5 September 1807. The *Description of Denmark* which precedes it in the second edition focuses its topographical descriptions more or less entirely on Copenhagen and its surroundings, reasonably enough in the context. 'Denmark Proper' it encouragingly writes off as: 'a flat country, abounding in bogs and morasses, and surrounded by the sea, fogs are extremely frequent there, and the air is in many parts unwholesome'.[131] In its account of Copenhagen, the *Description* follows quite closely the positive assessments offered by Coxe and Swinton. Copenhagen 'makes a magnificent appearance at a distance' and is 'adorned' by many fine buildings; the police are so efficient 'that people may walk through it at midnight in perfect safety'; and 'justice [. . .] has been always impartially administrated'.[132] The 'encouragement of arts and sciences' by successive kings is also emphasised.[133] This, in other words, is most certainly not Wollstonecraft's Copenhagen – and of course, in the context of this particular publication, the positive assessment of the Danish capital serves to reinforce the sense of outrage at the destruction wrought by the British.

Sommer's *Account* of that destruction is introduced by the curious final paragraph of the *Description*, which observes that:

> In 1780, his Danish Majesty acceded to the armed neutrality established between the Northern powers, which he observed inviolate, 'till the British fleet appeared in the Sound, in August, 1807, and forced him to have recou[r]se to arms.[134]

Not only is this summary historically inaccurate in that it conflates the First and Second Leagues of Armed Neutrality, and partisan in that the phrasing suggests a mutual rather than a solely British aggression, but it also neglects entirely to mention the battle of 2 April 1801, about which all of its readers must surely have known. One can only wonder as to why so striking an omission was made.

Sommer's *Account* proper begins, as we have already seen, with the assertion that 'the siege and bombardment of Copenhagen by the English, are, both, in their causes and consequences, one of the most remarkable events of modern times'.[135] Sommer then offers an extended, positive assessment of the condition of Copenhagen in 1807, presumably with a view to emphasising for those unfamiliar with the country the scale of the physical and cultural violence done by the bombardment:

> It was the golden age of our island [meaning Sjaelland] and our capital. Unconcerned for more, we confined our wishes to our native shore and lawful advantages, which our trade and a most impartial neutrality could afford. Our efforts were blessed by providence, and our happiness had reached its summit, when the English threatened our shores.[136]

Sommer also stresses the great disproportion of force involved, implicitly evoking the battle of 2 April 1801 which had left Denmark 'defenceless' but which had also established an 'honourable peace' between the two countries: 'so formidable and unexpected a force as that which was brought by the English must necessarily obtain a victory over a defenceless nation, who founded its whole grandeur and glory on the happy enjoyment of an honourable peace'.[137]

Sommer's *Account* dwells in considerable detail on the political backdrop to the bombardment and includes transcripts of various correspondence and declarations. It also provides detailed accounts of troop and ship movements and of the technicalities of various engagements on land and sea in the run-up to the bombardment. Explicit mention, too, is made of the Congreve Rockets: 'It deserves to be remarked, that the English, besides their bombs, threw a kind of rocket, which civilised nations never made use of before'.[138] 'Civilised', in this context, refers not just to the use of incendiary weapons against an urban target, but also to the fact that the Congreve Rocket was a British copy of the Mysore Rocket used by Hyder Ali (1720–82) and his son the notorious Tipu Sultan (1750–99) against the British in India. There is thus a kind of reverse Orientalism in Sommer's comparison, the inverse of the trope used by Wraxall and other early British accounts of Denmark, where it is now the British who behave like the uncivilised 'Other'.

Alongside this quite dispassionate, empirical discourse, however, there is another, more visual, affective discourse in Sommer's *Account*, which describes unflinchingly the horrors of the British attack, and it was this discourse which was to have so profound an influence on British literary responses to the bombardment. This visual-affective discourse is first evident in Sommer's description of the British fleet, which 'appeared like a forest' off Copenhagen:

> They would have afforded us the finest sight in the world, had we not unhappily been informed, that these superb monuments of British valour were destined to destroy our unhappy capital and annihilate our old maritime power.[139]

That ironic reference to the 'monuments of British valour' is made fully evident when Sommer's *Account* turns to the uses to which they were put, and it is here that the visual-affective discourse really comes to the fore. 'It is with the utmost grief', he writes, 'that I am going to describe the horrible scenes which the bombardment of Copenhagen has offered':

> Shame to the world, I said to myself, when about seven and a half in the evening I heard the thunder of the mortars breaking out, and saw a large rocket fly like an arrow through the streets and killing in its way a poor innocent child, who stood at a window opposite to my house. O! Britain! I cried out in despair – Queen of nations! Mother of such noble and manly sons! Is this thy work?[140]

As his *Account* proceeds, Sommer details the 'horrors' that follow. A 'blind man who was killed in his bed' by British shot.[141] People 'wounded and crushed to death both in the streets and houses'.[142] The burning buildings and the 'unfortunate' firemen 'killed at their post, in nobly attempting to do their duty'.[143] A 'mother giving suck to her child' who 'was killed together with her offspring by a shell'.[144] This last, particularly harrowing image evidently influenced that section of 'A Danish Tale', from the *Morning Chronicle*, which notes that while 'The English had the victory' it 'was a shocking sight':

> To see the fearful mother's flight,
> While with frantic care she prest
> Still closer to her throbbing breast
> That babe that pass'd, with transient breath
> From instant life to instant death.[145]

It clearly also influenced Percy Shelley's 'Fragment of a Poem', with its similar vision of 'a lone female' who 'lists to the death-shrieks that came on the air, / The pride of heart to her bosom she pressed, / Then sunk on his form in the sleep of the blest'.[146] 'All the scenes of horror', Sommer concludes, 'which appeared in every quarter, cannot be described'.[147] Surrender, in such circumstances, was inevitable: the alternative was 'the total destruction of Copenhagen and all that it contains'.[148]

In addition to supplying British responses to the bombardment which a series of recurrent images, Sommer's *Account* also emphasises the extent to which the British attack on Copenhagen was felt in Denmark to be a violation of the cultural bonds between the two countries, a violation of the 'brotherhood' re-established through mutual respect in April 1801. Sommer quotes a declaration made by Frederik VI of Denmark following the bombardment, in which the Danish Crown Prince lamented that Britain had not hesitated before 'dissolving the ancient and sacred connections which united Denmark to Great Britain'.[149] The bombardment, Frederik continued, was 'an act of violence, which even in England, every virtuous and generous mind will disown; which deforms the character of a virtuous sovereign, and which will ever remain a scandal in the annals of Great Britain'.[150] Once again, then, while the events of April 1801 had forged a new relationship between Britain and Denmark on the grounds of common valour and humanity, the bombardment of 1807 was represented as fracturing that relationship and signalling a fall from that 'virtuous' conduct which in 1801 had enabled the Danes and the English to recognise each other as brothers with a common foe in the French.

As well as drawing on the imagery of Sommer's *Account*, British literary responses to the events of September 1807 – both patriotic and critical – often also invoked this sense of common cultural identity between Britain and Denmark. As an example of a patriotic account, we might take the aforementioned *Particulars of the Expedition to Copenhagen*, the title page of which identifies its author, as we have seen, as one Septimus Crookes, 'private in the Fourth, or King's Own Regiment'.

For a supposedly eyewitness account – the British fourth infantry landed in Denmark as part of the expeditionary force, and the dedication to 'my fellow soldiers & countrymen' is dated 'Citadel of Copenhagen, Oct. 10, 1807' – the *Particulars* contains some striking instances of the 'Romantic' reimagining of Denmark that we have been tracing in Wollstonecraft's *Short Residence* and Shelley's 'Fragment of a Poem'. Consider, for example, Crookes's account of his first sight of the Danish west coast: 'it appeared to be very desolate and sandy, and very mountainous; it is called Jutland' – now Jutland might well be 'desolate and sandy', but 'very mountainous' it most certainly is not![151] And indeed, the authenticity of Crookes's *Particulars* might further be called into question by the fact that, on occasion, it seems to be directly plagiarised from Sommer's *Account*, as, for example, in Crookes's description of the British fleet at anchor off Copenhagen: 'I endeavoured, if possible, to count *these superb monuments of British valour* [. . .] a sight that conveyed to the mind of the beholder, a sensation truly sublime.'[152]

Crookes's frankly rather jingoistic account of the attack itself lays the blame for 'the dread fate of Denmark' firmly at the door of what he describes as 'the obstinate rashness' and 'pride of haughty Denmark', for 'which they paid full dear'.[153] But Crookes also inscribes this supposed Danish hubris and its consequences within a longer history of the cultural bonds between Britain and Denmark. Specifically, he very often invokes the Viking conquest of England and represents the British attack of 1807 as a redress for that perceived indignity. Hence, of his regiment's first landing, Crookes records: 'How inspiring the sight to the breast of each British soldier, to witness our landing on those shores from which our forefathers often experienced a similar invasion.'[154] And of the Danish officers and infantrymen taken prisoner after an engagement at Køge (then a small town, south-west of Copenhagen) on 29 August 1807, Crookes notes, with similar triumphalism:

> It was a sight highly gratifying to my feelings, to see in our possession the descendents of those proud progenitors, who often rejoiced in the distress of our forefathers, on similar occasions: Such is the fate of war![155]

In Crookes's *Particulars*, then, Britain is no uncivilised 'Other' breaking the 'ancient and sacred' bonds of cultural brotherhood with Denmark, to use Frederik VI's phrase, but rather a country driven by 'noble ambition and fixed determination' to redress both current and historical wrongs stemming from Danish 'pride'.[156] The passing reference made by Walter Scott (1771–1832) to the bombardment in the third canto of *Marmion* (1808) strikes a similar, historical note:

> 'Tis said, that, in that awful night,
> Remoter visions met his sight,
> Foreshowing future conquests far,
> When our son's sons wage northern war;
> A royal city, tower and spire,
> Reddened the midnight sky with fire,
> And shouting crews her navy bore,
> Triumphant to the victor shore.[157]

But significantly, in Crookes's *Particulars*, once hostilities have ended, Crookes returns to that more familiar idiom of cultural common ground, noting of Copenhagen that it 'is well built' – a curious observation given the condition in which he must have seen the city – and that 'the citizens are great imitators of the English, in both manners and dress'.[158] And in the final sentence of his *Particulars*, Crookes even identifies 'the Gallic Emperor' as the true villain of the piece.[159]

While Crookes's account of the British attack of 2–5 September 1807 expresses no doubt at all concerning either the motivation for or the conduct of the bombardment, British literary responses which were critical of the attack tended, conversely, to invoke the trope of cultural brotherhood to cast the British as an uncivilised 'Other' in contrast to the noble Dane, effectively, again, in a kind of reversal of the Orientalist tropes used by earlier commentators like Wraxall to describe Denmark. I want to conclude this chapter by examining one such response: *The Siege of Copenhagen. A Poem; With Notes* (1808), by the Scottish poet James Grahame (1765–1811).

Grahame, who later became an Anglican curate, tended to write on Scottish and religious themes, and hence Byron described him, in *English Bards and Scotch Reviewers* (1809), as 'the Sabbath Bard, / Sepulchral GRAHAME' who 'pours his notes sublime / In mangled prose, nor e'en aspires to rhyme'.[160] *The Siege of Copenhagen*, however, is in heroic couplets throughout (of which Byron, at least, should have approved). This form was far less popular in 1807 than it had been in the eighteenth century, but its continued associations with epic allowed Grahame, no doubt, to make a pointed contrast between the style of his poem and the subject which it describes: *The Siege of Copenhagen* is unflinching in its depiction of the British attack as an act of betrayal and barbarity against a friendly nation. Like many other British literary responses, Grahame's poem, too, draws in various ways on Sommer's *Account*, but to that picture it adds a sense not just of the physical but also of the *cultural* violence done to Denmark by Britain – and of the implications of that violence for British culture.[161] So explicit, indeed, is Grahame's description of the horrors of the bombardment that the reviewer of the poem in the *Anti-Jacobin Review* felt obliged to point out that:

> While we give to Mr. Grahame's Muse the just tribute of applause for the poetic merit of this plaintive effusion, we regret that she [i.e. the Muse] should be so short-sighted in her political views, as not to see the necessity of the energetic and decisive measure which is the subject of her song.[162]

The majority of the review is concerned less with Grahame's poem than with justifying this supposed 'necessity'.

The Siege of Copenhagen opens by invoking, for the reader, the memory of the battle of April 1801:

> Calm was the eve; the sun had set in gold,
> And silent to the beach the billows rolled,
> When England's banners, rising on the view,
> Awakened half-forgotten fears anew.[163]

The arrival of the fleet – a spectacle noted, as we have seen, in Sommer's *Account* – draws 'the veterans' of 1801 to 'the ramparts', where they 'gaze fearless on the force they cannot count'.[164] Denmark's unpreparedness is emphasised by the 'empty embrasures' on the fortifications, to which the veterans 'apply / The long-drawn tube, to aid the failing eye', a clear echo of Nelson's famous turning of a blind eye to Parker's signal during the height of the battle on 2 April 1801.[165] These early apprehensions subside as the Danes recall the 'love and friendship' between the two countries, forged out of that earlier conflict.[166] But this reassurance is short-lived and the Danish response turns to 'hate and fear' as the land assault begins and British intentions are revealed: 'perfidious foes approach the guardless strand'.[167]

As the bombardment begins, Grahame emphasises the indiscriminate nature of the attack: 'one ruin showering on the princely dome, / And on the poor man's low, once happy home'.[168] He, like so many others following Sommer, describes the fate of a mother and child in a house struck by a Congreve Rocket:

> The mother, safe, looks round in horror wild,
> And, lifting from the ground her darling child,
> Frantic beholds two sightless eyeballs roll,

Where beamed those orbs, that spake a seraph soul:
Another's limbs lie quivering in their blood,
While hissing fragments drink the reeking flood.[169]

He describes another 'cradled infant' surrounded by 'lambent' fire, 'leaden' roof tiles turned to 'molten currents', hospitals destroyed, and even long-buried corpses unearthed by the explosions: 'the grave is entered by the mining bomb: / [. . .] In awful caverns yawns the peopled mould, / Disclosing sights 'twere impious to unfold'.[170]

As I noted earlier, however, Grahame draws the reader's attention not just to the cost in civilian suffering of the bombardment, but also the cultural devastation wrought by the British attack. 'Behold yon edifice', he says of the university library, then at the Trinitatis buildings in central Copenhagen, which also includes the aforementioned Round Tower, 'whose summits tower / Through clouds of smoke':

there, in one little hour,
The British Vandals with relentless rage,
Destroy the mental labours of an age;
Extinguish Iceland's half rekindled light,
And shroud in treble gloom the Arctic night.[171]

In his commentary on this passage, Jørgen Sevaldsen reads it as evidence that Grahame thought that the bombardment had destroyed the classical Icelandic manuscripts ['de islandske hånskrifter'] which had played such a key role in the Antiquarian Revival of the eighteenth century, and which, as Sevaldsen points out, had already been damaged in the Copenhagen fire of 1728.[172] However, in his own note to the passage, Grahame explains: 'an immense public library was destroyed by the bombardment; and in it were all the copies of an Icelandic Dictionary, the preparation of which had been the labour of thirty years.'[173] Grahame would seem to refer, then, not to the destruction of the saga manuscripts, but rather to the work on those manuscripts of the Icelandic–Danish philologist Grímur Jónsson Thorkelín (1752–1849), who was Professor of Antiquities at Copenhagen University. In addition to his philological work on Icelandic, for some twenty years prior to 1807, Thorkelín had been transcribing and preparing for publication a translation of the Old English epic *Beowulf* and the two manuscripts of Thorkelín's translation were destroyed in the bombardment, though thankfully not the original manuscript transcription, which enabled him finally to publish an edition of the poem in 1815. The cultural violence to which Grahame points here, then, is not just directed against the Danes, but also, inadvertently, against the British themselves, to the extent that it could potentially have resulted in the destruction of a key text in English literature. Such acts mark the British out as 'Vandals': the enemies not just of Denmark, but of civilisation per se.

Sevaldsen also notes as 'interesting' in this passage what he sees as evidence that Grahame was 'fascinated with Copenhagen as a symbol of the world of the sagas' ['optaget med København som et symbol på det sagaverden'].[174] I would suggest, however, that Grahame's reference to 'the arctic night' rather marks this poem as part of that 'Romantic' tradition, which also includes Shelley's 'Fragment', which involves the reimagining of Copenhagen as an 'Arctic' city, as part of an imagined, sublime 'North' rather than an actual, contemporary Scandinavia. It is almost as if, in Grahame's lines, the British do violence not only against the legacy of classical Scandinavian culture, but also against a *natural* space (as in Shelley's 'Fragment'). Even the library, in Grahame's image, has 'summits', and an exactly similar blurring of architectural, natural and Arctic imagery can be seen a few lines later when Grahame refers to 'the spire' of Vor Frue Kirke [Our Saviour's Church], which burned down during the bombardment, as a 'pinnacle sublime' which 'seems with its point to kiss the polar star'.[175]

As *The Siege of Copenhagen* draws towards a close, Grahame reflects on the consequences of the bombardment for the British. These amount, in the first instance, to the turning of Danish friendship into enmity and the breaking of the sense of cultural brotherhood forged out of the conflict of 1801. Grahame imagines the case of a condemned prisoner set fortuitously at liberty by the destruction of his prison. But rather than feel 'the joys of freedom', this man is 'confounded' by the 'scene' in the city, where 'he death in every dreadful form surveys':

> Infuriate for revenge his eyeballs roll,
> And patriot feelings fire the felon's soul:
> Upon the ramparts, in the battle's strife,
> He ends with honour ignominious life;
> And feels, even with the latest gasp he draws,
> How sweet to suffer in an honest cause![176]

As was the case in the battle of 1801, then, the bombardment of Copenhagen also provides the opportunity for a display of Danish bravery and honour. Unlike in 1801, however, in 1807 there is no British honour to match the Danish. Rather, there is only ignominy and disgrace for the victor on this occasion. 'But subjugation is not always shame', Grahame writes of the Danish surrender after three days, in a passage which again echoes Sommer's *Account*, 'Nor conquest always honourable fame':

No: Britain, blush! and, Denmark, look erect!
And duly prize the blessing, self respect:
No blood of infants murdered at the breast,
No mother slaughtered, as she lulled to rest
Her babe affrighted by a world of fire,
Against thee calls for heaven's avenging ire:
Against the weak, from sex, disease, and age,
Thy arm was never raised in dastard rage.[177]

It is not difficult to see, here, why the ultra-conservative *Anti-Jacobin* review would baulk at Grahame's politics while acknowledging the power of his verse. Grahame's message is unambiguous: Britain's conduct in the bombardment has cost the country its honour, its 'self respect', among nations. And this is the note on which *The Siege of Copenhagen* concludes. In the final stanza of the poem, Grahame – rebuffing those political arguments that the bombardment was justified on the grounds of pragmatic necessity – notes that it has cost Britain not only a friend and an ally against a common foe, but also the opportunity for a heroic victory against that foe through noble conduct 'in open war', the opportunity, as he puts it, for 'a second Trafalgar'.[178]

In terms of the cultural history of Anglo-Danish relations which I am charting in this book, then, the shifting representation of Copenhagen can be seen to exemplify the changing place of Denmark in the British imagination during the late eighteenth and early nineteenth centuries. For the first British *tourists* in the mid-eighteenth century, Copenhagen is emblematic of an 'Oriental' polity, of the oppressive absolutism which had been condemned in early modern histories of Denmark, such as Molesworth's *Account of Denmark* (1693). This is a Copenhagen which is the antitype of London, a synecdoche for a Denmark which is the antitype of Britain. Later travellers, however, increasingly break down this sense of Denmark as 'Other', a process which reaches its apex in the sense of cultural brotherhood and alliance against a common foe which emerges from the Battle of Copenhagen in April 1801. Parallel to these responses to the contemporary cultural and political life of the Danish capital is a trend in British writing about Denmark, most visible in Wollstonecraft's *Short Residence*, to situate the country – with varying degrees of success – within an emergent, 'Romantic' discourse of 'the North' as a sublime, natural space. And both these interwoven discourses come under immense strain in the aftermath of the British bombardment of Copenhagen in September 1807, when critics of the attack in both countries consistently represent Britain as having broken the bonds of cultural brotherhood and violated a 'Romantic' valorisation of 'the North'. In other words, if the first British tourists in the city saw Copenhagen as emblematic of an 'Oriental' polity which was the opposite of British liberty, then, thirty years later, critics of the bombardment were all too likely to represent Britain as the 'Oriental' other of a progressive and heroic Denmark, as the 'Vandal' enemies of civilisation, to use Grahame's expression. Not until fifteen years after the signing of the Treaty of Kiel and the formal cessation of Anglo-Danish hostilities would works like Richard Jones's *Copenhagen and its Environs* begin again to recommend Copenhagen as a destination for mainstream British tourism.

Chapter 2

'The dwelling-place of a mighty people': Travellers beyond Copenhagen

Murray's *Hand-Book for Travellers in Denmark, Norway, Sweden, and Russia* (1839) reminds the reader early on that the attractions of Denmark are not limited to the capital but extend across the entire country, 'whose fertile lowlands have ever been the dwelling-place of a mighty people'.[1] However, if Copenhagen received comparatively few British tourists during the late eighteenth and early nineteenth centuries, then the rest of Denmark – that 'flat country' which Sommer's *Description of Denmark* portrays, rather less encouragingly than Murray's *Hand-Book*, as 'abounding in bogs and morasses' – received even fewer.[2] But by no means none at all. Prior to the publication of Mary Wollstonecraft's (1759–97) *Letters Written during a Short Residence in Sweden, Norway, and Denmark* (1796), for example, at least eight other English-language accounts of travel in Denmark had appeared. These include the brief but informative descriptions of key places on the land route from Hamburg to Copenhagen given in the *Grand Tour* (1749) of Thomas Nugent (1700–72), and the much more substantial discussion offered by William Coxe (1748–1828) in his *Travels into Poland, Russia, Sweden, and Denmark* (1784), which Wollstonecraft used, and which had gone to three editions by the time of her visit.[3] And, of course, many other accounts would follow Wollstonecraft's, written by everyone from wealthy tourists through prisoners of war to the author of the controversial *Essay on the Principle of Population* (1798).

Like Wollstonecraft's *Short Residence*, however, most British observations of places outside Copenhagen focus on the surrounding environs of Zealand and were made en passant, as it were, to and from the capital, at the beginning or the end of a larger Nordic tour. And the majority of these describe the east coast of Zealand between Copenhagen and Helsingør (Elsinore), the latter famous in Britain, of course, as the setting for *Hamlet*, as the prison of Caroline Matilda (1751–75), and as the main crossing point between Denmark and Sweden, 'the grand turn-pike gate to the Baltic', as Andrew Swinton (dates unknown) describes it in his *Travels* (1792).[4] But increasing numbers of British travellers did in the late eighteenth and early nineteenth centuries describe the rest of the Denmark, often as far west as the moors along the Jutland coast, including the likes of William Coxe and Edward Daniel Clarke (1769–1822), both of whom who made the journey from Germany to Copenhagen overland rather than by sea.

Nor, interestingly, were English-language accounts of travel in Denmark limited to those produced by British travellers. In 1792–3, the Danish writer Jens Baggesen (1764–1826), for example, published his two-volume *Labyrinten; eller Reise giennem Tydskland, Schweiz og Frankerig* [Labyrinth; or Journey through Germany, Switzerland and France] (1792–3). In this semi-fictional, semi-autobiographical novel – the first major work of travel writing to be published in Danish – Baggesen urged his contemporaries to 'always travel south as far as you can' ['Reis bestandig mod Syden saa langt du kan'], along the routes of the classical Grand Tour towards Italy.[5] Such journeys played an important role in the development of Romanticism in Denmark and lie behind important works of Danish Romanticism, such as the sculptures of Bertel Thorvaldsen (1797–1838) and the paintings of Italian scenes by Christen Købke (1810–48). But the early part of the nineteenth century also saw increasing numbers of Danes exploring their own country, often on state-funded trips, as well as journeying to England and Scotland. A key figure in this respect is the Danish traveller, author and editor Andreas Andersen Feldborg (1782–1838), whose work has yet to receive much attention in either anglophone or Danish scholarship.[6] Feldborg's *Tour in Zealand*, *A Dane's Excursions in Britain* and *Denmark Delineated* were published, in English, in 1805, 1809 and 1824, respectively, with the explicit intention of correcting what Feldborg saw as the 'unjust delineation' of many earlier accounts of Denmark and of emphasising the shared cultural and historical bonds between the two countries.[7] All received favourable notices in both Britain and Denmark, with the author of an eight-page review of *Denmark Delineated* in *Blackwood's Edinburgh Magazine* for September 1821 – possibly James Hogg (1770–1835), whom Feldborg knew – for example, praising that book 'as undoubtedly destined to render the name of its author immortal'.[8]

These travellers and their stories about Denmark and Britain are the subject of this chapter. And these are stories which have, hitherto, remained largely unexamined by those who have written about British travellers to the Nordic countries. Coupled to the assumption by many scholars that few British travellers came to Denmark is the assumption that most who did merely passed through this comparatively southern country as quickly as possible on their way farther north, in quest of the actual and imagined sublimities of 'the North', or on business of one sort or another to Oslo (then called Christiania), Stockholm or Moscow.[9] But British travel accounts of Denmark are actually very significant for understanding the development of Britain's imaginative investment in 'the North' during the late eighteenth and early nineteenth centuries. For one thing, the responses of British travellers to what they found in Denmark is often a revealing index of what they expected 'the North' to be, expectations which Denmark either did or (often) did not fulfil, being, in the opinion of some, as Hildor Barton also notes, neither sufficiently sublime nor sufficiently polished.[10] For another, one can clearly trace in British accounts of Denmark the emergence, in parallel with the development of wider 'Romantic' attitudes to 'the North', of the notion of a common, 'Northern' cultural identity encompassing the two countries. British accounts of Denmark routinely draw comparisons with Britain and, as in the descriptions of Copenhagen discussed in Chapter 1, a shift from a tendency to see Denmark as an exotic 'Other' towards finding it increasingly familiar is markedly visible. Late eighteenth- and early nineteenth-century British travel writing, which has so often been understood by scholars as a genre which registers difference, became, in the case of writing about Denmark, increasingly a space for registering and constructing cultural commonality as war with Revolutionary and Napoleonic France forced a reassessment in both countries of their relations with the Classical South of Europe. And, as exemplified in the work of Andreas Feldborg, this was a two-way process: Feldborg's writings about Britain and Denmark are explicitly concerned with highlighting the culture which the two countries share, even though, as we shall see, he is not always successful in maintaining that international emphasis in the face of national political crises.

Such is the extent of British travel writing about Denmark in the late eighteenth and early nineteenth centuries that some selection is necessary given the restrictions of scope in a single monograph. This chapter will therefore focus its attention on three key areas of that writing in which the emergence of a sense of common, 'Northern' culture is most readily visible. These are: accounts of the prehistoric monuments which travellers frequently encountered in Denmark; accounts of Helsingør and its environs; and Andreas Andersen Feldborg's account of his experiences as a Danish traveller in Britain.

'In a manner a *terra incognita* of little interest': British Travel Writing about Denmark

As we have seen, in the Preface to his *Tour in Zealand, in the Year 1802*, the Danish traveller Andreas Andersen Feldborg sets out to correct what he sees as the 'unjust delineation' which Denmark has 'suffered' in many 'bulky volumes' of travel writing – particularly, he says, by German authors – which combine 'incomprehensible falsehood' with 'visionary details'.[11] In *Denmark Delineated*, published almost twenty years after *Tour in Zealand*, although quarried in part from that earlier work, Feldborg restates this ambition, in both his 'Advertisement' and 'Preface', noting the 'injustice which Denmark has, in general, sustained from the ignorance and prejudice of travellers'.[12]

Feldborg points to un-named German authors, of course, so as not to alienate from the outset the intended English readership of his own travel books: once they get going, both *Tour in Zealand* and *Denmark Delineated* often take aim at English accounts, sometimes even directly quoting them to repudiate problematic passages. But Feldborg also makes it clear in his Preface to *Denmark Delineated* that, as well as performing a patriotic duty to provide a 'satisfactory' account of 'the country and the people', he has also a wider, transnational agenda.[13] This, Feldborg says, is 'to obey a call, at once just and generous, lately made in one of the eminent literary journals of Britain':

> requiring every man to contribute his mite to make nations better acquainted with each other, in the hope of repairing the breach which the fourth part of a century, spent in war and devastation, has made in mutual courtesy.[14]

Feldborg is slightly misquoting, here, sentiments expressed in the *Quarterly Review* for May 1820, in a review of the first volume of *De l'Angleterre*, just published at Paris by Maurice Rubichon (1766–1849). But the 'call' made by the *Quarterly* clearly chimes with what had been the consistent ideological project of Feldborg's writings since the publication of his *Tour in Zealand*: namely to emphasise and to shore up the sense of common cultural ground in Anglo-Danish relations during a period of trauma which had begun with the Battle of Copenhagen in 1801 and which had seen the two countries at war for seven years following the British bombardment of Copenhagen in 1807, a fourteen-year period during the majority of which Feldborg was himself in Britain. And Feldborg's expression of these sentiments met with approbation in British periodicals, with the reviewer of *Tour in Zealand* in the *Annual Review*, for example, noting of Feldborg's stated desire for renewed 'harmony' between the two nations that 'in this devout wish we most sincerely join'.[15]

We have already seen in Chapter 1 how Feldborg's 'historical account' of the events of April 1801, first published in his *Tour in Zealand*, seeks to deploy a notion of common, Anglo-Danish culture in opposition to the threat posed by Napoleonic France. But the rest of Feldborg's *Tour* is similarly concerned not just to familiarise British readers with Denmark but also to find and to describe exactly such common cultural ground between the two countries – and, as we shall see later in this chapter, Feldborg's *Denmark Delineated* and *A Dane's Excursions in Britain* are designed to serve this same purpose. Equally, as we shall see in Chapter 3, Feldborg's edition of *Poems from the Danish* (1815) was intended not only to introduce British readers to contemporary Danish poetry, but also to emphasise the common literary traditions linking the two countries, extending to the present-day work done on the influence of classical Scandinavian literature by antiquarians such as Feldborg's friends Robert Jamieson (1772–1844) and David Laing (1793–1878). Feldborg evidently thought of himself as a kind of cultural ambassador between Britain and Denmark, something which the influential Danish *saloniste* Karen Margrethe Rahbek (1775–1829) registered, albeit rather unkindly, when she described Feldborg as someone who 'was – or tried to be – a success in Denmark by being English and in England by being Danish'.[16] Hence Feldborg, in his Preface to *Denmark Delineated*, dwells with pleasure on 'the interest' which his projected volume 'has excited' among the Danes, as well as observing:

> That the British residents in the Danish dominions should have regarded the present undertaking with a friendly eye, was to be expected from men, who have so many motives for strengthening the good understanding which now happily subsists between the two countries.[17]

'The true friends of both nations', Feldborg concludes, 'can never sufficiently lament that it should have been interrupted.'[18]

What is perhaps most striking from Feldborg's 'advertisements' and 'prefaces', then, is that he could still feel, in the early 1820s, that Denmark was 'a kind of *terra incognita*' for the British, the perception of which continued to be influenced by the 'injustice' of travel accounts.[19] Certainly, the kind of mass British tourism in Denmark to which Murray's *Hand-Book* and Robert Jones's (dates unknown) *Copenhagen and its Environs* (1829) were designed to cater had yet to arise. But, as we shall see, a good number of descriptions of Denmark had been published by British travel writers by the early 1820s. What

Feldborg actually registers here, then, is the extent to which influential early *political* engagements with Denmark by British writers still tended to influence the perception of travellers, or at least to provide a baseline against which travellers needed to position themselves. Foremost among such engagements was the aforementioned *Account of Denmark* published by Robert Molesworth (1656–1725) over a century earlier, in 1692.

Molesworth, an Anglo-Irish Whig and former envoy to the Danish court, offers an unmitigated criticism of the absolutist monarchy which had been established in Denmark by Frederik III (1609–70) in 1660 and which remained in force, in theory at least, until 1848. The debate about Danish politics which Molesworth began will be considered in detail in Chapter 5 – although it is worth pointing out already now that his *Account* seems designed at least as much to *enable* comment, by comparison, on the current political state of England, as to engage with Danish politics: Molesworth repeatedly points to Denmark as a model which England must avoid. But Molesworth's *Account* is also in part a work of travel writing and almost everything is seen through the lenses of his political critique, as, for example, in his remarks on the 'frequent and grievous' taxation of 'the poor country people' in Zealand and the 'indifferent' quality of the air in Copenhagen, which he, as we have seen, says is 'constantly troubled with the plague of flies' in summer.[20] Political, social, economic and environmental ill-health all go hand in hand, it seems, in Molesworth's *Account*.

Molesworth's description of Denmark was controversial from the moment of its publication, and in that same year, *Denmark Vindicated: Being an Answer to a Late Treatise called An Account of Denmark* was published at London by 'a Gentleman in the Country, to his friend in *London*', as the title page ran. But, as both Hildor Barton and Karen Klitgaard Povlsen have observed, Molesworth's treatise continued to exert an influence over British perceptions of Denmark over a century later and was one of the main reasons 'that Denmark fared least well', as Barton puts it, in British travel writing about Scandinavia in the late eighteenth and early nineteenth centuries.[21] Both Nathaniel Wraxall and the anonymous author of *Narrative of the Expedition to the Baltic* (1808) draw on Molesworth in their accounts of Copenhagen, with the latter, for example, repeating the dubious claim that the city is, in summer, 'much troubled with swarms of flies'.[22] Wraxall's near contemporary Joseph Marshall (dates unknown), by contrast, notes in his description of Denmark that 'the reader cannot gain any just intelligence from former books; for the old ones are no longer true'.[23]

That Feldborg, too, had Molesworth and his legacy in mind when he attacks the 'injustice' with which Denmark had been treated by earlier travel writers is sufficiently evident from the fact that, in *Denmark Delineated*, Feldborg makes no fewer than twenty-two specific corrections of Molesworth, along with a number of others offered to British travellers writing is a similar vein, notably including Nathaniel Wraxall. What Feldborg's preface makes clear, then, is that Denmark in the 1820s remained an ideologically and imaginatively contested space in British travel writing. What we shall see, in the remainder of this chapter, is that the focus of this contestation continued to be, as it had been for Molesworth, a comparison, for better or for worse, between Denmark and Britain. We have already seen, in Chapter 1, how the terms of this comparison shifted as the eighteenth century drew to a close. A tendency to view Denmark as an exotic, 'Oriental' other – premised on often explicit comparisons with the absolutism of Ottoman Turkey – gave way increasingly to a tendency to emphasise the common cultural ground between the two countries and their shared, Northern liberties. And exactly this same shift is visible in those focal points of British travel writing about Denmark to which I want, now, to turn.

'[O]bjects of the highest interest': The Afterlife of Danish Antiquity

In describing the 'environs' of Copenhagen and the wider island of Zealand, Murray's *Hand-Book for Travellers* observes:

> *The Sepulchral Tumuli*, of which such numbers still exist in Denmark, and from the spoil of which the museums of the capital have derived many of their choicest specimens, must ever be objects of the highest interest, both to the antiquarian and the traveller.[24]

The study and representation of these monuments by Danish antiquarians and travellers played a substantial role in the development of Romanticism and Romantic nationalism in Denmark in the early-mid nineteenth century.[25] On 22 May 1807, the Danish Royal Commission for the Preservation of Antiquities [Den kongelige Kommission til Oldsagers Opbevaring] was founded with the express purpose of protecting and promoting the study of such sites. The Commission was the result of lobbying by Rasmus Nyerup (1759–1829), who became the first secretary, and who also, later in 1807, founded the first museum of Nordic antiquities in the Trinitatis church in central Copenhagen – only to see it badly damaged when the British bombarded the city on 2–5 September.[26] Reflecting on the subsequent effects of this 'excellent plan' in his *Travels in Norway, Sweden, Denmark, Hanover, Germany,*

Netherlands (1826), the Scottish solicitor, antiquarian and traveller William Rae Wilson (1772–1849) affirms that the establishment of the Royal Commission was 'most judicious on the part of the government':

> and ought to be adopted in our own country, as it would stimulate enterprize, and lead to the discovery of many curious pieces of antiquity that will otherwise, perhaps, remain forever concealed.[27]

While the Royal Commission was working to catalogue and to preserve prehistoric monuments, the remains of Danish antiquity also became a key motif in contemporary Danish poetry and painting, the latter spurred further by the foundation in 1827, by the Danish art historian Niels Lauritz Høyen (1798–1870), of the Danish Art Union [Dansk Kunstforeningen], which called for the development of a Danish national art addressing characteristic landscapes and themes. Hence Denmark's preeminent contemporary poet, Adam Gottlob Oehlenschläger (1779–1850), frequently takes the remains of Danish antiquity for his subject, as in his poems 'Guldhornene' [The Golden Horns] (1802) and 'Sanct Hansaften-Spil' [Midsummer Night's Play] (1803), while so-called *oldtidshøj* [ancient mounds] are a central motif in the work of the prominent Danish Golden Age painters Dankvart Dreyer (1816–52) and Johan Thomas Lundbye (1818–47).[28] The connection between this new 'Romantic' investment in the representation of Danish landscape and history and the development of Danish nationalism is well exemplified in Thomas Lundbye's celebrated painting *Hankehøj* (1847), in which the spirits of the past, in the form of clouds, look down upon a peasant tending cattle near an old tomb, bathed in autumn sunshine.[29]

These connections between the study of prehistoric monuments and the development of Romanticism and Romantic nationalism in mid-nineteenth-century Denmark have been well-documented by Danish scholars, writing in both Danish and in English.[30] What has not yet received attention in these discussions, however, in either anglophone or Danish scholarship, is the extent to which the representation of the remains of Danish antiquity has a substantial prehistory in British travel writing about Denmark in the late eighteenth and early nineteenth centuries. And significantly, while the study of prehistoric monuments and artefacts in Denmark was linked in the mid-nineteenth century to the rise of Romantic nationalism, the writing about these same topics by earlier British *and* Danish authors tended to see them not so much as evidence of a *national* tradition as evidence of a common, ancient culture, spreading across 'the North' between Denmark and Britain.

The emergence of this way of representing the prehistoric monuments dotted around the landscape of Zealand can be traced at least as far back as the account given by Nathaniel Wraxall (1751–1831) in his *Tour through Some of the Northern Parts of Europe* (1775). As we have seen in Chapter 1, Wraxall – doubtless influenced to some extent by the *Account of Denmark* (1694) of Robert Molesworth (1656–1725) – offers a highly critical account of the Danish capital, which he sees the embodiment of an 'Oriental' polity in marked contrast to British liberties. On 8 May 1774, however, Wraxall left Copenhagen for a three-day 'tour through the North part of Zealand', in which he took, he says, 'great pleasure'.[31] Outside the capital, Wraxall seemed to be able to relate more appreciatively to Denmark through the overlapping and increasingly influential eighteenth-century discourses of ruin, of the Gothic and of the picturesque. This ability is evident, for example, in his description of the 'pleasing aspect' of the Zealand countryside and of the 'most forcible effect on the mind' produced by the royal tombs in the 'sublime and awful' crypt at Roskilde Cathedral.[32] Wraxall's different attitude is arguably most visible, however, in his observations on 'the great number of tumuli' which he saw 'scattered on all sides' as he travelled around Zealand.[33]

Wraxall's initial response to these prehistoric 'tumuli' is to note that they reminded him of similar sites on 'the Wiltshire and Hampshire Downs', that they 'exactly resemble in size and appearance those in England, and are probably antient Saxon sepulchres'.[34] 'Several collections of stones in circular form', he says, 'some of which are very large', similarly 'reminded' him of Stonehenge, 'though on a smaller scale'.[35] These observations are the closest that Wraxall ever comes in his *Tour* to articulating any sense of cultural common ground between Britain and Denmark, and even as he does so, he is eager also to demarcate the difference between the countries. Wraxall says that, when he enquired whether any 'curious Antiquarians' had examined these sites 'as many of ours have been', the locals 'only stared in answer'.[36] 'Here', Wraxall concludes, 'are no Dr. Stukelys [*sic*], to investigate the monuments of our ancestors', about which, Wraxall claims, the Danes 'are totally ignorant; and it would only be lost time to attempt to gain any account of their origin or construction from the people who live near them'.[37]

Wraxall is referring, here, to the work of the antiquarian William Stukeley (1687–1765) who began, in the early decades of the eighteenth century, the serious archaeological investigation of stone circles and other prehistoric sites in England, notably including those at Stonehenge and Avebury. In his landmark work *Stonehenge: A Temple Restor'd to the British Druids* (1740), Stukeley 'combat[s]' the generally held opinion

– voiced, for example, by the 'celebrated' architect Inigo Jones (1573–1652), whose work Stukeley notes in his Preface – that such monuments were the work of the Romans.[38] By arguing that they were, rather, the work of prehistoric British Druids, Stukeley laid the foundations for subsequent speculation that the stone circles and similar monuments to be found across the north of Europe could all be traced, ultimately, to the same, pre-Christian culture of the North. Through his allusion to Stukeley, then, Wraxall's account of the ancient sites which he visited in Zealand both registers and refutes the idea of a common Northern culture encompassing Britain and Denmark. In Wraxall's view, though, the shared culture signalled by these monuments – and registered in Wraxall's telling phrase 'the monuments of *our* ancestors' – is now a matter of the past: Britain has advanced beyond Denmark in antiquarian research, as in almost everything else.[39]

Given the fact that, as we have seen, the Danish Royal Commission for the Preservation of Antiquities was not established until 1807, one might, at first glance, suspect that there was some justice in Wraxall's view of the state of antiquarian knowledge in Denmark, beyond the consistency of that view with the kind of patriotic jingoism of which Wraxall's *Tour* has more than its fair share. Wraxall's assessment is certainly not consistent in this respect, however, with that given by William Coxe in his account of 'those regular circles of stones which are so frequently scattered over the face, not only of these countries [meaning Denmark and Sweden], but our own'.[40] 'Many' of these, Coxe says, he and his companions 'remarked, with attentive curiosity', and he describes a number in detail, including one near Korsør, on the western coast of Zealand:

> About three or four English miles from Corsoer, at the extremity of a wood, standing on a promontory, I found one of the most perfect of those antient monuments. I observed a large mound of earth, on the summit of which large conical granite stones, standing at small intervals from each other, enclosed an oval space of a very considerable extent. In the centre and highest point, a huge, shapeless, mass of granite was laid horizontally on four other stones, almost buried beneath the surface of the ground. Near it was another mound, on the top of which another large stone was placed in a similar manner on four others. I remarked some vestiges of trenches; but as the place was covered with underwood, and as night approached, I could not trace their direction.[41]

Coxe records speculation about such sites by 'peasants', whom he says called them 'Gothick stones; and it seemed to be a general tradition amongst them, that they were erected by the Goths, whom they represented as a race of giants formerly inhabiting these countries'.[42] He also notes that they have been the subject of enquiry by academicians such as the Danish historian and natural philosopher Ole Worm (1588–1654), who had written pioneering studies of runic and runestones.⁴³

What Coxe does share with Wraxall, however, is a tendency to deploy these 'rude monuments' as topoi for both cultural commonality and cultural difference.⁴⁴ He notes repeatedly that 'we have many similar monuments in our island', and, as we have seen, that they are 'frequently scattered over the face, not only of these countries, but our own'.⁴⁵ But he also says that 'Olaus Wormius, and other authors, highly exaggerate when they deduce any resemblance between the stupendous fabrick of Stone Henge, and these trifling, though genuine, remains of high antiquity', and are 'still more erroneous in concluding, from that fanciful resemblance, that Stone Henge was constructed by our Anglo Saxon ancestors, who migrated from these Northern parts'.⁴⁶ The sublime ('stupendous') Stonehenge, it would seem, is to be set apart, as a matter of national distinctiveness, from any common Northern culture of the past.

Ultimately, however, Coxe's position on prehistoric monuments and what they may or may not reveal about any ancient cultural links between Britain and Denmark is agnostic. 'Endless controversies', he says:

> have arisen among the learned concerning their origin and destination; and each author maintains that they were raised by that particular nation, or sect, as best suits his favourite hypothesis. Thus they are styled, by different authors, Celtick, Cambrian, Gothick, Danish, Saxon, Picktick; and by others have been solely attributed to the Druids, a favourite order of men, under whom we are too apt to shelter our ignorance.⁴⁷

This last quip is aimed directly at Stukeley, whom Coxe, in a footnote, says 'amply overturned' the 'systems of former writers; but is equally not successful in establishing his favourite hypothesis' that Stonehenge 'was a Druidical temple'.⁴⁸

What Coxe's summation of the 'endless controversies' surrounding such prehistoric sites makes clear, then, is the extent to which those sites were beginning to become key components of emergent Romanticism and Romantic nationalist debates, in Britain and in Denmark, about 'the North', whether they were interpreted as evidence of a common, cultural inheritance, or as evidence of national distinctiveness. That a variety of theories continued to be proposed by travellers can be seen from the account of the prehistoric 'tumuli' given by the Scottish traveller and man of letters James MacDonald (1771–1810) in his *Travels Through Denmark, and Part of Sweden* (1809).⁴⁹ Denmark and Britain had been at war since the British bombardment of Copenhagen in September 1807 and MacDonald and his shipmates were taken in prisoner in late November 1809 when the ship in which they were travelling to Gothenburg, the *Johns*, was wrecked off Skagen, near the northern tip of Denmark – the early pages of MacDonald's *Travels* are full of praise for the 'noble' locals who saved him and his fellows at considerable risk to their own lives.[50]

Having spent some days (under guard) in Skagen recovering from his ordeal, where MacDonald affirms that he was treated 'with the greatest kindness', he was escorted (still under guard) to Copenhagen.[51] In Letter V of his *Travels*, dated 7 December at Aalborg, MacDonald notes how 'In almost the whole of Jutland, the traveller is struck with the number of earthen tumuli, or hillocks, which obtrude themselves constantly on his view' and which, he says, 'are exactly similar to those we have in Dorsetshire, and other parts of the south of England'.[52] 'The Danes', he continues, reminding us of Wraxall, 'have no answer when asked about them, but that they were made long, long ago, perhaps at the creation'.[53] MacDonald was an at least partly qualified witness here: he was familiar with the ancient Gaelic poetry of Scotland and his father, Hugh, had given evidence about the authenticity of James Macpherson's (1739–96) 'Ossian' poems before the Highland Society of Scotland.[54] And, in MacDonald's opinion, it was 'highly probable' that these 'tumuli were erected in honour of persons of note in Jutland, in the same manner as similar ones were created by the Greeks and Trojans in the Troad, and as cairns of stones were piled above the remains of heroes in the Highlands and isles of Scotland'.[55]

Overall, though, while influential early travellers like Wraxall and Coxe were sceptical about the extent to which the apparent similarity of prehistoric monuments in Britain and Denmark could be read as evidence of a common, Northern culture in the past, in the early nineteenth century, as 'Romantic' attitudes to 'the North' began to gain traction in Britain, British travellers to Denmark tended to read such sites in exactly those terms. In his *Travels*, for example, William Rae Wilson remarks en passant that he saw, near Roskilde, 'a number of tumuli, and sometimes small heaps of stones, presumed to be druidical remains', thereby alluding casually, almost taking for granted, the idea that such monuments originated in a prehistoric, common culture of 'the North'.[56] Among the most prominent and sustained articulations of this idea in British travel writing about Denmark can be found, however, in the account of these monuments of 'Danish antiquity' given by the celebrated traveller Edward Daniel Clarke (1769–1822) in his (no less) monumental *Travels in Various Countries of Europe, Asia and Africa* (1810–24), which had reached its fourth edition by 1824.[57]

Although Clarke's description of his Scandinavian journey was first published only in 1818, he had travelled to Denmark in the summer of 1799, 'when *Englishmen*', as he reminds us, 'were excluded from almost every part of the *European* Continent, by the distracted state of public affairs'.⁵⁸ His group of four included Thomas Robert Malthus (1766–1834), who had published anonymously the previous year the first edition of his soon-to-be notorious *Essay on the Principle of Population* (1798). Malthus's account of this trip in his private diary remained unpublished until 1966.⁵⁹ But Clarke's was widely read, including by Percy Bysshe and Mary Shelley in 1818 and by their friend Edward Ellerker Williams in November 1821, when he noted in his journal entry for Wednesday, 21 November: 'Take up "Clarke's travels in Scandinavia" – he seems to work by square and rle, & writes by the yard, sawing thro' nations as a carpenter thro' deal.'⁶⁰

In his *Travels*, Clarke begins to register comparisons with England and the English, and contrasts with Germany and the Germans, almost as soon as his party has crossed the border into Denmark. On the approach to Kiel, part of Denmark until 1866, he recalls:

> We had perceived a very visible alteration in the features of the inhabitants, from the time that we left *Lubeck*; and it was now evident that they differed markedly from the *Germans*; that is to say, they had lighter hair, fairer complexions, and a milder cast of countenance [. . .] To these were added so much of the *English* air and manner, that we really believed many whom we met were actually from our own country, until their ignorance of our language convinced us of our error.⁶¹

Such perceptions of physical and cultural ('so much of the *English* air and manner') commonality are then immediately consolidated by Clarke's account of 'the first monument of *Danish* antiquity' which his party 'observed'.⁶² This, he says, 'was a *Cyclopéan* structure of the kind which is called, in *Wales*, *Cromlech*; consisting of three upright stones, supporting, horizontally, an enormous slab of granite'.⁶³ 'It would be easy', Clarke continues, 'to enumerate many antiquities of the same form which exist in our own country', and he points in a footnote, by way of supporting evidence, to the *Tour in Wales* (1778) of the Welsh antiquarian and natural philosopher Thomas Pennant (1726–98).⁶⁴

Clarke acknowledges that 'for what purpose, and by whom' these structures were built remains unknown.⁶⁵ But he finds it 'evident that they are the works of the same people who have left other stupendous vestiges of *Cyclopéan* architecture, which are exhibited in *England* by the remains at *Stonehenge*; in *Greece*, by the walls of *Tiryns*; and in *Italy*, by the walls of *Cortona*'.⁶⁶ Clarke, in other words, rejects the arguments for the essential distinctiveness of *Stonehenge* from the 'monuments of Danish antiquity' advanced by Coxe and others and appeals, instead, to the so-called 'Odin migration legend' which was gaining increased traction among antiquarians around the turn of the century: the belief that the Scandinavian peoples had originally come from the east to the north, before further settling in prehistoric Britain.[67] 'There is nothing, therefore, *Gothic* about them', Clarke says of the builders of these monuments, insisting on a distinction from Southern and Central European cultures:

> nothing denoting the *Cimbri*; or the *Franks*; or the old *Saxons*; but rather the antient *Gaulish*, the antient *British*, and the antient *Irish*: and if this be admitted, they were the *Titan-Celts*; the *Giants* of the *sacred*, and CYCLOPS of the *heathen* historians.[68]

Clarke's archaeology, anthropology and ethnography, here, are a little muddled and certainly don't bear close scrutiny today. But the point which Clarke is trying to make is clear. The similarities between megalithic monuments in Denmark and Britain are evidence that both originated in a common, prehistoric culture which Clarke names 'the antient *Celts*': a culture which he represents as 'far more antient' than the Goths.[69] Megalithic ('Cylopéan') monuments map, in Clarke's opinion, 'the march they took' across Northern Europe.[70]

To emphasise this point about common origins, Clarke immediately reminds his reader that the part of Denmark in which he finds himself 'between *Flensburg* and *Alpenrade*' is 'particularly interesting to *Englishmen*; because the very name of their country, the features of its inhabitants, and many of its manners, were hence derived'.[71] This is Anglia, in western Jutland: 'Angeln', in Clarke's account, which word, he informs the reader, 'is pronounced exactly as we pronounce *England*, or *Engelonde*'.[72] 'We were surprised at the number of *English* faces we met', Clarke continues, 'and resemblance is not confined to features. Many articles of dress, and many customs, are common to the two countries. The method of cultivating and dividing the land is the same in both.'[73] In fact, even the physical environment seemed to remind Clarke and his party of home: 'the natural appearance of the country is also like the South of *England*; being diversified by numerous hills and valleys, adorned with flourishing woods and fertile fields.'[74] 'And throughout the whole district', Clarke reminds the reader, cementing the argument, 'one sees the *mounds*, or *tumuli*, of the antient *Celts*.'[75]

Clarke's speculations about the 'rude monuments' of Denmark are certainly not, as I have said, without their vagaries, and by no means do they represent the sole, uncontested opinion on the matter at the time.[76] In his account we do find, however, a prominent and very popular instance of the mediation through British travel literature of that strand of antiquarianism which read such sites as evidence that Britain and Denmark shared a common ancestry, equally visible in archaeological, cultural and even physiological similarities. And this strand lingered on in travel writing through the 1820s and 1830s. As noted, Murray's *Hand-Book* quotes at length from the detailed description of a 'Tumulus at Udleire [Udlejre]', given by Feldborg in Part II of his *Denmark Delineated*. Feldborg notes of the excavations under the auspices of the Royal Commission that 'there is not now that want of Doctor Stukeleys, of which Sir Nathaniel Wraxall complains'.[77] 'Since these remarks [i.e. Wraxall's] were made', Feldborg affirms, 'a host of learned men have arisen [who] have distinguished themselves in researches of that kind, with a degree of industry and skill which has been highly appreciated by the antiquaries of England and Germany', and he cites Rasmus Nyerup and others as examples.[78] Feldborg does not speculate, himself, about the origins or purposes of this and the other tumuli which he describes, but he does quote approvingly 'the sentiments of my learned friend' the Scottish antiquary Robert Jamieson (1772–1844), whom Feldborg had met in Edinburgh, from his *Illustration of Northern Antiquities* (1814) that monuments 'of this kind are every where pointed out at this day in Norway, Sweden, and the Highlands of Scotland'.[79]

While antiquarians and travellers continued to discuss the significance of Denmark's megalithic monuments, however, in the late eighteenth and early nineteenth centuries, another part of Denmark provided a much more immediate and concrete space for exploring the cultural common ground between Britain and Denmark: this was the town of Helsingør and its famous castle, Kronborg, on the north-eastern tip of Zealand.

'Englishmen will find themselves on classic ground': Helsingør and Its Environs

'Englishmen will find themselves on classic ground': thus writes Andreas Andersen Feldborg of Kronborg castle, outside Helsingør, in his *Denmark Delineated*.[80] Feldborg identifies two reasons for Kronborg's 'strong claim' on the English cultural imagination.[81] It is 'inseparably associated', he says, 'with one of the noblest works of human genius', Shakespeare's *Hamlet*, 'which has', he continues, 'affected English hearts more than any other dramatic production'.[82] And, more recently, Kronborg had been the setting for 'a still deeper' royal 'tragedy', as the prison of Caroline Matilda, the English wife of Christian VII of Denmark, whose 'chief enjoyment' during her captivity was, Feldborg says, 'to ascend the square tower, which commands one of the finest prospects in the world'.⁸³

In addition to this cultural common ground, Feldborg also points to more immediate, material links between Britain and Helsingør, as he had already done in his *Tour in Zealand*. 'On landing at Elsinore', Feldborg affirms:

> an Englishman might easily conceive that he is in some seaport town in his own country. He is perpetually accosted in his own language by slopsellers, butchers, fishwomen, and trades-people of all descriptions. The streets close to the harbour bear a striking resemblance to the streets nearest the Thames, the Humber, the Wear, and the Tyne. The public-houses display signs with a Danish man-of-war on one side, and an English on the other. The houses of the English merchants resident here are either built or fitted up in the style of their country.⁸⁴

While Feldborg's comparisons pay, perhaps, no great compliment to English 'seaport' towns, he does point to the fact that, by the early part of the nineteenth century, Helsingør had developed into a focal point in Denmark not just for the British imagination but also for British commercial activity.⁸⁵ My primary focus in this section will be on the overlap between these two areas of engagement, that is to say, on the emergence of what we might call a 'culture industry' in Helsingør, aimed specifically at British visitors, and focused around those two royal tragedies, Caroline Matilda and *Hamlet*.⁸⁶

The extent to which these associations had been commoditised by the 1830s is clearly visible from account given in Murray's *Hand-book* of sites at Marienlyst, outside Helsingør, which had, for the past twenty years at least, been routinely identified, for British tourists, as the 'garden' and the 'grave' of Hamlet:

> On being asked by a lady, in 1837, where the king was poisoned by his brother, the worthy cicerone professed his entire ignorance of such an event having occurred. He will, however, no doubt, take the hint; and in the course, perhaps of the present year, some appropriate spot will be selected [. . .] and English travellers will derive additional pleasure from gazing on the actual tree beneath which the monarch was sleeping when his unnatural brother stole upon his slumber [. . .] The fame of Ophelia is alike unknown, and the scene of her disastrous 'muddy death' has not yet been provided by the caterers for the appetite of English travellers.⁸⁷

While enterprising 'Zealand *artistes*' might have been responsible for 'catering' to these 'appetites', however, it was certainly late eighteenth- and early nineteenth-century British travel writing about Denmark which had created them in the first place.[88] And it is that process that I want, now, to examine.[89]

For beginnings, we can turn, once again, to Nathaniel Wraxall, who arrived in Helsingør on 19 April 1774. That same day he was shown around Kronborg by a servant of Nicholas Fenwick (1729–99), the English consul general. Wraxall describes Kronborg as 'a fine Gothic chateau, or palace', a characterisation which might have perplexed the more architecturally minded of his readers, and reports that he 'desired to see the chambers' occupied by Caroline Matilda 'during her confinement here' – but was told that this was not possible, as they were being used by the head of the garrison.[90] Curiously, Wraxall says nothing at all about *Hamlet*, but he does note, as did virtually all visitors after him, that the 'prospect' across the Øresund towards Sweden 'is beautiful beyond all expression'.[91]

When Matthew Consett (1757–1831) passed through Helsingør in late July 1786 he, likewise, made no mention of *Hamlet* in his account of Kronborg, observing only that the castle 'will excite a sigh in the Breast of an Englishman [. . .] to reflect that here was confined a few years ago the Sister of his Sovereign, Matilda, the unfortunate Queen of Denmark'.[92] And Mary Wollstonecraft, who acknowledges during her account of Copenhagen that 'poor Matilda!' had 'haunted me ever since my arrival', makes no mention at all of either Kronborg or *Hamlet*, despite having landed at Helsingør.[93]

Already by the mid-1780s, however, the history of Caroline Matilda had become part of a nascent tourist industry at Helsingør. When the Dutch cavalry officer Jean Frédéric Henry de Drevon (1734–97) visited Kronborg in the summer of 1785, for example, he 'desired to be shewn the apartments formerly occupied by the Queen'.[94] '[T]he manner in which I was gratified', he affirms, 'shewed the request to be by no means unusual.'[95] During the first decade of the nineteenth century, however, sentimental reveries on *Hamlet* and Caroline Matilda became de rigueur for British travel writing about Helsingør. This is partly due to the fact that the memory of the harsh treatment of Caroline Matilda, who had died in exile in Germany in 1775, was less fresh and of less urgent political consequence. It also reflects the growing, Romantic-period investment in Shakespeare in Britain around the turn of the century, an investment which was to an increasing extent paralleled in Denmark (see Chapter 3). But, and perhaps above all, it is indicative of the extent to which new 'Romantic' attitudes to 'the North' were transforming the place of Denmark in the British imagination, making *Hamlet*, in particular, one more topos for expressing the rhetoric of cultural bonds which had featured so prominently in the run-up to, and in the aftermath of, the Battle of Copenhagen in 1801.

Hence John Carr, in his very popular *Northern Summer* (1805), moves smoothly between these two 'affecting' royal tragedies in his account of Helsingør, an account in which the boundary between imaginative and physical place is decisively blurred.[96] Carr begins with a description of 'the gardens of Marie Lyst, or Maria's Delight [Marienlyst], which are within half an English mile of Elsineur'.[97] These, he says, 'cannot fail to prove very interesting to every admirer of our immortal Shakespeare'.[98] 'I have trod on the very spot', Carr tells his reader, 'where, with all the uncertainty of antiquity, tradition asserts that the Father of Hamlet was murdered.'[99] Carr then quotes from Act 1, Scene 5 of *Hamlet*, where the ghost of the murdered king reveals his fate to his son, before concluding that 'a more beautiful spot for such a frightful conference could not have been selected'.[100] From this 'celebrated scene', a phrase which allows Carr to blend the 'beauties' of *Hamlet* with the 'beauties' of physical geography – he uses the same term for both play and place – Carr moves, via an 'enchanting' walk, to the fate of 'the hapless Matilda'.[101] Reaching a 'tower' with a view of the castle, he points out to the reader the 'battlements' where she 'was permitted to walk during her confinement'.[102] This view, Carr says, 'excited an irresistible wish to lay before my reader the most affecting circumstances, which passed under [Kronborg's] gloomy roof during her captivity'.[103] Carr, then, would style himself as a latter-day Shakespeare, inspired to stage for his reader the more recent royal tragedy which had played out at Helsingør.

What we can see in Carr's account of Marienlyst and Kronborg, then, is the process by which British travel writing about Helsingør began to fuse romance and history, imaginative and physical geography, to create the kind of 'classic ground' to which Feldborg points in *Denmark Delineated*; to create, in a very real sense, a British imaginative investment in this particular part of Denmark, made British, as it were, through its cultural and historical associations. But this kind of imaginative investment in Helsingør by British travellers could also be the occasion of frustration and disappointment. In his description of 'the very haunts of Shakespeare's northern hero', for example, the Scottish painter and traveller Robert Ker Porter (1777–1842) recounts an experience not unlike the report given by William Wordsworth (1770–1850), in Book VI of *The Prelude* (1805), of the disappointment he felt when he saw Mont Blanc for the first time.[104] For Porter, the *imagined* Helsingør cannot survive the encounter with the actual town.

Porter's expectations of Helsingør were substantial. He describes for the reader his 'impatience' to make landfall as the ship on which he was travelling from England approached the 'city which had been immortalized by the pen of our matchless Shakespeare'.[105] 'Eager to traverse every part of this consecrated ground', he tells the reader, 'I had already followed Hamlet everywhere.'[106] With his 'fancy thus raised' in expectation of a 'memorable and once regal city', Porter is immediately disappointed by the reality of Helsingør.[107] 'But "what a falling off was there!"', he records, quoting *Hamlet* 1.5.47: 'Wapping possesses the splendour of ancient Rome, when compared with the modern aspect of Elsineur.'[108] 'Judge then', he tells the reader, in a passage which, though lengthy, is worth quoting for the emphasis which it lays on the conflict between the corporeal and the imaginary:

> how soon my eye and mind were called back to the narrow footpaths of dull matter-o'-fact; but you cannot judge, for you cannot imagine, how much more rapidly I was made to forget the sweet-scented flowers of the 'pretty Ophelia', in the *hauts gouts* which now assailed my senses. The weather being so hot, various effluvia and exhalations sported about so pesteriferously, that it was impossible to proceed without the shield of a handkerchief to the nose, if you wished to prevent actual sickness [. . .] In vain I sought for decayed battlements and mouldering towers; not a single vestige presented itself that bore the smallest trace of this town ever having been hallowed by the mausoleum of Ophelia.[109]

Hoping to alleviate his disappointment, Porter seeks out a local 'informer' and is directed to 'a place, a mile from the town, that bears the name of Hamlet's Garden'.[110] But here, too, he was frustrated by 'ruins' which turned out, on closer inspection, to be 'a modern wretched building' and which 'retained no relic of ancient interest, excepting the tradition, which affirms that to be the spot where once stood the Danish palace'.[111]

Once again, then, for Porter, the actual experience of Helsingør frustrates his imaginative investment in the idea of Helsingør, the 'eager' 'meditations' and 'raised' 'fancy' with which he had arrived. However, in a move which, as I have said, recalls Wordsworth's response to Mont Blanc in Book VI of *The Prelude*, Porter, faced with this disappointing reality, turns back to imagination for redemption. Although the physical space or 'degenerated aspect' of Helsingør falls short of his expectations, the fact that the place 'has been so gloriously immortalized by the genius of our great dramatic bard' enables 'the mind to look through what is, to what was, and once more ennobles the scene'.[112]

What Porter ends by seeing, in other words, is not the actual Helsingør but an *imagined* Helsingør, and it is Shakespeare's drama which enables for him this transcendence of the physical scene. The actual, historical, *Danish* Helsingør is effaced, for and by Porter, by the English *imagining* of

Helsingør – and this exemplifies the process by which that 'classic ground' described by Feldborg in *Denmark Delineated* is marked out for travellers and endorsed by the locals. Helsingør is a physical space progressively inscribed with cultural Englishness by and for English travellers, a part of Denmark which becomes, we might say, through its associations with Hamlet and Caroline Matilda, forever England.

Feldborg's account of this 'classic ground' at Helsingør in *Denmark Delineated* reflects, as we have seen, these same, persistent imaginative links between the tragedy of *Hamlet* and the 'still deeper tragedy' of Caroline Matilda. But, like Porter before him and like Murray's *Hand-Book* after him, Feldborg does also register some scepticism about the potential conflict between the actualities of early nineteenth-century Helsingør and the imaginative investment in it by travellers and tourists – and, again, the so-called 'garden' of Hamlet is the focal point here.

'Most travellers, especially English, take the earliest opportunity', Feldborg says, 'of bending their steps to the King's, or as it is more poetically called, Hamlet's Garden, where, according to tradition, Hamlet's father was murdered by his brother.'[113] 'The lower garden, it must be confessed', he continues, 'is not very favourable to the illusion, being laid out in the old, stiff, French style, and of course at variance with nature and Shakespeare.'[114] The striking opposition which Feldborg draws here between 'the old, stiff, French style' and 'nature and Shakespeare' recalls immediately the similar oppositions established in various responses (including Feldborg's own) to the Battle of Copenhagen in 1801, where the French were consistently identified as the true enemies of the Northern 'brothers' (to use Nelson's phrase), the English and the Danes. And this sense of the need to reassert the 'natural', cultural common ground between the English and the Danish in the face of French influence is immediately extended by Feldborg in his account of the shortcomings of Hamlet's garden, when he observes that 'an Englishman will recollect, that greater violence has been done in his own country to Hamlet, when he was brought on stage in a French court-dress, and that by Garrick himself'.[115] Feldborg is referring, here, to the influential Shakespearean actor, playwright and producer David Garrick (1717–79), who began playing Hamlet in 1742, who organised the Shakespeare Jubilee in Stratford-upon-Avon in 1769, and who was the dominant impetus behind the resurgence of interest in Shakespeare in mid- and late eighteenth-century England. Against Garrick's 'French' 'violence' to the character, however, Feldborg immediately marshals the work of the later actor John Richard Kemble (1757–1823), whom, Feldborg says, 'brought back the costume of Hamlet and of Shakespeare generally to nature and truth'.[116]

In Feldborg's account, then, the movement from the 'old, stiff, French style' towards a more 'Romantic' fidelity to 'nature and truth' represents a move back towards the common cultural ground between England and Denmark embodied in the relationship between *Hamlet* and Helsingør. Nor is this only true for performances of Shakespeare's tragedy. '[A] similar revolution', Feldborg assures his reader, 'has taken place in gardening in Denmark; and the upper parts of Hamlet's garden will be found to be as favourable to the traditional character of the place as the most enthusiastic admirer of Shakespeare can desire.'[117] The 'revolution [. . .] in gardening in Denmark' to which Feldborg points here – the shift from the eighteenth-century, Neoclassical style towards the so-called English, 'Romantic' style – had begun, as we will see later in this chapter, already in the 1790s. But the point that Feldborg wishes to make is clear: English Shakespeare and English gardening are the 'Romantic' foundations on which the 'classic ground' of Helsingør should now rest. And to emphasise the Danish investment in this process, Feldborg concludes his account of Marienlyst with the hope that 'this interesting spot will soon [. . .] receive a most appropriate embellishment': a monument to Peter Foersom (1777–1817), the Danish actor who had begun the first Danish translations of Shakespeare in 1803 (see Chapter 3).[118] The Danish reviewer of *Denmark Delineated* for the Copenhagen weekly *Nyeste Skilderie af Kjøbenhavn* for 28 August 1821 singled out Feldborg's account of Marienlyst as exemplary of his ability 'to give', as Jørgen Erik Nielsen renders it, 'the English a more favourable impression of Denmark than Molesworth had done and without destroying their innocent belief that Marienlyst is Hamlet's garden'.[119]

'The story of this retired spot': British Travellers and British Poets in Zealand

In *Denmark Delineated*, Feldborg observes that it was not only at Helsingør that an English traveller might 'easily conceive' himself 'in his own country'.[120] On the contrary, not only does Feldborg compare the landscapes of northern Zealand with 'the meadows of Worcestershire' or 'the banks of the Thames about Richmond and Twickenham' – places which he had himself visited – but he also notes that 'some of the English merchants have villas' north of Copenhagen and 'a number of Scottish and English farmers have also settled in the neighbourhood'.[121] The country seat in Zealand of a Dutch merchant, however, has a surprising and hitherto undocumented connection with one of the key figures of the second generation of English Romantics: the poet, essayist, editor and de facto leader of the so-called 'Cockney school', James Henry Leigh Hunt (1784–1859) – and the episode as a whole is further evidence of the range and of the complexity of the cultural connections between Britain and Denmark in the early nineteenth century.

In his *Tour in Zealand*, Feldborg gives a brief description of 'a villa belonging to the Counsellor of state', commenting on the 'excellent' condition of the farm ('constantly improving by his intercourse with England') and noting that the 'beautiful' 'park' included an 'artificial hermitage'.[122] This 'villa' was Dronninggaard (now called Næsseslottet) on the shore of Furesø, the summer residence of the wealthy, Copenhagen-based Dutch merchant Frédéric de Coninck (1740–1811), who had purchased and restored it in 1781–2. John Carr visited Dronninggaard as part of his 'northern summer', describing it as 'the first [i.e. pre-eminent] private residence in Denmark' and assuring his reader that 'the story of this retired spot deserves to be told'.[123]

The main focus of Carr's 'story' about Dronninggaard is not the house, however, but the gardens. These had been designed by none other than Jean Frédéric Henry de Drevon, whose experiences at Helsingør we have already discussed, who visited the estate at the start and end of his travels in Scandinavia, and who composed part of his *Journey through Sweden* while he was staying there.[124] De Drevon was a childhood friend of de Coninck and had been invited by him to stay at Dronninggaard while he recovered from a disastrous love affair. In his *Journey through Sweden*, de Drevon points discreetly to the contrast between 'the activity and turbulence of my life for some months past' and 'the peaceful state in which I now enjoy the kindness of my friends' at Dronninggaard.[125] Drevon 'laid out' the gardens 'entirely' in the new 'English taste', thereby creating one of the earliest 'Romantic' gardens in Denmark.[126] He published a detailed account of his improvement work, featuring illustrations by the Danish painter Erik Pauelsen (1749–90), as *Description de Dronning-gaard, terre située dans l'isle de Zelande en Dannemark* (1786), dating the dedication at Copenhagen on 25 April of that year.[127]

John Carr's account of 'the romantic beauties of Dronningaard' mentions first an 'elegant marble column' which he found 'at the end of a beautiful walk', bearing an inscription in Danish which he translates as 'This Monument is erected in gratitude to a mild and beneficent Government, under whose auspices I enjoy the blessings that surround me'.[128] This 'monument' (still standing today) was designed by the Westminster-born, Anglo-Danish Neoclassical sculptor Carl Frederik Stanley (c. 1738–1813), and raised by de Coninck in 1784. The main objects of Carr's interest, however, he found 'in a spot of deep seclusion': 'the ruins of a hermitage, before which was the channel of a little brook, then dried up; and a little further, in a nook, an open grave and a tomb-stone'.[129] Carr expands in some detail on the explanation for this Gothic-sounding discovery, in a passage which I also need to quote at some length here:

> one who, weary of the pomp of courts and the tumult of camps, in the prime of life, covered with honours and with fortune, sought from [Dronning- gård's] hospitable owner permission to raise a sequestered cell, in which he might pass the remainder of his days in all the austerities and privation of an anchorite. This singular man had long, previous to the revolution of Holland, distinguished himself at the head of his regiment, but in an unhappy moment the love of aggrandisement took possession of his heart, and marrying under its influence, misery followed: and here, in a little wood of tall firs, he raised this simple fabric: moss warmed it within, and the bark of the birch defended it without; a stream of rock water once ran in a bed of pebbles before the door, in which the young willow dipt its leaves; and at a little distance from a bed of wild roses the labernum gracefully rose and suspended her yellow flowers; he selected an adjourning spot for the depository of his remains [. . .] Every day he dug a small portion of his grave until he had finished it: he then composed his epitaph in French, and had it inscribed upon a stone [. . .] In this singular solitude he passed several years, when the plans of his life became suddenly reversed, by a letter of recal from his prince, which contained the most flattering expressions of regard. The wishes of his sovereign and his country were imperative, he flew to Holland, and at the head of his regiment fought and fell.[130]

The 'singular man', never identified by Carr, was in fact de Drevon himself, who had constructed the ruined hermitage as part of his 'Romantic' improvement work on the grounds at Dronninggaard and who had, of course, never lived in it.[131] As Margrethe Floryan observes, de Drevon drew partly on 'his own life story and philosophy as a leitmotif' for this part of the garden, but also upon the tomb and cabin of Jean-Jacques Rousseau (1712–78) at Ermenonville.[132] De Drevon himself, in his *Description*, makes it clear that the whole area had been designed ('a place where art imitates nature to perfection') and Feldborg, as we have seen, was in no doubt that the 'hermitage' was 'artificial'.[133] Carr, however, was either unable or perhaps simply unwilling to distinguish between history and fantasy in his account of the hermitage, and he retold his version of the story four years later in a footnote to his 'Lines written in a Hermitage, At Dronningaard, Near Copenhagen', published in *Poems* (1809), which repeats in substance, and mostly verbatim, the account quoted above from *A Northern Summer*.[134]

The question, then, is from where Carr drew the details of his account of the hermit of Dronninggaard in *A Northern Summer* and 'Lines'. The answer would seem to be that he based both entirely upon two poems in French by de Drevon, which he had incorporated into monuments raised during his improvement works on the estate. Through Carr's agency, these poems became the basis for translations by William Hayley (1745–1820), the friend and biographer of William Cowper (1731–1800), and Leigh Hunt – both of which remain, essentially, unknown.[135] They are included as an appendix to *British Romanticism and Denmark*.

The first poem is introduced by Carr as the 'epitaph' of the 'hermit', which, Carr says, he had 'inscribed upon a stone'.[136] This 'stone' – described in detail by de Drevon, and illustrated in plate 15 of his *Description* – was in fact a tablet of white Norwegian marble, inclined against a crucifix, which was planted by an open grave.[137] Carr does not include the original, nineteen-line, French text of the 'epitaph' in *A Northern Summer*, 'but the reader I think will be pleased with it', he says, 'in the English dress which it has received from the distinguished pen of William Hayley, Esq.'.[138] Hayley's faithful translation makes clear that this 'epitaph' contains much of the detail from which Carr drew his 'story' about the life and fate of the 'hermit' of Dronninggaard, although the original text can evidently be read as (at least) combining the conventional with the personal as part of de Drevon's incorporation of himself, as a kind of latter-day Rousseau, into his improvements to the estate. Since Carr nowhere mentions either de Drevon or his *Description*, he presumably transcribed the French original from the monument on the spot and, on his return to England, showed it to Hayley, whom Carr describes in a footnote to 'Lines Written in a Hermitage' as 'my respected and distinguished friend'.[139] It would certainly not have been the first literary collaboration between the two men: in his Preface to *The Stranger in France* (1803), Carr places Hayley, 'a name familiar and dear to every elegant and polished mind', foremost among those whose 'emendations, and [. . .] cherishing spirit of approval' played a key role in preparing the text for publication.[140]

A similar process must have led to the second translation of a Dronninggaard text, with Carr transcribing a French original on the spot, and subsequently asking Leigh Hunt to make a translation. A letter from Hunt to his future wife, Marianne Kent, of 23 March 1807, records 'I have been here to breakfast with Sir John Carr', so the two men clearly were in contact then and probably had been for some time, since Leigh Hunt's *Juvenilia* (1801) lists Carr among its subscribers.[141]

The source text in this case is a poem by de Drevon entitled 'Les Adieux de l'Hermite de Dronning-Gaard'. It is engraved on a monument designed by the Danish Neoclassical sculptor Johannes Wiedewelt (1731–1802), which also features emblems of de Drevon's regiment and of the Dronninggaard estate. Neither poem nor monument is mentioned in de Drevon's *Description*, which raises the possibility that the latter, at least, dates from after that work was sent to press. In *A Northern Summer*, Carr introduces the 'translation' of this text as the product of 'the poetic and elegant mind of Leigh Hunt, Esq'.[142] Entitled 'Farewell of the Hermit of Dronningaard', Hunt's text, however, is twelve lines longer than the original, and less a 'translation' of de Drevon's 'Les Adieux', than a 'Romantic' extempore based upon it. Hunt, in composing, clearly drew also on Carr's recollections of the estate, and he introduces allusions which would seem to be of more obvious relevance to his own situation, and to the political climate in England, in 1804–5, than to de Drevon's in 1786, although Hunt must have completed the poem well prior to the death of his mother in November 1805, which affected him so profoundly.[143] Hunt's text, which received positive notices in the reviews of *A Northern Summer* carried by *The Monthly Mirror* (1805) and *Anti-Jacobin Review* (1806), is, then, another example of the diverse forms of cultural exchange which took place within the context of British travel to, and travel writing about, Denmark.[144]

A Dane's Excursions: Conflict and Community in Feldborg's Travels in Britain

Travel between Britain and Denmark in the late eighteenth and early nineteenth centuries was by no means, of course, a one-way traffic. The most celebrated Danish traveller to Britain in the nineteenth century was, undoubtedly, the priest and man-of-letters Nikolaj Frederik Severin Grundtvig (1783–1872), one of the major cultural architects of modern Denmark, who visited the country four times in 1829–31 and 1834. But others had gone before him, naturally. In Scotland in 1810, for example, Andreas Andersen Feldborg found in the visitors' album of an inn near Melrose Abbey inscriptions dated 23 June 1807, in Danish and English, made by 'three Danish gentlemen', comprising 'poetical extracts' and 'original remarks'.[145] Foremost among Grundtvig's predecessors, however, was, of course, Feldborg himself. Feldborg first came to England in November 1802 and he remained there until 1808. After some time in Denmark and a tour in Sweden, Norway and northern Germany, he returned to England in November 1810, staying until the summer of 1816. He began a third visit in 1820 and stayed, excepting some brief visits home, until 1825.

During this time, Feldborg worked actively to promote Anglo-Danish relations. In addition to the travel books already noted and his edition of *Poems from the Danish*, he published a translation of *Great and Good Deeds of Danes, Norwegians, and Holsteinians* (1807) by the Danish historian Ove Malling (1747–1829), which received very favourable notice in British periodical reviews (see Chapter 4). Following the bombardment of Copenhagen in September 1807, Feldborg also worked on behalf of Danish prisoners of war in Britain, publishing in 1813 his *Particulars Relevant to the Danish Prisoners of War*. And the following year, after the Treaty of Kiel had ceded control of Norway from Denmark to Sweden, a move which Norway tried to reject, Feldborg published 'An Appeal to the English Nation in behalf of Norway', asking that Norwegian independence be granted (which would, in practice, have amounted to a return to Danish rule).[146]

Feldborg also travelled extensively in Britain, spending considerable time in the north-east and at Edinburgh. And he made the acquaintance of many leading cultural figures, in both Britain and Denmark: not for nothing did the reviewer of *Denmark Delineated* in *Blackwood's Edinburgh Magazine* for September 1821 open with the question 'who is there in Edinburgh or Copenhagen that knows not Feldberg [sic], the Dane?'.[147] As we saw in Chapter 1, Feldborg's 'Historical Account of the Battle of Copenhagen', published with *A Tour in Zealand*, earned him an audience with Admiral Nelson (1758–1805) and Emma Hamilton (1765–1815). Feldborg met Robert Southey (1774–1843) in 1821, who had drawn some of the details of his description of the Battle of Copenhagen in his *Life of Nelson* from Feldborg's 'Historical Account' – and on 19 October 1814, Southey wrote to his publisher John Murray (1778–1843) that he had 'just received a very gratifying letter from the author of the Tour in Zeeland, whose account of the Battle of Copenhagen was of such use to me in my Life of Nelson. He is about to translate the Life into Danish.'[148] Feldborg does not seem to have made this translation, but in Edinburgh, to which he travelled after his meeting with Southey, he met and became friends with a number of eminent antiquarians and academics, including, as we have seen, Robert Jamieson and David Laing. 'Feldborg the Dane' even features in Book V of *Queen Hynde*, the comic-epic poem published by James Hogg in 1824, where he beats the 'athletic bard' of 'Albyn' in a race, earning him, 'although an enemy and a Dane', the title of 'Illustrious man of tale and chart! / Professor of the running art!'[149]

Feldborg gives an account of his first visit to England and Scotland in *A Dane's Excursions in Britain*, which he published in 1809, under the name J. A. Andersen, although the title page also credited him as

'Author of a Tour in Zealand, &c. &c.', that earlier work having on its title page been attributed to 'A Native of Denmark'.[150] Feldborg's *Excursions* exemplify well the extent to which not only British travel writing about Denmark but also Danish travel writing about Britain could serve as a space for exploring and articulating the idea of a shared 'Northern' culture uniting the two countries, in the past and in the present. Feldborg, with his consistent agenda to promote Anglo-Danish relations in this strained period, points, whenever he thinks that he sees it, to the evidence of cultural commonality. But he also struggles, at times, to maintain his faith in this idea, with the effect that his attempts to forge an Anglo-Danish identity in *Excursions* more than once become the occasion, conversely, of disappointment and a retreat into a more nationalistic position.

A few examples from the lengthy, two-volume *Excursions* should suffice to illustrate this process well enough. We can begin with Feldborg's account of Northumbria, in the north-east of England, part of the old Danelaw, which Feldborg visited in October 1807, less than a month after the British bombardment of Copenhagen, and where he found many 'vestiges of the Danes'.[151] The first point of comparison which Feldborg makes here is that the locals 'strikingly resemble the Danes and Norwegians' in their 'extraordinary care and attachment for their horses'.[152] From this apparently quite specific perception of similarity, however – although, in fairness to Feldborg, British travellers to Denmark did often comment on how well the Danes treated their horses – Feldborg draws a much more substantial picture of a common culture in the past and of its persistence into the present day. 'Independently of the aids of history', he says:

> I discovered, by a similarity of features, customs, and language, the strongest affinity between the northern inhabitants of England and those of Denmark and Norway. I never beheld a more truly Norwegian countenance than that of my worthy and much-esteemed host; the dialect he spoke was also evidently of a similar origin.[153]

The 'similarity' with Feldborg discovers, as it were, empirically, involves not just physical ('features') but also cultural ('customs') and even linguistic continuity, reminding us of Clarke's experiences in Jutland. Notably, some ten years before Thomas De Quincey (1785–1859) published his theories about 'The Danish Origin of the Lake District Dialect' in *The Westmorland Gazette* (which I discuss in Chapter 3), Feldborg argues that 'in Northumberland there are examples without number of words of similar import in the Norwegian and Icelandic language; and the guttural pronunciation is eminently Danish'.[154] All over Northumbria, then, in Feldborg's analysis, evidence of the common 'Northern' culture which united Denmark and Britain in the past can be seen and heard.

But, before very long, this perception of cultural common ground begins to give way in Feldborg's account to a sense of difference between contemporary Britain and Denmark, as he reflects on the social hierarchy around him and, in particular, on what he describes as the 'unquestionably highly disgraceful' tendency of 'the superior classes of society' towards 'ill-treatment of the humbler parts'.[155] 'During my intercourse with the landed gentry of England', Feldborg continues:

> I have had some occasions to notice, with peculiar astonishment, an unnecessary want of gentility in comportment towards the lower orders [. . .] I may presume to know something of the pretensions of Danish and German aristocracy; but I do not remember having in Denmark or Germany witnessed more absurd and insufferable instances of contumely in predial tyrants, than in this favourite land of Liberty.[156]

From perceptions of cultural commonality, then, Feldborg moves quickly to the perception of difference. The contrast that he draws here is all the more striking when we recall the respective, contemporary views of England ('this favourite land of Liberty') and Denmark, an absolutist monarchy – and yet it is in the latter, Feldborg insists, that the ancient Northern traditions of 'liberty' and 'nobility' and the 'imperious duty to resist such tyranny by all consistent means' persist, while in England they are on the decline.[157]

If we are to try to understand the wider dynamics at play, here, in Feldborg's *Excursions*, if we are to try to understand why he so often establishes, only so soon thereafter to seemingly dismantle, a sense of common cultural ground between Britain and Denmark, then we need perhaps only to remember that Feldborg's book was published less than two years after the British bombardment of Copenhagen, which had occurred while he was himself in Britain. In fact, Feldborg makes only very slight, direct, *personal* reference to the events of September 1807 in *Excursions*, although he does on one rare occasion note how 'Denmark was convulsed by the most exquisite sensations of horror and indignation', a 'convulsion' that we must imagine he shared.[158] Feldborg does, however, record a number of conversations on the subject with the English and the Scots. Sometimes these are more sympathetic, as in Feldborg's recollection of a conversation with an 'honest tar' at Newcastle, who had been to Copenhagen on a collier, and who had told him: 'I never shall forget, the longest day o' my life, how the poor Danes shed tears as we hauled their ships out of the harbour. I don't know why we took 'em; but they say, if we had not, Bony would.'¹⁵⁹ But often such conversations were more difficult. Feldborg recalls meeting a retired captain at Newcastle, for example, one of whose vessels had been 'employed as a transport' during the British expedition, who told him that the Danish fleet was 'better where it now is; Denmark is but a poor and a small coontry [sic], and we did her a piece of real service by taking away the navy; it was an useless expensive burden upon the people' – the 'novelty' of which 'argument', Feldborg recalls discreetly, 'struck me very forcibly'.¹⁶⁰ And Feldborg also describes at some length a particularly awkward after-dinner conversation in Scotland, where one of the party complained about the current 'rigorous treatment to which Englishmen in that country [Denmark] were exposed', before going to enquire '"whether the Danes had not harboured a rancorous feeling towards this country, ever since the battle of Copenhagen, in 1801?"' – an enquiry which Feldborg managed deftly to defuse by proposing a toast to 'the speedy restoration of peace and good-will between the English, and their brothers, the Danes', with a helpful nod towards the terms of Nelson's address to Frederik VI during the height to that battle (see Chapter 1).¹⁶¹

Feldborg is more willing to offer his thoughts about the events of 1801, however, and it is in these moments that we can, perhaps, gain some sense of his personal response to the bombardment, since his remarks on 1801 in *Excursions* often differ in tone from those given in his 'Historical Account'. Exemplary, in this respect, are Feldborg's observations of and responses to British naval power. Almost from the moment of his arrival in Britain, Feldborg had been struck by and sought to express his admiration for 'Britain's naval glory'.¹⁶² He, like many other travellers who took the same route, describes the 'grandeur' of 'a forest of masts' as he made his way up the Thames, 'passing some of the most delightful scenes that ever engrossed my attention'.¹⁶³ 'I had under the most tremendous circumstances', he says, meaning the Battle of Copenhagen in 1801, which he witnessed, 'beheld the navy of England in commission; it now lay before me divested of the "pride, pomp, and circumstance of glorious war". What a goodly sight! It suggested a thousand pleasing ideas.'¹⁶⁴ Up until this point, Feldborg's tone is very much in keeping with that of his 'Historical Account', where the emphasis was unequivocally on the mutual displays of heroism by the Northern 'brothers', the English and the Danes, which set them apart from their true, common enemy, the French. But immediately, in Feldborg's *Excursions*, the tone shifts as these 'thousand pleasing ideas', he tells us, 'alas! vanished the moment sober Reflection resumed her empire'.¹⁶⁵

Feldborg's figurative coupling of 'Reflection' and 'empire' here is presumably not accidental, since what he describes is the transition from an appreciation of the aesthetic spectacle of the British fleet to the recollection of the uses to which it had been put against his own country, first in 1801 and again, more recently, in 1807. And exactly this same transition is visible in Feldborg's account, in *Excursions*, of his visit to the *Holsteen*, at Blackwall, in the summer of 1805. The *Holsteen*, a former Danish ship of the line, had, as Feldborg tells the reader, been taken from Copenhagen as a prize after the battle in April 1801 and was still undergoing repairs.[166] When he boarded the ship, Feldborg tells us, he 'found everywhere some honourable mark of the share she had borne on the 2d of April, 1801'.[167] 'Entering her lower cabin', Feldborg continues: 'my memory forcibly retraced a scene which had occurred in that very place, but under circumstances calculated to inspire feelings very different from those which now had possession of my mind.'[168] The 'scene' which Feldborg then describes for the reader concerns the surrender of the *Holsteen*. He had been on board the ship at Copenhagen in March 1801, a month before the battle, and had, on that occasion, 'entered into conversation with an ensign of the King's regiment, who had been sent on board with a party to do the duty of marines': 'he was not more than sixteen years old, a Norwegian by birth, and his name was Holm'.[169] After the battle, Feldborg says he 'made the earliest enquiry respecting the fate of the gallant youth'.[170] Holm had, Feldborg learned, 'behaved throughout the action with a degree of valour and coolness which could not be surpassed', and 'the ship having struck, he descended into the lower cabin, and very calmly sat down to read a volume of Voltaire, in which situation he was founded by the British officer who demanded his sword.'[171]

For Feldborg, then, the 'feelings very different' inspired by his being in that same 'lower cabin' of the *Holsteen* are marked not by the sense, so often present in his 'Historical Account', of common cultural ground between Denmark and Britain, but rather by a sense of difference between the two nations, by a sense of Danish 'valour and coolness' now explicitly associated with French revolutionary ideas, signalled by Holm's reading of Voltaire.

The *Holsteen* thus emerges from Feldborg's *Excursions* – like so many of the places described in British travel writing about Denmark, and Danish travel writing about Britain – as a space not only of physical but also of ideological contestation, a space where the desire to forge a model of transnational 'Northern' unity struggles against feelings of national pride. In this respect, the episode exemplifies well not only the complexities of an entire genre of writing, but also the difficulties faced by Feldborg personally in his attempts to repair Anglo-Danish relations. We are reminded again of Kamma Rahbek's quip about Feldborg's identity as a key, perhaps, to the very real sense that Feldborg, despite his diplomatic agenda and evident wishes, always felt himself to be, and always remained, Danish in Britain.

Chapter 3

'A mine yet to be explored': Romanticism and Anglo-Danish Literary Exchanges

On 1 July 1819, *The New Monthly Magazine* ran a six-page article entitled 'Notices of Danish Literature'. It consists, for the most part, of 'extracts translated' from a book in German about 'those Danish poets who have flourished during the last 35 years', written by the Danish lawyer Jens Kragh Høst (1772–1844), who had been one of the founders of the Nordic Literature Society [Det skandinaviske litteraturselskab] at Copenhagen in 1796.[1] The author of the 'Notices' remains unidentified and seems markedly unsure, themselves, about the 'merits' of contemporary Danish literature – and very possibly did not actually read Danish.[2] The final paragraph of the 'Notices' suggests, circumspectly, that because of 'the partiality of patriotism', Høst might 'have somewhat over-rated' the writers whom he discusses, but also allows that 'upon examination, some might doubtless be found worth translating' – the implication being that the author of the 'Notices' has themselves little or no independent familiarity with contemporary Danish literature.[3] 'The recent poetry of that country', the 'Notices' concludes, more encouragingly, 'may at least be regarded as a mine yet unexplored by the literati of Great Britain.'[4]

The mixture of scepticism and apparent unfamiliarity with which the author of the 'Notices' handles contemporary ('recent') Danish poetry is, to a certain extent, indicative of wider British attitudes to modern Danish arts and letters in the late eighteenth and early nineteenth centuries. In her *Letters Written during a Short Residence in Sweden, Norway, and Denmark* (1796), for example, Mary Wollstonecraft (1759–97) suggests that there were 'few literary characters, and fewer artists' to be found at Copenhagen and that those 'few' lack 'encouragement'.[5] Such assumptions have found a legacy, too, in a story often told by scholars in the twentieth century and which has only recently begun to be challenged: namely, the idea that while British Romantic-period literature, in original and translation, found an increasing audience in Denmark in the early nineteenth century, the reverse was not true for contemporary Danish writing in Britain. As Lis Møller puts it: 'Anglo-Danish literary relations in the romantic period are usually thought of as a strictly one-way affair with Britain as the centre from which influence flowed and Denmark as the receiving periphery.'[6]

This chapter of *British Romanticism and Denmark* subjects to further scrutiny the 'one-way' paradigm discerned by Møller in existing scholarship – building, in part, on work already done by her, and by myself, in the collection *Romantic Norths*.[7] Specifically, the chapter argues that the discussion and circulation in late eighteenth- and early nineteenth-century Britain of contemporary Danish literature, in both original and in translation, constituted a more significant axis of cultural exchange between the two countries than has yet been recognised in either anglophone or Danish scholarship. Equally, certain key elements of the transmission of British literature to Denmark in the early nineteenth century remain relatively unconsidered. Foremost among those which will be examined here are the accounts in British Romantic-period writing of the nascent reception of Shakespeare in Denmark, which, as Kristian Smidt observes, was closely 'allied with the growth of the romantic movement' in that country.[8] These accounts cast a revealing light on the development of Romanticism and Romantic nationalism, in both countries, around a paradigm of cultural connection. The 'mine' of contemporary Danish culture was not nearly so unexplored in late eighteenth- and early nineteenth-century Britain, then, as the author of the 'Notices of Danish Literature' might lead one to believe.

'Good books are seldom found': Danish Literature in British Travel Writing

In my introduction to this chapter, I stress a focus on *contemporary* Danish literature. I do so not only to signal what the chapter *will* consider, but also, and perhaps no less importantly, to signal what it will *not* consider: namely, the reception of classical Danish writing, in original and translation, in late eighteenth-century and Romantic-period Britain. A great deal of significant scholarly work has been done and continues to be done on the widespread role of ancient Norse texts in the so-called ballad and antiquarian revivals of the late eighteenth century.[9] The (re)introduction of these classical Scandinavian texts to a wider European readership began, in earnest, with the work of the Swiss historian and philologist Paul Henri Mallet (1730–1807), who became professor of belles lettres at Copenhagen in 1752. With the official sponsorship of the Danish government, Mallet published two monumental studies of classical Scandinavian history and culture: *Introduction à l'histoire du Danemarch où l'on traite de la religion, des mœurs, des lois, et des usages des anciens Danois* (1755) and *Monuments de la mythologie et de la poésie des Celtes, et particulièrement des anciens Scandinaves* (1756). The second of these books included French texts of the Icelandic *Eddas*, skaldic poetry, and a range of other classical Scandinavian writings, and was quickly translated into Danish and German.

The widespread reception of these texts in Britain was begun soon thereafter by the antiquarian Thomas Percy (1729–1811), who published an adapted translation of Mallet's two volumes, in 1770, as *Northern Antiquities: Or, An Historical Account of the Manners, Customs, Religion and Laws, Maritime Expeditions and Discoveries, Language and Literature of the Ancient Scandinavians*. Further key milestones in the reception of classical Danish poetry in Britain include the publication in 1806 of *Popular Ballads and Songs from Tradition, Manuscripts and Scarce Editions with Translations of Similar Pieces from the Ancient Danish Language,* by the Scottish antiquarian Robert Jamieson (1772–1844), and, in 1814, of a collection edited by Jamieson, Walter Scott (1771–1823) and Henry William Weber (1783–1818) under the title *Illustrations of Northern Antiquities from the Earlier Teutonic and Scandinavian Romances*. The titles of these various works illustrate well the slippage between terms like 'Norse', 'Scandinavian' and 'Danish', which is such a marked feature of both the ballad and the antiquarian revivals, and which reflects the ongoing attempts, which I have traced elsewhere in this book, to map anew the cultural and geographical boundaries of 'the North'.[10]

As noted, scholars like Møller and Rix have documented the role played by these classical Scandinavian texts, newly made available through translation into modern European languages, on the development of Romanticism and Romantic nationalisms in Britain and Denmark. In a very straightforward way, these texts provided artists and writers with a rich new repertoire of images, motifs and narratives, whose close connection to the vernacular past gave them a specific national resonance not to be found in the textual artefacts of Classical Greece and Rome, or in their eighteenth-century, Neoclassical remediations.[11] But such ancient Norse texts could also function as (pseudo-)historical documents, enabling comparative cultural histories and speculation about cultural origins – as they do, for example, in James Macpherson's (1736-96) *Introduction to the History of Great Britain and Ireland* (1770) and in Thomas Percy's essay 'On Ancient Metrical Romances', part of his *Reliques of Ancient English Poetry* (1765).[12] And it was in this latter respect, in particular, that the recovery of the classical Scandinavian past enabled speculation within both the ballad and antiquarian revivals about a common 'Nordic' culture of the past, whose present-day legacies could be found in the vernacular culture of Britain and Denmark.[13]

In the *Grammar of the Danish Language for the Use of Englishmen* which he compiled in 1830, the influential Danish linguist and philologist Rasmus Rask (1787–1832) noted that there were by then available Danish 'translations of many celebrated works of English and American authors, as: Shakespeare, Fielding, Sir Walter Scott, Cooper, Washington Irving &c. which may afford an agreeable introduction' to the language for would-be learners.[14] The reception of British Romantic-period authors (including Scott) in early nineteenth-century Denmark has also begun to be documented by scholars. Pioneering, in this respect, was the work of Jørgen Erik Nielsen, who followed his *Den Samtidige Engelske Litteratur og Danmark 1800–1840* [Contemporary English Literature and Denmark, 1800–1840] (1976) with a range of English-language essays on the subject, and on the reception of Byron and Scott in particular.[15]

As Nielsen notes in 'English Literature in Denmark', British Romantic-period writing had some obstacles to overcome in early nineteenth-century Denmark, since the English language was not widely spoken 'even among educated people' (only French and German were taught in school) and English books were expensive; interestingly, though, Nielsen suggests that 'there are no indications that the animosity against Britain [following the attacks of 1801 and 1807] in any way lessened interest in English literature'.[16] In this context, then, as Nielsen observes, the key forum for the reception of British Romantic-period literature in Denmark was the nascent literary periodicals, which 'testify to a widespread interest in things English'.[17] And a central figure in this respect was the influential Danish *littérateur* Knud Lyne Rahbek (1760–1830), who founded the periodicals *Minerva* (1785–1808) and *Det Danske Tilskuer* [The Danish Spectator] (1791–1806), and who produced some of the earliest translations of British second-generation Romantic-period writers. Both publications would have been familiar to at least some British readers, if only by name. Reviewing contemporary Danish periodicals in his *Travels through Denmark*, Pierre-Marie-Louis de Boisgelin de Kerdu (1758–1816), for example, noted that *Minerva* was 'remarkable for being written in a philosophical style', while the Danish traveller and Anglophile Andreas Andersen Feldborg (1782–1838), in his *Tour in Zealand* (1805), informs his readers that Rahbek's monthly *Minerva* and weekly *Tilskuer* have both 'flourished' since their foundation.[18] As Nielsen argues, Rahbek almost certainly used the two-volume anthology *Modern English Poems* (1815–16) compiled by Christian Wiedemann (1770–1840), which contains work by Byron, Scott, Campbell (1777–1844) and William Wordsworth (1770–1850).[19]

Building on Nielsen's work on the reception of British Romanticism in Denmark, Gertrud Oelsner has recently explored the influence of Scott's historical fiction on the depiction of the Jutland heath by Danish Romantic-period painters.[20] Karsten Engelberg, for his part, has established that Percy Bysshe Shelley's (1792–1822) poetry did not really gain any audience in Denmark during the Romantic period: 'in the first half of the nineteenth century', Engelberg writes, '[Percy] Shelley rarely appeared in print in Denmark, and when he did, it invariably happened in brief mentions in texts discussing other poets, primarily Scott and Byron.'[21] What still remains relatively unconsidered by literary scholars and cultural historians, however, is the reception and influence in late eighteenth- and early nineteenth-century Britain of contemporary Danish poetry, in original or translation, which is not concerned with the classical Scandinavian past. The 'one-way' paradigm discerned by Lis Møller still very much prevails in this respect. Indeed, we might cite as exemplary, here, the fact that Diego Saglia's recent *European Literatures in Britain, 1815–1832: Romantic Translations* (2019) makes no mention at all of Denmark or of any of the other Scandinavian countries. And yet interest and influence there most certainly were.

As I have already said, the tendency of critics to assume a 'one-way' model of literary influence between Britain and Denmark during the late eighteenth and early nineteenth centuries has a prehistory in British writing about Denmark at the time, visible, for example, in the scepticism expressed by Wollstonecraft and others about the supposedly poor state of Danish arts and letters. As late as 1839, Murray's *Hand-Book for Travellers* suggested that 'the literature of Denmark presents few living names of European reputation', and mentions Adam Oehlenschläger (1779–1850), certainly Denmark's pre-eminent contemporary poet, as 'alone' enjoying the 'distinction' of such a 'reputation'.[22] Previous, influential British accounts of Denmark strike a similar note. In his description of Copenhagen in his *Travels in Various Countries of Europe, Asia and Africa* (1810–19), for instance, the celebrated traveller Edward Daniel Clarke (1769–1822) laments that 'good books are seldom found in any of the booksellers' shops', before going on to observe that 'literature is more advanced in *Norway* than in the *Danish* Isles'.[23] And the Scottish prisoner of war James Macdonald (1771–1810) is even more scathing in his *Travels through Denmark, and Part of Sweden* (1810), claiming that, when he inquired at Copenhagen about the state of Danish drama, he 'had such vague and contradictory answers, that I soon formed my opinion and suppressed my curiosity'.[24] 'The case is pretty much the same',

Macdonald suggests, 'with regard to the performances of this country, in other departments of literature' – and this conclusion he reached, he says, from the testimony of 'the most enlightened and candid Danes with whom I have conversed; for I cannot pretend to judge the literature of the nation, from my own imperfect acquaintance with the language'.[25] For the same reason, Macdonald graciously declines to pass judgement on the poets Jens Baggesen (1764–1826) and Friederike Brun (1765–1835), 'whose names are often mentioned with respect by this people', whom he says 'have attempted of late to force their language into elegance and popularity'.[26] And then he suggests, again, that 'in the belles lettres, eloquence, and the higher poetry, however, they [i.e. the Danes] confess themselves far behind the four European nations'.[27]

Those travellers who offered such sceptical assessments of Danish arts and letters tended to ascribe their condition either to environmental or socio-political causes, or often to the combination of both. Hence, in his *Travels Through Denmark*, de Kerdu suggests that when it comes to the 'state of the arts and sciences [. . .] if we compare Copenhagen [. . .] to the other cities of Europe, the advantage will undoubtedly not be on her side', a lack which he attributes 'to two principal causes': 'the climate', which both effects the Danes directly and deters 'learned and ingenious foreigners' from taking up residence there, and 'the poverty of the country, which cannot be remedied'.[28] A short 'Account of Copenhagen' published in *The Monthly Magazine* for 1 June 1801 suggests, in a similar vein, that 'literature appears to meet with but little encouragement in Denmark': 'the fact is, that little patronage is given to literature, and no notice is taken of literary men: if they have not the title of professor, or do not stand high in the church, they may rot in obscurity.'[29]

Very often, then, the supposedly atrophied condition of arts and letters in Denmark was presented by British writers as a symptom of the underlying cultural malaise which they believed to be a consequence of the absolutist system of government. Attitudes to the state of the arts in Denmark can function, in this way, as a key indicator of the broader, cultural and political assumptions made by a given writer. Hence, this was very much a matter of individual perspective, and just as there were dissenting voices among British travellers about the nature and influence of Danish absolutism, so, too, did some British commentators paint a rather different picture of the state of the republic of letters in Denmark. In his *Tour through Sweden, Swedish-Lapland, Finland, and Denmark* (1789), for example, Matthew Consett (1757–1831), who visited Denmark in 1786 and who was very sympathetic to the country, affirms that 'literature flourishes at Copenhagen' and benefits from the 'attention' of the 'amiable' and 'much and deservedly respected' crown prince Frederik VI (1768–1839).³⁰ Almost fifty years later, John Barrow (1808–98), the son of the celebrated traveller and secretary to the British Admiralty, in his account of Denmark, reports that:

> Literature, the sciences, and the arts were at an early period encouraged in the Danish capital; and few cities can boast of a greater number, or more respectable societies for the encouragement of arts, sciences, and various branches of literature and the fine arts, than Copenhagen.³¹

One thing which both sceptical and more enthusiastic British visitors to Denmark could agree about, however, when it came to the state of Danish letters was the impressive holdings of the Royal Library in Copenhagen. In his *Tour*, for example, Edward Daniel Clarke – who had lamented the lack of 'good books' in the bookshops at Copenhagen – notes, with admiration, that the Royal Library 'contains above a hundred thousand volumes of printed books, and some thousand manuscripts'.³² John Carr (1772–1832), in *A Northern Summer* (1805), put the number at 'one hundred and thirty thousand volumes and three thousand manuscripts', and suggested the library 'is too enormous for that of the capital and kingdom'.³³ A quarter of a century later, Richard Jones (dates unknown), in *Copenhagen and its Environs* (1829), one of the first modern tourist guides to the Danish capital, describes it as 'one of the finest Royal libraries in Europe', affirming not only that it has an 'extensive collection of literature' but also that 'few public libraries have a more extensive collection of manuscripts, atlasses, and engravings'.³⁴ By 1839, Murray's *Hand-Book* was estimating the number at 'about 400,000 volumes and a large and valuable collection of manuscripts'.³⁵

As the reference by each of these travellers (and by many others) to the manuscript holdings of the Royal Library make clear, most British visitors to Danish reading rooms were primarily interested not in contemporary Danish writing, but in the textual artefacts of the classical Scandinavian past. William Coxe (1748–1828), for example, in his account of Copenhagen in *Travels into Poland, Russia, Sweden, and Denmark* (1784), observes that 'the Danish literati have particularly turned their researches upon the history and antiquities of the North', aided by 'such a number of Icelandick manuscripts as are contained in the Danish libraries', and he gives an extended account of how these 'tend to throw considerable light upon the antiquities, history, and mythology of the northern nations'.³⁶ Clarke records that he and his companions were shown in the Royal Library 'the manuscript copy of the *Edda*, by *Snorro*, and [. . .] also a manuscript collection of histories in the *Icelandic* language'.³⁷ And Macdonald, commenting on the same 'extensive collection of manuscripts in the Icelandic tongue', records that, 'contrary to my expectation, I found a considerable analogy betwixt that language and the Danish'.[38]

Mary Wollstonecraft, as so often, constitutes an exception here. In her *Short Residence*, she records only of the Royal Library that 'of the value of the Icelandic manuscripts I could not form a judgement, though the alphabet of some of them amused me, by shewing what immense labour men will submit to, in order to transmit their ideas to posterity'.[39] Generally speaking, however, the responses of British travellers to the textual artefacts of the classical Scandinavian past which they saw in the Royal Library at Copenhagen tended to parallel wider concerns and debates within the antiquarian and ballad revivals, including the widespread hypothesis of a common 'Northern' culture from which the modern Scandinavian countries and Britain had inherited significant characteristics, visible, for example, in vernacular literatures and national characters. Indeed, the role played in the antiquarian and ballad revivals by the remediation of these classical Scandinavian texts through contemporary British travel writing about Denmark (and 'the North' more generally) has not yet received scholarly attention on a par with that which has been devoted to British antiquarian writing or to British poems which affect a Nordic style or have Nordic themes, like those examined by Rix in *Norse Romanticism*. As noted, however, my concern, here, is not with the reception in Britain of classical Scandinavian texts, but rather with the reception of contemporary Danish literature, in original or translation, which is not concerned with the Nordic past. And it is to that subject that I want, now, to turn.

'Our Westmorland-Copenhagen': Danish Literature in Romantic-Period Britain

If it is familiar at all, then British interest in Danish literature during the Romantic period will probably be most familiar to scholars from the work of Thomas De Quincey (1785–1859), the 'English Opium-Eater'. De Quincey seems to have come to Danish literature, and to the Danish language, through a family connection, of sorts. In the first of his 'Letters to a Young Man whose Education has been Neglected', serialised in *The London Magazine* in May 1823, De Quincey observes that he has 'some acquaintance with the Danish literature', which, he says, he began to study, along with the Danish language, 'about twelve years ago'.[40] The occasion then seems to have been the return to England from Denmark of De Quincey's younger brother Richard (b. 1789), known to the family as 'Pink'. As De Quincey explains in 'My Brother', the twelfth chapter of his posthumously published *Autobiographic Sketches* (composed in 1853), Richard had been taken prisoner by the Danes following the British attack on Copenhagen in 1807 when he, and some of his crewmates from the fireship *Prometheus*, had 'landed on the coast of Jutland' – rather ill-advisedly, and probably against orders, as De Quincey himself observes.[41] 'Wyborg [Viborg] in Jutland was the seat of his Danish captivity', De Quincey recalls, 'and such was the amiableness of the Danish character, that, except for the loss of his time, to one who was aspiring to distinction and professional honour, none of the prisoners who were on parole could have had much reason for complaint.'[42]

Richard was released as part of an exchange of prisoners in August 1809 and returned to London in September of that year.[43] As further evidence of the 'amiableness' of Richard's former captors – a trait which, as we have seen in Chapters 1 and 2, is almost universally applauded in accounts by British prisoners of war of their time in Denmark – Thomas De Quincey records that:

> through long years after my brother's death, I used to receive letters, written in the Danish (a language which I had attained in the course of my studies, and which I have since endeavoured to turn to account in a public journal for some useful purposes of research), from young men as well as women in Jutland; couched in the most friendly terms, and recalling to his remembrance scenes and incidents which sufficiently proved the terms of fraternal affection upon which he had lived amongst these public enemies.[44]

Some of these letters De Quincey says he 'preserved', as 'memorials that do honour, on different considerations, to both parties alike'.[45]

The 'useful purposes of research' to which De Quincey says he turned his knowledge of Danish is almost certainly a reference to a series of articles which he published in *The Westmorland Gazette* in November and December 1819 and in January 1820.[46] Over the course of four letters to the editor, De Quincey announces and expands upon what he calls his 'remarkable discovery' that 'the dialect spoken in Westmoreland and Cumberland, in so far as it is peculiar to those counties, is borrowed wholly from the Danish'.[47] 'I do not mean simply that it has some affinity to the Danish,' De Quincey continues, 'what I mean – is that all the *words* peculiar to the Lake District, at least, and most of the *names* attached to imperishable objects (as mountains, lakes, tarns, &c.) are pure Danish.'[48]

De Quincey advances two kinds of argument in support of this claim 'that as good Danish will be spoken in Kendal market next Saturday as by any professor at Kiel or Copenhagen'.[49] The first argument is empirical, based on a variety of words currently in use in the Lake District, which, De Quincey says, are 'radically distinct from such as belong to the universal English and wholly unintelligible to a southern Englishman', and on 'the peculiar pronunciation of many words common to the Cumbrian and the classical English'.[50] In both categories, De Quincey says, Danish 'furnishes a master key which unlocks nearly all'.[51] De Quincey's second argument is more theoretical, based not only on the fact that 'the Danes settled a colony' in the area in the ninth century, but also on wider theories about the 'affiliation of languages' which had been developed in Britain during the Antiquarian Revival of the late eighteenth century.[52] Specifically, De Quincey points to the hypothesis of a pan-Northern language in the past, which he calls 'Teutonic (or Gothic)', and which, he says, following a number of eighteenth-century philologists, was originally of 'Asiatic birth'.[53]

At the core of De Quincey's arguments about the Danish origins of the Lake District dialect, then, are not only empirical data but also that now-familiar hypothesis which I have been tracing in this book of a common, Nordic culture of the past, traces of which were still visible in the similarities between the two languages. Hence it is not surprising that De Quincey argues that the closest resemblances between the Lake District dialect and modern Danish are to be found in those more remote areas of the area (comparatively) less touched by what De Quincey calls 'universal English'. 'There it is', De Quincey suggests, 'that the Danish is spoken in its purity: there lies our Westmorland-Copenhagen'.[54]

Referring to these arguments in a footnote to his 'Letters to a Young Man whose Education has been Neglected', De Quincey expresses the hope that 'for the amusement of the lake-tourists, Mr Wordsworth may do me the favour to accept it as an appendix to his work on the English Lakes'.[55] In fact, as both Barry Symonds and Daniel Sanjiv Roberts point out, De Quincey had already offered Wordsworth the essay for the revised version of his 'Topographical Description of the Country of the Lakes in the North of England' which was published with *The River Duddon* in 1820, and which he subsequently worked up into his *Guide through the District of the Lakes* (1835) – but Wordsworth had declined it.[56] As Roberts recognises, Wordsworth's rejection must have been prompted, at least in part, by the fact that the foundation of De Quincey's linguistic hypothesis in the idea of a common, pan-Nordic culture of the past was directly antithetical to 'the nationalistic, truly *British*' configuration of the Lake District in Wordsworth's poetry, as a place where one could observe the natural, unmediated evolution of what Wordsworth famously calls, in his Preface to *Lyrical Ballads* (1800), 'the language really used by men'.[57]

De Quincey's engagement with the Danish language and literature was not confined, however, to his speculations about the possible linguistic artefacts of a pan-Nordic culture in the past. In his 'Letter to the

Editor of the *Westmorland Gazette*' of 4 December 1819, De Quincey affirms also that he has 'a great attachment to Northern literature', and he did, during his career, make a number of engagements with contemporary Danish literature.⁵⁸ In 1822, for example, De Quincey began a loose, incomplete and never-published translation of *Nicolai Klimii Iter Subterraneum* (1741) by the influential Danish man of letters Ludvig Holberg (1684–1754), a satirical travel narrative very much in the mode of Jonathan Swift's (1667–1745) *Gulliver's Travels* (1726). As Musgrove points out in his edition of De Quincey's manuscript, a Danish translation had been made by Hans Hagerup (1717–81) in 1742, and an anonymous English translation appeared in the same year, which was reprinted in Edinburgh in 1812 by Henry William Weber (1783–1818), the friend and assistant of Walter Scott.⁵⁹ De Quincey used as his source, however, neither the Latin original nor the Danish translation of 1742, but rather the second Danish translation which had been made in 1785 by the contemporary Danish poet Jens Baggesen under the title *Niels Klims Underjordiske Rejse* [Niels Klim's Subterranean Journey].⁶⁰

Musgrove argues convincingly that De Quincey did not make this translation 'as an academic exercise, nor as a piece of self-instruction in Danish, but in order to produce a readable English version for publication' – and may very well have done so at the instigation of his friend the antiquarian and editor Robert Pearse Gillies (1788–1858), who had begun to run translations of Danish literature in *Blackwood's Edinburgh Magazine* in the summer of 1820.⁶¹ De Quincey's translation of *Niels Klim* never saw the light of day during his lifetime, but, as David Groves observes, in May 1829 De Quincey almost certainly authored a review, in the short-lived *Edinburgh Gazette*, of which he was co-editor, of a recent history of Danish literature.⁶² This was the first volume of the projected *Dansk Bibliothek* [Danish Library] which had been published at Copenhagen in 1827 by Christen Thaaarup (1795–1849), an 'enterprise' which the reviewer concluded would 'be very popular, not only in Denmark, but also in Germany'.⁶³ Be this as it may, De Quincey's acquaintance with Danish literature, and his attempt to make it better known in England, is most evident from his most substantial, published translation of a contemporary Danish work: Jens Baggesen's account of the poet Friedrich Gottlieb Klopstock (1724–1803). And this translation by De Quincey, though interesting enough in itself, also provides some tantalising clues about Baggesen's possible wider influence on British Romantic-period poetry.

Born in Germany, Klopstock was in 1750 invited by Frederik V of Denmark (1723–66) to move to Copenhagen, where he received an annuity enabling him to complete his epic poem, *Der Messias* [The Messiah]

(1748–73): the invitation was motivated by Johann Bernstorff (171–22), the Danish statesman and diplomat, who was keen to cement German–Danish cultural relations. De Quincey's 'Klopstock, from the Danish' was published in the *Edinburgh Saturday Post* for 11 August 1827. In his brief introduction, De Quincey notes that Samuel Taylor Coleridge (1772–1834) had already published in *The Friend* a 'private and anonymous memorandum of two visits' to Klopstock by 'Mr Wordsworth, the poet' in 1798.[64] De Quincey identifies the source of his new 'memorial' as the account given by Baggesen of his meeting with Klopstock in Hamburg, in 1789, in the first volume of his *Labyrinten; eller Reise giennem Tydskland, Schweiz og Frankerig* [Labyrinth; or Journey through Germany, Switzerland, and France] (1792–3).[65]

Baggesen's semi-fictional, semi-autobiographical novel was the first major work of travel writing to be published in Danish, and De Quincey notes that Baggesen 'holds a conspicuous place in the modern Danish literature; and, judging from my own limited acquaintance with his works, I am disposed to think not undeservedly'.[66] But 'A Danish book, which has never been translated', De Quincey continues:

> although printed and well published at Copenhagen, Kiel, and Altona, may fairly be considered a sealed book to the world at large; there being probably not twenty people in Great Britain, merchants excepted, who cultivate any acquaintance with the Danish language or literature.[67]

De Quincey praises 'the unaffected sensibility', 'enthusiasm', 'good sense' and 'no inconsiderable originality of thought' in Baggesen's work, but he also stresses for the reader that he 'would not be understood to compare Mr. Baggesen with Mr. Wordsworth', author of the earlier memoir, as Baggesen 'has no pretensions of that magnitude'.[68] De Quincey's comparative evaluation aside, however, there is, I think, the distinct possibility that Klopstock acted as a conduit of influence between Baggesen and Wordsworth.

I have noticed elsewhere the close verbal and thematic similarities between Baggesen's poem 'Da jeg var lille' ['When I was young'] (1785) and the first version of Wordsworth's 'Ode. Intimations of Immortality from Recollections of Early Childhood', composed in March 1802.[69] In neither of my previous discussions of the potential relationship between the two poems could I trace any direct line or point of contact. But Klopstock might well connect the two works. Baggesen visited Klopstock in 1785: the year in which 'Da jeg var lille' was first published in the anthology *Poesier*, compiled by Hans Wilhelm Riber (1760–96), and as De Quincey's translation makes clear, the two poets discussed Danish literature and their own work (as one would expect). Wordsworth visited Klopstock in 1798 and, of course, the two also discussed literature.[70] Baggesen was by then one of the luminaries of contemporary Danish poetry and 'Da jeg var lille' one of his most popular works. It would seem not unreasonable to conclude, then, although of course we cannot be certain, that Klopstock might have introduced Baggesen's work to Wordsworth as part of any discussion of contemporary Danish literature and that Wordsworth later echoed 'Da jeg var lille' when he came to compose his 'Ode'.

Whether or not De Quincey counted Wordsworth or Coleridge among those 'twenty people in Great Britain, merchants excepted, who cultivate any acquaintance with the Danish language or literature', that number certainly included De Quincey's friend Robert Pearse Gillies, who, Musgrove suggests, 'more than any other man after [Walter] Scott was responsible for the popularisation of contemporary northern European literature in England and Scotland during the first part of the 19th century'.[71] Gillies is probably best remembered by scholars today for his work with German literature. Together with John Gibson Lockhart (1794–1854), the magazine editor and biographer of Walter Scott, Gillies compiled the 'Horae Germanicae' which ran in *Blackwood's* from 1819 until 1828: an occasional series of essays on, and translations from, a range of contemporary German literature.[72] Gillies also published his own three-volume anthology of *German Stories* in 1826, which De Quincey reviewed, somewhat equivocally, for *Blackwood's* in December of that same year.

As I noted earlier, Gilles might have been the author of the 'Notices of Danish Literature' which was published in *The New Monthly Magazine* for 1 July 1819. But he was certainly responsible for the 'Horae Danicae' series which ran to four instalments in *Blackwood's* in 1820–1 and for which, as we have seen, De Quincey's translation of *Niels Klim* might originally have been intended. Like the more extensive 'Horae Germanicae' series, the 'Horae Danicae' consist of commentary and translated extracts. All four instalments focus on contemporary Danish drama, and cover three works by Adam Oehlenschläger and one by Bernhard Severin Ingemann (1789–1862).[73]

The first instalment, in April 1820, deals with *Hakon Jarl, a Tragedy* [Hakon Jarl hin Rige, et Sørgespil], (1805), by Oehlenschläger, whom Gillies characterises as 'a great poet of Denmark, whose compositions, in his native language, have rendered him the chief living pride of his own country'.[74] The subject of Oehlenschläger's play is Haakon Sigurdsson (937–995), whose 'history', Gillies assures the reader, will be 'well known to all those who have read the Scandinavian ballads', and Oehlenschläger's treatment of it displays 'the audacity of genius' and 'all the delicacies of perfect skill'.[75] But before turning to the play itself,

Gillies offers a reflection on the distinctive nature of Danish literature and, in particular, seeks to decouple it from the German, noting that the two are 'as different [. . .] as the literature of Germany is from that of England'.[76] For Gillies, the distinctiveness of contemporary Danish literature is rooted in its close connections to the classical Scandinavian past, to 'the kindred, but far purer sources of Scandinavian mythology and romance'.[77] Oehlenschläger, Gillies suggests, 'of all the modern Danish Poets [. . .] is the most deeply and essentially imbued with this prevailing spirit of Scandinavian thought':

> The wild unbridled spirits of those haughty Sea-kings that carried ravage and terror upon all the coasts of Europe – the high, warm, unswerving love of those northern dames that welcomed them on their return to their native ice-girt fastnesses – the dark ferocious superstitions which made these bold men the willing sport and tools of demons – their sacrifices of blood – their uprootings of tenderness – their solemn and rejoicing submission when fate irresistible arrests them in their buoyant and triumphant breath of strife – their hot impetuous lawless living – their cold calm dying – and their desperate ignorance of the name of despair – such are the characters and such the passions that Oehlenschläger has delighted to contemplate as an antiquarian, and dared to depict as a Tragedian.[78]

According to Gillies, then, contemporary Danish literature, at least as exemplified in this play by Denmark's foremost contemporary poet, not only inherits but also embodies the virtues of the classical Scandinavian past.

The second instalment of the 'Horae Danicae' ran in *Blackwood's* in December 1820. It, however, took an altogether different direction. The focus here is not on a work with a classical Scandinavian theme, but rather on the tragedy which Oehlenschläger wrote about the life of the Italian painter Antonio da Correggio (1489–1534) while he was staying with the celebrated Danish sculptor Bertel Thorvaldsen (1770–1844), in Rome, in the spring of 1809. Gillies evidently felt the need to justify this choice to *Blackwood's* readers for whom the expectation, clearly, was that contemporary Danish literature was more or less connected to the classical Scandinavian past – as Gillies had, himself, argued in the previous instalment. He notes, referring back to the first of the 'Horae Danicae', that he has 'already introduced the great Danish poet to our readers by abundant quotations from one of the best of these tragedies, which he has devoted to the stern genius of the heroic north'.[79] *Corregio*, by contrast, was 'composed so far as we can judge, upon a set of principles as remote as may well be imagined from those exemplified' in *Hakon Jarl* and 'devoted certainly to the illustration of a set of manners altogether different'.⁸⁰ Gillies justifies its inclusion, then, 'from the beauty of its conceptions, the facility of its execution [and] above all, from the exquisite touches of Nature scattered with a careless hand of lavishness over its dialogue'.⁸¹ These factors, he says, mean that *Correggio* is 'entitled to be classed amongst the most brilliant productions' of Oehlenschläger.⁸² But not only these. *Correggio* is also worthy of the reader's attention, Gillies argues, because 'the true object of the poet in this piece, seems to have been the embodying of his own main conceptions concerning the character of the artist-mind'.⁸³ And the key here, says Gillies, lies in the nuances of Oehlenschläger's characterisation: he is 'too great a man to have only one conception of greatness' and hence the reader will not find, in *Correggio*, definitive support for 'any one favourite theory' of artistic creativity.⁸⁴ Ultimately, then, Gillies presents *Correggio* as valuable not merely because of its artistry and historical interest, but because of its engagement with wider debates in contemporary philosophy about what he calls 'the character of the artist-mind'.

The third instalment of the 'Horae Danicae' (incorrectly labelled the fourth) was published in *Blackwood's* in March 1821. It returns to a work with a classical Scandinavian theme: Oehlenschläger's tragedy *Hagbarth and Signa* [Hagbarth og Signe] (1815), the story of a woman who falls in love with the man who, unbeknown to her, has killed her brother. This is not now regarded as one of Oehlenschläger's more successful works, and Gillies, too, seems aware of insufficiencies, compared to earlier works. He notes that 'several poets (Wordsworth for example)' have 'deemed it advisable to publish prefatory dissertations, in order that their works might be properly understood and appreciated'.⁸⁵ Oehlenschläger might have done the same in this case, Gillies thinks, to ensure that the reader 'may not condemn the poet for missing a mark at which he had never aimed'.⁸⁶ *Hagbarth and Signa* is included, Gillies says, as exemplary of the genre of 'heroic poems' and 'the characters, however rude and wild, are in strict keeping with the manners of the times'.⁸⁷ The work, Gillies suggests, is also typical of Oehlenschläger's handling of source materials: 'as if by chance (if the metaphor is here allowable) he finds the pillars of some ancient Scandinavian temple, seizes the massy fragments, and, by one mighty spell, combines them into a great and graceful whole'.⁸⁸

Gillies takes his leave of Oehlenschläger by assuring the reader that 'the works of this highly-gifted Dane, are indeed a rich mine of inspiration for others', a phrase which (though hardly recondite) certainly recalls the closing injunction of the 'Notices of Danish Literature' in *The New Monthly Magazine*.⁸⁹ He then introduces Bernhard Severin Ingemann, whom he says 'in *some respects* (though a much younger author) is even superior to his countryman'.[90] A poet and novelist, Ingemann was much influenced by the work of Walter Scott and, starting in the mid-1820s, began to author the earliest historical poems and novels in Danish. Ingemann's earlier work is not, now, highly regarded, but it is the tragedy *Masaniello* (1815) which forms the subject of the fourth and final instalment of the 'Horae Danicae', which was published in *Blackwood's* in April 1821: the story of the Neapolitan fisherman Tomasso Aniello (1620–47) who led a revolt against Habsburg rule in 1647.

Gillies presents his translated extracts as a first. 'Of the tragedies of Ingeman[n]', he says, 'so far as we can learn, no translation has yet appeared in this country; nor indeed have we ever observed his name noticed by any of our pretenders to foreign scholarship.'[91] He stresses that Ingemann is 'yet but a young man, from whose riper genius much may be expected' (in which prediction Gillies was certainly correct) and that he has, since the composition of this work, been 'sedulously improving his mind by travels in Italy, and by tranquil and laborious study, of which the fruits may soon be looked for'.[92] Gillies's source for this biographical information was probably Feldborg, who knew Ingemann and corresponded with him.

Gillies observes that *Masaniello* may be 'unfavourably contrasted with some of the modern writers of Germany' because there are 'no blendings of the magnificent scenery of Naples with delineation of the mind's internal conflicts'.[93] And following his extracts from the drama, Gillies closes the instalment on a similar note, reflecting that 'we cannot expect that the admirers of our "Horae Germanicae" will in a like degree approve the productions of the *Danish* school. There is a wide difference indeed in the style and taste of the two nations.'[94] Ultimately, then, it seems that for Gillies, contemporary Danish literature was still at its strongest when it engaged with the themes and the landscapes of the classical Scandinavian past, when it was, in other words, most 'Romantic', in the Germanic sense of that term. Or such, at least, is how Gillies imagined that his readers would respond to a literature from the North which did not openly engage with 'Romantic' constructions of 'the North' as a place where sublime national and natural characters were intimately intertwined.

Although no further translations from Ingemann or other Danish dramatic poets by Gillies are extant, in 1822 the antiquarian, poet and botanist William Herbert (1778–1847), who had already published two volumes of *Select Icelandic Poetry, Translated from the Originals* (1804, 1806), brought the Dane's name again before the British public when he published his well-received play *The Wierd Wanderer of Jutland*. In his Appendix, Herbert informs the reader that 'the subject first suggested itself to me in reading a Danish play by Ingemann'.[95] The dramatic poem in question is Ingemann's *Løveridderen* [The Lion Knight] (1816), of which Herbert also provides an abstract, noting that the story actually 'originates in a Danish ballad, founded on circumstances which are said to have occurred towards the end of the fourteenth century'.[96]

For Herbert, the engagement with classical and contemporary Danish writing also seems to have been intended to emphasise the common cultural ground between Britain and Denmark. The dedication to his *Select Icelandic Poetry*, for example, written three years after the Battle of Copenhagen, asserts that Denmark 'is intimately allied to England in ancient blood and language' and 'should ever continue joined to it by the closest ties of uninterrupted amity'.[97] However, the critical reception of Herbert's *Wierd Wanderer* exemplifies, rather, the continuing association of Denmark, in British Romantic-period writing, with the characters and landscapes of classical Scandinavian myth, which we also traced in the 'Horae Danicae'. *The Monthly Repertory*, for instance, notes Herbert's 'love of the wild, the violent, and the supernatural' and says that 'his genius is like the sun of the northern climes in which it delights to indulge'.[98] And exactly this same collocation of contemporary Danish writing with the textual artefacts of the classical Scandinavian past is visible in the anthology of *Romantic Ballads, Translated from the Danish* which was published by George Henry Borrow (1803–81) at Norwich in 1826.

Borrow's volume contains thirty-four poems, divided equally into 'ballads' and 'miscellanies'. His table of contents makes for interesting and instructive reading. In the category of 'ballads', all the poems have explicitly classical Scandinavian themes. Four are identified as by Oehlenschläger, twelve as 'from the old Danish' and one only by title. Among the 'miscellanies', two are identified as by Oehlenschläger, two as by Ewald and a further seven by title alone; the remainder comprises one 'from the Norse', one 'from the Gaelic', and two each 'from the German' and 'from the Swedish'. From Borrow's table of contents alone, then, we can see not only the fluidity of the contemporary British conception of 'Danish' and its relation to wider constructions of 'the North', but also the fluidity of the contemporary understanding of the boundary between classical and contemporary Danish writing. Interestingly in this latter respect, of the eleven actually Danish poems which Borrow includes among the seventeen 'miscellanies', only eight do not openly engage with classical Scandinavian themes – that is to say, only eight poems out of the thirty-four in the volume as a whole. Such figures are by no means representative of the themes of contemporary Danish literature per se but are extremely indicative of the kinds of contemporary Danish literature that was mediated to Britain.

Of the eight Danish poems not concerned with classical Scandinavian culture, the most significant, from the point of view of the making available to British readers of contemporary Danish poetry, are certainly the four poems by Oehlenschläger and Ewald. The former Borrow describes in his Preface as 'a poet who is yet living, and who stands high in the estimation of his countrymen'.[99] Both of the poems which Borrow includes are early works, published in Oehlenschläger's *Digte* [Poems] (1803). The first is 'Nature's Temperaments' [Natur-Temperamenter], a highly allusive consideration of the four humours. Borrow's translation follows faithfully enough the tetrameter couplets of the original, but addresses only two of the four humours (styled 'Sadness' and 'Madness' by Borrow) which Oehlenschläger describes. The second poem, 'The Violet-Gatherer' [Violsamleren], has a Gothic feel and tells the story of a young man called Louis who picks violets in anticipation of soon being reunited with his recently deceased beloved, Emma.

Of the two poems by Ewald (who had died in 1781), the first, the short 'Bear Song', is extracted and translated, without the context being given, from Evald's Norse-themed verse-drama *Balders Død* [The Death of Balder] (1775). But the second poem is much more significant. Entitled 'National Song' by Borrow, this was the poem beginning 'Kong Christian stoed ved hoien Mast' [King Christian stood by the lofty mast] which Evald had composed in 1779 as one of the songs in his play *Fiskerne* [The Fishermen]. Evald's play was first performed at Copenhagen in January 1780 to mark the birthday of Christian VII of Denmark (1749–1808) and the song was adopted that same year as the Danish royal anthem.[100] It is one of the oldest national anthems still in use, and Borrow's is the second-earliest, extant English-language translation of it. The first English translation was made, as we shall see later in this chapter, by a Dane.[101]

Even though the emphasis in Borrow's *Romantic Ballads* lay very much, then, on contemporary Danish literary engagements with the classical Scandinavian past, his volume did also play a role in introducing some other major works of Danish Romanticism to British readers. Throughout, however, Borrow tends to perceive the value of contemporary Danish writing to be in direct proportion to the extent to which that literature reflects the textual artefacts of the past. 'However defective their poetry may be in point of harmony of numbers,' Borrow argues of classical Scandinavian poets in his Preface:

> it describes, in vivid and barbaric language, scenes of barbaric grandeur, which in these days are never witnessed; and, which, though the modern muse may imagine, she generally fails in attempting to pourtray, from the

violent desire to be smooth and tuneful, forgetting that smoothness and tunefulness are nearly synonymous with tameness and unmeaningness.[102]

In Borrow's suggestion, here, that the 'tuneful' muse of contemporary Danish writing suffers in comparison with the 'vivid' muse of Denmark's 'barbaric' past, we see a version of the argument often made by British writers about the Danish national character: namely that modern Danes suffered by comparison with their heroic ancestors (see Chapter 4). We see, in other words, a further instance of the extent to which British Romantic-period constructions of 'the North' tended to influence perceptions of present-day Denmark and Danishness. But not all contemporary commentators were in agreement, of course, that the literary glories of Denmark lay firmly in its past.

'The introduction of Danish literature into this country': The Danish Contribution

In April 1820, the first instalment of the 'Horae Danicae' had concluded with praise (presumably penned by Lockhart) for the work being done by Gillies in disseminating the literature of modern Denmark in England, for his 'diligence' as a translator, and for his potentially bright future as 'a writer of English tragedies'.[103] 'The day may perhaps come', we are told, 'when German and Danish poets may be proud to repay in kind, the services which Mr Gillies is now rendering to the genius of the North.'[104] But Gillies, Herbert and Borrow were not the only ones rendering that service during the Romantic period. Some Danes, too, writing in English, sought to increase the reputation of their national literature in Britain. One of these was the aforementioned linguist Rasmus Rask, who, in his *Grammar of the Danish Language for the Use of Englishmen*, directs those of his readers 'who wish for a thorough knowledge of the Danish and Norwegian' literature to the *Dansk Læsebog* [Danish Reader] (2 vols, 1799, 1804) compiled by Knud Lyne Rahbek, 'a book which', Rask affirms, 'presents a view of the best authors, in the elegant branches of Literature, together with copious specimens of their writing'.[105] The most prominent example of a Dane attempting to promote contemporary Danish literature in Britain was, however, the expatriate Danish Anglophile Andreas Andersen Feldborg.

'Who is there in Edinburgh or Copenhagen that knows not Feldberg the Dane?'[106] Thus opens the review in *Blackwood's Edinburgh Magazine* for September 1821, presumably written by Gillies or Lockhart, of the first part of Feldborg's *Denmark Delineated*, which had been published earlier that year. 'Feldberg, the companion of Oehlenschläger, the beloved of Thorvaldsen, the bosom friend of Baggesen', the review continues, somewhat exaggeratedly:

> When *he* comes forward to vindicate the literature of his country from the neglect under which it is the reproach of the European nations that it should so long have laboured, who is there that will not 'lend him his ears'?[107]

The playful tone of the reviewer is slightly difficult to gauge here: is the phrase from *Antony and Cleopatra* being used to laud Feldborg as a noble orator or actually to tease him as a besotted Bottom, who was granted ass's ears in *A Midsummer Night's Dream* as a mark of his foolishness? Either way, the reviewer draws immediate attention to the considerable efforts made by Feldborg to promote contemporary Danish literature in Britain. I will return to how Feldborg prosecutes that task in *Denmark Delineated* later in this chapter. To begin with, however, I want to consider his first, serious attempt at 'the introduction of Danish literature into this country': his anthology *Poems from the Danish* (1815).[108]

The anthology is dedicated by Feldborg to James de Windt (1772–1834), for the 'support which you have been pleased to give' to this 'attempt which I ventured to conceive for the introduction of Danish literature into this country'.[109] The De Windts were an influential family on the island of Saint Croix in the Danish West Indies (see Chapter 5). James de Windt seems to have acted as a long-term patron of Feldborg, all of whose published works are dedicated to him. The exact nature of their connection and of the 'support' offered remains unknown. But, in his three-page dedication, Feldborg praises De Windt's 'patriotic devotion', which, he says, he hopes to emulate 'with the execution of a design which will, I trust, prove creditable to Denmark, and meet with the countenance of England'.[110]

Once again, here, we see Feldborg stating explicitly his desire to act as a kind of cultural liaison between Britain and Denmark during a time of prolonged crisis in the relations between the two countries, by promoting Danish culture in Britain. After the two British attacks on Denmark in 1801 and 1807, 1814–15 was another low point in Anglo-Danish relations: under the Treaty of Kiel (1814), which brought to an end the state of war which had existed between Britain and Denmark since 1807, Denmark had to cede possession of Norway to Sweden. That this situation was foremost in Feldborg's mind as *Poems from the Danish* went to press is evident (if evidence were needed) not only from the fact that he published in 1814 an *Appeal to the English Nation in Behalf of Norway*, arguing for the reuniting of that country with Denmark. Rather, it is also made explicit by the companion volume to *Poems* which Feldborg also published in 1815 under the title *Danish and Norwegian Melodies*. This volume was prepared with the assistance of one C. Stokes and consists of thirteen of the texts from *Poems* set to musical accompaniment.[111] The volume is dedicated by Feldborg at London, on 24 July 1815, as follows:

> To the Danish and Norwegian Nations, in token of the dutiful regard felt by one who rejoiced with them in the days of their prosperity, and who has not been prevented in the enemy's country, from manifesting his sympathy in their sufferings, these melodies are inscribed, with sanguine hopes for a return of the times when Denmark and Norway presented a picture of public and private happiness which but few countries have enjoyed.[112]

Appropriately enough, then, in view of Feldborg's stated wish to promote Danish interests by shoring up Anglo-Danish relations, *Poems from the Danish* is itself an Anglo-Danish collaboration – between Feldborg and William Sidney Walker (1795–1846), the future Shakespearean critic who was then beginning a distinguished residence as a Classical scholar at Trinity College Cambridge. In his Preface, Feldborg expresses gratitude on behalf of 'my country and myself' to Walker, 'a young gentleman, who bids fair to become a great poetical ornament to England'.[113] Quite when and how the two met is unclear, but Nielsen refers to a letter from Feldborg to the Danish historian and critic Christian Molbech (1783–1857) in which Feldborg says that Walker produced the verse on the basis of English prose translations which he had made from the original Danish texts.[114]

Poems from the Danish contains twenty poems and fifteen 'historical notes and illustrations', essentially short essays by Feldborg on various connected topics, such as 'Character of Archbishop Absalon' and 'Character of Christian the Fourth'. Explaining, in his Preface, 'the principle of selection which [he] thought proper to adopt', Feldborg says that he 'was chiefly influenced by recollections of that happy period when my country appeared to me the greatest, as she ever will remain to me the best, of countries on earth'.[115] From the original composition dates of the poems involved, this 'happy period' can be said to correspond, approximately, to the end of the eighteenth and the beginning of the nineteenth century: there are a few exceptions, but the majority of poems are from the 1780s–90s, prior to the Battle of Copenhagen in 1801.

Unlike Borrow's *Romantic Ballads*, which emphasised, as we have seen, Danish verse dealing with classical Scandinavian culture, *Poems from the Danish* offers the reader a much wider range of contemporary

Danish poetry and authors. Only one of the twenty poems has a dominant mythological subject or motif: Oehlenschläger's 'The Bard' ['Til Danmark's Frederik'] (1805). Many, by contrast, are nascent works of Romantic nationalism predicated on the beauties of the Danish landscape, such as 'The Wishes' [Det Nye Aar] (1779) by Johannes Evald, 'The Love of our Country' [Fødelands-Kærlighed] (1782) by Thomas Thaarup (1749–1821) and 'To my Country' [Til mit Fædreneland] (1792) by Jens Baggesen. Others have more conventional themes and motifs, such as 'To a Girl Beloved' [Til Den Elskede] (date uncertain) by Ingemann and 'On Fortitude' [Bedre at leve blant isklædte Bjerge'] (date uncertain) by Ove Malling, or celebrate national characteristics, such 'The Women of Denmark' [Til Søstrene] (1803) by Knud Lyne Rahbek.

Four poems in the collection are of especial interest and significance, the full texts of which my reader can find in the appendix to *British Romanticism and Denmark*. The first, which opens the volume, is titled 'The Popular Naval Song of Denmark' and credited to 'the late Johannes Evald, of Copenhagen'.[116] This is a translation of Evald's aforementioned song from *Fiskerne* which had been adopted as the Danish royal anthem in 1780: Feldborg and Walker's version is, in fact, the earliest English translation of the song, predating Borrow's by some eleven years. The song celebrates the victories over Sweden of three great Danish naval heroes of the past: Christian IV of Denmark (1577–1648), Niels Juel (1629–97) and Peter Tordenskiold (1690–1720), whose lives and achievements Feldborg describes in the 'Historical Notes and Sketches' which he included in *Poems from the Danish*. Sweden, which had failed to come to the aid of her ally Denmark during the Battle of Copenhagen in 1801, and which had taken possession of Norway under the Treaty of Kiel in 1814, must have seemed liked fair game to Feldborg in 1815, and publishing the 'Naval Song' as the lead entry in *Poems from the Danish* was, no doubt, an assertion of national pride and patriotism on his part.[117] However, at an historical moment when Danish military and political influence in the North was at a low ebb, following the defeats by the British in 1801 and 1807, and the loss of Norway in 1814, recollections and assertions of Danish naval power must have seemed ironic to British readers.

The second text in *Poems from the Danish* of especial significance is 'The Negro's Song', a translation of an untitled song from the seventh scene of Thomas Thaarup's operetta *Peters Bryllup* [Peter's Wedding] (1793), which was part of the growing campaign in Denmark during the 1790s to abolish the Danish slave trade – and which is accompanied in *Poems* by a brief account, from Feldborg, of 'Particulars Relative to the Abolition of the Slave Trade in Denmark'.[118] *Poems* also contains the earliest English-language translation of Jens Baggesen's 'Da jeg var lille', under the title 'Infancy'. This is the poem which, I argue, may have influenced the conception and vocabulary of Wordsworth's first, 1802 version of 'Ode. Intimations of Immortality from Recollections of Early Childhood', although the translation in *Poems* is evidently too late by some thirteen years to have been the source of that influence. The other poem in the volume which has a specific, British resonance, is 'Dedicatory Lines prefixed to a Danish Translation of Hamlet and Julius Caesar', by Peter Thun Foersom (1777–1817), which Feldborg glosses with 'Particulars concerning, and Extracts from, a Danish Translation of Hamlet and Julius Caesar, by Mr. Foersom' and with 'Notices relative to Mr. Foersom's efforts for the diffusion of English Literature in Denmark' (I return to these texts when I discuss the Danish reception of Shakespeare in the final section of this chapter).

Taken as a whole, then, *Poems from the Danish* introduces British readers to a much wider range of authors and topics from contemporary Danish literature and shifts the focus away from engagements with classical Scandinavian culture. It serves well its stated purpose of 'the introduction of Danish literature into this country', and it was well received. Even six years after *Poems from the Danish* had been published, the reviewer of Feldborg's *Denmark Delineated* in *Blackwood's* in September 1821 took the time to note that 'those of our readers who have had the good fortune to meet with a small volume of admirable translations from the Danish [. . .] will agree with us, we think, in forming a very high estimate of the poetical talent now existing in Denmark'.[119]

That 'poetical talent' was addressed again by Feldborg in *Denmark Delineated*, where he republished a good number of the texts from *Poems*. The review in *Blackwood's* discusses only 'Part the First' of *Denmark Delineated*, which had been published earlier in 1821; parts two and three followed in 1824. 'Part the First' deals with Danish painting and literature as well as with a range of landscapes and historical locations.[120] But the reviewer in *Blackwood's* focuses almost entirely on Feldborg's treatment of the arts, notably the celebrated sculptor Bertel Thorvaldsen ('the Phidias of Denmark', as the reviewer calls him), and on literature in particular.[121] 'In truth', the reviewer suggests, 'the task of introducing us to the literature of Denmark could not have fallen into better hands than those of Mr Feldberg.'[122] And this is a literature, the reviewer assures us, which is both worthy of and in need of introduction:

> With respect to the world at large, the literary offspring of Denmark may be said to have been hitherto confined in the womb in which it was originally engendered. A healthy bantling, indeed, full formed, and of robust

proportions [. . .] and waiting only for so accomplished an accoucheur as Mr Feldberg, to breathe a purer atmosphere, and to become the grace and ornament of a more extended region.[123]

Whether or not Feldborg would have appreciated the slightly patronising humour here, in *Denmark Delineated* he makes it quite clear that he intends not merely to introduce contemporary Danish literature to British readers, but also to correct exactly those negative perceptions about Danish arts and letters which we noted earlier in this chapter – and this forms part of his wider project, in *Denmark Delineated*, of correcting the 'injustice' with which Denmark has been treated, by 'the ignorance and prejudice of foreign travellers'.[124]

In the first sentence of his 'Introduction' (in effect, a thirty-five-page essay on Thorvaldsen), Feldborg paraphrases the outright condemnation offered by Sydney Smith (1771–1845) in his approving review of Jean-Pierre Catteau-Calleville's (1759–1819) three-volume *Tableau des états danois* (1802): 'It would be a loss of time to speak of the fine arts in Denmark: they hardly exist.'[125] This 'assertion' Feldborg immediately dismisses as 'hearsay'.[126] But later, in 'Part the Third', Feldborg returns again to this claim in his account of the time which he spent at Copenhagen with 'one of the remarkable men of the age', the famous explorer and archaeologist Giovanni Belzoni (1778–1823).[127] Feldborg says that, after the two men had visited to the Royal Academy of Arts together, 'I could not suffer the opportunity to slip of asking him':

> Now, Mr. Belzoni, if you should chance to hear some reviewer of great authority say, 'It would be loss of time to speak of the fine arts in Denmark; they hardly exist'. 'He should not repeat so flippant an assertion in my hearing', replied Belzoni, 'unless he could efface the recollection of what I have seen here to-day'.[128]

This is an example, then, of Feldborg's tendency, in 'Part the Third' of *Denmark Delineated*, to use Belzoni's undeniable cultural authority to shore up his own arguments about the merits of contemporary Danish culture. And although, in this specific instance, the arts in question are sculpture and painting, Feldborg also informs the reader that he introduced Belzoni to Oehlenschläger, whom he describes as 'the greatest of living Danish poets'.[129] Their 'interview was extremely animated', Feldborg records – he couldn't understand it, as the two men spoke French – and afterwards, Belzoni 'assured me that he had been impressed with a very high opinion of the poets and poetry of Denmark'.[130] And if they are good enough for Belzoni, Feldborg implies, then they deserve greater attention and admiration from British critics.

In 'Part the First' of *Denmark Delineated*, Feldborg introduces his readers to the work of Evald, Oehlenschläger and Ingemann, and notes, as we have seen, the good work done by Gillies in translating them for the 'Horae Danicae' series. He also incorporates into his topographical descriptions the translations of Evald's aforementioned song 'Kong Christian stoed ved hoien Mast', of Ingemann's 'To a Girl Beloved' and of Baggesen's 'Infancy', from *Poems from the Danish*.[131] The *Blackwood's* reviewer of *Denmark Delineated* remarks approvingly on these extracts and confirms Feldborg's positive evaluations of his countrymen, describing Evald, for example, as 'a poet of considerable powers', and comparing Baggesen favourably with Thomas Moore (1779–1852).[132] In fact, the only 'regret' which the *Blackwood's* reviewer expresses about Feldborg's handling of Danish literature in *Denmark Delineated* is that 'this subject occupies so small a portion of Mr. Feldberg's work': 'we [. . .] trust', the reviewer says, 'that in the future numbers of his work, this cause of complaint will be obviated.'[133] And this Feldborg did indeed do in the complete version of *Denmark Delineated* which he published in 1824, and which includes, as a seventy-four-page appendix, an 'Historical Sketch of Danish Literature, from 1588 to the Present Time'.

Feldborg's 'Historical Sketch' is, in a very real sense, a kind of cultural history of Denmark, in which the condition of the arts and the sciences is consistently linked to the more or less progressive tendencies of national polity. That is to say that Feldborg repeatedly stresses that arts and the sciences flourished in Denmark during periods of benevolent governance and languished under repressive rule, to the extent that he even finds himself in agreement, on occasions, with the assessments of one of his arch antagonists, Robert Molesworth (1656–1725), whose *Account of Denmark* (1694) continued to exert a substantial, negative influence over British perceptions of Denmark in the early nineteenth century.[134]

Feldborg begins his 'Sketch' with the reign of Christian IV (he of Evald's song), under whose 'enlightened and patriotic' influence, Feldborg says, 'the literary regeneration' of Denmark was 'accomplished' following 'a long interval of ignorance and barbarism'.[135] Reasons both of scope and of my focus in this book forbid a detailed discussion of the lengthy and detailed survey which follows, which encompasses such historical luminaries of Danish culture as the astronomer Tycho Brahe (1546–1601), the historians Ole Worm (1588–1654) and Eric Pontoppidan (1698–1764), the poets Anders Arrebo (1597–1637) and Peter Syv (1631–1702), and the dramatist Ludwig Holberg. I want to concentrate, rather, on the final part of Feldborg's 'Sketch', in which he traces the

'Rapid Advance of Science and Literature, from the Year 1746 to the Close of the Last Century'.[136]

In his account of this period, Feldborg emphasises, above all, how an increasingly progressive polity (albeit not without occasional setbacks) created the conditions for the arts and sciences to flourish and to reach that eminence at which they now stand. Hence, while Feldborg allows the justice of some of Molesworth's critiques of early modern Denmark, here he is at pains to point out that narratives of the continuing political and cultural decline of Denmark are simply mistaken, if not actively malicious. He singles out, as the most recent example of such a narrative, Smith's review of Catteau-Calleville's *Tableau des états danois*, which claims that the French work is 'too cautious for the interests of truth' by suggesting that, although 'Denmark is in theory one of the most arbitrary governments on the face of the earth', it 'in fact [. . .] enjoys a great reputation its forbearance and mildness; and sanctifies, in a certain degree, its execrable constitution, by the moderation with which it is administered'.[137] Such a perspective on Danish absolutism is, Smith insists, 'timid and sterile'.[138]

Writing back against this kind of negative stereotype, Feldborg, in the final part of his 'Historical Sketch', lists various political and cultural developments during the reigns of Frederik V, Christian VII (1749–1808) and Frederik VI, which drove a second renaissance in Danish letters. These include the making of 'Danish translations from the classics'; the increasing number of 'booksellers' who 'began to find their interest in catering for the public at large'; the 'abolishing of vassalage and the slave trade'; the 'LIBERTY OF THE PRESS' and the subsequent growth of periodical reviews such as Rahbek's *Minerva*; and the 'well authenticated fact' that 'the principles of the French Revolution did not make great impression on the people of Denmark'.[139] In support of this latter claim, Feldborg quotes approvingly Macdonald's praise, in his *Travels*, for the 'active and devoted patriotism' of the Danes 'between 1795 and 1805', and confirms that 'the Danish poetry of the period in question, likewise bears testimony to the cordiality subsisting between the government and the people'.[140]

Feldborg's remarks about the lack of revolutionism in Denmark recall, of course, the rhetoric he and many others, in both Denmark and Britain, deployed in the wake of the Battle of Copenhagen in 1801, which portrayed Britain and Denmark as Northern 'brothers' in fact fighting against a common enemy in France.[141] And in his 'Historical Sketch', Feldborg underlines, too, both the role of Anglo-Danish cultural relations in spurring the growth of Danish literature and the role of literature as a vehicle for promoting and cementing those same relations.

Noting, for example, that 'men of learning were sent to travel in foreign countries at the public expense', Feldborg takes as a representative literary figure the Icelandic-Danish antiquarian Grímur Jónsson Thorkelín (1752–1829) who went to Britain in 1786 and 'staid several years'.[142] The purpose of Thorkelín's visit was, of course, exactly to investigate the textual artefacts of Anglo-Danish relations in the Middle Ages, an investigation which would lead to the transcription, translation and eventual publication, under the sponsorship of the Danish government, of *Beowulf*.[143] Curiously, Feldborg also suggests that 'Messrs Oehlenschläger, Baggesen, and Rahbek travelled to Germany, Switzerland, Italy, England, and France, for objects exclusively connected with their favourite studies, the *Belles Lettres*' – the fact that none of the three did actually visit England (as far as anyone knows) is further testament to the strength of Feldborg's wish to identify literature as a key vehicle of Anglo-Danish cultural relations.[144]

And the role of literature in registering and promoting Anglo-Danish cultural relations is very much the note on which Feldborg closes his 'Historical Sketch'. He moves towards a close by recognising (perhaps with the *Blackwood's* review of the first part of *Denmark Delineated* in mind) that 'it would be desirable to furnish a comprehensive view of Danish literature from the beginning of this century to the present day'.[145] To do so adequately, however, Feldborg says, would require him to deal extensively with 'the varied difficulties with which the Danish Literati have had to contend'.[146] Foremost among these, of course, was 'the disastrous war [with Britain] which commenced in 1807 and terminated in 1814', 'the awful reverses of fortune which Denmark has experienced during that period', including the state bankruptcy of 1813 and 'the dismemberment of Norway'.[147]

Despite the central role played by Britain in these 'difficulties', however – or perhaps, indeed, because of it – Feldborg is nevertheless keen to emphasise the continuing importance of Anglo-Danish cultural relations. 'It is impossible for me to close this paper', he says in his 'Historical Sketch', 'without noticing the beneficial effects likely to arise to Danish literature, from an extended intercourse with Britain'.[148] And this 'intercourse', as Feldborg describes it, is very much a process of *exchange* rather than the 'one-way' paradigm which, as Lis Møller points out, has so often been suggested by modern critical responses to Anglo-Danish literary relations in the late eighteenth and early nineteenth centuries. Feldborg notes that 'since the re-establishment of peace in 1814', following the Treaty of Kiel, 'very considerable collections of Danish books have been introduced' to Britain.[149] 'The Bodleian library', Feldborg says, 'possesses a choice collection of Danish works', while the

Advocate's Library at Edinburgh, he says, 'has a collection of not less than 1200 volumes of Danish, Icelandic, and other northern books'.[150]

Primarily, of course, these are antiquarian works, dealing with the classical Scandinavian past: Feldborg mentions the efforts of Walter Scott, Robert Jamieson and the 'elegant poet' William Herbert, as examples of British writers who 'have so successfully excited an interest in this country for the literature of Denmark'.[151] But Feldborg also registers that contemporary Danish literature has 'been duly appreciated in Edinburgh' – a reference, presumably, to the 'Horae Danicae' – and although he does not mention it, his own efforts in *Poems from the Danish* and *Denmark Delineated* itself are, of course, part of that same project. 'At no former period of Danish history', Feldborg concludes, 'was there a more animated correspondence' than at present 'between the literati of the two countries'.[152] And indeed, as Jørgen Eric Nielsen points out, Feldborg himself constituted a sustained and substantial link, in private correspondence, between British and Danish authors, for instance sending Byron's *Childe Harold's Pilgrimage* to Christian Molbech on 27 September 1814, and acting as liaison between Scott and Oehlenschläger in early 1822.[153]

In the final paragraph of his 'Historical Sketch', Feldborg turns to the continued influence of British literature in Denmark, which, he says, 'has never excited a deeper interest than during the last twenty years'.[154] He notes with pleasure – striking that now familiar cord about Britain and Denmark as Northern 'brothers' with a common enemy in the French – that 'the Author of Waverley', for example, has 'extended the sphere of the British language, even to the strongholds before exclusively occupied by the "conventional language of courtiers and waiters", as French has been called'.[155] And Feldborg's 'Historical Sketch' concludes on exactly this same, Anglo-Danish theme, promoting cooperation rather than rivalry between the two countries in the arts, and quoting, in support of this idea, the 'generous effusion on behalf of the people of Denmark' offered by a 'celebrated British poet':

> May we struggle not who shall in fight be the foremost,
> But the boldest in sense, in humanity warmest!
> As our nations are kindred in language and kind,
> May the ties of our blood be the ties of our mind,
> And perdition on him who our peace would unbind.[156]

The 'celebrated British poet' might be Thomas Campbell who had, in 1801, published his *The Battle of the Baltic* in response to the events of April of that year, and the 'effusion' taken from a poem written by Campbell for Feldborg himself.[157] Whatever their origin, however, the sentiments which the lines express are certainly clear and consistent with Feldborg's own: an assertion of Anglo-Danish brotherhood, in both 'blood' and culture ('language'), which recalls exactly the rhetoric which (as I show in Chapter 1) developed in Britain and Denmark following the Battle of Copenhagen in 1801. And of all the contemporary writers whom Feldborg identifies as instrumental in the representation and promotion of that brotherhood through literature, the one to whom he points with the greatest emphasis, in both *Denmark Delineated* and *Poems from the Danish*, is the Danish poet and translator Peter Thun Foersom, whose 'translations from Shakespeare', Feldborg says, 'were highly favourable to a more general diffusion of the literature and language of Britain'.[158]

'Exalted fair, in every charm complete': Bringing Shakespeare to Denmark

As I have shown in Chapter 2, the late eighteenth and early nineteenth centuries saw the growth of a Shakespeare industry around Helsingør (Elsinore) to cater to the increasing numbers of British tourists coming to the area as a result of growing, Romantic-period interest in Shakespeare in Britain. In his account of one of the key sites of that industry in Part the First of *Denmark Delineated*, the so-called 'Hamlet's Garden', Feldborg takes the opportunity to introduce his late friend Peter Foersom.[159] But this was not in fact the first time that Feldborg had presented Foersom to British readers. As noted above, in *Poems from the Danish*, Feldborg and Walker provide a translation of Foersom's 'Dedicatory Lines prefixed to a Danish Translation of Hamlet and Julius Caesar', in which Foersom offers to Louise Auguste of Denmark (1771–1843), who was, as Feldborg notes, the daughter of Caroline Matilda (1751–75), these 'gems' from Shakespeare, 'exalted fair, in every charm complete'.[160]

As Kristian Smidt points out, the earliest extant, complete translation into Danish of a work by Shakespeare is the *Hamlet* published by Johannes Boye (1757–1830) in 1777, and this was followed, in 1790–2, by translations of *All's Well That Ends Well, Cymbeline, King Lear, Macbeth, Othello* and *The Merchant of Venice*, by the Norwegian Niels Rosenfeldt (1761–1804).[161] But these were all *prose* renditions. Foersom's great innovation was to produce complete translations of Shakespeare's plays into idiomatic Danish *verse*.[162] Hence, in his note on Foersom's 'Lines Dedicatory' in *Poems from the Danish*, Feldborg affirms that Foersom's 'masterly translation of Shakespeare [. . .] has made an epoch in the dramatic history of Denmark' and points out that Foersom himself had already played the role of Hamlet 'on the Danish stage'.¹⁶³ Feldborg then includes a translation of Foersom's own 'Preface' to the translation, dated Copenhagen 1806, as well as Foersom's texts of *Hamlet* 3.1 and 3.4, and of *Julius Caesar* 4.3.¹⁶⁴ Foersom, in his Preface, presents his translations as part of the second renaissance in Danish literature which Feldborg would later describe in his 'Historical Sketch': 'we all clearly perceive the rise of a bright morning', Foersom writes, 'which may dispel the gloom that has so long overshadowed the Danish Parnassus. The time therefore seems to be auspicious to my undertaking.'¹⁶⁵

Following his texts of *Hamlet* and *Julius Caesar*, Foersom went on before his death in 1817 to produce, in addition, complete translations of *Henry IV 2*, *Henry V*, *Henry VI 1* and *2*, *King Lear*, *Richard II* and *Romeo and Juliet* – evidently understanding, as Smidt puts it, 'his romantic generation's preface for the tragedies and the histories'.¹⁶⁶ But, as Smidt also observes, the timing of Foersom's translations is 'peculiarly interesting against the backdrop of political events in the first decade of the century', namely the British attacks on Copenhagen in 1801 and 1807 and the leading role taken by Britain in the drawing up of the Treaty of Kiel in 1814.¹⁶⁷ Shakespeare, paradoxically, could be enlisted behind a Danish Romantic nationalist banner, in opposition to England. As Alf Henriques first noted, Knud Lyne Rahbek, writing in his periodical *Ny Minerva* [New Minerva], shortly after the British bombardment of Copenhagen in 1807, proposed a version of *Macbeth* in which the three witches would be allegories of the British ministers George Canning (1770–1827), Spencer Perceval (1762–1812) and Arthur Wellesley, Duke of Wellington (1769–1852), while Foersom published in the Copenhagen daily *Dagen* [The Day], in 1808, a translation of Gaunt's claim in *Richard II* (2.1.65–6) 'That England that was wont to conquer others / Hath made a shameful conquest of itself'.¹⁶⁸

In *Poems from the Danish*, however, Feldborg brings in the work of his friend Foersom for an entirely opposite purpose: namely to identify the translation of Shakespeare as exemplary of the positive role played by English literature in the rejuvenation of Danish literature, in despite of the fractured military and political relationship between the two countries. And to emphasise the ongoing and widening connection, Feldborg points out that Foersom 'is likewise engaged in a translation of Thomson's Seasons, of which the Spring and the Hymn have already been published in a style equally creditable to the English and Danish language'.¹⁶⁹

Alongside Foersom's pioneering texts, Danish translations of Shakespeare gathered pace in the early decades of the nineteenth century. In his essay 'Shakespeare's Sonnets in Danish Translation', Holger Scheibel makes the puzzling claim that 'private attempts to recreate a single sonnet or two in Danish may have been made before, but nothing had been *published* until 1885'.[170] In point of fact, Knud Lyne Rahbek, to take just a single example, published Danish translations of seven of Shakespeare's sonnets (25, 29, 30, 32, 37, 73 and 74) in his *Asterkrandsen* [The Aster Wreath] in 1817, the year of Foersom's death, along with a translation of Desdemona's 'Willow Song' from *Othello* 4.3, and various lyrics by Byron, Scott and Johann Wolfgang von Goethe (1749–1832). But by the time that Feldborg published Part the First of *Denmark Delineated* in 1821, it was still Foersom's name which was synonymous with Shakespeare in Denmark – and hence it is no surprise that Feldborg should return to him in his account of 'Hamlet's Garden', outside Helsingør.

Feldborg introduces his fifteen-page biographical sketch of Foersom by noting that 'this interesting spot will soon, it is hoped, receive a most appropriate embellishment – a monument in honour of the man who has succeeded better than any other in transferring the "wood-notes wild" of "Fancy's child" into a foreign language'.[171] And throughout, as in *Poems from the Danish*, Feldborg tries to deploy Foersom's work as evidence of Anglo-Danish cultural exchange and connection, making no mention at all of the ways in which Shakespeare had been marshalled behind a Danish Romantic nationalist agenda. Feldborg begins by comparing Foersom's work to that of the sculptor Bertel Thorvaldsen, whose pieces – including busts of Byron and Scott – played a significant role in producing the material legacy of Romanticism in both Britain and Denmark.[172] 'Mr Foersom's translation of Shakespeare', Feldborg writes:

> is as much a work of genius as a statue of Thorvaldsen's, or a tragedy of Oehlenschläger's. Indeed he might be said to have been born to be the translator of Shakespeare. He did not simply give the words, but preserved the very spirit of Shakespeare.[173]

Feldborg's line of argument is quite clear, then. Unlike earlier renditions of Shakespeare in Danish prose, Foersom's idiomatic, verse translations successfully *translate* Shakespeare – not merely linguistically, but also in 'very spirit' – to Danish. And this is only possible, Feldborg affirms, because of Foersom's close understanding of the English language and of English literature.

Feldborg assures his reader that 'Foersom had from his infancy loved the English language, which he regarded as the most philosophical language in the world – the language of profound thought, fearless expression, and the vehicle of the noblest sentiments that ever gave dignity to human nature'.[174] Foersom 'loved' English, in other words, as a language which encapsulates national virtues shared by Britain and Denmark ('profound thought, fearless expression') and encompasses general human nature. In support of his claim, Feldborg then prints part of a letter written in English from Foersom to an unnamed 'friend' (almost certainly Feldborg himself) in which Foersom describes his introduction to English literature through 'Gray's matchless Elegy [and] Ossian'.[175] That Foersom's introduction to English literature should have been through authors and works with Scandinavian connections is, of course, not surprising, and in his letter, Foersom says that *Ossian* 'naturally proved less difficult' for him to understand.[176] But his first acquaintance with Shakespeare, he says in his letter, was what he describes as 'the perfidious edition' of *The Tempest* which was published by William Warburton (1698–1779) in 1747.[177]

In *Denmark Delineated*, then, Feldborg is eager to establish that the success of Foersom's translations of Shakespeare is founded upon his friend's wider embrace of English literature and culture. But Feldborg is not content merely with this point. Rather, as he had already done in *Poems from the Danish*, Feldborg is here, too, keen to marshal Foersom's translations as evidence of the salutary influence of English literature on Danish cultural life. He remarks on how the works of earlier Danish dramatists of note, including Holberg and Evald, have 'been nearly discarded from the stage in favour of French and German writers'.[178] Foersom, says Feldborg, 'determined to do his utmost to put an end to the dominion usurped by the dramatists of France and Germany', and to restore to Danish literature what he saw as its more natural connections with Britain: 'with this view', Feldborg tells us, 'he projected a translation of Shakespeare, beginning, as was natural to a Dane, with Hamlet.'[179] And just to be sure that the reader does not miss this note of cultural connection, Feldborg goes on to report that Foersom said, in conversation, 'that a Dane enjoyed peculiar facilities in translating from the English', presumably, the implication is, on account of the close linguistic and cultural ties between the two countries.[180]

Feldborg concludes his account of Foersom with discussion of his other translations from Shakespeare and their warm reception in Denmark, as well as with some discussion of his translations from Thomson and planned translations from Robert Burns (1759–96), which were never completed. In this latter instance, Feldborg once again emphasises Anglo-Danish cultural connections: when asked about reading Burns (whose poems Feldborg had sent to him from Scotland, at his request), Foersom supposedly replied that he needed no 'glossary' to understand the Scottish dialect because 'all the difficult words are derived from South Jutland, where I was born' – an assertion which might be read interestingly alongside De Quincey's aforementioned arguments about the Danish influence on the dialect of the English Lake District.[181] Feldborg also includes two poems by Foersom. The first is the text of 'Lines Dedicatory', which Feldborg reproduces from *Poems from the Danish*. But the second is of especial relevance to Feldborg's ideological agenda in his account of Foersom and, indeed, in *Denmark Delineated* more generally. These are 'lines' which Foersom supposedly 'wrote in English, in the album of a friend going to England'.[182] Once again, the 'friend' is almost certainly Feldborg himself. The lines are as follows:

> Go, son of Denmark, to that lofty shore
> Our bloody banners flouted once of yore;
> Go to the nation which I deem the best,
> (Though Dane, I must its ministers detest);
> That land where Shakespeare rose 'midst darkest night,
> And still pours forth his mighty streams of light;
> Where gallantly once Christian champions fought,
> And always home unspotted laurels brought;
> That land, refined by science, arts, and taste,
> The lofty ruler of the wat'ry waste,
> That, proud and free, ere she will be a slave,
> Sinks in the ocean, as her family grave.[183]

The poem, as given in *Denmark Delineated*, is dated by Foersom at Copenhagen on 4 May 1810. Feldborg says that he includes it 'as British readers may be pleased to have an opportunity of judging of his [Foersom's] familiar acquaintance with their language'.[184] But his real purpose in doing so was, evidently, to promote again the close cultural connections between Britain and Denmark and to advertise to 'British readers' the continuing respect for English culture in Denmark, despite the (unrepresentative) actions of its current government ('ministers') – and Foersom's choice of words, here, recalls both his and Rahbek's aforementioned marshalling of Shakespeare *against* England in the wake of the bombardment of Copenhagen in 1807.

Feldborg's point was well made, at least to the reviewer of Part the First of *Denmark Delineated* in *Blackwood's* in September 1821. 'Of the Danish poets', the reviewer affirms, 'we are inclined to rank none before Mr Foersom, the translator of Shakespeare.'[185] Following Feldborg's lead, the reviewer, who quotes at length from Feldborg's account of Foersom, emphasises the 'difficulties' which Foersom 'had to encounter in the progress of his work':

> Much of Shakespeare is untranslatable. Many, very many, of his beauties are so embodied in the language in which he wrote, so entwined with its idiom, so essentially English, as to be altogether unconvertible into another tongue. No one knew this better than Mr Foersom, and no one was more sensible of the difficulties of his undertaking.[186]

Despite the 'boldness' of Foersom's 'attempt', then, the reviewer argues that Foersom at times 'failed' to overcome these 'difficulties', but only 'where success was impossible' because of the 'essentially English' nature of Shakespeare's work, which, in the reviewer's opinion, encapsulates a kind of national 'idiom' that cannot be translated to any other language. But, for the most part, the reviewer is keen to point out that Foersom is 'eminently successful' and, taken as a 'whole', his 'work is *Shakespearian* to a degree not attained by any other translator'.[187] In explanation of this success, the reviewer gives Feldborg the stage, quoting from the passages in *Denmark Delineated* which describe how 'natural' it is for a Dane to translate *Hamlet* and how Foersom himself emphasised that 'a Dane enjoyed peculiar facilities in translating from the English'.[188]

*

The review of *Denmark Delineated* in *Blackwood's Edinburgh Magazine* for September 1821 concludes with the following affirmation:

> We have now discharged a public duty, in calling the attention of the literary world thus early a work destined to render the name of its author immortal. We once more call upon Mr Feldberg to proceed fearlessly in his high career, till he reaches the goal of glory and of fame, to which the completion of his labours must inevitably conduct him.[189]

That Feldborg's work has been, essentially, and unjustifiably, forgotten takes nothing from the fact that the *Blackwood's* reviewer – most probably a friend of Feldborg – both understood and appreciated what Feldborg was trying to achieve in *Denmark Delineated* and *Poems from the Danish*. This was to promote contemporary Danish culture – and Danish Romantic-period writing in particular – in Britain in order to reinforce the common cultural ties between the two countries during a time of prolonged strain and outright war. But Feldborg's project, ambitious and impressive as it was, is only one example of the ways in which Romantic-period literature served as a vehicle of mutual, cultural influence and exchange between Britain and Denmark during the late eighteenth and early nineteenth centuries. As I have shown in this chapter, such exchange was by no means restricted to British antiquarian interest in the textual artefacts of the classical Scandinavian past but extended also to exchanges and influences between living writers, and to a sense of Shakespeare as, at least in some respects, the embodiment not just of an English but also of a 'Northern' cultural identity which Britain and Denmark had in common.

Chapter 4

'The brothers of Englishmen': British Reflections on the Danish National Character

Not the least striking of the many striking passages in that most sensational of Gothic novels, *The Monk* (1796), by Matthew Lewis (1775–1818), is found in Chapter I of Volume III, where two nuns discuss the Danes, inhabitants of a country which, they are told, is 'terribly infested by Sorcerers, Witches, and Evil Spirits'.[1] One nun asks, '[A]re not the People all Blacks in Denmark?', to which the other replies, 'By no means, reverend Lady; They are of a delicate pea-green with flame-coloured hair and whiskers.'[2] 'Mother of God!' replies the first: 'Pea-green? [. . .] Oh! 'tis impossible!', at which point the Porteress, who has been listening, interjects with 'contempt': 'Impossible? [. . .] Not at all: When I was a young Woman, I remember seeing several of them myself.'[3]

In Lewis's novel, this humorous passage is merely one of many which serve to illustrate the credulity of the Spanish Catholic nuns, and presumably, by implication, of Catholics more generally. But the conversation between the nuns should also be seen in a wider context, because discussion of the national character of the Danes was a persistent and surprisingly extensive strand of British writing about Denmark during the late eighteenth and early nineteenth centuries – and Lewis, as we have seen in Chapter 3, was certainly familiar with at least some of that writing.[4] Nor, indeed, is Lewis's vision of exotic Danes altogether unique. The Scottish historian and traveller William Thomson (1746–1817), for example, in his *Letters from Scandinavia* – published in 1796, the same year as Mary Wollstonecraft's (1759–97) *Letters Written during a Short Residence in Sweden, Norway, and Denmark* – remarks that 'the Danes are rather bizarre in their appearance [. . .] They have many of them a sickly appearance and others look as if they painted [i.e. used makeup]', something stereotypically associated, at the time, with the French.[5] And, of course, this British discussion of the Danish national character itself took place within the still-wider context of the ongoing debate about national character in Scottish Enlightenment philosophy, which can be traced back at least as far as the essay 'Of National Characters' first published by David Hume (1711–76) in 1748, in which Hume uses the 'supposed' contrast between an Englishman and a Dane as one of his early, illustrative examples.[6]

As I write, at the beginning of the third decade of the twenty-first century, the particular nature of Danishness is still a recurrent theme of British writing about Denmark. The fascination in Britain with *hygge*, and, in particular, the attempt to understand what it is that explains the self-image of Denmark as 'the happiest country in the world', still permeate a diverse range of cultural texts.[7] It is an interest which would have been familiar to British writers during the late eighteenth and early nineteenth centuries. That phrase, 'the happiest country in the world', I quote not from current travel journalism or a Carlsberg commercial, but from Wollstonecraft's *Short Residence*, in which she recalls, provoked, 'the men of business' whom she met in Copenhagen who 'dogmatically assert that Denmark is the happiest country in the world'.[8] Nor was she alone in representing this view of Denmark: in the apocryphal sequel published to the *Candide, ou l'Optimisme* (1759) of Voltaire (1694–1778) in 1760, for example, Candide comes finally to settle in Copenhagen, concluding that while things were not so good there as in El Dorado, 'everything was not bad'.[9]

This chapter of *British Romanticism and Denmark* looks at descriptions of the Danes and Danishness in late eighteenth- and early nineteenth-century British writing about Denmark. In so doing, it charts the early history of a current fascination. But it also recovers the terms of a debate which was central to British thinking about Denmark at the time and examines the relationship between that debate and the larger, ongoing philosophical investigation into the origins, the nature and the implications of national character. British descriptions of the Danish national character during the late eighteenth and early nineteenth century usually share with British writing about Denmark more generally a tendency to find comparisons or to draw contrasts: between the Danish and the Germans, between the Danish and the French, between the Danish and other Scandinavians, and, not least, of course, between the Danish and the English. But, within this broadly comparative discourse, certain key and overlapping questions were recurrent. Foremost among them was the question of whether or not it was possible to discern a 'Northern' national character, elements of which Britain and Denmark had in common – an idea visible, for example, in Nelson's address to the Danes, in 1801, as 'the brothers of Englishmen' – or whether it only really made sense to talk about separate and distinct national characters.[10]

The attempt to answer that question in British writing about the Danish national character played, it goes without saying, an important role in the development of Romantic nationalism in Britain, as part of the wider process of defining what it meant to be British. And within the context of this speculation about a shared 'Northern' national character, with its roots in the classical Scandinavian past, an important corollary question arose concerning where that character was now most visible, in Britain or in Denmark. Late eighteenth- and early nineteenth-century British writing about Denmark was no less concerned to map the relationship between ancient and modern Danes than contemporary British writing about the Mediterranean world was concerned to map the relationship between ancient and modern Greeks, and between the Romans and the Italians. And, in both genres, British writers very often, though by no means always, positioned contemporary Britons as the inheritors of glorious national characters and cultural traditions no longer visible on the soils from which they had first sprung.

A further, significant and closely related concern of British writing about the Danish national character was the attempt to determine to what causes that national character could be attributed: to the relatively constant physical environment or to the continually shifting socio-political environment? The attempt to answer this question meant that British writing about Danishness not only played an important role in the development of Romantic nationalism in Britain, but also paralleled, as I have said earlier, the ongoing debate in eighteenth- and early nineteenth-century philosophy about the nature and the origins of national character.

'Some particular qualities': National Character and Romantic Nationalism

In his essay 'Notions on National Character in the Eighteenth Century', John Hayman documents not only the extent to which speculation about national character was a key element of eighteenth-century travel writing, but also how philosophical discussions of national character and race often turned to travel writing for ostensibly empirical data in support of theoretical arguments.[11] Discussion of how national character was formed and about how (or if) the notion of distinct national characters could 'be reconciled with the premise of a universal human nature' gave the topic, as Hayman puts it, a 'central importance' in eighteenth-century philosophy.[12]

In their introduction to *Character, Self, and Sociability in the Scottish Enlightenment,* Thomas Ahnert and Susan Manning draw attention to the 'distinctive contribution' made by Scottish philosophers to this wider eighteenth-century debate about 'national character', especially once Scottish philosophy embraced the stadial model of societal development set out by Adam Ferguson (1723–1816) in his influential *Essay on the History of Civil Society* (1767), according to which 'all societies progressed through a uniform sequence of development'.[13] As Silvia Sebastiani puts it in her discussion of 'National Characters and Race' in the same volume, the debate about national character became 'central to the philosophical histories produced by the Scottish Enlightenment, where characters – and national characters in particular – appeared as a product and mirror of different stages of civilization and manners'.[14] As Sebastiani also makes clear, however, the inquiry into national character by Scottish Enlightenment philosophers did not begin with Ferguson's *Essay* but rather with earlier responses to the ideas put forward by Montesquieu (1689–1755) in his *De l'esprit des loix* (1748), where he argues that natural environment and climate play a decisive role in shaping the dominant characteristics of individual cultures and peoples.[15] Montesquieu's work was quickly translated into English by the Irish historian and travel writer Thomas Nugent (1700–72), author of the four-volume *Grand Tour* (1749), and published in 1750 as *The Spirit of the Laws*. Only one month after the publication of *De l'esprit*, however, David Hume responded to these ideas with his essay 'Of National Characters', which he would refine in subsequent iterations as he made clearer his opposition to Montesquieu's ideas about the influence of environment and climate and those similar ideas subsequently advanced by Georges-Louis Leclerc, Comte de Buffon (1707–88) in his *Histoire naturelle* (1749–1804).[16]

Hume opens by attacking the 'vulgar' tendency to view national character in terms of 'extremes' which admit of no variety, that is, the tendency to see all individuals in a given nation as possessing essentially the same dominant character traits.[17] However, he does grant that 'each nation has a peculiar set of manners, and that some particular qualities are more frequently to be met with among one people than among their neighbours'.[18] Hence, Hume suggests, among a list of examples drawn from European countries, that 'An ENGLISHMAN will be naturally supposed to have more knowledge than a DANE; though TYCHO BRAHE was a native of DENMARK.'[19] The presence of these 'supposed' differences has variously been accounted for, Hume says, by what he calls 'moral causes' and 'physical causes'.[20] The latter, Hume defines as 'those qualities of the air and climate' which, he says, influence the 'temper', 'tone and habit of the body', in other words, those environmental factors which Montesquieu had argued determine national character.[21] For Hume, however, such 'physical causes' have at best a secondary influence and he admits that he is 'inclined to doubt altogether their operation in this particular'.[22] 'That the character of a nation will much depend on *moral* causes', Hume argues, 'must be evident to the most superficial observer.'[23] And 'moral causes', in Hume's analysis, are socio-political and cultural: 'of this kind', he argues, 'are the nature of the government, the revolutions of public affairs, the plenty or penury in which the people live, the situation of the nation with regard to its neighbours, and such like circumstances'.[24]

As Hume began to refine his ideas about national character in response to the work of Buffon, in particular, subsequent iterations of his essay accept that environmental conditions could influence the extent to which universal human traits are emphasised or de-emphasised in particular nations, an idea also taken up by Henry Home, Lord Kames (1696–1782) in his *Sketches of the History of Man* (1774). Again, however, as Silvia Sebastiani points out, this concession granted, the Scottish tradition following Hume tended to prioritise historical and social ('moral') rather than environmental ('physical') explanations for national character, as exemplified in the 'wholly historicized' explanations given by Adam Smith (1723–90) in his *Theory of Moral Sentiments* (1759) and *Lectures on Jurisprudence* (1763), with the quintessential statement of this position being Ferguson's aforementioned *Essay on the History of Civil Society*, and its stadial model of progressive societal development.[25]

Such debates about the origins, causes and destinies of national characters clearly had bearing upon Britain's emergent status as a global power, and were deeply implicated in narratives of supposed racial superiority. In his essay 'On National Character', for example, Hume (notoriously) argues that:

> there is some reason to think, that all the nations which live beyond the polar circles or between the tropics, are inferior to the rest of the species, and are incapable of all the higher attainments of the human mind. The poverty and misery of the northern inhabitants of the globe, and the indolence of the southern, from their few necessities, may, perhaps, account for this remarkable difference.[26]

Although Hume does conclude that this speculation requires 'our having recourse to *physical* causes' as a means to account for national character, he is nevertheless one among many eighteenth-century thinkers who point to a supposed link between specific global regions and specific racial, rather than *national*, characteristics.[27]

These same debates about *national* character also had, however, a more local, European application. More specifically, speculation about national character played, of course, a key role in the rise of Romantic nationalisms in various European countries, including Britain and Denmark. Building on Benedict Anderson's argument that the modern concepts of 'nation' and 'nationality' were first formulated as 'cultural artefacts' in late eighteenth-century Europe, the cultural historian Joep Leerssen has argued that Romantic nationalism can best be described as 'the celebration of the nation (defined in its language, history, and cultural character) as an inspiring ideal for artistic expression; and the instrumentalization of that expression in political consciousness-raising'.[28] Central to the emergence of this phenomenon, Leerssen argues in *National Thought in Europe*, was the shift from an Enlightenment view of 'the nation as the locus of sovereign power' towards a tendency to see 'nations as natural human categories, each defined in its individual identity by a transcendent essence, each self-perpetuating that identity through history, each deserving its own self-determination'.[29] The 'backbone' of this Romantic nationalist 'ideology', Leerssen suggests, is 'a belief in ethnotypes: essential individual dispositions giving each nation a separate character, identity, or "soul" and setting it apart from others'.[30] Consequently, Romantic nationalists and Romantic nationalist cultural texts routinely turn to the vernacular and the historical as a means of identifying, or of constructing, what Georg Wilhelm Friedrich Hegel (1770–1831) and Friedrich Carl von Savigny (1779–1861) would call the *Volksgeist*, or national character: 'the national essence', as Leerssen puts it, 'can be understood or intuited from its expressions in the collective history, the subsisting vernacular culture (always seen as a remnant from the primordial past), or its language.'[31]

In Denmark, we can see an example of this quest for the *Volksgeist* in the work of the statesman and historian Ove Malling (1747–1829), who was commissioned to write, for use in schools, a patriotic history of Danish national heroes and virtues. Published in 1777, the intention behind Malling's *Store og Gode Handlinger af Danske, Norske og Holstenere* [Great and Good Deeds of Danes, Norwegians and Holsteinians] was exactly to promote Danish cultural values and to counteract the perceived growth in German cultural influence which had developed during the de facto rule of Johann Friedrich Struensee (1737–72) in 1770–2 (see Chapter 5). The Danish traveller and writer Andreas Andersen Feldborg (1782–1838) published a translation of Malling's work in 1807 as part of his ongoing attempts to promote Anglo-Danish relations, but it received a somewhat indifferent response, with the *Anti-Jacobin*, for example, lamenting – rather unfairly – that no 'modern' Danes were discussed and suggesting that 'the translator' would 'find a greater consolation in his motives than in the extent of the good effects which his translation will produce'.[32]

This said, the *Anti-Jacobin* did praise Malling's apostrophe to patriotism and the promotion of public welfare, noting that 'such sentiments', though they 'have long been familiar to Englishmen', could not be 'too frequently urged' in the current political climate 'when we have seen the people of the continent of Europe tamely yield their necks to the yoke of a vulgar usurper, merely for want to the virtue of patriotism'.[33]

As I have argued in Chapters 2 and 3, the rise of Romantic nationalism in the late eighteenth and early nineteenth centuries was also connected with new antiquarian interest, in Denmark, in the physical and textual remains of the classical Scandinavian past: archaeological sites, vernacular ballads and 'popular' cultural forms. In Britain, too, as has been well documented by critics and historians, the development of Romantic nationalism went hand in hand with an emergent, antiquarian interest in vernacular, regional culture, understood as an index of national character, in a marked shift away from the internationalism of the earlier eighteenth century. Hence, in *Mapping Mythologies*, Marilyn Butler, for example, points to the role played by the study of 'popular and local antiquities' in the development not only of regional but also national 'pride and patriotism'.[34] 'Implicitly', Butler writes:

> this scholarly activity contained the notion of culture as in essence, especially in its pure early phases, 'autochthonous', generated on the spot among the native population, rather than imported or diffused from the classical southern European, Catholic regions of ancient Rome, Italy and France.[35]

Katie Trumpener, in a similar vein, argues that the 'new forms of cultural nationalism' which developed in Britain during the late eighteenth and early nineteenth centuries were predicated upon the 'historicizing turn' of 'antiquarian practice'.[36] These new Romantic nationalisms, Trumpener writes, 'stress the survival of cultural memory from one epoch to the next' and share the 'elementary' conviction of antiquarianism at the time that 'the past [. . .] can be reconstructed through the analysis of the artifactual traces it has left behind'.[37] And this shared conviction is, in Trumpener's analysis, one of the key factors distinguishing Romantic nationalisms from the stadial theories of Enlightenment historiography, which emphasise, rather, 'the necessary discontinuities of culture'.[38]

Of course, the surge of interest in the physical and textual artefacts of the past, in both Britain and Denmark, during the late eighteenth and early nineteenth centuries, was also closely related to what Jonathan Sachs has described as 'the Romantic cult of ruins and the aesthetic fascination such material decay held for so many Romantic writers'.[39] This 'cult', characterised by Laurence Goldstein as 'an undeniable mania for physical representations of decay', had a complex relationship with emergent Romantic nationalisms and the ongoing philosophical considerations of national character.[40] In *England's Ruins*, for example, Anne Janowitz documents the connections between this so-called 'ruin sentiment' and nascent British nationalism. 'The paradox of the eighteenth-century ruin', Janowitz argues, 'was that the figure of decay was at the same time the image used to authorize England's autonomy as a world power.'[41] This was possible, Janowitz explains, because ruin 'provides an historical provenance for the conception of the British nation as immemorially ancient' and, 'through its naturalization' in the landscape, effectively 'subsumes cultural and class difference into a conflated representation' of a shared national past.[42]

But, of course, as Janowitz and others have also observed, interest in the ruins of past civilisations and cultures also fed into the 'anxieties about *decline* – national and imperial, economic and political, cultural and literary – which are', as Sachs puts it, 'a pervasive feature of British public discourse in the later eighteenth and early nineteenth century'.[43] Enquiry into the nature, causes and consequences of 'decline', as Sachs shows, 'spanned a variety of discourses and concerns around the turn of the nineteenth century'.[44] But certain concerns are common to these already interconnected areas of enquiry, notably including speculation about whether the fall of earlier, sophisticated civilisations implied that a similar fate awaited the nascent British Empire; about what had caused the fall of previous civilisations; and about whether such decline was inevitable or could be prevented.

The seminal exploration of these questions in the eighteenth century was, of course, the six-volume *History of the Decline and Fall of the Roman Empire* (1776–88) by the English historian Edward Gibbon (1737–94), which identified the gradual transformation of the Roman national character as foremost among the causes for the collapse of the empire. 'The story of its ruin is simple and obvious', Gibbon writes in his 'General Observations on the Fall of the Roman Empire in the West':

> and, instead of inquiring *why* the Roman empire was destroyed, we should rather be surprised that it had subsisted so long. The victorious legions, who, in distant wars, acquired the vices of strangers and mercenaries, first oppressed the freedom of the republic, and afterwards violated the majesty of the purple. The emperors, anxious for their personal safety and the public peace, were reduced to the base expedient of corrupting the discipline which rendered them alike formidable to their sovereign and to the enemy; the vigour of the military government was relaxed, and finally dissolved, by the

partial institutions of Constantine; and the Roman world was overwhelmed by a deluge of Barbarians.⁴⁵

In short, the gradual undermining of civic virtue by 'vices' and self-interest was what enabled the military defeat of the Roman Empire and the subsequent collapse of Roman civilisation.

As Sachs points out, Gibbon does not extrapolate from the collapse of the Roman Empire a similar and similarly inevitable fate for the British Empire. Conversely, he seeks to relocate the fall of Rome within a longer-term 'pattern of progress' in European civilisation, a strategy also deployed on a more local level by Gibbon's contemporary Adam Smith, who deals similarly with anxieties about a shrinking national economy in his *Inquiry into the Nature and Causes of the Wealth of Nations* (1776).⁴⁶ But the link between decadence and national decline formulated by Gibbon remained a powerful trope of late eighteenth- and early nineteenth-century 'ruin sentiment' and is often visible in British writing about Denmark. Exemplary, in this respect, are Mary Wollstonecraft's remarks about the 'deserted' Rosenborg Castle, in Copenhagen, which (as we saw in Chapter 1) she visited shortly after the city had been ravaged by fire in July 1795.⁴⁷ 'Diffused with a gloomy kind of grandeur throughout', Wollstonecraft recalls, 'every object carried me back to past times, and impressed the manners of the age forcibly on my mind.'⁴⁸ 'Could they be no more', Wollstonecraft asks of 'the shadowy phantoms' of 'departed greatness' to whom her 'imagination [. . .] gave life' in the 'vast tomb' of the castle: 'these beings, composed of such noble materials of thinking and feeling, have they only melted into the elements to keep in motion the grand mass of life?'⁴⁹

What Wollstonecraft's almost Wordsworthian comparison between the 'departed greatness' of Danes-past and 'the grand mass' of Danes-present makes clear, then, is that the discussion of the Danish national character in British writing about Denmark during the late eighteenth and early nineteenth centuries needs to be seen against the backdrop of the complex discursive network I have been charting here, in which speculation about national character in a European context is intimately bound up with attention to the past and its perceived legacy in the present. As Jonathan Sachs points out in *The Poetics of Decline in British Romanticism*, attempts to identify and to quantify 'national decline' in late eighteenth- and early nineteenth-century British writing routinely had resort to a comparative methodology:

> Sometimes, in debates about national decline [. . .] this comparison is between two extant nations, often where one is understood as rising and the other as declining; at other times, the comparison can be between a

contemporary power and a past example of decline. Such comparisons can also be internal, as when aspects of a nation's present are judged negatively against its past.[50]

This is no less true in the case of British writing about the Danish national character. Discussions and comparisons of Danishness and Englishness were integral not only to the development of Romantic nationalisms in both countries, but also to questions of whether or not it was meaningful to talk about a common, 'Northern' culture inherited from the past, which Denmark and England, or Danes and Britons, could still be seen (or at least be said) to share.

'Of English mould as well as English blood': Comparing the English and the Danes

As we saw in Chapter 1, Robert Southey (1774–1843), in his account of the Battle of Copenhagen in his *Life of Nelson* (1813), dwells at some length on the arrangement of the ceasefire and the note sent by Nelson to the Danish crown prince, Frederik VI (1768–1839), which he addressed 'To the Brothers of Englishmen; the Danes'.[51] Southey misquotes or paraphrases the note (he could have used a number of sources) by incorporating a version of the salutation as the final lines: 'The brave Danes are the brothers, and should never be the enemies, of the English.'[52] And he emphasises the key point again in his commentary on the events. 'The Danes were an honourable foe', Southey concludes: 'they were of English mould as well as English blood; and now that the battle had ceased, [Nelson] regarded them rather as brethren than as enemies.'[53]

Southey, expanding on Nelson's original sentiment, makes in fact two claims here: that the Danes are the racial 'brethren' of the English ('of English blood') and that the Danes are also the cultural 'brethren' of the English ('of English mould'). The first claim, for racial brotherhood, was not infrequently made in British travel writing about Denmark and Danish travel writing about Britain, as we have seen in Chapter 2. Edward Daniel Clarke (1769–1822), for example, in his account of Denmark, pointed to the physiological similarities between the Danes and the English, while Andreas Andersen Feldborg, in his account of his travels in Britain, noted comparable similarities among the population of northern England. The historical underpinnings for such claims is, of course, as Feldborg makes clear, the Danish occupation of the north and east of England during the ninth century and the establishment of the so-called 'Danelaw'.[54]

Neither of these claims would have seemed particularly controversial to Southey's readers in 1813, although we do remember (as we saw in Chapter 1) that some few commentators on the British bombardment of Copenhagen in 1807 represented that attack as a reversal of the Viking conquest of England. But neither claim had an especially long history, either. In fact, we can see both emerge from British writing about the Danish national character during the late eighteenth and early nineteenth centuries, and again, as so often in British writing about Denmark, what we see is a progressive move away from perceptions of difference and towards perceptions of similarity. In short, the Danish become more English and the English more Danish in direct parallel with the emergence in Britain of 'Romantic' attitudes to 'the North'. And, once again, the writings about Denmark by Robert Molesworth (1656–1725) and Nathaniel Wraxall (1751–1831) effectively bookend the beginnings of this process, drawing, as we have already seen in Chapters 2 and 3, sustained and unflattering contrasts between England and Denmark across a range of different points of comparison, including descriptions of national character.

Molesworth's remarks on 'The Conditions, Customs, and Temper of the People' in his *Account of Denmark* (1694) is no less informed than the rest of that book by his desire to critique the absolutist rule which had been established in Denmark under Frederik III (1609–70) in 1660 and carried on by his successor, Christian V (1646–99), and to contrast it with English liberties.[55] Molesworth does not pull his proverbial punches in his assessment of the peasants of Zealand, claiming flatly that 'they are all as absolute slaves as the negroes are in Barbadoes, but with this difference, that their fare is not so good'.[56] Writing some fifty years before the Montesquieu–Hume debate about the origins of national character, Molesworth points to the influence of environmental factors on the people, noting, for example, that 'in all Denmark' there 'are but two seasons of the year, winter and summer', the 'indifferent' air, the 'gloomy heat', and, as we have seen, 'the plague of flies'.[57] But Molesworth's primary explanation for the Danish national character would put him firmly on the side of what Hume would later call 'moral causes'. 'All these', Molesworth says of 'the condition, customs, and temper' of the Danes, 'do so necessarily depend upon, and are influenced by, the nature and change of government, that it is easily imagined, the present condition of these people of all ranks must be most deplorable.'[58] 'Slavery', he continues:

> like a sickly constitution, grows in time so habitual, that it seems no burden nor disease; it creates a kind of laziness, and idle despondency, which puts men beyond hopes and fears: It mortifies ambition, emulation, and other

troublesome as well as active qualities, which liberty and freedom beget; and instead of them affords only a dull kind of pleasure of being careless and insensible.[59]

Hence, while Wollstonecraft would suggest almost a century later, in the *Short Residence*, that 'to be born here [at Risør, on the Norwegian coast] was to be bastilled by nature – shut out from all that opens the understanding, or enlarges the heart', for Molesworth, the prison that forms the Danish national character is unequivocally one of social and political institutions.[60]

Everywhere, Molesworth points to what he sees as evidence of decline from 'antient riches and valour' consequent upon 'the late alteration in the government'.[61] 'Expensiveness in coaches, retinue, clothes, etc.', he says, anticipating the kind of arguments which Gibbon would later make about the relationship between decadence and decline in his *History* of the Roman Empire, 'is nowhere more common, nor more extravagant in proportion to their income, than in this country.'[62] Even the poor people, Molesworth suggests, 'have a degree of vanity; pride and poverty often being companions', and hence 'many of the ancient families' and 'trading towns and villages [. . .] are all fallen to decay'.[63] Danes of all rank and both sexes 'are much addicted to drinking', he claims – and, somewhat more curiously, 'extremely addicted to gardening'.[64] 'The common people' are supposedly 'mean-spirited, not warlike in their tempers, as formerly; inclined to gross cheating, and to suspect that others have a design to cheat on them.'[65] 'The seasons of jollity', apparently, 'are very rare', and it seems that 'not so much as a song, or a tune, was made, during three years that I stayed there' (perhaps unsurprisingly, one might think, given his attitude).[66] Even the Danish language earns Molesworth's opprobrium. It is, he says, 'very ungrateful, and not unlike the Irish in its whining tone', although he does acknowledge that:

> Very many of the monosyllables in this tongue are the same with the English; and without doubt we owe the original of them to the Danes, and have retained them ever since they were masters of our country.[67]

The malicious effects of absolutism extend, in Molesworth's *Account*, even so far as to influence the population. In the past 'extremely populous', as evidenced 'by the vast swarms that in former ages, from these northern parts, over-ran all Europe', Denmark is 'at present', he says, 'but competently peopled; vexation of spirit, ill diet, and poverty, being great obstructions to procreation'.[68] Little help, then, that 'the women' are 'exceedingly fruitful' and their 'winter-dress [. . .] very becoming', as Molesworth remarks in a rare moment of praise.[69]

Molesworth's – at times almost comically – negative portrait of the Danes and Danishness in his *Account* was immediately called into question by the author of *Denmark Vindicated* (1694) who affirms that Denmark is 'very well known to me' and that Molesworth's remarks on the Danes are 'utterly contrary to the Experience of all understanding People'.[70] *Denmark Vindicated* offers an extended, point-by-point rebuttal of many of Molesworth's claims, especially those concerning hospitality, diet and lifestyle, and includes also a very effective countering of Molesworth's afore-mentioned argument about the abrupt change from summer to winter in Denmark by pointing out that the latitudes of Denmark and Copenhagen are broadly equivalent to those of northern England and Edinburgh, where no such extremes are visible.[71] But the damage had been done, and Andreas Andersen Feldborg was (as we have seen in Chapter 2) correct to identify Molesworth's *Account* as still, in the early nineteenth century, a significant interlocutor to be overcome in the promotion of Anglo-Danish relations. We can see why if we look at John Carr's (1772–1832) brief, patronising summation of the Danish 'national character' in Chapter 3 of his *Northern Summer* (1805):

> It is scarcely necessary for me to observe that the government of Denmark is despotic. The Dane is a good natured, laborious character; he is fond of spirits, but is rarely intoxicated; the severity of the climate naturalizes the attachment, and his deportment in the indulgence of it, is inoffensive.[72]

And this after Carr had already noted that 'the alertness and activity of the British tar [whom he met at the harbour in Husum], afforded a striking contrast to the sluggishness of the Danish seamen who surrounded him'.[73]

Hence, certain key climatological and socio-political elements of Molesworth's seminal characterisation of the Danish national character, and its contrast with the English, remained points of controversy in British writing about the topic a century later. These included, of course, ongoing questions about the relative influence of the climate and the political system. But two, interconnected focal points stand out: the idea that the Danish national character has declined from 'antient' glories and the claim that the modern Danish character is defined, primarily, by what Molesworth calls 'a kind of laziness, and idle despondency'.[74] The extent to which British writers subscribe to this latter point in particular – that is, to the idea that the Danish national character was marked above all by *indolence*, as the preferred term became – is a revealing index of the gradual shift away from an early tendency to represent Denmark as an exotic, 'Oriental' other, and towards constructions of a common, 'Northern' cultural identity encompassing Britain and Denmark.

'They are now slaves': The Decline and Fall of the Danes

We have already noted the assessment offered by Jonathan Sachs of the extent to which attempts to identity and to quantify national decline by eighteenth-century British writers deployed comparative methodologies, comparing not only nation with nation but also the past and present state of individual nations. This kind of comparative strategy is routinely visible in British writing about the Danish national character, which often contrasts the supposed glories of the past with the perceived debasement of the present.

One of our English trailblazers in Denmark, Nathaniel Wraxall, is surprisingly unrepresentative in this respect, to the extent that he suggests, entirely characteristically, that Denmark never really had a great past from which to decline. The almost wholly negative appraisal of Denmark offered by Wraxall in his *Tour through Some of the Northern Parts of Europe* (1775) – a work informed as much by Molesworth's ideas as by Wraxall's own response to fate of Caroline Matilda (1751–75) – extends to his account of the Danes themselves. 'Every nation has produced her heroes and patriots, on whom history delights to dwell', says Wraxall: 'some countries are, however, more fruitful in great and sublime spirits. In Denmark, they have had very few to grace their annals.'[75] The 'few' whom Wraxall notes are in fact only two: the kings Christian IV (1577–1648) and Frederik IV, the latter of whom abolished serfdom in 1702.

Other travellers, however, were much more eager to draw attention to the past achievements of the Danes and to estimate to what extent a continuity of national character could or could not be seen in the present day. Sometimes this involved pointing – against the backdrop of Scottish Enlightenment historiography – towards the apparently arrested development of Danish society at an earlier stage than that currently enjoyed by England. Hence Edward Daniel Clarke, whose enthusiasm for the genetic and archaeological remains of Danish antiquity I discussed in Chapter 2, says in his *Travels* – with a clear nod towards Adam Fergusson's stadial model of societal development – that, in 1799, 'to our eyes, it seemed, indeed, that a journey from *London* to *Copenhagen* might exhibit the retrocession of a century; every thing being found, in the latter city, as it existed in the former a hundred years before.'[76] 'This observation' extends not only to the amusements, the dress, and the manners of the people', Clarke continues, 'but to the general state of every thing connected with *Danish* society; excepting, perhaps, the commerce of the country, which is on a good footing.'[77] 'There is', Clarke concludes, 'a littleness in every thing that belongs to them.'[78]

More frequently, however, comparisons between the national character of the modern and the historical Danes amounted to tracing a supposed narrative of decline inversely proportional to the rise of the English. To a certain extent, the first part of this narrative is visible in Danish history, too. In his *Journey through Sweden* (1790), for example, Jean Frédéric Henry de Drevon (1734–97) says that 'with respect to the military character of the Danes, one of their own historians writes thus':

> 'The Danes, though no longer that sanguinary and ferocious people, who thought it a disgrace to die in their beds, are still a brave nation, and have signalised their courage in some unhappy wars, in which their want of success by land has been recompensed by their victories at sea.'[79]

However, the tendency to contrast modern and ancient Danes, and modern Britons, is, of course, much more visible in British writing about the Danish national character, and its frequency is closely bound to the rise, in Britain, of 'Romantic' imaginings of 'the North' and the classical Scandinavian past, imaginings to which modern Scandinavians, more often than not, struggled to live up in the opinion of British travellers.[80] Hence, when Mary Wollstonecraft went to Scandinavia in 1795, for example, she admits that her expectations 'carried me back to the fables of the golden age: independence and virtue; affluence without vice; cultivation of mind, without depravity of heart; with "ever smiling liberty", the nymph of the mountain' – and all to be found amid landscapes 'most romantic, abounding in forests and lakes, and the air pure'.[81] And twenty-five years later, in his poem *Hedin* (1820), 'a tale from the Danish history', the poet and botanist William Herbert (1778–1847) offered a similar, imaginative collocation of the sublimities of nature and society in 'the North':

> Thy steeps yclad with fir-trees evergreen,
> Thy torrents roaring the huge rocks between,
> Thy broken glens and crags sublimely piled,
> O Norway, beauteous Nature's rudest child,
> Who can survey, and lash'd by the stormy wind
> Mark thy bleak coast, and climate nothing mild,
> Nor deem such scenes by Freedom's power design'd
> To steel her sons with strength, and brace the generous mind![82]

Hedin's speaker, however, immediately contrasts the historical achievements of Norway's ancient 'sons of the rock', who formerly 'roam'd, like seamews, o'er the waves', with the present state of the country, ceded from Denmark to the 'foreign yoke' of 'Sweden's hateful banners', by the Treaty of Kiel in 1814.[83] And Wollstonecraft, for her part, tells the reader of the *Short Residence* that she was soon reminded 'that the world is still the world, and man the same compound of weakness and folly, who must occasionally excite love and disgust, admiration and contempt'.[84]

Of course, both Wollstonecraft and Herbert are talking, in the extracts which I have just considered, about the Norwegians, inhabitants of the High North. But British writers about the Danish national character routinely made similar comparisons, and a similar dynamic of expectation and reality is often visible. As late as 1826, for example, William Rae Wilson (1772–1849), who left Denmark with 'the best opinion' of the Danes – whom he found 'tall and well-made, with strong limbs and fair complexion' and generally to 'resemble the English' – remarked upon the 'striking [. . .] contrast' between 'the character of the modern Danes, and that of their ancestors, who were bold and adventurous; infested the coasts of Europe, settled in Ireland, and became masters of England and part of Scotland'.[85] The anonymous 'officer' who authored *Narrative of the Expedition to the Baltic* (1808), for his part, took as evidence of the 'degeneracy' of modern Danes, their increasing adherence to 'French principles' in national and international politics: a supposed decline, in other words, from Northern to Southern values.[86]

In point of fact, however, this tendency to compare ancient and modern Danes can be traced back at least as far as 1784 and the anonymous travel account *Observations on the Present State of Denmark, Russia, and Switzerland*. The author of *Observations* includes a series of (quite possibly fictitious) letters, ostensibly written by 'a young student, of the university at Copenhagen, to his Friend at St. Thomas', which he praises as the 'effusions of a noble mind, and a feeling heart', imbued with 'such a spirit of liberty' in marked opposition to the prevailing absolutist climate.[87] The supposed student correspondent claims that 'the national character of the Danes may be said to exist no more, and though it may still preserve an allowed value in the political scale of Europe, yet, like a worn-out coin, it is sunk in weight, and has lost both its image and superscription'.[88] This perceived decline encompasses the entirety of society:

> the lower classes of people are ignorant and ill-shaped, and their bodies, in general, as inactive as their minds. The middling rank, or petit bourgeois, present a ludicrous picture of dirt and pride [. . .] The court presents a most gloomy picture of fallen majesty, and disgraced dignity.[89]

And the contrast between this 'fallen' condition of the modern Danes and their forebears is made explicit when the letter writer turns to the 'many specimens of Runic poetry' which, he says, are 'records of our ancient genius and valour'.[90] But now, the letter writer concludes, 'I fear the poet and the hero alike, are for ever dead to the remembrance of our future annals [. . .] We are fit subjects for elegy.'[91]

The author of the *Observations* (and perhaps of the enclosed letters) shares with Molesworth and Wraxall a tendency to view and to represent Denmark negatively as part of a critique of absolutism contrasted with English liberties. But even an author rather more well-disposed towards Denmark, such as William Thomson (1746–1817), whose *Travels* was published in 1792, has recourse to the comparison. Thomson opens his account of the Danish national character by calling into question the claim by 'My Lord Molesworth, and some other writers who have treated of the Danes [. . .] that they possess no great share of intellect'.[92] 'If this be the case,' Thomson continues, 'it proves that wit is not requisite in the composition of a warrior, as no country is more famous than Denmark for producing heroes.'[93] Thomson then goes on to refute Nathaniel Wraxall's above-mentioned claim that Denmark produced 'few' great national figures.

Thomson begins his own appraisal of 'the Manners and Customs of the Modern Danes', however, by noting that to understand 'the character of the modern Danes, it is necessary to consider their ancient and present situation, to prevent drawing an unjust likeness from a figure of which little more than a skeleton remains'.[94] 'They were formerly free,' Thomson continues, again pointing to the supposedly deleterious effects of absolutism of the Danish national character:

> They are now slaves. That nation which first pulled down the Roman tyranny, and spread the flame of liberty throughout Europe, now behold every other European nation free, or attempting to be free; while they, driven back to their northern provinces, are again deprived of the natural as well as the political sun.[95]

Thomson's ethnography is a little off here, but, as we have seen, he was certainly not alone at the time in equating the ancient Danes with 'the Goths'.[96] We can detect echoes in his account of the theories of Montesquieu and Buffon about the influence of climate and environment on the formation of national character. But what is undoubtedly most striking in Thomson's characterisation of the modern Danes is his sense that 'the flame of liberty' which was once 'spread' by the inhabitants of the 'northern provinces' of Europe has now been extinguished there while it burns brightly elsewhere. And indeed, given that Thomson's travels were made in the late 1780s and published in 1792, one might wonder whether or not he implicitly includes England among those 'northern provinces' for whom the 'flame of liberty' has grown dim even while it burns brightly in Revolutionary France and across Europe.

In any case, having explained this caveat to his readers – that the national character of the modern Danes must be distinguished from that of their forebears – Thomson goes on to paint a predominantly negative picture, citing uncleanliness and intemperance ('a drunken Dane is proverbial') among the national vices, although he attributes these not just to poverty but also to 'the coldness of the northern climate'.[97] And the Danes themselves are affected, in Thomson's opinion, by that same perceived contrast between what he calls 'their ancient and present circumstances'. In a passage which recalls the student letter writer from *Observations*, Thomson affirms that 'the modern Danes have not forgot their former name; and the recollection occasions sullen pride, or, as frequently, despondency'.[98] Hence, he suggests, some writers 'describe' the Danes as 'proud' while others see them 'as a spiritless, tame, and abject people'.[99]

One final example should suffice adequately to represent the tendency to chart narratives of decline in British writing about the Danish national character, and to illustrate the various ways in which that tendency interacted with other, contemporary discourses not only about Denmark but also about European politics more generally. This is the account given by James MacDonald (1771–1810) in his *Travels through Denmark and Part of Sweden* (1810). MacDonald, as we have seen in Chapter 2, came to Denmark as a prisoner of war when the ship in which he was sailing, the *Johns*, was wrecked off Skagen, the northernmost point of Jutland. Despite these doubly inauspicious circumstances, however, MacDonald's *Tour* is full of praise for the heroism of the Danes who saved him and his comrades from the sea and for 'the greatest civility and politeness' and 'humane treatment' which he subsequently experienced during his captivity.[100]

MacDonald's account of the Danish national character is for the most part, then, appreciative and, on occasion, even affectionate. He points light-heartedly to some curious quirks, including 'a delight in red and purple colours' and 'a peculiar delight in mirrors', and he claims that 'there is no nation that I know of, which spends so much money in [sic] tomb-stones as the Danish'.[101] But he also notes, more seriously, the rise of nationalism in consequence of the British bombardment, claiming that the Danes 'are not a little addicted' to 'patriotic hyperboles regarding their country' – 'hyperboles' presumably including those of the kind which, as we shall see later in this chapter, Mary Wollstonecraft found so irritating during her stay in Copenhagen.[102] 'In no country in Europe', he says '(some parts of the Austrian empire, perhaps excepted), have I seen such active and devoted patriotism, as in Denmark.'[103]

This patriotic spirit could have its downsides, of course, especially for an English prisoner of war. On more than one occasion, MacDonald records his being subjected to 'harrangues on the bravery and power of the Danish nation' and, 'sometimes', to 'absolutely rude' comparisons between the Danish and the English.[104] He stoically (and prudently, given his circumstances) puts these sentiments down to the Danes being 'enraged' by the British bombardment and now finding themselves trapped between 'allies and enemies equally dangerous'.[105]

Again prudently, MacDonald refrains from offering any real comparisons of his own between England and Denmark, except the occasional reminder that the latter is 'an unlimited, despotic, continental monarchy', whose people cannot enjoy the same freedoms as those afforded 'by a country like Great Britain'.[106] Nor does MacDonald explicitly contrast ancient and modern Danes. But he does point to what he sees in 'present' Danish society as 'alarming symptoms of decay', evidence of a society arrested at an earlier stage of development than Britain.[107] He even anticipates the state bankruptcy which Denmark would be forced to declare in 1813, concluding, after a discussion of population and revenues in various European states, that the country 'cannot possibly maintain, for any length of time, her present establishments. Her credit is almost annihilated, and all her resources are in rapid decline.'[108]

In line with the arguments advanced by Montesquieu, Buffon and others, about the role of environmental factors in determining national character, MacDonald points to what he sees as the deleterious influence of climate and physical geography on the prospects for political and social development in Denmark. 'There must surely, at bottom', he says:

> be some sore evil connected with her climate, soil, produce, and cultivation, to account for this blighting of Denmark's political tree. May not the cause, perhaps, be traced to the deadly stagnation of the Baltic winter, the disjointed state of the provinces, and the extreme difficulty of intercommunication?[109]

Environmental and political 'stagnation' are thus causally related, in MacDonald's account, and he even permits himself to wonder 'what inconveniences would Britain not be subject to' if it had to contend with similar geophysical hardships.[110]

But, of course, MacDonald also takes aim at the 'blighting' effects of the absolutist system of government in Denmark and a misconceived 'idea of shining as a military state', which he attributes first and foremost to economic motivations.[111] Conversely, MacDonald urges the Danish government now to 'return to its old habits and connexions' and to 'renew its amicable relations with Britain, even at the risk of Bonaparte's vengeance'.[112] In so doing, MacDonald invokes that now familiar idea of England and Denmark as Northern brethren who ought to be allied against France, the true enemy of both. 'The spirit of nationality and patriotism' which is so 'conspicuously' visible in Denmark and Norway, MacDonald argues, if correctly directed, could again 'support national independence' and provide Denmark with a 'powerful preservative' against national decay.[113] '[E]very impartial philanthropist', he concludes, 'must wish that it may prove effectual.'[114]

If for MacDonald, however, the social, political and economic difficulties which he felt Denmark needed to overcome were the combined outcome of harsh environment and misdirected polity, for others, it was the Danish national character itself which was to blame for these afflictions, a character very frequently classified in British writing as defined by *indolence*.

'Our national lethargy': Indolence and the Danish National Character

In *Observations on the Present State of Denmark, Russia, and Switzerland*, the supposed student at Copenhagen university who laments, in his letters, the decline of the Danish national character, also points specifically, on a number of occasions, to what he calls 'our national lethargy', to the 'lethargy' into which the country has 'fallen'.[115] The fact that these remarks echo and ostensibly support the claims already made by the anonymous author of *Observations* about the 'indolence or weakness' which he finds characteristic of the present 'state' of Denmark is one of a number of reasons to question the authenticity of the letters and to suspect them, rather, to be a rhetorical device on the part of the author to strengthen his argument through its supposed corroboration by a local.[116] Taken as a whole, however, *Observations* is indicative of the extent to which the supposed 'indolence' of the Danish national character, whether it originated in climate or in polity or in some combination of the two, is a recurrent refrain of British writing about Denmark at the time. In her account of Copenhagen, for example, Mary Wollstonecraft – despite ostensibly eschewing any attempt 'to sketch a national character' – points to what she sees as the 'indolence of mind, and dull senses' of the inhabitants, and concludes that 'indolence, respecting what does not immediately concern them, seems to characterize the Danes'.¹¹⁷ Later, arrived in Schleswig-Holstein, she contrasts the 'chearfulness of the people in the streets' with 'the deathlike silence of those of Denmark, where every house made me think of a tomb'.¹¹⁸ In a similar vein, just a few years earlier, in his *Journey through Sweden*, Jean Frédéric Henry de Drevon had suggested that the Danes 'have an inclination to repose, and a serious, phlegmatic disposition'.¹¹⁹ We have already noted the contrast John Carr perceived between 'the sluggishness of the Danish seamen' and 'the alertness and activity' of 'British tar'.¹²⁰ In his account of the British attack on Copenhagen in 1807, the anonymous author of *Narrative of the Expedition to the Baltic* also points, more than once, to what he describes as the 'inactivity by the Danes' in their own defence.¹²¹

Two things, in particular, are striking about the tendency of British writers to characterise the Danes as indolent. The first is the frequency with which the characterisation is made. As we shall see, even those writers who offer more positive assessments, routinely feel the need also to rebuff the charges of indolence. The second is the fact that in various eighteenth-century discourses surrounding race and national character, accusations of indolence are usually levelled not just at ostensibly primitive peoples but, quite specifically, at *Southern* or *Eastern* peoples. We remember, for example, the precise contrast drawn by David Hume in his essay 'Of National Character' between 'the poverty and misery of the northern inhabitants of the globe, and the *indolence* of the southern'.¹²²

Hume is, in this respect, entirely typical. To cite just two further instances, here, both Jean-Jacques Rousseau (1712–78) in Book III of *The Social Contract* (1762) and Montesquieu in Book IV of *The Spirit of the Laws* make sustained connections between geophysical environment, racial characteristics and polity. Hence, Montesquieu argues that, since 'cold air constringes' and 'warm air relaxes' the human body, 'people are therefore more vigorous in cold climates [. . .] The inhabitants of warm countries are, like old men, timorous; the people in cold countries are, like young men, brave', while Rousseau claims that 'from the influence of climate [. . .] [w]arm countries should be the seat of despotism, and cold ones the haunt of barbarous people; while civilization and good policy should dwell with the inhabitants of the intermediary regions.'¹²³ Even Adam Ferguson, in his aforementioned *Essay on the History of Civil Society* – whose stadial model follows Hume rather than Montesquieu in emphasising the importance of 'moral' rather than 'physical' causes for social development – argues that:

> Great extremities, either of heat or cold, are, perhaps, in a moral view, equally unfavourable to the active genius of mankind, and by preventing

alike insuperable difficulties to be overcome, or strong inducements to indolence and sloth, equally prevent the first applications of ingenuity, or limit their progress.[124]

In further support of this idea, Ferguson then quotes, approvingly, from Rousseau's assessment of the relationship between the arts and environmental conditions in his *Discourse on the Arts and the Sciences* (1750).

The strong and consistent – effectively ubiquitous – association in eighteenth-century philosophy of indolence and tropical climate raises, then, the question of how we might account for the repeated characterisation of the Danes as indolent by late eighteenth- and early nineteenth-century British writers about Denmark, since the Danish climate is not obviously tropical. It is certainly no coincidence that those writers who most effectively originate and perpetuate the indolence trope – Molesworth and Wraxall – do in fact, as we have seen, greatly exaggerate the heat of the Danish summer. But rather than in any tracing of indolence to climate à la Montesquieu and others, the primary origin of the Danish indolence trope appears to lie in the perception by writers like Molesworth and Wraxall of Denmark as an exotic, Oriental country – not in a geographical sense, but rather, and moreover, in *political* sense. In eighteenth-century philosophy, as we have seen, indolence is associated not only with the South and the East, but also with the despotism routinely assumed to characterise Southern and Eastern politics: we remember, for example, Rousseau's suggestion in *The Social Contract* that 'warm countries' are 'the seat of despotism'.[125] It is the tendency to see Denmark as despotic, as a kind Oriental state in 'the North', then, which drives the representation of the Danes as indolent – and that representation is surprisingly long-lived, even in the face of emergent 'Romantic' attitudes to 'the North' in Britain, with the new cultural investment in the classical Scandinavian past, and the tendency to describe Danes and Britons as Northern 'brothers' following the Battle of Copenhagen in 1801.

The discursive complexities surrounding the trope of Danish indolence are well exemplified in the early account of the Danes and the Danish national character given by Joseph Marshall in his *Travels* (1772). Little information survives concerning Marshall, and at least one contemporary review raised the 'violent suspicion' that 'Squire Marshall' was a nom de plume.[126] Marshall's remarks about the Danish national character are divided between his own observations and the reported observations of one 'Count Roncellen' (a markedly un-Danish name) whom Marshall says he met when his carriage broke down while he was travelling across Jutland.[127] Marshall reports that Roncellen 'made several enquiries into the motives of my journey', to which he replied that he:

did not come to the North to see pictures and statues, or to hear operas, but to observe the manners of the people, the state of agriculture, the nature of manufactures, and the general appearance of the country.[128]

On hearing that the Briton was travelling 'philosophically', Roncellen invited Marshall to stay on his estate, where he showed him the various agricultural improvements in which he was involved and explained their 'wonderful efficacy' in transforming the conditions of the local peasantry.[129]

Roncellen began his account, Marshall says, by observing that his British guest 'must see a great difference' in 'the industry of the inhabitants, between England and their country' and subsequently explained to him that he knew of 'no people naturally more indolent than the common people in Denmark'.[130] The use of the word 'natural' here suggests an environmental rather than a political basis for this indolence, and much of Roncellen's subsequent narrative is concerned precisely to illustrate the role of polity in either exacerbating or correcting this supposedly innate characteristic. Much of that narrative is a critique of absolutism and its depressing effects, not only on agriculture but also on trade, with Roncellen affirming that 'what we want in Denmark is a market' – and all this reads very much like the similar strictures offered by Molesworth and Wraxall on the lack of trade and commerce in Denmark.[131]

But the whole point of Roncellen's narrative is, of course, that under the *correct* form of polity, this 'natural' indolence can be corrected: that is the lesson of the improvement works on Roncellen's own estate, run by a 'manager' from Essex with a team of English and Danish workers, where 'the native Danes, as well as the Englishmen, carry on their work with quickness and intelligence'.[132] Here, then, we have not the later idea of Britons and Danes as Northern 'brothers', but rather the clear implication that 'indolent' 'native Danes', under the correct (and in this case explicitly *English*) form of governance, can achieve English efficiency. Roncellen himself (again, explicitly) contrasts the Danish form of governance practiced by other landowners with his own, English style. 'I have adhered', he says:

> to the rule of proceeding on the very contrary conduct which is common among nine tenths of nobility of the kingdom. They keep their peasants as poor, and as humble as possible; I, on the contrary, do every thing to enable them to enrich themselves.[133]

And the 'advantage' which accrues from this 'conduct' apparently speaks for itself: 'my peasants', Roncellen concludes, 'grow into wealthy farmers, or, at least, are all in easy and happy circumstances.'[134]

Taken as a whole, then, whether the Roncellen episode is fictional or not, the introduction of the trope of Danish indolence into Marshall's *Travels* – ostensibly by a Dane, like the student correspondent in *Observations* – serves to enable political comparison between the effects of absolutism in Denmark and the more progressive polity of England. 'Indolence' and tyranny are mutually related. As with Molesworth's *Account*, however, one also wonders whether the real purpose of this part of Marshall's reflection on the Danish national character is less to comment on Denmark than to comment on England and the potentially deleterious effects of politic abuses there. In other words, not so much a case of 'Danes and Britons share a common culture' as a case of 'be careful, or Britain could end up like Denmark'.

Whatever the case may be, in his 'own' account of the Danish national character, Marshall certainly continues Roncellen's theme of the potential for national improvement and takes specific aim at Molesworth's version of the country, which he suggests is now outdated. Marshall starts by acknowledging the influence of Molesworth's *Account* which has, he says, 'been transcribed over and over again by every author that has written anything concerning Denmark' – and the justice of that observation we have confirmed more than once in this book.[135] 'But almost every circumstance to be gathered from that writer', Marshall continues, 'is changed essentially since his time.'[136] Again, as in Roncellen's early narrative, then, the leitmotif of Marshall's own account of the Danes is improvement. 'I do not apprehend', he says, 'there is a kingdom in Europe in which greater changes have been made.'[137] And these meliorative 'changes' Marshall attributes firmly to altered polity: 'the throne of Denmark has of late years', he affirms, 'been filled with three or four very able princes, who have shewn, in every department of the state, such a spirited conduct, with so much attention to the welfare of their subjects.'[138] These 'princes', in other words, have not abused their absolute power: 'the laws have been well and impartially executed.'[139] 'But what would they be', Marshall concludes, with that familiar note of warning, 'under a weak or a wicked Prince, or even a negligent one?'[140]

Taken in total, then, Marshall's account of the Danish national character in his *Travels* introduces the familiar trope of Danish indolence only to attribute this supposed characteristic firmly to the political rather than to the physical environment, both as an argument about the potential for national renewal in Denmark under better government and, perhaps, as an allegorical reflection on current and future British polity. Marshall certainly leaves his reader in little doubt about what he perceives as the rejuvenation of the Danish national character under those 'able princes'. The Danes 'appear', he says, 'to be a brave, courteous, and humane people'.[141] Far from indolent, 'the superior classes are of an high spirit, and have as much vivacity in them as any people in Europe', with a lifestyle 'in a mean between the English and the Germans, more sumptuous than the latter, but not with such general consistency as the former'.[142] Weighted comparisons between the Danes and the English are (as always) present, then, and these become especially visible when Marshall discusses the 'lower classes' of Danish society.[143] These, he says, 'are not comparable to ours, in ease and happiness; but they are by no means in that state of absolute slavery they were in Molesworth's time'.[144] But, though they can be 'ignorant and clownish', Marshall says, 'their manners have nothing of disgusting brutality in them', and he remains convinced – following his time with Roncellen – that 'with proper instruction, I believe that there are none in Europe, would make better husbandmen and farmers'.[145]

Not only, then, does Marshall's account of the Danish national character illustrate the complexity of the discourse of Danish indolence: its connections to debates in European philosophy about the nature of national character, and to increasingly urgent domestic debates, in Britain, about good governance. Rather, Marshall's account of Danish indolence also gives rise – almost paradoxically – to that other familiar trope of late eighteenth- and early nineteenth-century British writing about Denmark: the trope of the happy Danes. And this is a paradox still visible in writing about Denmark today, indeed about the Nordic countries in general, where complex evaluations of the relationship between the quality of life and the quality of economic productivity often go hand in hand.

'The happiest country in the world': Now, and Then

As I noted earlier in this chapter, Denmark has, over the last ten years, consistently scored highly in the annual index compiled by the World Happiness Report, and has, while I write in 2021, held the top spot three times since 2012. But this idea of the happy Danes is not, as I have said, an especially recent phenomenon. Writing in his *Travels* in 1810, for example, the prisoner of war James MacDonald describes the Danes as 'uncommonly good-humoured and obliging', while Murray's *Hand-Book for Travellers*, written nearly three decades later, characterises them as 'a kind-hearted and friendly people', who are 'courteous and obliging to the English traveller', albeit noting that they remain 'enraged' – 'and it must be owned not without just cause' – by the British bombardment of Copenhagen in 1807.[146] Among the most sustained analyses of Danish happiness to be found in late eighteenth- and early nineteenth-century British writing about Denmark is undoubtedly, however, that offered by Mary Wollstonecraft in her *Letters Written during a Short Residence* – an analysis not less interesting in that Wollstonecraft sees the happiness of the Danes as grounds for criticism rather than commendation of the Danish national character![147]

The *unhappiness* from which Wollstonecraft herself suffered throughout her Scandinavian journey came to a head as she neared the end of that journey in Copenhagen, when the hoped-for reconnection with her erstwhile lover, the American businessman Gilbert Imlay (1754–1828), seemed increasingly unlikely to occur.[148] It is in the Danish capital, we remember, that Wollstonecraft admits that she 'may be a little partial, and view everything with the jaundiced eye of melancholy – for I am sad – and have cause'.[149]

This sadness and its effect on Wollstonecraft's perceptions goes some way towards explaining why she finds fault with so many things which we might expect a radical feminist otherwise to extol. She notes, for example, the comparative personal freedoms enjoyed by 'young people, who are attached to each other [. . .] and are permitted to enjoy a degree of liberty together, which I have never experienced in any other country'. She continues: 'The days are courtship are therefore prolonged, till it be perfectly convenient to marry: the intimacy often becomes very tender.'[150] And yet she also argues that 'love here seems to corrupt the morals without polishing the manners', and laments somewhat prudishly 'the gross debaucheries into which the lower order of people fall; and the promiscuous amours of men of the middle class with their female servants'.[151]

These particular strictures on sexual (mis)conduct we might understand to have less to do with the Danes and more to do with Gilbert Imlay, then living with an actress. But Wollstonecraft also takes aim at more strictly social and political attitudes. She argues, for example, that 'an adoration of property is the root of all evil' and yet remarks pointedly that 'wealth does not appear to be sought for, amongst the Danes, to obtain the elegant luxuries of life; for a want of taste is very conspicuous at Copenhagen' – and then goes on to complain about the 'parsimony' of 'the court' which 'seems to extend to all the other branches of society', concluding that 'nothing can give a more forceful idea of the dullness which eats away all activity of mind, than the insipid routine of a court, without magnificence or elegance'.[152] Observing that 'one of the best streets in Copenhagen is almost filled with hospitals, erected by the government', the best Wollstonecraft can do is to wonder only whether such institutions 'are any where superintended with sufficient humanity'.[153] And, despite having registered early on in her journey that 'the inhabitants of Norway and Denmark are the least oppressed people in Europe', 'that the press is free' and that 'on the subject of religion they are likewise becoming more tolerant', Wollstonecraft still seems more concerned to stress, in her account of Copenhagen, that 'the men of business are domestic tyrants', who drink too much ('the pleasure of savages'), and the women 'simply notable housewives', who spoil their children, and who lack 'accomplishments, or any of the charms that adorn more advanced social life'.[154] Again, we might detect barbs aimed more at Imlay here than at the Copenhageners, but the overall impression one gets from Wollstonecraft's account of the Danish capital is that the Danes simply *cannot* be so happy as they themselves 'dogmatically assert' that they are.[155] For it is at those Danish claims to happiness that some of Wollstonecraft's sharpest shafts are aimed.

According to Wollstonecraft, the Danes enjoy what she calls a 'negative happiness' because the 'liberty' which they possess they consider a 'boon' from their absolutist government rather than 'their right by inheritance'.[156] In Wollstonecraft's opinion, then, Danish happiness is not only an illusion but also predicated upon a fundamental misconception of the true nature of political freedom. Those 'men of business', whom she characterises as 'domestic tyrants', and who must, surely, have reminded her of Imlay, are, she says:

> So coldly immersed in their own affairs, and so ignorant of the state of other countries, that they dogmatically assert that Denmark is the happiest country in the world; the prince royal the best of all possible princes; and count Bernstorff the wisest of ministers.[157]

Wollstonecraft's sarcastic adjectives ('the best of all possible', 'wisest') are certainly intended to recall, for the reader, those deluded but irrepressibly cheerful optimists imagined by Voltaire: Candide and his philosopher-tutor, Pangloss. Hence, the overall point of Wollstonecraft's analysis of Danish happiness is, again, clear: it is predicated upon 'ignorance' of true political freedom; it is an effect of an absolutist system which grants as a privilege what it should protect as a right. Danish absolutism, in other words, creates 'negative happiness', a happiness rooted not in aspirational activity but in that conservative 'indolence' which Wollstonecraft thinks 'seems to characterize the Danes': a 'concentration in themselves', Wollstonecraft says of the Danes, 'makes them so careful to preserve their property, that they will not venture on any enterprise to increase it, in which there is a shadow of hazard'.[158]

What seems clear, then, is that, while Wollstonecraft's critique of Denmark and Danishness may well, as she suggests, have been coloured by her own unhappiness, it is also influenced by the tendency which we have often seen in eighteenth-century British writing about Denmark to find evidence, everywhere, of the ills of absolutism. In this respect, while Wollstonecraft's *Short Residence* is in many ways a deeply 'Romantic' book about 'the North', in its assessment of Danishness and the Danish national character, it is still very much a product of the eighteenth century, of that genre of British writing, coming from Molesworth, which would see Denmark as a quasi-Oriental 'Other' rather than as a culture with which Britain had much in common. And in this, of course, Wollstonecraft very much anticipates some of the loudest critical voices in Britain today of the Danish social model, who argue that the Danes are happy because they have low expectations, and that Danish society is conformist, discouraging individual ambition or distinction – a set of values often said to be embodied in the concept of *Janteloven* [Law of Jante].[159] The happy inhabitants of a free and progressive society, or an indolent nation living by the grace of 'big government' – it seems that in some respects, at least, British debates about Danishness and the Danish national character have not moved on a great deal from the late eighteenth and early nineteenth centuries.

Coda: 'One of the remarkable men of the age': Belzoni on Denmark and the Danes

In the third part of his *Denmark Delineated* (1824), the Danish traveller and translator Andreas Andersen Feldborg draws the reader's attention to the 'Hotel of England' on Kongens Nytorv, in central Copenhagen, noting that, if those earlier English travellers who had complained about the standard of accommodation in the city – such as the late Edward Daniel Clarke – had 'put up' there instead, they would have found 'cheerful company' and 'the greatest of all luxuries'.[160] But Feldborg's main reason for mentioning the Hotel d'Angleterre (which is still in business in 2021) is not to recommend it to travellers: 'I am besides very partial to this house', he says, 'for it was my good fortune to meet here one of the remarkable men of the age.'[161] This 'remarkable' man was none other than the celebrated explorer and archaeologist Giovanni Belzoni (1778–1823).

Belzoni passed through Copenhagen in May 1822 on his way back to England from Saint Petersburg. By that time, of course, he was already famous across Europe, as an excavator and exhibitor of the remains of Egyptian antiquity. In 1815–16, Belzoni rose to celebrity when he oversaw the transportation of the colossal bust of Ramesses II (c. 1303 BCE – c. 1213 BCE) to the British Museum in London, Napoleon (1769–1821) having previously tried and failed to send it to France in 1798. This, of course, is the statue which may have inspired Percy Bysshe Shelley's (1792–1822) famous sonnet 'Ozymandias' (1818) and which certainly did inspire celebrated passages in the *Suspiria de Profundis* (1845) and 'System of the Heavens' (1846) of Thomas De Quincey (1785–1859), the 'English opium-eater'. Following this success, Belzoni subsequently opened key archaeological sites in Egypt, including the temple of Abu Simbel, the tomb of Seti I (thirteenth century BCE), and the Pyramid of Khafre at Giza, and published in 1820 his influential *Narrative of the Operations and Recent Discoveries within the Pyramids, Temples, Tombs and Excavations in Egypt and Nubia*. The reason for Belzoni's journey to Saint Petersburg in 1822 remains unclear, but he may well have been attempting, as one of his biographers plausibly suggests, to promote an exhibition there like those which he had organised in London in 1820–1 and in Paris earlier in 1822.[162]

The only substantive, contemporary witness of Belzoni's time in Copenhagen is that provided by Feldborg in *Denmark Delineated*: the two spent most of Belzoni's short time in the city together after 'he kindly accepted my offer', Feldborg recalls, 'to be his Cicerone'.[163] We know that Belzoni could not have met there the equally famous Danish sculptor Bertel Thorvaldsen (1770–1840), who was in Italy at the time, but Feldborg confirms that he did introduce Belzoni to Adam Oehlenschläger (1779–1850), 'the greatest of living Danish poets', as Feldborg describes him.[164] This 'interview', Feldborg recalls, 'was extremely animated', but he could not 'judge of the degree of interest it possessed' as the two men conversed in French, which he did not understand.[165]

Of primary interest to me here, however, are the ways in which Feldborg enlists Belzoni into the wider project of *Denmark Delineated*: namely, to rebuff the 'injustice' with which Feldborg felt his country had been treated by the 'ignorance and prejudice' of previous travel accounts.[166] Belzoni functions in this part of *Denmark Delineated* as a kind of expert witness – whose qualifications could scarcely be doubted – to the true nature of Denmark and Danishness. Indeed, it is tempting to see Feldborg's narratological use of Belzoni as a deliberate writing back against those other local witnesses who had appeared in earlier British accounts of Denmark, such as the student letter writer from *Observations* or Count Roncellen from Marshall's *Travels*.

This strategic use of Belzoni begins almost immediately in Feldborg's account of his brief stay in Copenhagen. On their first evening together, Feldborg says he enquired directly of Belzoni:

> 'Well, Sir, I should like to know what you will say of us, in addition to what Shakespeare, Molesworth, Yorick, Coxe, Wraxall, Dr. [Edward Daniel] Clarke, Mary Wollstonecraft, Sir John Carr, and Mr. Macdonald have already said.'[167]

This question is interesting not only because it identifies for us Feldborg's sense of his primary antagonists in *Denmark Delineated* but also, and indeed moreover, because it evidences his conviction that, from an international perspective, 'Denmark' was still a textual construct of British writing. Belzoni, who had come straight from the theatre, gives, in Feldborg's account, an appropriate response:

> 'From what I heard and saw at the play, I should say you were a very quiet, good-natured people, who are very fond of a hearty laugh. You have reason to be proud of a dramatist, who can shake your sides in the manner I noted tonight: as for your music, I fancied myself in my own country.'[168]

In thus invoking the now familiar trope of the happy Danes, then, Belzoni manages simultaneously to praise not only the national character but also the artistic traditions of Denmark as well, which had so often been, as we saw in Chapter 3, the object of censure by British travellers. 'Belzoni spoke this', Feldborg assures the reader, anticipating and seeking to allay any suspicions, 'in a tone, and with a look, which satisfied me that the words were not the badinage of a captain of compliments.'[169]

From these auspicious beginnings, Belzoni has nothing but praise for Copenhagen and its inhabitants as Feldborg leads him on a tour of the city's cultural landmarks, including the Academy of Arts, the Botanic Garden, the University Library and Museum of Northern Antiquities, where they met the 'profound and skilful' antiquarian Rasmus Nyerup (1759–1829).[170] And, as Belzoni left the city, Feldborg made sure that he noticed the 'monument' raised to 'acknowledge the enlightened and liberal sentiments of the government, and breathe most fervent gratitude of the citizens'.[171] This was Frihedsstøtten, an obelisk placed on what is now Vesterbrogade, to commemorate the emancipation of the peasantry in 1788, and which, Feldborg had already said, 'cannot fail to impress the mind of a stranger with ideas favourable to Danish art'.[172] Their final stop before Belzoni left the city was Frederiksberg, were the two men viewed the Royal Gardens. Here, again, Belzoni says exactly what Feldborg, the self-styled cultural liaison between Denmark and Britain, would wish: 'Bless me,' cried Belzoni,' Feldborg reports, 'how much this is like England.'[173] Though evidently only a comparison between styles of landscape gardening, Feldborg must nevertheless have been happy to be able to promote, once again, and this time with the support of an objective witness, his key argument about the cultural common ground between Britain and Denmark. As the two men parted, Feldborg recalls he 'could not but feel happy' because Belzoni 'expressed himself so kindly of the persons he had become acquainted with in Denmark' and his 'best wishes' for 'the prosperity of Denmark'.[174] Belzoni's final words 'as the carriage moved away' were '*We shall soon meet again in old England*' – and indeed they did, as Feldborg tells us in a footnote, on 14 July 1822.[175]

There is, of course, no reason to doubt the veracity of anything which Feldborg reports of Belzoni's visit. But it is also clear, as I have said, that Feldborg deploys Belzoni in *Denmark Delineated* as an expert witness against earlier, British accounts of Denmark and the Danes. Belzoni becomes, in other words, part of the rhetorical apparatus of *Denmark Delineated*, becomes, as I have said, a counter to those local voices brought into evidence in the anonymous *Observations* and in Marshall's *Travels*.

Nor, remarkably, is this rhetorical use of Belzoni by Feldborg confined within the parameters of the Italian's *actual* visit to Copenhagen. Rather, Feldborg also provides a five-page account of the other places to which he *would* have 'conducted' Belzoni if he had had 'a couple of days more' in the city.[176] Only on one occasion in his account of this imagined tour, on a visit to some schools, does Feldborg allow himself explicitly to state that this 'would have afforded Belzoni pleasure'.[177] But as Feldborg describes how he would have taken Belzoni to see the 'magnificent prospect' of 'the sea' and 'the beautiful environs of Copenhagen', which have 'a degree of life and interest which no other capital can boast of', and 'the improvements generally introduced into the prisons', the reader is given little alternative but to assume that these experiences would only have augmented the Italian's expressed praise for the city and people.[178]

Feldborg's rhetorical use of Belzoni even extends to his onward journey from Copenhagen. Feldborg assures the reader that 'As Belzoni proceeded on his journey' he would have passed through 'well cultivated country', although 'he might occasionally be roused into a malediction against' the 'very bad' road to Roskilde.[179] Having seen Belzoni thus far in imagination, Feldborg then continues, for a further seven pages, to describe that city and other key cultural sites in Zealand, describing not just the places themselves but also commenting upon what they reveal about Danishness and Danish polity. And, although in these pages

Feldborg no longer refers to Belzoni by name, but to a generic 'traveller', the reader is again prompted to imagine Belzoni in these places and to accept that Belzoni would share the appreciative sentiments expressed by Feldborg.[180]

Feldborg's defence of his country in *Denmark Delineated* concludes, then, with the extensive, legitimating testimony – both actual and imagined – of one of the foremost and most celebrated travellers of the early nineteenth century, brought in to rebuff the strictures of earlier British accounts of both Denmark itself and of the Danish national character. With one of 'the remarkable men of the age' to back him up in this way, Feldborg must have felt himself to be on solid, rhetorical ground.

Chapter 5

'No trifling kingdom': Anglo-Danish Politics beyond the Revolutionary and Napoleonic Wars

As will by now be evident, Anglo-Danish political relations during the period covered by *British Romanticism and Denmark* were defined, to a very considerable extent, by the events of the Revolutionary and Napoleonic Wars: by the two British attacks on Copenhagen in 1801 and 1807, and by the British role in the drawing up of the Treaty of Kiel and the subsequent forced cession of Norway to Sweden in 1814 – an outcome which Murray's *Hand-Book for Travellers* (1839) characterised as 'a death blow to the prosperity of Denmark, and a transaction but little reputable to England'.[1] To these calamities, must be added the bankruptcy of the Danish state in 1813, a consequence of the expensive war with Britain and the attendant loss of trade and overseas revenue, a scenario anticipated by, among many others, the Scottish prisoner of war James MacDonald (1771–1810), who remarks in his *Travels* in 1810 that 'Denmark cannot possibly maintain, for any length of time, her present establishments. Her credit is almost annihilated, and all her resources are in rapid decline.'[2]

As we have also seen, the flowering of Romanticism and Romantic nationalism in Denmark – the so-called 'Golden Age' in literature, painting and music – has been linked by scholars and historians to a turning inwards towards national landscapes and vernacular cultural forms in the wake of this diminishing Danish presence on the European stage, to Denmark having 'lost its importance as a European power', as Murray's *Hand-Book* puts it.[3] For all their undoubted significance, however, the events of the Revolutionary and Napoleonic Wars do not by any means delimit the extent of British engagement with Danish political life during the period covered by this book. Conversely, before a single shot was fired on Copenhagen Roads in April 1801, British writers had expressed considerable interest in what Joseph Marshall (dates unknown) had described in his *Travels* (1776) as 'no trifling kingdom'.[4] Within this extensive British discourse about Danish politics, three main focal points are visible: the nature and effects of absolute monarchy in Denmark; the collapse and aftermath of the marriage between Christian VII of Denmark (1749–1808) and Caroline Matilda of Great Britain (1751–75), sister of the future George III of England (1738–1820); and the extent and value of Danish territorial possessions overseas, including Danish involvement with the slave trade. In this final chapter, I show how British writing about these topics is a revealing barometer of changing British attitudes to Denmark and Danishness in the late eighteenth and early nineteenth centuries, exhibiting many of the same trajectories and concerns which we have discerned in other areas of Anglo-Danish cultural relations at the time.

'The most absolute monarch in Europe': British Liberty and Danish Despotism

In her *Letters Written during a Short Residence in Sweden, Norway and Denmark* (1796), Mary Wollstonecraft (1759–97) seems uncertain about the consequences of 'the king of Denmark being the most absolute monarch in Europe'.[5] She grants, for example, that 'though the king of Denmark be an absolute monarch, yet the Norwegians [Norway was then ruled by Denmark] appear to enjoy all the blessings of freedom'.[6] She even notes that 'the arbitrary government' of Denmark 'seeks to hide itself in a lenity that almost renders the laws nullities' and 'that fearing to appear tyrannical, laws are allowed to become obsolete, which should be enforced, or better substituted in their stead'.[7] And yet, in the Appendix to her *Short Residence*, Wollstonecraft also observes how 'the gigantic evils of despotism and anarchy' have ensured that 'slavery has retarded the improvement of every class in Denmark' and that, although the country is 'advancing', 'innumerable evils still remain to afflict the humane investigator' like herself.[8] Denmark became an absolute monarchy in 1660 during the reign of Frederik III (1609–70), after victory in the Dano-Swedish War (1658–60), and remained so until 1848, when a constitutional monarchy was established following the death of Christian VIII (1786–1848). And the uncertainties which we see in Wollstonecraft's account – whether absolutism 'retarded' Danish society and culture, or whether, despite or perhaps even paradoxically because of its 'arbitrary government', Denmark was in fact a remarkably progressive society – had been, for a long time, a key factor in British debates about the country's politics.

The seminal British critique of Danish absolutism was Robert Molesworth's (1656–1725) *Account of Denmark, as it was in the Year 1692* (1694).[9] Reaching multiple posthumous editions, Molesworth's *Account* was so extensive in its influence that, over a century after its publication, the Danish traveller and Anglophile Andreas Andersen Feldborg (1782–1832), writing in 1824, still felt the need to refute as 'no longer extensively applicable' (if ever true at all) Molesworth's claim that 'the Danes do now really love servitude; and [. . .] could not make use of liberty if it were offered them'.[10] Molesworth is uncompromisingly critical both of the establishment of an absolute monarchy and of the deleterious effects which he perceives monarchy to exert on the nation and the people of Denmark. In his discussion of 'The Conditions, Customs, and Temper of the People', for instance, he argues that since 'all these do so necessarily depend upon, and are influenced by, the nature and change of government, that it is easily imagined, the present condition of these people of all ranks must be most deplorable'.[11] 'Slavery', he affirms:

> like a sickly constitution, grows in time so habitual, that it seems no burden nor disease; it creates a kind of laziness, and idle despondency, which puts men beyond hopes and fears: It mortifies ambition, emulation, and other troublesome as well as active qualities, which liberty and freedom beget; and instead of them, affords only a dull kind of pleasure of being careless and insensible.[12]

In passages such as this, then, we can find the origins of those assertions of the inherent indolence of the Danish national character which, as we saw in Chapter 4, can be found in the works of British travellers to Denmark as diverse as Nathaniel Wraxall, and Mary Wollstonecraft. For Molesworth, national character is understood as the product of the prevailing socio-political situation rather than of the natural environment.

Not all, of course, agreed: James MacDonald, for instance, in his *Travels*, suggests that 'there must surely, at bottom, be some sore evil connected with [Denmark's] climate, soil, produce, and cultivation, to account for this blighting of Denmark's political tree'.[13] 'May not the cause', he argues, 'perhaps, be traced to the deadly stagnation of the Baltic winter, the disjointed state of the provinces, and the extreme difficulty of intercommunication?'[14] For Molesworth, however, the establishment of an absolute monarchy in Denmark signalled a dramatic break with the values of the classical Scandinavian past: he emphasises 'how great the rights of the people were very lately in the elective kingdoms of

Sweden and Denmark', something which he attributes to 'the antient form of government in this kingdom, which continued with very little interruption [. . .] till about two and thirty years ago'.[15] This 'antient form of government' in Denmark, Molesworth explains, 'was the same which the Goths and Vandals established in most, if not all, parts of Europe [. . .] and which in England is retained to this day for the most part'.[16]

By identifying England as the inheritor of classical Northern liberty, then, Molesworth establishes a political geography in which Britain and Denmark now represent binary opposites rather than sharing in a common culture. And this political geography is further visible in two significant and persistent strands of Molesworth's argument, which connects freedom with the North and links absolutism and oppression to the South and the East. The first of these strands is Molesworth's consistent tendency to attribute the blame for the collapse of the 'antient form of government' in Denmark to French influence, to the fact that Denmark 'has often had the misfortune to be governed by French counsels' (and we must remember that Molesworth is writing in the 1690s, since similar arguments would be made a century later).[17] The second is Molesworth's tendency to associate the polity of Denmark with Southern and Eastern countries, and often, though not exclusively, with Ottoman Turkey – for many commentators at the time, the embodiment of despotic rule. Hence, for instance, Molesworth's assessment that Denmark is now governed 'after the Turkish manner', that the people suffer 'most of the Mischiefs of a Turkish Government in an infinitely worse Climate', and that 'in Zealand [the people] are all as absolute slaves as the negroes are in Barbadoes, but with this difference, that their fare is not so good'.[18] Indeed, 'the *Turks* themselves', Molesworth suggests, 'who are Lords and Masters, live well and pleasantly, and it is their conquered Slaves whom they use in the manner above mentioned.'[19]

From Molesworth's *Account*, in other words, emerges a paradoxically (given its geographical position) 'Oriental' Denmark, a Denmark which is represented as, in almost all respects, the absolute (pardon the pun) 'Other' of England – and this, of course, is exactly that image of Denmark which, as we have already seen, would change so utterly during the late eighteenth and early nineteenth centuries. So insistent, indeed, is Molesworth that 'an Englishman should be shewn the misery of the enslaved parts of the world, to make him in love with the happiness of his own', that it is distinctly possible (as I have noted earlier in this book) that Molesworth meant less to provide an 'account' of Denmark per se than to provide an object lesson in the kind of governance which England ought to avoid, following the recent civil war (1642–51) and

Glorious Revolution (1688).[20] Exemplary, perhaps, of this possibility, is Molesworth's extended discussion of taxation in Denmark, for which he apologises to the reader but justifies as exactly such an object lesson. 'I suppose by this time', Molesworth writes:

> an English reader has taken a surfeit of this account of the taxes which the subjects of Denmark do pay. But it ought to be a great satisfaction to him to reflect, that through the happiness of our constitution, and the prudence and valour of our king, the people of this nation [. . .] do not [. . .] pay towards the carrying on of the most just and necessary war, the third part in proportion to what the king of Denmark's subjects do in time of a profound peace.[21]

It is difficult not to see, in such encomiums, at least some admonitory reference to England's involvement in the Nine Years' War, ongoing since 1688.

The possibility that Molesworth 'did not intend to give us a just account [of Denmark], but under a Romantick Cover of Arbitrary Power, to represent Tyranny in its worst shape to the English Nation' was in fact first raised by Jodocus Crull (1660–1713), whose instant refutation of Molesworth's *Account*, entitled *Denmark Vindicated*, was published the same year.[22] Such a motivation was the only possible explanation, Crull suggests in his prefatory letter, for the 'extravagances and groundless assertions, so little suitable to the rules of true History, wherewith [Molesworth's *Account*] is filled up from the beginning of the Preface'.[23] Particularly problematic, Crull thought, is 'the gross and unaccountable Comparison especially, made betwixt the Northern Parts of the world and the Turkish Government, nay, even preferring the latter'.[24] What follows in *Denmark Vindicated* proper is a 216-page, point-by-point refutation of Molesworth's 'ill-grounded' *Account*, which Crull characterises as neither 'true' nor 'impartial', based on Crull's own 'memory', 'observations' and 'correspondence from friends'.[25] And though by no means an unmitigated panegyric on the Danish state, Crull's account is far more balanced and presents a nation progressing towards political and cultural modernity, as these were then understood, praising everything from the food to the 'academies' and other institutes of learning receiving royal support at Copenhagen.[26] 'As the Kingdom of *Denmark* is very well known to me,' Crull concludes, 'so I am sure I have related nothing, but what I not only very well know, but also can easily prove, by unquestionable Witnesses who are not ashamed to own their Names' (a dig at Molesworth's 'suspicious' anonymity).[27]

In this seminal debate between Molesworth and Crull in the early to mid-1690s, then, we find the two poles which would continue to dominate British writing about Danish polity for more than a century after. Only towards the end of the eighteenth century, with the emergence of new 'Romantic' attitudes to 'the North' do we begin to see a more determined shift towards an image of Denmark as less the opposite than the analogue of Britain, less the embodiment of a foreign culture than the representative of shared values rooted in a common past.

Many eighteenth-century British (and French and German) travellers and commentators echoed both Molesworth's strictures and his version of an 'Orientalised' Denmark. As we have seen in Chapter 1, Nathaniel Wraxall, for example, in his *Tour through Some of the Northern Parts of Europe*, describes the decoration of Christian IV's chamber at Rosenborg as better fitted to a 'mussulman' than a 'Lutheran' monarch.[28] Equally, and again as we saw in Chapter 1, the anonymous author of *Observations on the Present State of Denmark, Russia, and Switzerland* (1784) compares the conditions of the peasantry in Denmark with 'the despotism of a Turkish bashaw' and later notes, 'as a curious specimen of Danish liberty', that:

> In Turkey few can read; in Denmark, as few dare write: the despotism, in both countries, equally completes its purpose; and of the two, the former, I think, is the happiest way for the individual.[29]

The form of government in Denmark, the *Observations* insist, embodies 'a most gloomy picture of fallen majesty, and disgraced dignity', in marked contrast to Denmark's 'zenith of glory' in the eleventh century, and offers only 'obstacles to the advancement of cultivation'.[30] Equally attributable to 'prejudicial [. . .] genius of [the Danish] government' are 'the present state of Danish agriculture', which is 'painful' in comparison with 'the operations of the English farmer', and 'the manufactures of the country', which are much below the 'superiority of our own [i.e. the English]'.[31]

In addition to *Denmark Vindicated*, however, the eighteenth century also saw some early, dissenting voices about the nature and implications of absolutism in Denmark. The celebrated traveller William Coxe (1747–1828), for example, gives in his *Travels* (1785) an extended account of the transition from the 'form of government antiently established in Denmark' to 'an hereditary and absolute, monarchy', but does not draw any orientalising comparisons with England or other European nations – and moreover is, as we have seen, generally quite positive about Danish polity and society.[32] Foremost among the earliest eighteenth-century responses to Molesworth, however, is Joseph Marshall's account of Denmark in his *Travels*. Marshall assures his reader that 'they cannot gain any just intelligence from former books; for old ones are no longer true, and modern travellers have, in general, slighted all the North.'[33] And Molesworth's *Account* is, for Marshall, a case in point here. 'Most of the people with whom I conversed [about 'this kingdom and its inhabitants'], Marshall affirms, 'generally quoted Mr. Molesworth':

> whose book has been transcribed over and over again by every author that has written any thing concerning Denmark; but almost every circumstance to be gathered from that writer, is changed essentially since his time; insomuch, that although his book is a very able performance, yet it is little more than an old almanack for turning to, to gain information of the present times; for I do not apprehend, that there is a kingdom in Europe in which greater changes have been made.[34]

In support of this claim that 'the affairs of this country are on the flourishing hand', Marshall cites an 'increase', 'improvements' in agriculture ('a husbandry superior to the common run of the North') and industry ('government had established manufactures in various places'), and 'a general improvement in the riches and welfare of the nation [achieved without] the addition of taxes'.[35] Marshall's description of Denmark is very much focused on matters of political economy ('the state of agriculture, the nature of manufactures') rather than on descriptions of landscapes and architecture, or 'pictures and statues'.[36] The centrepiece of his *Travels* is his extended (and, as I have argued in Chapter 4, quite possibly fictional) account of a four-day stay on the estate of a Danish count by the name of 'Roncellen' whom Marshall says he met, by chance, on the road near Rinkøbing, and who expressed an interest in the 'philosophical' purpose of his journey.[37] It is to his discussions with this Count that Marshall attributes most of his knowledge of Danish polity, and Marshall is also keen (as I have shown in Chapter 4) to emphasise the extent to which Roncellen was employing English methods and English workers, including an estate manager from Essex whom he recruited during his travels in England.[38] Throughout Marshall's *Travels*, then, 'improvements' in Denmark are closely allied to a movement towards Englishness across a range of different activities, from farming to industry, and towards a laissez-faire economics markedly in contrast to what one might expect from an absolute monarchy. On Roncellen's estate, for instance, Marshall records 'farm houses and cottages, the inhabitants of which seemed as easy, chearful, and happy, as if they had been resident in England instead of Denmark'.[39] And all of this can be explained, Marshall concludes, following Roncellen, because, although the monarchy in Denmark is absolute, the government is in fact moderate. 'The throne of Denmark', he affirms, 'has, of late years, been filled with three or four very able princes, who have shewn, in every department of the state, such a spirited conduct, with so much attention to the welfare of their subjects.'[40]

Around the turn of the nineteenth century, as British attitudes to Denmark shifted away from the perception of difference and towards an emphasis on common cultural values rooted in a classical Scandinavian past, exactly this point was increasingly made. The conflicted response to Danish polity exhibited by Wollstonecraft in her *Short Residence* gives way to more confident and optimistic assertions by British travellers and commentators that, while Denmark was in law an absolute monarchy, in practice, the government was benevolent and comparatively progressive. Hence John Carr (1772–1832), in his *Northern Summer* (1805), could remark without contradiction that 'it is scarcely necessary for me to observe that the government of Denmark is despotic' while at the same time praising at length 'the mildness of the Danish government'.[41] In *Copenhagen and its Environs* (1829), Richard Jones (dates unknown) similarly confirms that the Danish monarchy has 'absolute and uncontrouled authority', but also emphasises the 'paternal affection for all his subjects' of 'the present Sovereign', religious toleration, and that 'the laws are simple and excellent, and justice is administered in its several courts with equity'.[42]

Most telling, perhaps, in this regard, is William Rae Wilson (1772–1849), who dedicates his *Travels* to the Duke of York 'in the hope that you will be interested in seeing other states adopting nearly similar principles' to 'our own noble and excellent constitution', 'principles which, while they form the safeguard of the subject, shed a moral dignity around the monarch, which despotism must ever remain an utter stranger to'.[43] Wilson goes on, like Carr and Jones, to describe Frederik VI of Denmark (1768–1839) as a 'father' to his 'people' and even to note (as we have seen in Chapter 4) that the 'cast of his features appeared to me to be not unlike those of the royal family of Great Britain'.[44] Wilson insists that 'it behoves us to discriminate between a monarch vested with supreme power and absolute authority, and the despot who tyrannically abuses those privileges'.[45] 'If by the expression "despotism"', Wilson affirms:

> is to be understood absolute and unlimited monarchy, then it unquestionably follows that the government of this country is in reality despotic. At the same time, let it never be lost sight of that this right is more nominal than practical. The constitution of Denmark, it is true, is denominated an absolute monarchy: but the slightest investigation will clearly prove that few governments coming under this description will be found more distinguished for moderation, and few people that enjoy greater liberties and privileges.[46]

In Wilson's account, then, we can see how radically the pendulum has swung from an estimation of Denmark as an 'Oriental' 'despotism' to a view of the country as, in practice, despite its absolutist constitution, on a par with England in its promotion of the 'liberties and privileges' of its people. And as I have argued in Chapter 1, in the wake of the British bombardment of Copenhagen in 1807, in particular, it had become difficult to sustain the old opposition between British liberty and Danish despotism.

For all that British attitudes to Danish absolutism did change in line with new, 'Romantic' attitudes to 'the North' and because of the events of the Napoleonic Wars, however, old prejudices were by no means altogether forgotten. In *Denmark Delineated*, as we have seen, Feldborg still felt the need to rebut Molesworth's century-old *Account of Denmark*, assuring his readers, for instance, that Molesworth's assertion that 'the Danish peasants were as absolute slaves as the negroes in Barbados' was really only valuable, now, as a testimony to their 'present improved condition'.[47] But Feldborg also had more recent commentators to deal with. In his Appendix to *Denmark Delineated*, he sets out again to 'correct various erroneous impressions concerning the practical character of a government little known to the British public'.[48] Feldborg takes issue in particular with Jean-Pierre Catteau-Calleville's (1759–1819) *Tableau des états danois* (1802), which had been reviewed approvingly by Sydney Smith (1771–1845) in the *Edinburgh Review* for July 1803 – a review from which Feldborg quotes, verbatim, at some length. In point of fact, neither Catteau-Calleville's book (which one suspects Feldborg had not read) nor Smith's review is nearly so hostile to Denmark as Feldborg's reaction seems to imply. But Smith does note approvingly what he sees as the 'great diligence and good sense' of Catteau-Calleville's book, which points to a steady decline in 'the spirit of the Danish nation [. . .] for the last two or three centuries' – and Smith does suggest that Catteau-Calleville has been 'too timid and sterile' in his discussion of Danish absolutism, is 'occasionally too cautious for the interests of truth', and 'manages the Court of Denmark with too much delicacy'.[49] And those old, 'Orientalising' comparisons with 'Turkey' and the idea of 'blind and slavish submission [. . .] to the foot of the Sultan' do also raise their heads again in Smith's review.[50] Part of the reason for the persistence of hostility in Britain towards the absolutist government in Denmark – rather than, necessarily, to the Danish people in the wake of 1801 and 1807 – was, of course, the still comparatively fresh memory of the collapse of the marriage between Caroline Matilda and Christian VII. Indeed, even the extended and very flattering review of Feldborg's *Denmark Delineated* which ran in *Blackwood's Edinburgh Magazine* in September 1821 quoted at length from his account of Kronborg Castle, which the reviewer affirms 'will be interesting to our readers from the knowledge that it formed the prison of the unfortunate Queen Caroline Matilda'.[51] Hence, it is to British eighteenth-century and Romantic-period responses to that particular crisis in Anglo-Danish relations that I want, now, to turn.

'Hurried into an untimely grave': British Romanticism and Caroline Matilda

'Poor Matilda! thou hast haunted me ever since my arrival; and the view I have had of the manners of the country, exciting my sympathy, has increased my respect for thy memory!'[52] Thus Mary Wollstonecraft, miserable in Copenhagen – rejected by her former lover Gilbert Imlay (1754–1828), and having attempted suicide before she began her journey to Scandinavia – signals in her *Short Residence* her ability to empathise, even to identify, with the 'hapless' English princess whose unhappy union with the king of Denmark had 'hurried [her] into an untimely grave'.[53]

Caroline Matilda, the daughter of Frederick, Prince of Wales (1707–51), married Christian VII of Denmark in Copenhagen on 8 November 1766 and was crowned queen on 1 May the following year – the culmination of a long-sought-for political union between the houses of Hanover and Oldenburg. A son, the future Frederik VI of Denmark (1768–1839), was born to the couple in January 1768. But the marriage was troubled from the start, with rumours of infidelity by both parties, and it gradually collapsed as the mental health of the king, unstable at the time of the marriage, grew worse and worse. Christian VII was absent from Copenhagen on a grand tour of Europe during the second half of 1768, and when he returned in January 1769, he brought with him the German physician Johann Friedrich Struensee (1737–72). Caroline Matilda and Struensee became closely attached and were assumed to have become lovers by 1770, although Wollstonecraft (not an altogether unbiased commentator) insisted, in her *Short Residence*, that:

> many very cogent reasons have been urged by her friends to prove, that her affection for Struensee was never carried to the length alledged against her [. . .] and if she an attachment for him, it did not disgrace her heart or understanding, the king being a notorious debaucher, and an idiot into the bargain.[54]

At the same time, Struensee, who was officially created royal advisor in May 1770, gained enormous influence in the Danish court, and, as the king's mental health deteriorated, effectively became ruler in all but name. Much influenced by Jean-Jacques Rousseau (1712–78) and French Enlightenment thought, Struensee attempted to make an array of progressive reforms to the Danish political, social and economic system, including a ban on the slave trade in Danish colonies overseas and the abolition of both capital punishment and the censorship of the press. However, these reforms and his assumed affair with the queen also earned him powerful enemies, and the situation was further exacerbated when Struensee created himself and his friend, the judge and royal chamberlain Enevold Brandt (1738–72), counts in November 1771. In January 1772, Struensee's enemies in the royal court moved against him: he and Brandt were arrested and Caroline Matilda was taken as a prisoner of state to Kronborg Castle, in Helsingør (Elsinore). Brandt and Struensee were tried and found guilty of *lèse majesté* and usurpation of royal authority and executed at Copenhagen on 28 April 1772. Caroline Matilda confessed to an affair with Struensee (although it is thought under pressure); her marriage to Christian VII was dissolved and she went into exile in Celle Castle, in Germany, leaving her children behind in Denmark. She died there of scarlet fever on 10 May 1775.

Wollstonecraft, as we have seen, believed Caroline Matilda innocent of any impropriety (of the heart, at least, if not altogether of custom), being 'convinced' rather (and rightly) that she was a 'victim' of Struensee having 'attempted to overturn some established abuses before the people, ripe for the change, had sufficient spirit to support him when struggling in their behalf'.[55] 'Disgusted with many customs which pass for virtues', Wollstonecraft concludes, 'she probably ran into an error common to innovators, in wishing to do immediately what can only be done by time.'[56] It is certainly not difficult to detect again, here, in the author of the soon-to-be notorious *Vindication of the Rights of Woman* (1796), an element of self-identification with the former queen of Denmark and the high price which she paid for desiring to be an 'innovator'. And, indeed, Wollstonecraft recalls hearing in Copenhagen 'invectives thrown out against the maternal character of the unfortunate Matilda', who 'was censured, with the most cruel insinuation, for her management of her son', and she compares her fate with the fate of women in society in general.[57] 'Still harping on the same subject, you will exclaim,' Wollstonecraft quips ironically to the reader of *Short Residence* in general and to Imlay in particular, 'how can I avoid it, when most of the struggles of an eventful life have been occasioned by the oppressed state of my sex.'[58]

Wollstonecraft's feminist take on the fate of Caroline Matilda in her *Short Residence* is coupled, then, not only with an element of self-identification, but also with a sense of the former queen as a kind of sentimental, one might even more properly say *Romantic*, heroine, undone by her passion and virtue, which the unsympathetic (and patriarchal) world deems improper. Wollstonecraft was, of course, not the first British traveller to Denmark to take up the fate of Caroline Matilda. But her account does illustrate well the ongoing transition, in parallel with the broader shift in British attitudes to Denmark, towards representing the former queen in this 'Romantic' fashion, as the victim of a formerly French-influenced Denmark which was now increasingly returning to the classical Scandinavian values it had earlier shared with Britain.

Nathaniel Wraxall, who visited Copenhagen in the summer of 1774, and who composed his *Tour* while Caroline Matilda was still alive, gives an extended account of 'the late extraordinary revolution which expelled a queen from her kingdom, and brought the ministers to the scaffold', noting in conclusion that the 'skulls and bones of these unhappy men [Struensee and Brandt] are yet exposed on wheels about a mile and a half out of town', that he had himself 'viewed them with mingled commiseration and horror', and that 'they hold up an awful and affecting lesson for future statesmen'.[59] Of 'her present majesty [. . .] I mean the queen Matilda', however, Wraxall has relatively little to say, noting only his pleasure in hearing her, whom he describes pointedly as 'an English and an injured queen', complimented during his visit to Kronborg.[60]

William Coxe, however, writing in 1785, gives a rather more sentimental portrait of 'the late unfortunate queen Matilda', which he begins by noting how she would walk 'upon the side-batteries, or upon the leads of the tower', during her imprisonment in Kronborg, while 'she was uncertain of the fate that awaited her'.[61] Coxe describes the 'spirited conduct' of 'the English minister at Copenhagen' in securing her release and how, forced to leave her son and infant daughter behind, 'she retired to the vessel [which to take her from Kronborg] in an agony of despair'.[62] In Celle Castle, Coxe affirms, though 'naturally of a lively disposition', she 'became extremely fond of solitude; and, when alone, indulged her grief in the most bitter lamentations [and] retained, to her last moments, the most unaffected attachment to her children in Denmark', portraits of whom she acquired and 'often apostrophized them as if they were present, and addressed them in the tenderest manner'.[63]

As noted, this kind of sentimental or 'Romantic' portrait of Caroline Matilda increasingly came to dominate in British responses over political analyses of the events which had led to her exile and death. In his account of the 'neglect and suffering the Queen, in the bloom of youth and beauty, endured', for example, John Carr describes her arrest in terms which echo Edmund Burke's (1729–97) well-known account of the seizure from their bedroom of the French royal family in his *Reflections on the Revolution in France* (1790).[64] 'They opened the door of the Queen's bedchamber',

Carr writes, 'and awoke her from profound sleep to unexpected horror. These savage intruders are said upon her resisting to have struck her: the indecency and indignity of the scene can scarcely be imagined.'[65] And having described what he calls Caroline Mathilda's 'mock trial' and the 'agony' of her separation from her children and departure from Denmark, Carr closes his account by asking the reader: 'shall we follow the wretched Matilda a little farther? The path is solitary, very short, and at the end of it is her tomb.'[66]

With the passage of time and the proliferation of such sentimental accounts, Kronborg Castle became increasingly a destination for British travellers to Denmark on account of its associations with Caroline Matilda, which often rivalled if not altogether eclipsed the older connection with *Hamlet*. As we have seen in Chapter 2, in *Denmark Delineated* Feldborg says of Kronborg that 'Englishmen will find themselves on classic ground'.[67] This is partly because the castle has 'a strong claim on his [i.e. an Englishman's] best feelings, from its being inseparably associated with one of the noblest works of human genius: for *Hamlet* [. . .] has more affected English hearts than any other dramatic production'.[68] 'But a still deeper tragedy', Feldborg affirms, 'will awaken the sympathies of an Englishman on his visit.'[69] Feldborg then quotes a paragraph from Robert Southey's (1774–1843) *Life of Nelson* (1813) on the 'foul and murderous court-intrigue' to which Caroline Matilda fell 'victim', before providing his own description of how 'during her imprisonment' she used to 'ascend the square tower, which commands one of the finest prospects in the world. No spot could better soothe the anguish of her mind'.[70]

By the mid-1820s, the rooms where Caroline Matilda were imprisoned were well established as a site on the tour of Zealand.[71] When William Rae Wilson published his *Travels* in 1826, he noted that, while he was generally underwhelmed by the interior of Kronborg Castle:

> [t]hose apartments, however, once inhabited by the unfortunate Caroline Matilda, will always preserve a high degree of interest for every honest Englishman, whose feelings cannot fail to be affected by the unparalleled injuries experienced by that exalted individual.[72]

Wilson, like Carr twenty years earlier, also recalls for his readers how Caroline Matilda's 'bed chamber was most indecently invaded at an early hour of the morning'.[73] Sentiment, appeals to 'honest' 'feelings' rather than political analyses, had by then become the leitmotif of British Romantic-period responses to that 'beautiful and animated' 'princess' who had wandered the ramparts at Kronborg Castle, having 'suffered in no ordinary degree such a train of persecution, malignity, and injustice, to forward schemes of ambition, and accomplish the most base purposes'.[74] This is Caroline Matilda as Gothic heroine, a transformation made possible not only by the passing of time but also by the transformation in British attitudes to Denmark.

'A few India goods': British Writing about Danish Territories Overseas

Danish activity outside Europe during the period covered by this volume is probably best remembered today, if indeed it is remembered at all, for the Danish Arabia Expedition to Egypt and the Near and Middle Easts in 1761–7, funded by the Danish crown and led by the German-born Carsten Niebuhr (1733–1815). This six-man expedition, which only Niebuhr survived, was celebrated at the time and made significant contributions to various debates in those areas of enquiry which would now be called ethnography and linguistics.[75] Niebuhr's *Beschreibung von Arabien* [Description of Arabia] (1772) and *Reisebeschreibung nach Arabien und ander umliegender Ländern* [Description of a Journey to Arabia and Other Adjacent Lands] (1778), published in Copenhagen, were both translated into Dutch, English and French before the end of the eighteenth century and widely read. William Coxe, for instance, in his *Travels*, praises this 'curious and interesting journey', which, he says, 'reflects the highest honour upon the crown of Denmark, and holds up an example to be imitated by other sovereigns', and notes Niebuhr's 'much esteemed account'.[76]

As Nathaniel Wraxall observes in his *Tour*, Denmark could 'boast', in the late eighteenth century, 'a vast extent of dominion' in the Nordic and Arctic regions – although Wraxall, ever the cynic, proceeds immediately to undercut this 'boast' by asking 'of what importance are the barren and uninhabited mountains of Norway and Lapland stretching to the pole; or the plains of Iceland [. . .]?'[77] For all Wraxall's cynicism, though, Norway, rich in timber and ore, was a valuable possession, 'the brightest jewel in the Danish crown', as William Thomson (1746–1817), writing under the pseudonym 'Andrew Swinton', described it in his *Travels* (1792).[78] Hence the forced cession of Norway to Sweden under the Treaty of Kiel in 1814 was a cruel economic as well as cultural blow to Denmark, which had declared state bankruptcy the previous year. However, as James MacDonald and many other British writers noted, Denmark did also have in the late eighteenth and early nineteenth centuries a 'valuable East- and West-India trade, and colonies': nothing to compare with the possessions of Britain or other large European countries, of course, but still generating revenue and trade rather more than the 'few India goods' which Swinton dismisses in his *Travels*.[79] British visitors to the royal palace of Amalienborg in Copenhagen, for example, very often had occasion to remark not only upon the quality of the bronze equestrian statue of Frederik V (1723–66) in 'the Octagon' but also on the fact that this statue had been paid for by the Danish East India Company 'and is said to have cost 80,000l', as John Carr puts it.[80] Indeed, even the sceptical Molesworth had granted in his *Account of Denmark* that, while 'the king of Denmark's factories in the East and West Indies, and in Guinea, are esteemed of very little worth [. . .] I have seen several East-India ships return home to Copenhagen well laden with the merchandise of those countries.'[81]

Danish West and East India Companies were established and granted monopolies by royal charter in the seventeenth century, but financial and other operational difficulties led to both being taken under state control in the 1770s.[82] During the period covered by *British Romanticism and Denmark*, Danish colonies overseas were gathered in three regional groupings: the Danish Gold Coast, the Danish East Indies and the Danish West Indies. The Danish Gold Coast consisted of a series of forts and outposts along the south-east coast of what is today Ghana, on the Gulf of Guinea, with the first, Fort Christiansborg, established in Accra in 1658. Early trade was mainly in gold and ivory, but slavery came to dominate during the eighteenth century until it was abolished in 1802, although the law prohibiting it had been passed a decade earlier (see discussion below). In his account of Danish 'Commerce to the Coast of Africa' in his *Travels through Denmark* (1810), Pierre-Marie-Louis de Boisgelin de Kerdu (1758–1816) estimated the Danish trade in slaves during the 1770s and 1780s at 'from two thousand to two thousand five hundred slaves' annually, and cited weapons, brandy and tobacco as other important goods.[83] Denmark sold all its territories in the region to Great Britain in 1850, when they became part of the British Gold Coast. The Danish East Indies also dated from the early seventeenth century and the establishment of Fort Christiansborg in Tranquebar (Tharangambadi) in 1628, on land granted to the Danish admiral Ove Gedde (1594–1660) by Raghunatha Nayak, who ruled Thanjavur from 1600 to 1634. By the end of the eighteenth century, Denmark had established further settlements in Serampore, Achne and Pirapur, and had also taken possession of the Nicobar Islands (dubbed 'New Denmark'). The late eighteenth and early nineteenth centuries witnessed both enormous growth and catastrophic decline in Danish East India trade. As a member of the League of Armed Neutrality during the Anglo-French War (1778–83), Danish vessels carried out trade with and between England, France and the Netherlands, often at great profit. De Kerdu estimated Danish East India trade in tea alone, during 1776–8, to have generated 'twenty millions eight hundred and ninety-seven thousand rix-dollars'.[84] But the situation became unsustainable during the Revolutionary and Napoleonic Wars, when Britain moved decisively to break up the League in order to enforce a blockade on French trade. Moreover, as MacDonald, among others, noted in his *Travels*, 'in times of war with Britain [Denmark] loses her valuable East and West India trade, and her colonies': following the British attack on Copenhagen in 1801 and the seizure of the Danish fleet, British troops also took temporary possession of Denmark's East India settlements, returning control in 1802, and this situation was repeated following the British bombardment of Copenhagen in 1807 and the seizure and destruction of the remaining Danish fleet.[85] By the time that Britain finally returned to Denmark possession of its East India colonies in 1815, following the defeat of Napoleon, Danish East India trade had been dealt a hammer blow from which it never recovered – and the Danish East India territories were eventually sold off piecemeal to Britain in the 1840s. Settlement of the Danish West Indies (now the US Virgin Islands) began with the acquisition of the island of Saint Thomas in 1672; Saint John was added in 1718 and, in 1733, Saint Croix was bought from the French West India Company, 'for 164,000 rix-dollars' according to Wilson in his *Travels*.[86] 'These', as the anonymous author of *Observations on the Present State of Denmark* somewhat sardonically puts it, 'are the whole of [Denmark's] possessions in this part of the world.'[87] The islands were hub of the so-called 'triangular trade' in slaves, sugar and tobacco, between Africa, the Caribbean and Europe, although de Kerdu estimated the annual production of sugar on Saint Croix in the 1780s as 'no more than eighteen thousand hogsheads; indeed they only made seven thousand in 1790s', with 'half' sent to Copenhagen, one-quarter to North America 'and the rest to Holland'.[88] As with the Danish East Indies, the Danish West Indies were also occupied by the British in 1801–2 and again from 1807 to 1815, when Britain and Denmark were on opposite sides in the Napoleonic Wars. These occupations, together with the abolition in 1802 of the slave trade on which such much of the colony's economy depended, effectively ended the profitability of the Danish West Indies, but the islands remained Danish territory until 1917, when they were sold to the United States for US$25 million.

As noted, from Molesworth onwards, British commentators about Denmark expressed interest in the extent and value of the country's overseas possessions – effectively proving the justice of Molesworth's early observation that the expansion of Danish trade in the West and East Indies 'will in time be worth the inquiry of those kingdoms and states whose interest it is to preserve in the Indians and Persians a good opinion of the honesty and fair dealing of the Europeans'.[89] In his response to Molesworth's *Account*, for example, Joseph Marshall, having noted the importance to Altona of Danish East India trade, goes on to recall an extended discussion, with the count whom he says he visited, of Danish ambitions to 'set heartily about an increase in their India commerce', with plans afoot to acquire territories in Mozambique from the Portuguese and even, potentially, 'to open a commerce with the great southern unknown continent, called the Terra Australis', whose existence was often posited during the eighteenth century.[90] 'The plan', Marshall records the count affirming, was 'to throw Denmark upon a par with other nations in commerce' through 'the opening of new discoveries, erecting a few forts, establishing factories among populous nations of Indians, unknown to Europeans, and the carrying on an extensive commerce with them', which 'would not only pour in a flood of wealth upon this kingdom, but, what is also of vast consequence, keep numbers of stout ships and hardy seamen in constant employment'.[91]

If such assertions seem unrealistic or even naive today, they should, of course, be seen in the context of Marshall's attempts to rebuff Molesworth's highly negative account of Denmark and, indeed, read alongside assertions such as that made by John Carr some thirty years later that 'Nature, which has broken the kingdom [of Denmark] into islands, has instinctively made the Danes, merchants and sailors'.[92] The growth of Danish trade in the East and West Indies would, in other words, merely be a return to the expansionism of the Viking past. As the eighteenth century wore on, however, it was not just the revenues generated by Danish West and East India trade which were of interest to British commentators but also, as the movement towards abolition of the slave trade gained momentum, the condition of the slaves in Denmark's colonies. Writing in 1784, for example, the author of *Observations on the Present State of Denmark* – which, as we have seen, is generally critical of Danish polity – appended a footnote to a discussion of Danish West Indies and Africa trade affirming that:

> when I think of the fate of these wretched negroes, the tears of humanity convince me that I am not patriot; and, I believe, I could read with less emotion the massacre of a ship's crew on the coast of Guinea, than its bill of lading at Barbadoes, or Antigua.[93]

One of the most extended and informative English-language engagements with slavery in the Danish colonies during the period covered by *British Romanticism and Denmark* was not penned by a British writer, however, but by the Dane Andreas Andersen Feldborg.

Three of Feldborg's works – *A Tour in Zealand* (1805), *Poems from the Danish* (1815) and *Denmark Delineated* (1821–4) – are dedicated to one James de Windt of Saint Croix (1772–1834), who evidently acted as a sponsor and patron for Feldborg in his attempt to familiarise British readers with Denmark and Danish culture in the wake of the British attacks on Copenhagen in 1801 and 1807 (see Introduction and Chapter 1). The De Windt family owned a plantation in the Prince Quarter of Saint Croix, at the south-west of the island. How precisely Feldborg made the acquaintance of James de Windt remains unclear, but in *A Dane's Excursions in Britain* (1809), Feldborg recalls that he 'enjoyed the happy privilege of a most hearty welcome' from the 'opulent and hospitable' De Windt at his cottage on the Terrace at Barnes, in south-west London, in August 1805, where he stayed for some days.[94] Feldborg's *Tour in Zealand* is dedicated to De Windt on 1 August 1805 in recognition of 'that patriotic ardour, which incites you to promote whatever can in any way conduce to the honour and welfare of Denmark', while in his Preface to *Denmark Delineated*, dated at Edinburgh on 9 September 1824, Feldborg records 'his particular acknowledgements' for the 'very handsome and patriotic conduct' of his 'old and highly valued friend' in acting as patron for the work.[95]

Feldborg's engagement with slavery in the Danish colonies comes, however, in the anthology *Poems from the Danish*, which he edited with William Sydney Walker (1795–1846) in 1815, and it is this volume, too, which contains Feldborg's most extensive and most revealing dedication to De Windt. The dedication is dated at London on 14 July 1815. Feldborg thanks De Windt for 'the generous support which you have been pleased to give for the space of nearly twelve years, to an attempt which I ventured to conceive for the introduction of Danish literature into this country [i.e. Britain]' and praises his 'patriotic devotion', 'lofty public spirit' and 'goodness of heart' in supporting the volume, which, Feldborg hopes, will 'prove creditable to Denmark, and meet with the countenance of England'.[96] As noted, then, what all these various dedications make clear is that De Windt supported Feldborg's attempts to act as a kind of cultural liaison between Britain and Denmark and to shore up the faltering relations between the two countries during the Napoleonic Wars by reminding British readers of their common cultural values, rooted in a shared past. And Feldborg's account, in *Poems from the Danish*, of the history of the abolitionist movement in Denmark is very much part of that project, intended to emphasise the shared humanitarianism of Britons and Danes. The occasion of that account is the inclusion in *Poems from the Danish* of 'The Negro's Song' by the Copenhagen-based poet and playwright Thomas Thaarup (1749–1821), to which Feldborg appends some 'Particulars relative to the Abolition of the Slave Trade by Denmark'.

'The Negro's Song' is in fact a translation of some lines from Thaarup's highly successful operetta *Peters Bryllup* [Peter's Wedding], which was first performed in Copenhagen in 1793 and which was part of a growing campaign in Denmark during the 1790s to abolish the trade in slaves in the Danish West Indies. It appeals on the grounds of sentiment and religious duty rather than through the kind of rationalist, Enlightenment arguments made by abolitionists like Josiah Wedgwood (1730–95) in England. Feldborg and Walker retain the form of the original: the tetrameter variant of the so-called 'Venus and Adonis stanza', which became a popular lyric mode in both Britain and Denmark during the Romantic period. The speaker is 'Martin', an African slave who has been rescued at sea by the Dane Peter, with whom he returns to Copenhagen. Martin, the son of an African chief, had been due to marry the daughter of another chieftain, but both are taken prisoner on the eve of their wedding. Martin escapes but assumes that his beloved has been sold into slavery in the Danish West Indies. His story is modelled, to an extent, on historical figures like the newly famous Olaudah Equiano (1745–97), whose *Interesting Narrative* (1789) of his life played a key role in the abolitionist movements in America and Europe.

'The Negro's Song'[97]

> I will fly the social room,
> I will weep in lonely sadness;
> The poor negro's cherish'd gloom
> Must not mar the hour of gladness.
> 5   Let my fate your sighs command,
> Fetter'd in a distant land.
>
> Say, what is the negro's crime,
> Ye who in our blood engrave it?
> Can the colour of our clime
> 10 Plead for sin with him who gave it?
> Gloomy is the negro's breast,
> Robb'd of her he loves the best.
>
> God of Christians, God of men!
> Thou canst melt the heart of scorn;
> 15 May none e'er the bridegroom chain,
> From his new-espoused torn!
> Let our fate thy pity move,
> Robb'd of country and of love!

In his commentary on the 'Song' in the 'Historical Notes' appended to *Poems from the Danish*, Feldborg opens by reminding the reader that 'Denmark, it is well known, was the first European country which took any effectual measures for the abolition of the Slave Trade'.[98] As Feldborg explains, in 1792 Denmark had passed a law 'that no more negroes should be imported into her West India Colonies' and this law had come into force in 1802, by which time the Danish government had 'provided the planters with the necessary pecuniary means for establishing a permanent supply of domestic labourers in the plantations'.[99]

In point of fact, while the *trade* in slaves had been prohibited in Danish territories since 1802, slavery itself continued until the late 1840s and was certainly still an active component of the Danish West Indies economy when Feldborg and Walker published their anthology. Feldborg's focus, though, is rather on the history of abolition than on its current status, and he is keen to point out that, even during 'an earlier period of Danish history', when the West and East India companies were most active,

> private individuals engaged in that most horrid traffic will be found to have entitled themselves to a considerable degree of that praise which has subsequently fallen to the lot of their countrymen at large, as being the first nation to redress the wrongs of Africa.[100]

In support of this claim, Feldborg then quotes some three-and-a-half pages (pp. 22–5) from his own English translation of *Store og gode Handlinger af Danske, Norske og Holsterne* (1777) by the Danish historian Ove Malling (1747–1829), which he had published in 1807 as *Great and Good Deeds of Danes, Norwegians, Holsteinians*.[101]

Malling's book, which was intended for use in Danish schools, is a compilation of the lives of exemplary historical figures, with interpretative commentary, grouped under eighteen thematic headings – and was very much part of an emergent national Romanticism in Denmark. The examples which Feldborg cites in *Poems from the Danish* come from the section of *Great and Good Deeds* entitled 'humanity' [Menneskekierlighed, or 'love of mankind', in the original]. Since Malling's Danish-language original was published before the law banning the trade in slaves in Danish territories had been passed, his account is part of the history of Danish abolitionism which Feldborg wants to bring to the attention of his British readers – and the fact that Feldborg cites at such length from his own translation might be brought forth as evidence for just how *much* he wanted his readers to be made aware of that history. 'The hardships which the devoted inhabitants on the coasts of Africa and America have experienced from the insatiate thirst of European avarice', Malling argues, in Feldborg's translation:

> are so various and melancholy in their nature, that every human being alive to the sensibilities of the heart, must revolt at a mere recital of these atrocities. – Our fellow-creatures have been treated by the polished nations of Europe, not only as slaves, but they have also been degraded into brutes – bought and sold to gratify lust, ambition, and avarice.[102]

Slavery, according to Malling, has 'shamefully compromised' what he calls 'the honour of mankind' – and 'Danish merchants' have not been 'exempt' from this 'guilt calculated to level the more enlightened part of the human race far beneath the wretched victims of their disgraceful superiority'.[103]

Malling finds some 'consolation', though, in the fact that even in these 'horrid' circumstances, 'there have been men whose exalted minds [. . .] listened to the tale of human woe, and whose benevolent hearts sought to retrieve the outrages committed on the laws of nature.'[104] Standing 'foremost' among such men 'in the ranks of worth and philanthropy', Malling argues, are two administrators of the Danish Gold Coast during the late seventeenth and early eighteenth centuries: Christian Cornelisen (d. 1684), 'whose intercourse with the Negroes, was', according to Malling, 'so marked by gentleness and urbanity, that he was considered more their friend and father, than their master', and Severin Schilderup (d. 1736), who 'completely gained the affections of the natives; by whom he was, indeed, beloved'. 'Never has the death of a European been so lamented in that country,' says Malling of Schilderup, who died in post on 14 June 1736.[105]

Very little historical information now survives about either man, and of course caution is always advisable in dealing with such panegyrics, especially in a postcolonial context. What we can be sure of, however, is the purpose of Malling's original account and of Feldborg's two translations of it, both as part of *Great and Good Deeds* and in *Poems from the Danish*: to emphasise the 'humanity' of the Danes. For Malling, this emphasis was part of a nascent Romantic nationalist project of educating Danish youth in the patriotic and civic virtues of their recent forebears, rather than harking back to examples from the classical past, be that Scandinavian or Mediterranean. For Feldborg, by contrast, writing for an international audience, such exemplary Danish figures served his purpose of countering British prejudices, deriving from Molesworth and others, about Danish polity as absolutist and despotic in character and practice. The history of the abolitionist movement in Denmark becomes, precisely, another case in point of the common cultural values, of the 'humanity', shared by Britons and Danes – indeed, an even more effective example in that in this case, as Feldborg emphasises, Danes led the way. No longer, in other words, are Danes themselves slaves in an absolutist system; rather, they are pioneers in extending freedom to 'those robb'd of country and of love', as Martin puts it in 'The Negro's Song'.

Coda: The 'German' Oehlenschläger

British Romanticism and Denmark has traced a multifaceted discourse about modern Denmark across a wide range of different areas of enquiry and genres of cultural productivity in late eighteenth- and early nineteenth-century Britain. In so doing, the book has had a twofold purpose. First: to recover a significant but still largely unfamiliar aspect of the cultural history of Britain during the Romantic period. Second, and by extension: to further scholarly understanding of Romanticism as a European phenomenon by exploring how individual national Romanticisms interacted across political and linguistic borders. This book has shown how the idea of a 'Northern' cultural identity shared between Britain and Denmark, and rooted in constructions of the classical Scandinavian past, played an important role in the emergence and development of Romanticism and Romantic nationalism in both countries.

In order to shed some final light on the extent to which British Romantic-period writers themselves invoked this paradigm of a regional or transnational Romanticism, while at the same time showing themselves aware of the many complexities which that paradigm involved, I want to turn, in this Coda, to an essay on the Danish poet Adam Oehlenschläger (1779–1850) which was published in Charles Ollier's (1788–1859) *Literary Miscellany* in the autumn of 1820. Ollier is chiefly remembered today as the publisher of Percy Bysshe Shelley (1792–1822) and John Keats (1795–1821). Ollier's *Literary Miscellany*, which ran to only a single number, is remembered, if it is remembered at all, because it carried Thomas Love Peacock's (1785–1866) essay 'The Four Ages of Poetry'. This, of course, was the essay which prompted Peacock's friend Percy Bysshe Shelley to compose his 'Defence of Poetry' (1821), one of the best-known works of Romantic-period criticism, and a work very much concerned to examine the history of European literature, which Shelley planned to publish in the second number of the *Miscellany*. The 1820 number also carried what was intended to be the first of a series of essays 'On the German Drama', by the English theologian Julius Charles Hare (1795–1855), who would later translate into English some stories by the German Romantic-period writer Johann Ludwig Tieck (1773–1853). This first essay took as its subject the Copenhagen-born poet and playwright Adam Oehlenschläger, whom Hare characterises as 'the great poet of Denmark'.[1]

Hare opens with a relatively lengthy argument about the relationship between 'dramatic poetry' and the cultural health and maturity of a nation: 'whenever a mighty poetical instinct awakens in and actuates a nation that has reached an advanced stage of culture,' he writes, 'the dramatic department of poetry will ever be the one in which, above all others, it will infallibly strive to put forth its organising powers.'[2] This is so, Hare suggests, because 'it is the drama alone, wherein poetry can come into contact with and act upon the universal life of a cultivated age', when 'unadorned narratives of facts, or simple lyrical effusions of feeling can no longer appease the hunger of a more craving intellect'.[3] Given this conviction that 'dramatic poetry [is] the highest product of national genius', then, it is not surprising that Hare chooses to focus on two dramatic works by Oehlenschläger: his *Correggio* (1809) and, especially, *Aladdin* (1805), from which he quotes lengthy extracts in translation.[4] But Hare's selection of these particular texts is nevertheless striking: two works with, respectively, Italian and Oriental rather than Nordic settings and motifs. And once Hare turns from his general remarks about the relationship between drama and society to a consideration of Oehlenschläger proper, the tensions in his attempt to articulate a transnational paradigm for the understanding of Oehlenschläger's work become immediately apparent.

To begin with, Hare addresses the obvious question of what two works by 'the great poet of Denmark' are doing in an essay about 'recent German drama'.[5] 'It may indeed appear rather whimsical', Hare grants, 'that a series of criticisms on the most eminent German writers should commence with the account of a Dane.'[6] 'But there are few, if any, Germans, we believe,' he continues, 'who would hesitate about assigning to Oehlenschlaeger a very distinguished station upon their own Parnassus.'[7] This, of course, rather begs the question of what the *Danes* might think about the matter. But, in support of his claim, Hare appeals directly to the idea of a regional literature which crosses not only national but even linguistic boundaries. Oehlenschläger has, Hare points out, 'himself introduced a considerable portion of his compositions to them [i.e. the Germans] in translations' while some others 'have been originally composed in German'.[8] This interaction across languages and borders is, Hare insists, perfectly natural under the circumstances:

For though it be most true that his own mother language forms the natural element wherein every poet ought to breathe [. . .] yet the similarity between the two tongues is such, that for a Dane to write in German scarcely implies a greater desertion of his household Gods, than for an ancient Dorian, like Herodotus, to make use of the Ionic dialect. It is rather a migration from one region or sea into another, than a wilful and perverse confusion of that which nature has designed to be separate.[9]

Hare's appeal to Classical Greece for an illustrative comparison of this kind of 'regional' cultural identity is particularly apt because he points to 'the ancient brotherhood between Teutonic and Scandinavian' cultures as the foundation for the regionality exhibited in Oehleschläger's work.[10] In so doing, clearly, Hare parallels those many British Romantic-period cultural texts which, as we have seen, seek to articulate the notion of a 'Northern' culture shared by Britain and Denmark and rooted in the classical Scandinavian past. His characterisation of Oehlenschläger also contrasts with the bipartite paradigm developed by Germaine de Stäel (1766–1817), in her *De la littérature considérée dans ses rapports avec les institutions sociales*, of 'two distinct kinds of literature still extant [. . .] one derived from the east, the other from the north', which I discussed in my introduction to *British Romanticism and Denmark*.[11] The works by Oehlenschläger on which Hare chooses to focus, at least, seem markedly to blend motifs and modes from the North, the South and the East, and bear out, to an extent, Elisabeth Oxfeldt's arguments (also noted in my introduction) about the incorporation of Orientalist elements into Danish Romantic-period cultural texts.[12]

All this said, however, Hare's construction of Oehlenschläger as a Northern author whose writing transcends national and linguistic boundaries is far from unproblematic. Conversely, the most visible consequence of that construction is that it undermines the notion of national literatures and particularly, in this case, of exactly that Danish national Romanticism of which Oehlenschläger – who wrote the lyrics of what later became the national anthem – was a major proponent.[13] More precisely, Hare's argument leads, in his essay, less to the promotion of a Northern regional literature in which the Danish and the German partake as equal partners, but rather to the subsumption of Danish literature within the German. In support of this argument, Hare includes a lengthy (three-page) quotation, translated into English, from what he calls 'one of the most illustrious philosophers of Germany, himself a Norwegian'.[14] The work from which Hare quotes (accurately) is *Die gegenwärtige Zeit und wie sie geworden mit besonderer Rücksicht auf Deutschland* [The Present Age and How It Emerged, with Particular Regard to Germany] (1817), by the indeed 'illustrious philosopher' Henrik Steffens (1773–1845), who was born in Stavanger but who spent most of his academic career in Germany.[15] In 1802, Steffens gave nine lectures during a short stay in Copenhagen which sought to promote German Romantic literature and philosophy in Denmark as part of a wider movement to counter the perceived, deleterious influence of French culture – which, as we saw in Chapter 3, was also something which concerned the Danish Anglophile and travel writer Andreas Andersen Feldborg (1782–1838), among others.[16] While certainly consistent with such an agenda, the material which Hare quotes from *Die gegenwärtige Zeit* is also problematic in its tendency to subsume Danish letters to German. 'Though however we are compelled to deny,' Hare quotes:

> that there is a Danish literature, understanding by literature a peculiar, characteristical conformation, whereby the whole intellectual culture of a nation marks out itself and separates itself from others, it is by no means intended to assert, that the Danes are to be regarded as mere imitators of the Germans. They are much rather intellectual allies, and therefore the German independence of mind shows itself here also.[17]

Here, then, we see precisely illustrated the problems involved in the regional paradigm of 'intellectual allies' in which some, as George Orwell (1903–50) might have later put it, are understood to be more allied than others. 'When we assert that Denmark has no literature of its own,' Hare quotes further, 'this holds only so far, as the general, even the highest intellectual tendency cannot be represented separately from that of Germany.'[18] Hence, for Hare, still quoting Steffens, key Danish Romantic-period authors including Oehlenschläger can and should be classified as German: 'all Germany knows' Jens Baggesen (1764–1826), the passage continues, while 'the noble [Johannes] Evald [1743–81] was truly German'.[19] Indeed, of all the authors whom Steffens surveys in the passage quoted by Hare, only, pointedly, the *Neoclassical* writers Johan Herman Wessel (1742–85) and Ludwig Holberg (1684–1754) are 'truly *national*'.[20]

It perhaps needs to be emphasised, again, that in the passage which Hare quotes, this relationship is understood in wholly positive terms and is based, primarily, on a sense of cultural and linguistic 'alliance', on the conviction that the 'deepest' thoughts can be 'expressed with equal ease in both languages'.[21] 'This intimate [Danish] brotherhood with the nation in Europe intellectually the most important is', the quotation continues, 'a blessing, not a disgrace.'[22] What we can see, then, in Hare's justification of his choice of Oehlenschläger as an appropriate subject for an essay on German drama, and in the quotation from Steffens which Hare brings in to support that justification, is how the paradigm of a regional literature can, even when it is motivated positively in Romantic-period cultural texts, destabilise precisely those national Romantic literatures which it is meant to elevate. Hence the tortured recognition, in the passage which Hare quotes, that 'Denmark exhibits traces of a peculiar [i.e. distinctive] intellectual existence, and even if these are unable to constitute a peculiar literature, they yet impress their character upon many directions of intellectual activity.'[23] The difficulty, as I argued in my discussion of European Romanticism in my introduction to this book, consists precisely in the attempt to negotiate the respective and often rival claims of national and international traditions. This is a difficulty of which Romantic-period cultural texts are often intensely aware and at times explicitly thematise. But it is also, as we can see in the case of Hare's essay, a difficulty which besets the critic more than the artist, the commentator on Oehlenschläger more than Oehlenschläger himself, since it is the task, or the fate, of the critic to attempt to map the landscapes through which authors wander freely. As Hare puts it in his essay, there is 'one class of writers, who write *about* things, another who write *the things themselves*'.[24]

With this thought in mind, we might end by recalling Christoph Bode's insistence that 'Romanticism' is 'a *construct* (a concept which we have developed because we have reason to believe it is useful as a *tool*)'.[25] Taking the largely forgotten history of Anglo-Danish relations in the late eighteenth and early nineteenth centuries as a case in point, *British Romanticism and Denmark* has examined how we might 'reconceptualise', to use Bode's term, our understanding of the ways in which two individual national Romanticisms interacted across political and linguistic borders, even during a period of declared war between the two countries involved.[26] In doing so, I hope the book has never lost sight of the myriad complexities involved in the attempt to map those interactions or 'turned a bind eye' (to use an expression which derives from the Battle of Copenhagen in 1801) to the trees while seeking to describe the wood.

Appendices

Appendix to Chapter 2

Translations by William Hayley (1745–1820) and Leigh Hunt (1784–1859) of verses inscribed, in French, on various monuments at the Dronninggaard estate, north of Copenhagen, which were transcribed by John Carr (1772–1823) during his visit in 1804. The translations are reproduced from John Carr, *A Northern Summer; or Travels round the Baltic, through Denmark, Sweden, Russia, Prussia, and Part of Germany, in the Year 1804* (London, 1805).

'The Hermit's Epitaph'
[William Hayley's translation, from *A Northern Summer*, p. 67]

    Here may he rest, who, shunning scenes of strife,
    Enjoy'd at Dronningaard a Hermit's life;
    The faithless splendour of a court he knew,
        And all the ardour of the tented field,
5   Soft Passion's idler charm, not less untrue,
        And all that listless luxury can yield.
    He tasted, tender Love! thy chaster sweet;
    Thy promis'd happiness prov'd mere deceit.
    To Hymen's hallow'd fane by Reason led,
10   He deem'd the path he trod, the path of bliss;
    Oh! ever mourn'd mistake! from int'rest bred,
        Its dupe was plung'd in Misery's abyss.
    But Friendship offer'd him, benignant power,
    Her cheering hand, in trouble's darkest hour.
15   Beside this shaded stream, her soothing voice
        Bade the disconsolate again rejoice:
    Peace in his heart revives, serenely sweet;
        The calm content so sought for as his choice,
    Quits him no more in this belov'd retreat.

* * *

'Farewell of the Hermit of Dronningaard'
[Leigh Hunt's translation, from *A Northern Summer*, pp. 68–9]

    Vain would life's pilgrim, lingering on his way,
        Snatch the short respite of a summer's day;
        Pale Sorrow, bending o'er his sad repose,
        Still finds a tear in ev'ry shelt'ring rose:
5   Still breaks his dream, and leads th'unwilling slave
        To weep, and wander to a distant grave.
        E'en he, whose steps since life's ungenial morn
        Have found no path unfretted with rude thorn,
        From all he lov'd must turn his looks away,
10   Far, far from thee, fair Dronningaard, must stray,
        Must leave the Eden of his fancy's dreams,
        Its twilight groves and long-resounding streams;
        Streams, where the tears of fond regret have ran,
        And back return to sorrow and to man!
15   O yet once more, ye groves, your sighs repeat,
        And bid farewell to these reluctant feet:
        Once more arise, thou soft, thou soothing wave,
        In weeping murmurs, ere I seek my grave,
        Ere yet a thousand social ills I share,
20   Consuming war, and more consuming care,
        Pleasures that ill conceal their future pains,
        Virtue in want, blest Liberty in chains,
        Vice, proud and powerful as the winter's wind,
        And all the dire deliriums of mankind.

25   Yet e'en this heart may hail its rest to come:
        Sorrow, thy reign is ended in the tomb!
        There close the eyes, that wept their fires away;
        There drop the hands that clasp'd to mourn and pray;
        There sleeps the restlessness of aching hearts;
30   There Love, the tyrant, buries all his darts!
        O grant me, heav'n, thus sweetly to repose!
        'Tis thus my soul shall triumph o'er its woes;
        Spring from the world, nor drop one painful tear
        On all it leaves, on all it treasures here;
35   Save once, perhaps, when pensive moonlight gleams
        O'er Dronningaard's meek shades and murmuring streams,
        The sacred grief, to dear remembrance true,
        O'er her soft flow'rs may shed its gentlest dew,
        May once in sounds, that soothe the suff'ring mind,
40   Breathe its lorn murmurs through the solemn wind;
        Lament, sweet spot, thy charms must wither'd be,
        And linger e'en from heav'n to sigh for thee!

* * *

Appendix to Chapter 3

Four Danish Romantic-period poems translated by Andreas Andersen Feldborg (1782–1838) and William Sidney Walker (1795–1846) and published in *Poems from the Danish* (1815).

'The Popular Naval Song of Denmark'
[by Johannes Evald (1743–81); text from *Poems from the Danish*, pp. 9–11]

     KING CHRISTIAN took his fearless stand
     'Midst smoke and night:
     A thousand weapons rang around,
     The red blood spun from many a wound,
5   'Midst smoke and steam to the profound
     Sunk Sweden's might!
     'Fly, sons of Swedes! what heart may dare
     With Demark's Christian to compare
     In fight?'

10   NILS YULE beheld the storm roll nigh;
     'The hour is come!'
     He waves the crimson flag on high
     The blows in doubling vollies fly,
     ''Tis come,' the foes of Denmark cry,
15   'Our day of doom!
     Fly ye who can! what warrior dares
     Meet Denmark's Yule, that man prepares
     His tomb!'

     Sea of the North! aloft behold
20   Thy third bolt fly!
     Thy chilly lap receives the bold,
     For terror fights with TORDENSKOLD,
     And Sweden's shrieks, like death-bell toll'd,
     Ring through the sky.
25   Onward the bolt of Denmark rolls;
     'Swedes! to heaven commit your souls,
     And fly!'

     Thou darksome deep! the Dane's pathway
     To might and fame!
30   Receive thy friend! whose spirit warm
     Springs to meet danger's coming form,
     As thy waves rise against the the storm
     And mounts to flame!

> 'Midst song and mirth life's path I'll tread,
35 And hasten to my ocean-bed
> Through fame.

* * *

'The Negro's Song'
[by Thomas Thaarup (1749–1821); text from *Poems from the Danish*, pp. 42–3]

> I will fly the social room,
> I will weep in lonely sadness;
> The poor negro's cherish'd gloom
> Must not mar the hour of gladness.
5 Let my fate your sighs command,
> Fetter'd in a distant land.
>
> Say, what is the negro's crime,
> Ye who in our blood engrave it?
> Can the colour of our clime
10 Plead for sin with him who gave it?
> Gloomy is the negro's breast,
> Robb'd of her he loves the best.
>
> God of Christians, God of men!
> Thou canst melt the heart of scorn;
15 May none e'er the bridegroom chain,
> From his new-espoused torn!
> Let our fate thy pity move,
> Robb'd of country and of love!

* * *

'Infancy'
[by Jens Baggesen (1764–1826); text from *Poems from the Danish*, pp. 44–6]

> There was a time, and I recal it well,
> When my whole frame was but an ell in height;
> Oh! when I think of that, my warm tears swell,
> And therefore in the memory I delight.
>
5 I sported in my mother's kind embraces,
> And climb'd my grandsire's venerable knee;
> Unknown were care, and rage, and sorrow's traces;
> To me the world was blest as blest could be.

           I mark'd no frowns the world's smooth surface wrinkle,
10   Its mighty space seem'd little to my eye;
           I saw the stars, like sparks, at distance twinkle,
              And wish'd myself a bird, to soar so high.

           I saw the moon behind the hills retiring,
              And thought the while – Oh! would I were but there!
15   Then could mine eye examine without tiring
              That radiant thing, how large, how round, how fair.

           Wond'ring I saw the sun of God depart
              To slumber in the golden lap of even,
           And from the east again in beauty dart
20   To bathe in crimson all the field of heaven.

           I thought on him, the Father all-bestowing,
              Who made me, and that beauteous orb on high,
           And all the little stars, that nightly glowing
              Deck'd like a row of pearls the azure sky.

25   To him with infant piety I faulter'd
              The prayer my pious mother taught me:
           "Oh! gracious God! be it my aim unalter'd,
              Still to be wise and good, and follow thee!"

           For her I pray'd, and for my father too,
30   My sister dear, and the community,
           The king, whom yet by name alone I knew,
              And that mendicant that sighing totter'd by.

           Those days were matchless sweet – but they are perish'd,
              And life is thorny now, and dim, and flat;
35   Yet rests their memory – deeply – fondly cherish'd;
              God! in thy mercy take not – take not that.

                              *   *   *

'Dedicatory Lines, to Her Royal Highness, Princess Louisa Augusta, Princess
     Royal of Denmark; prefixed to a Danish translation of
          Shakespeare's *Hamlet* and *Julius Caesar*'
     [by Peter Foersom (1777–1817); text from *Poems from the
                    Danish*, pp. 64–5]

           Snatch'd from the scenic monarch's glorious crown,
              A few stray gems I bring. Before thy feet,
           xalted fair, in every charm complete,
              With rev'rence and delight I lay them down.

                Their home was ever in the princely breast;
5   That crowned vestal, western sun of fame,
                She loved them; and in their unfading flame
                The image of her brightness shines confess'd.
                As when the flow'rets of the spring unfold
10   Their censers, with the pearls of morn replete,
                Nature's sweet sacrifice, the lordly sun
                Joys to illumine them; on my offering bold,
                Sun of the North, from the resplendent seat,
                Of all thy countless rays, oh, shed but one!

Notes

Introduction: 'The country of our ancestors'

1. Andrew Swinton, *Travels into Norway, Denmark, and Russia, in the years 1788, 1789, 1790, and 1791* (London, 1792), pp. 11, 12. 'Andrew Swinton' is a pseudonym of William Thomson, who later published *Letters from Scandinavia* (1796) under his own name.
2. Swinton, *Travels into Norway, Denmark, and Russia*, pp. 11, 12. In Classical times, Jutland was known as the Cimbrian Peninsula, *Cimbricus Chersonesus*.
3. Thomas Percy, *Northern Antiquities: or, A Description of the Manners, Customs, Religion and Laws of the Ancient Danes*, 2 vols (London, 1770), vol. 1, pp. 260–1. Percy's book is a translation of Mallet's *Introduction à l'histoire du Danemarch où l'on traite de la religion, des mœurs, des lois, et des usages des anciens Danois*, 3 vols (Copenhagen, 1758–77).
4. Percy, *Northern Antiquities*, vol. 1, pp. 261–2. Hence 'when the Danes again inherited England about three or four hundred years after', Percy continues, 'and finally conquered it toward the latter end of the tenth century, they waged war with the descendants of their own ancestors' (p. 262).
5. As only the most recent of the many excellent works on this topic, see Marilyn Butler, *Mapping Mythologies: Countercurrents in Eighteenth-Century British Poetry and Cultural History* (Cambridge: Cambridge University Press, 2015). See also Rosemary Sweet, *Antiquaries: The Discovery of the Past in Eighteenth-Century Britain* (London: Hambledon & London, 2004).
6. Hildor Arnold Barton, *Northern Arcadia: Foreign Travellers in Scandinavia, 1765–1815* (Carbondale, IL: Southern Illinois University Press, 1998), p. 3. For the influence of antiquarian interest in the classical Scandinavian past on late eighteenth- and early nineteenth-century British literature, see, for example: Sigurd Hustvedt, *Ballad Criticism in Scandinavia and Great Britain during the Eighteenth Century* (New York: American Scandinavian Foundation, 1916); Peter Mortensen, *British Romanticism and Continental Influences* (London: Palgrave, 2004), Chapter 3, 'Romantic Writers among the Norsemen', pp. 173–207; Lis Møller, 'British and Danish Romantic-Period Adaptations of Two Danish Elf Ballads', in Cian Duffy (ed.), *Romantic Norths: Anglo-Nordic Exchanges, 1770–1842* (London: Palgrave, 2016), pp. 129–52; Robert Rix (ed.), *Norse Romanticism: Themes in British Literature, 1760–1830*, Romantic Circles: https://romantic-circles.org/editions/norse/index.html (accessed April 2021); and Robert Rix, '"The North" and "the East": The Odin Migration Theory', in Duffy (ed.), *Romantic Norths*, pp. 153–79. For antiquarianism and

Danish Romanticism, see Karen Sanders, '"On the bedrock of material things": The Journey to the Past in Danish Archaeological Imagination', in Karen Klitgaard Povlsen (ed.), *Northbound: Travels, Encounters, and Constructions, 1700–1830* (Aarhus: Aarhus University Press, 2007), pp. 151–70; and Robert Rix, '"In darkness they grope": Ancient Remains and Romanticism in Denmark', *European Romantic Review*, 26/4 (July 2015), pp. 435–51.

7. William Rae Wilson, *Travels in Norway, Sweden, Denmark, Hanover, Germany, Netherlands &c.* (London, 1826), p. 433.
8. Anon., 'On Feldberg's Denmark', in *Blackwood's Edinburgh Magazine*, 10 (September 1821), p. 172.
9. Nelson's despatch is preserved in the National Archives of Britain (ADM 1/4 (Ha 54)).
10. Mortensen, *British Romanticism and Continental Influences*, p. 1.
11. Mortensen, *British Romanticism and Continental Influences*, p. 2.
12. See René Wellek, 'The Concept of "Romanticism" in Literary History II: The Unity of European Romanticism', *Comparative Literature* 1/2 (Spring 1949), pp. 147–72. Mortensen himself grants that his 'revisionist claim that British Romantic-period writers owed considerable debts to Continental pre-Romanticism is far from unprecedented' (*British Romanticism and Continental Influences*, p. 6).
13. Diego Saglia, *European Literatures in Britain, 1815–1832* (Cambridge: Cambridge University Press, 2019), p. 4. 'Over the last ten to fifteen years', Saglia notes, 'Romantic-period scholarship and criticism in the Anglo-American tradition has seen a significant multiplication of studies about trans-Channel literary exchanges, cosmopolitanism, and Transatlantic cultural traffic' (4).
14. See https://www.euromanticism.org/project-reve/ (last April 2021).
15. Paul Hamilton (ed.), *The Oxford Handbook of European Romanticism* (Oxford: Oxford University Press, 2016), p. 1. See Arthur O. Lovejoy, 'On the Discrimination of Romanticisms', *PMLA* 39/2 (June 1924), pp. 229–53; and Wellek, 'The Concept of "Romanticism"'.
16. Stephen Prickett (ed.), *European Romanticism: A Reader* (London: Continuum, 2010), p. 11.
17. See, for example, Gertrud Oelsner, 'Inventing Jutland for the "Golden Age": Danish Artists Guided by Sir Walter Scott' (pp. 101–28) and Lis Møller, 'British and Danish Romantic-Period Adaptations of Two Danish "Elf Ballads"' (pp. 129–52).
18. Saglia, *European Literatures in Britain*, pp. 6, 14, vii.
19. Prickett, *European Romanticism*, p. 1.
20. Percy Bysshe Shelley, 'A Defence of Poetry' (1821), quoted from *Selected Poetry and Prose*, ed. Jack Donovan and Cian Duffy (London: Penguin, 2017), pp. 655–6.
21. Shelley, 'Defence of Poetry', p. 656.
22. Silvia Bordoni, 'From Madame de Staël to Lord Byron: The Dialectics of European Romanticism', *Literature Compass* 4/1 (2007), pp. 134–49 (135).
23. William Coxe, *Travels into Poland, Russia, Sweden and Denmark*, 2 vols (London, 1784), vol. 2, p. 599.
24. Aidan Day, *Romanticism* (New York: Routledge, 1996), p. xi.
25. Christoph Bode, 'Europe', in Nicholas Roe (ed.), *Romanticism: An Oxford Guide* (Oxford: Oxford University Press, 2005), pp. 126–36 (126; original emphasis)
26. Bode, 'Europe', p. 126; original emphasis.

27. Bode, 'Europe', pp. 134, 135.
28. Bode, 'Europe', p. 135.
29. Hamilton, *European Romanticism*, p. 2. For recent work in this area, see, for example, the essays in the festschrift presented to Bode himself on his retirement: Sebastian Domsch, Christoph Reinfandt and Katharina Rennhak (eds), *Romantic Ambiguities: Abodes of the Modern* (Trier: WVT, 2017).
30. Joep Leerssen, *National Thought in Europe: A Cultural History* (Chicago: University of Chicago Press, 2007), p. 21. See Duffy (ed.), *Romantic Norths*, pp. 3–4.
31. Leerssen, *National Thought in Europe*, p. 17. Cp. Leerssen's more recent definition of Romantic nationalism as 'the celebration of the nation (defined in its language, history, and cultural character) as an inspiring idea for artistic expression; and the instrumentalization of that expression in political consciousness-raising', in Joep Leerssen, 'Notes towards a Definition of Romantic Nationalism', *Romantik* 2 (2013), pp. 9–35 (28).
32. Colin Kidd, *British Identities before Nationalism: Ethnicity and Nationhood in the Atlantic World, 1600–1800* (Cambridge: Cambridge University Press, 1999), p. 215.
33. Linda Colley, *Britons: Forging the Nation, 1707–1837* (New Haven: Yale University Press, 1992; revised 2009).
34. Mortensen, *British Romanticism and Continental Influences*, p. 9.
35. Mortensen, *British Romanticism and Continental Influences*, pp. 12–13; William Wordsworth, 'Preface' to *Lyrical Ballads* (1802); quoted from William Wordsworth, *The Major Works*, ed. Stephen Gill (Oxford: Oxford University Press, 2011), p. 599. Unless otherwise indicated, Wordsworth's writings are quoted from this edition.
36. See, for example, Michael Roberts, *The Age of Liberty: Sweden 1719–22* (Cambridge: Cambridge University Press, 2003); and Bente Scavenius, *The Golden Age in Denmark: Art and Culture, 1800–1850* (Copenhagen: Gyldendal, 1994).
37. Prickett, *European Romanticism*, p. 5. See Katie Trumpener, *Bardic Nationalism* (Princeton: Princeton University Press, 1997) and Murray Pittock, *Scottish and Irish Romanticism* (Oxford: Oxford University Press, 2008). Other studies in this tradition include: Gerald Carruthers and Anthony Rawe (eds), *English Romanticism and the Celtic World* (Cambridge: Cambridge University Press, 2003). See also David Duff and Catherine Jones (eds), *Scotland, Ireland, and the Romantic Aesthetic* (Lewisburg: Bucknell University Press, 2007).
38. Saglia, *European Literatures in Britain*, p. 19.
39. Mortensen, *British Romanticism and Continental Influences*, pp. 15–16.
40. Saglia, *European Literatures in Britain*, pp. 4, 5.
41. Saglia, *European Literatures in Britain*, p. 5.
42. Thomas De Quincey, 'John Paul Friedrich Richter', quoted from *The Works of Thomas De Quincey*, gen. ed. Grevel Lindop, 21 vols (London: Pickering & Chatto, 2000–2003), vol. 3, p. 18.
43. De Quincey, 'Richter', p. 18. Saglia opens *European Literatures in Britain* with this same passage from De Quincey, though I disagree with Saglia's sense that it 'echoes with the fear of miscegenation and hybridization that permeates [De Quincey's] *Confessions of an English Opium-Eater*, published in the *London Magazine* in the same year' (p. 1).

44. Wordsworth, 'Preface' to *Lyrical Ballads* (1802), p. 597.
45. Germaine de Staël, *Germany*, 3 vols (London, 1813), vol. 1, p. 1.
46. Germaine de Staël, *The Influence of Literature upon Society*, 2 vols (London, 1812), vol. 1, p. 269.
47. Controversy concerning the authenticity of the poems which the Scot James Macpherson had published in the 1760s as the work of an ancient bard called Ossian broke out almost immediately and remained heated during the Romantic period; the cultural impact of the Ossian poems at the time, in both Britain and Europe, was, however, substantial. For an overview, see Howard Gaskill (ed.), *The Reception of Ossian in Europe* (London: Continuum, 2004).
48. De Staël, *The Influence of Literature*, vol. 1, p. 269.
49. De Staël, *The Influence of Literature*, vol. 1, p. 271.
50. De Staël, *The Influence of Literature*, vol. 1, pp. 271, 272.
51. De Staël, *The Influence of Literature*, vol. 1, p. 273.
52. De Staël, *The Influence of Literature*, vol. 1, p. 273.
53. De Staël, *The Influence of Literature*, vol. 1, p. 273.
54. Duffy (ed.), *Romantic Norths*, p. 2.
55. Duffy (ed.), *Romantic Norths*, p. 1.
56. See Povlsen, *Northbound*, pp. 16, 15; and Robert Rix, 'Introduction: Romanticism in Scandinavia', *European Romantic Review* 26/4 (July 2015), pp. 395–400 (395).
57. Peter Fjågesund, *The Dream of the North: A Cultural History to 1920* (Amsterdam: Rodopi, 2014), p. 17.
58. Hendriette Kliemann-Geisinger, 'Mapping the North – Spatial Dimensions and Geographical Conceptions of Northern Europe', in Povlsen (ed.), *Northbound*, pp. 69–88 (69).
59. Øystein Sørensen and Bo Stråth (eds), *The Cultural Construction of Norden* (Oslo: Scandinavian University Press, 1997), p. 1.
60. See Fjågesund, *Dream of the North*, p. 17. See also Sylvain Briens, 'Boréalisme: Le Nord comme espace discursif', in *Études germaniques* 71 (2016), pp. 179–88.
61. See Barton, *Northern Arcadia*; Mark Davies, *A Perambulating Paradox: British Travel Literature and the Image of Sweden, c. 1770–1865* (Lund: Lund University, 2000); and Peter Fjågesund and Ruth Symes, *The Northern Utopia: British Perceptions of Norway in the Nineteenth Century* (Amsterdam: Rodopi, 2003), p. 21.
62. Penny Fielding, *Scotland and the Fictions of Geography* (Cambridge: Cambridge University Press, 2008), p. 14.
63. Fielding, *Scotland*, pp. 10–11.
64. Robert Molesworth, *An Account of Denmark, as it was in the Year 1692*, sixth edition (Glasgow, 1752), p. xii.
65. Molesworth, *Account of Denmark*, p. 59.
66. Molesworth, *Account of Denmark*, p. xv.
67. Molesworth, *Account of Denmark*, pp. 64–5. National stereotypes, of course, always run both ways. In *A Northern Summer* (London, 1805), John Carr records a 'Danish gentleman' having told him that, while 'he had heard the English women were very pretty [. . .,] he was confident he could never love them [. . .] because he understood they were never seen without a pipe in their mouths!' (p. 76).

68. Molesworth, *Account of Denmark*, p. 68.
69. Molesworth, *Account of Denmark*, p. 8.
70. Molesworth, *Account of Denmark*, pp. 50, 183.
71. Molesworth, *Account of Denmark*, pp. xxi, 32.
72. Molesworth, *Account of Denmark*, p. 29.
73. Molesworth, *Account of Denmark*, p. xxxi.
74. Molesworth, *Account of Denmark*, p. xxx.
75. Compare, in this respect, Elisabeth Oxfeldt's argument in *Nordic Orientalism* (Copenhagen: Museum Tusculanum, 2005) that, far from defining themselves in opposition to an Oriental other, Danes themselves often 'embraced an imaginary Orient in an effort to identify and construct themselves as a modern, cosmopolitan nation' (p. 12).
76. Mary Wollstonecraft, *Letters Written during a Short Residence in Sweden, Norway, and Denmark* (London, 1796), pp. 214, 202.
77. Andreas Andersen Feldborg, *Denmark Delineated; or, Sketches of the Present State of that Country* (Edinburgh, 1824), 'Appendix', p. 58.
78. Jodocus Crull, *Denmark Vindicated: Being an Answer to a Late Treatise called An Account of Denmark* (London, 1694), pp. xvi, xxii, xxiii.
79. Crull, *Denmark Vindicated*, p. xxii.
80. Crull, *Denmark Vindicated*, p. xxiii.
81. Joseph Marshall, *Travels through Holland, Flanders, Germany, Denmark, Sweden, Lapland, Russia, the Ukraine, and Poland, in the Years 1768, 1769, and 1770*, 8 vols (London, 1772), vol. 2, p. 277.
82. Marshall, *Travels*, vol. 2, p. 277.
83. Marshall, *Travels*, vol. 2, p. 285.
84. Marshall, *Travels*, vol. 2, p. 167.
85. William Herbert, *Select Icelandic Poetry, Translated from the Originals: with Notes* (London, 1804), 'Dedication'.
86. Barton, *Northern Arcadia*, p. 59.
87. William Coxe, *Travels into Poland, Russia, Sweden, and Denmark*, 2 vols (London, 1784), vol. 2, p. 524.
88. George Gordon, Lord Byron, *The Curse of Minerva* (London, 1813), lines 213–16.
89. John Murray (ed.), *Hand-Book for Travellers in Denmark, Norway, Sweden, and Russia* (London, 1829), p. 28.
90. Murray, *Hand-Book*, p. 29.
91. Quoted from Just Mathias Thiele, *Af mit Livs Aarbøger. I. 1795–1838* (Copenhagen: C. A. Reitzel, 1917), pp. 157–8; my translation.
92. Anon., 'On Feldberg's Denmark', p. 172.
93. Barton, *Northern Arcadia*, pp. 83, 113.
94. Carr, *Northern Summer*, p. 4; Barton, *Northern Arcadia*, p. 147.
95. Anon., 'Notices of Danish Literature', in *The New Monthly Magazine*, vol. 11, number 61 (July 1819), pp. 487–92 (492).
96. Anon., 'Notices of Danish Literature', p. 492.
97. Kristian Smidt, 'The Discovery of Shakespeare in Scandinavia', in Dirk Delabastita and Lieven D'hulst (eds), *European Shakespeares: Translating Shakespeare in the Romantic Age* (Amsterdam: John Benjamins, 1993), pp. 91–103 (92).
98. Robert Southey, *Life of Nelson*, 2 vols (London, 1813), vol. 2, p. 143.

99. Anon., *Candide, ou, l'Optimisme. Traduit de l'Allemand de Mr. le Docteur Ralph, Seconde Partie* (1761; no place of publication given), p. 98: 'Tout n'est pas aussi bien que dans El Dorado; mais tout ne va pas mal.'
100. Marshall, *Travels*, vol. 2, p. 290.
101. Julius Charles Hare, 'The German Drama. No. 1. Oehlenschlaeger', in Charles Ollier's *Literary Miscellany, in Prose and Verse, by Several Hands*, 1 (1820), pp. 90–153 (104, 92).

Chapter 1: 'One of the finest capitals of Europe': Some British Romantic Views of Copenhagen

1. Robert Southey, *Life of Nelson*, second edition, 2 vols (London, 1814), vol. 2, p. 107.
2. Robert Southey, letter to Thomas Southey of 28 April 1797 (quoted from Lynda Pratt, Tim Fulford and Ian Packer (eds), *The Collected Letters of Robert Southey*, pt 1 (ed. Lynda Pratt), at: http://www.rc.umd.edu/editions/southey_letters/Part_One/HTML/letterEEd.26.213.html (last accessed April 2021).
3. William Coxe, *Travels into Poland, Russia, Sweden, and Denmark*, 2 vols (London, 1784), vol. 2, p. 524.
4. Richard Jones, *Copenhagen and its Environs. Compiled after the best Authors* (Copenhagen, 1829), pp. 1, 5.
5. Percy Bysshe Shelley, 'Fragment of a Poem; the original idea of which was suggested by the cowardly and infamous bombardment of Copenhagen' (1811), lines 14, 29, 15–21.
6. Nathaniel Wraxall, *A Tour through Some of the Northern Parts of Europe, particularly Copenhagen, Stockholm, and Petersburgh. In a Series of Letters*, third edition (London, 1776), p. 14.
7. Wraxall, *Tour*, p. 23. Wraxall suggests that 'a month or five weeks is fully adequate to the completion of these purposes' (*Tour*, p. 23).
8. Wraxall, *Tour*, pp. 36–7.
9. Wraxall, *Tour*, p. 22.
10. Wraxall, *Tour*, pp. 23–4.
11. Wraxall, *Tour*, pp. 21.
12. Wraxall, *Tour*, pp. 20, 53.
13. Wraxall, *Tour*, pp. 19, 30, 55, 57.
14. Wraxall, *Tour*, pp. 29, 60.
15. Wraxall, *Tour*, p. 24.
16. Wraxall, *Tour*, p. 61.
17. Wraxall, *Tour*, p. 61. Wraxall's claims about the absence of 'industry or business' at Copenhagen might also be read alongside stereotypical eighteenth-century representations of 'Oriental' indolence. Late eighteenth- and early nineteenth-century accounts of Istanbul, for example, often draws comparable conclusions about the failure of the Ottoman government to utilise the resources of the city to best advantage. See, for instance, Edward Clarke on Istanbul in *Travels in Various Countries of Europe, Asia, and Africa*, three parts, 6 vols (London, 1810–23), i, p. 691: 'Under a wise

government, the inhabitants [. . .] might obtain the riches of all the empires of the earth. Situated as they are, it cannot be long before other nations, depriving them of such important sources of wealth, will convert to better purposes the advantages they have so long neglected.' In Chapter 4, I discuss the role of 'indolence' in British discussions of the Danish national character.
18. Anon., *Observations on the Present State of Denmark, Russia, and Switzerland. In a Series of Letters* (London, 1784), p. 24n. There is some evidence to suggest that the *Observations* were authored by the Oxford Divine and anti-slavery campaigner Francis Randolph (1714–97).
19. Anon., *Observations*, p. 2.
20. Anon., *Observations*, pp. 2–3.
21. Coxe, *Travels*, vol. 2, p. 526.
22. Coxe, *Travels*, vol. 2, p. 525,
23. Coxe, *Travels*, vol. 2, p. 525.
24. Coxe, *Travels*, vol. 2, p. 525.
25. Coxe, *Travels*, vol. 2, p. 554.
26. Coxe, *Travels*, vol. 2, p. 554.
27. Coxe, *Travels*, vol. 2, pp. 554–5.
28. Coxe, *Travels*, vol. 2, p. 556.
29. Coxe, *Travels*, vol. 2, p. 557.
30. Coxe, *Travels*, vol. 2, p. 563.
31. Coxe, *Travels*, vol. 2, pp. 565, 564. For more on the *Flora Danica* compendium and the porcelain dinner service based on it, and intended as a gift for Catherine the Great of Russia (1729–96), see Cian Duffy, 'The Flora Danica Dinner Service', on *Rêve: The Virtual Exhibition*, 5 March 2021, http://www.euromanticism.org/the-flora-danica-dinner-service/ (last accessed April 2021).
32. Coxe, *Travels*, vol. 2, p. 568.
33. Coxe, *Travels*, vol. 2, p. 568.
34. Coxe, *Travels*, vol. 2, p. 569.
35. Matthew Consett, *A Tour through Sweden, Swedish-Lapland, Finland and Denmark. In a Series of Letters* (London, 1789), pp. 137, 141.
36. Consett, *Tour*, p. 137.
37. Consett, *Tour*, pp. 142, 143.
38. Consett, *Tour*, pp. 142, 140.
39. Consett, *Tour*, pp. 142, 144.
40. Consett, *Tour*, pp. 138, 140.
41. A. Swinton (pseudonym of William Thomson), *Travels into Norway, Denmark, and Russia, in the Years 1788, 1789, 1790, and 1791* (London, 1792), p. 1.
42. Swinton, *Travels*, v.
43. Swinton, *Travels*, v.
44. Swinton, *Travels*, v–vi.
45. Swinton, *Travels*, pp. 11, 36–7.
46. Swinton, *Travels*, p. 38. This 'misunderstanding' to which Thomson diplomatically refers is, of course, the controversy surrounding the treatment of Caroline Matilda (see Chapter 5).
47. Swinton, *Travels*, p. 25.

48. Swinton, *Travels*, p. 25.
49. Swinton, *Travels*, pp. 27–8, 25.
50. William Thomson, *Letters from Scandinavia*, 2 vols (London, 1796), vol. 2, pp. 450–1.
51. Thomson, *Letters*, vol. 2, p. 450.
52. Thomson, *Letters*, vol. 2, p. 451.
53. Thomson, *Letters*, vol. 2, p. 450.
54. Thomson, *Letters*, vol. 2, p. 449.
55. Thomson, *Letters*, vol. 2, p. 450.
56. Mary Wollstonecraft, *Letters Written during a Short Residence in Sweden, Norway and Denmark* (London, 1796), p. 197.
57. Christoph Bode, '"Imaginary circles round the human mind": Bias and Openness in Mary Wollstonecraft's *Letters Written during a Short Residence in Sweden, Norway, and Denmark* (1796)', in Cian Duffy (ed.), *Romantic Norths: Anglo-Nordic Exchanges, 1770–1842* (London: Palgrave, 2017), pp. 29–52 (47, 48). As Bode notes, Wollstonecraft herself acknowledges, on more than one occasion in *Short Residence*, that she may be 'jaundiced' or 'prejudiced' in her opinions. See also Cian Duffy, '"The happiest country in the world": Mary Wollstonecraft in Denmark', *The Wordsworth Trust* (https://wordsworth.org.uk/blog/2015/09/14/the-happiest-country-in-the-world-mary-wollstonecraft-in-denmark/); last accessed April 2021.
58. Bode, '"Imaginary Circles"', pp. 29–30. See Per Nyström, *Mary Wollstonecraft's Scandinavian Journey*, Acts of the Royal Society of Arts and Sciences of Gothenburg, Humaniora 17 (1980).
59. William Godwin, *Memoirs of the Author of A Vindication of the Rights of Woman* (London, 1798), p. 133.
60. Quoted from Janet Todd (ed.), *The Collected Letters of Mary Wollstonecraft* (London: Allen Lane, 2003), p. 320.
61. Todd (ed.), *Collected Letters*, p. 320.
62. For studies of the importance of ruin sentiment in eighteenth-century English literature, and of its relationship with discourses of travel, nationalism and empire, see Anne Jannowitz, *England's Ruins: Poetic Purpose and the National Landscape* (Oxford: Basil Blackwell, 1990); and Laurence Goldstein, *Ruins and Empire: The Evolution of a Theme in Augustan and Romantic Literature* (Pittsburgh: University of Pittsburgh Press, 1977).
63. For detailed discussion of Wollstonecraft's assessment of the Danish national character, as she found it exhibited at Copenhagen, see Chapter 4.
64. Wollstonecraft, *Short Residence*, p. 198. As Richard Holmes notes in his edition of *Short Residence* (London: Penguin, 1987), this is 'one of the earliest references to the recreation of camping under canvas' (p. 120 n.109).
65. Wollstonecraft, *Short Residence*, p. 198.
66. Wollstonecraft, *Short Residence*, p. 198. Cp. Letter 17 of *Short Residence*, in which Wollstonecraft, describing the waterfall of Trollhättan, near Gothenburg, laments the extent to which human industry had disturbed the 'solitary sublimity' of the view (p. 191). Civil society, in whatever form, is an almost constant disturbance to Wollstonecraft in her *Short Residence*.
67. Wollstonecraft, *Short Residence*, p. 199.
68. Wollstonecraft, *Short Residence*, p 199.

69. Wollstonecraft, *Short Residence*, p. 199.
70. Wollstonecraft, *Short Residence*, pp. 201–2, 230.
71. Wollstonecraft, *Short Residence*, pp. 226–7.
72. Wollstonecraft, *Short Residence*, p. 227.
73. Wollstonecraft, *Short Residence*, p. 225.
74. Wollstonecraft, *Short Residence*, p. 220.
75. Wollstonecraft, *Short Residence*, p. 223.
76. Wollstonecraft, *Short Residence*, p. 223.
77. Wollstonecraft, *Short Residence*, p. 224.
78. Wollstonecraft, *Short Residence*, p. 225.
79. Wollstonecraft, *Short Residence*, pp. 230–1.
80. John Carr, *A Northern Summer; or Travels round the Baltic, through Denmark, Sweden, Russia, Prussia, and Part of Germany, in the Year 1804* (London, 1805), p. 79.
81. Wollstonecraft, *Short Residence*, p. 227.
82. Wollstonecraft, *Short Residence*, pp. 221–2.
83. Wollstonecraft, *Short Residence*, p. 230.
84. For detailed discussions of the background to and events of the Battle, see Ole Feldbaek, *The Battle of Copenhagen 1801: Nelson and the Danes*, transl. Tony Wedgwood (Copenhagen: Politikens Forlag, 2002 [1985]).
85. For the Barkers' panorama of Copenhagen, see, for example, the obituary for him in *The Gentleman's Magazine* for 10 October 1856 (vol. 201; pp. 515–18), which notes that Nelson was 'much pleased' by it (p. 517). The Battle of Copenhagen also gave rise to the expression 'to turn a blind eye': during the height of the battle, Nelson – who was blinded in his right-eye during an attack on Corsica in 1797 – put that eye to his telescope so that he could claim not to have seem Hyde Parker's signal to withdraw out of range of the Danish guns.
86. Nelson's despatch is preserved in the National Archives of Britain (ADM 1/4 (Ha 54), and available at www.nationalarchives.gov.uk/nelson/gallery6/popup/ultimatum_trans.htm. (last accessed April 2021).
87. National Archives of Britain (ADM 1/4 (Ha 54)).
88. Thomas Campbell, 'The Battle of the Baltic' (lines 1–4), quoted from Thomas Campbell, *Gertrude of Wyoming, and Other Poems*, second edition (London, 1810).
89. Campbell, 'Battle of the Baltic', lines 10, 13, 23, 28, 30, 31–2.
90. Campbell, 'Battle of the Baltic', lines 37–45.
91. Campbell, 'Battle of the Baltic', lines 46–9.
92. Campbell, 'Battle of the Baltic', lines 60–3.
93. John Fairburn, *Authentic Account of the Bombardment of Copenhagen, and the Surrender of the Danish Fleet* (London, 1807), p. 48.
94. Thomas Rodd, *The Battle of Copenhagen; A Poem, with Notes* (London, 1806), p. vii.
95. Rodd, *Battle of Copenhagen*, p. 13 (no line numbers given).
96. Rodd, *Battle of Copenhagen*, p. 72.
97. Rodd, *Battle of Copenhagen*, p. 78 (emphasis added).
98. Rodd, *Battle of Copenhagen*, p. 85.
99. Rodd, *Battle of Copenhagen*, pp. 98–9.
100. Rodd, *Battle of Copenhagen*, p. 99n.

101. Anon., 'On Lord Nelson's sending a flag of truce to Copenhagen in the midst of victory', lines 7–8, 18–20; quoted from *The Scots Magazine*, lxiii (May 1801), p. 350. The text is also available, with commentary, in Betty T. Bennett and Orianne Smith (eds), *British War Poetry in the Age of Romanticism*, at: https://www.rc.umd.edu/editions/warpoetry/index.html (last accessed April 2021).
102. Southey, *Life of Nelson*, vol. 2, p. 141.
103. Andreas Andersen Feldborg, *A Tour in Zealand, in the Year 1802; With an Historical Account of the Battle of Copenhagen. By a Native of Denmark*, second edition (London, 1805), p. 3 (pagination restarts for the 'Historical Account').
104. Feldborg, *Tour*, p. 63.
105. Andreas Andersen Feldborg, *A Tour in Zealand* (Philadelphia, 1807), p. 131.
106. Feldborg, *Tour* (1805), p. xvi.
107. J. A. Andersen (pseud.), *A Dane's Excursions in Britain. By J. A. Andersen, Author of A Tour in Zealand, etc.*, 2 vols (London, 1809), vol. 1, p. 15.
108. Feldborg, *A Dane's Excursions*, vol. 1, p. 19. It is tempting to suspect that this was the passage (on p. 39) in which Feldborg describes how 'two British line of battle ships ran foul of each other, and in that situation got aground, where they were raked by red hot balls from the battery of the Three Crowns (Trekroner), on which account Lord Nelson sent us the flag of truce'.
109. Feldborg, *A Dane's Excursions*, vol. 1, pp. 19–20 and n.
110. Edmund Burke, *Reflections on the Revolution in France* (London, 1790), p. 11.
111. F. L. Sommer, *A Description of Denmark; And a Narrative of the Siege, Bombardment, and Capture of Copenhagen [. . .] From the Danish Account of F. L. Sommer*, second edition (Colchester, 1808), p. 17. I discuss the complex provenance of Sommer's *Narrative* below. Named after its designer, William Congreve (1772–1828), the incendiary Congreve Rocket became part of the arsenal of the British navy in 1805.
112. Septimus Crookes, *Particulars of the Expedition to Copenhagen* (Sheffield, 1808), 'Dedication', p. i. Although the full title declares the author to be a 'Private in the Fourth, or King's own Regiment', the name Septimus Crookes may well be a pseudonym.
113. The events of 2–5 September 1807 have received far less attention from academic historians than those of 2 April 1801. For a Danish perspective, published to mark the two-hundredth anniversary of the bombardment, see the collection of historical and cultural historical essays *Det venskabelige bombardement* (Copenhagen: Museum Tusculanum, 2007) edited by Rasmus Glenthøj and Jens Rahbek Rasmussen. The title of this collection, 'The friendly bombardment', indicates the extent to which it was seen in both Denmark and Britain, at the time, as an attack by a friendly power on a neutral ally.
114. The Danish historian Jørgen Sevaldsen gives a fascinating overview of British responses in his essay '1807 i Storbritannien: Reaktioner i samtid og nutid' [1807 in Great Britain: reactions then and now], in Glenthøj and Rasmussen (eds), *Det venskabelige bombardement*, pp. 199–226. While a broad and perceptive survey of the cultural and academic history

of the bombardment in Britain from 1807 until 2007, however, including a sketch of parliamentary debates and notices by canonical Romantic-period poets, Sevaldsen's essay does not consider the many contemporary English-language prose accounts (no mention is made of Sommer) of the attack – and hence I cannot quite agree with his conclusion that the subject of contemporary responses is quickly exhausted ['et emne, der hurtig er udtømt'] (p. 199).

115. George III of England, 'The Declaration of his Britannic Majesty, Westminster Sep. 25, 1807', quoted in John Fairburn, *Authentic Account of the Bombardment of Copenhagen, and the Surrender of the Danish Fleet* (London, 1808), p. 25.
116. Sevaldsen summarises the key positions in these debates in '1807 i Storbritanien', pp. 201-06. See also Burton R. Pollin, 'Southey's "Battle of Blenheim" Parodied in the *Morning Chronicle*: A Whig Attack on the Battle of Copenhagen', *Bulletin of the New York Public Library*, 72 (1968), pp. 507–17 (511–14).
117. Gillray's cartoon is available via the British Library here: http://www.britishmuseum.org/research/collection_online/collection_object_details.aspx?objectId=1640414&partId=1 (last accessed April 2021).
118. See David Erdman, 'Blake's transcript of Bisset's "Lines Written on hearing the surrender of Copenhagen"', in *Bulletin of The New York Public Library*, 72 (1968), pp. 518–21.
119. James Bisset, 'Lines Written on hearing the surrender of Copenhagen', lines 1, 21–3, 33; quoted from Erdman, 'Blake's Transcript', p. 519.
120. *The Spirit of the Public Journals: 1808*, 12 (1808), p. 62; original emphasis.
121. Pollin, 'Southey's "Battle of Blenheim" Parodied in the *Morning Chronicle*', p. 507.
122. Coleridge's defence of the bombardment in an allegory published in *The Friend* on 15 February 1810, and in a series of letters, are discussed by Pollin in 'Southey's "Battle of Blenheim" Parodied in the *Morning Chronicle*', p. 514.
123. 'Song on the New Affair of Copenhagen (Not Lord Nelson's)', lines 1–4; quoted from Betty T. Bennett and Orianne Smith (eds), *British War Poetry in the Age of Romanticism*, at: https://www.rc.umd.edu/editions/warpoetry/index.html (last accessed March 2020). Sevaldsen also discusses this 'Song' in '1807 i Storbritannien', p. 208.
124. George Gordon, Lord Byron, 'The Curse of Minerva' (1811), ll. 213–14.
125. De Quincey describes the circumstances of his brother's captivity and release in his essay 'My Brother', the twelfth chapter of the first volume of his posthumously published *Autobiographic Sketches*, which he composed in 1853; see *The Works of Thomas De Quincey*, gen. ed. Grevel Lindop, 21 vols (London: Pickering & Chatto, 2000–3), vol. 19, pp. 204–5.
126. William Wordsworth, 'The Sailor's Mother', lines 20–2.
127. *The Monthly Magazine*, 24 (1807), p. 24; see also the *Universal Magazine*, 3 (July–December 1807), p. 477.
128. Hence the reference to *The Danish Account of F. L. Sommer* in the title of this second edition signals a text published in Denmark by a Dane and not (as one might more reasonably expect) a text first published in Danish and now translated into English.

129. Anon., *An Authentic Account of the Siege of Copenhagen by the British, in the Year 1807. Containing the Danish Description of the Attack [. . .] And the Whole of the Official Dispatches Relating to the Expedition, as Published in the London Gazette* (London, 1807).
130. Although the name and background are a good fit, the Copenhagen-born Danish seaman Frederik Laurentius Fiedler Sommer (1813–78) could not have been the author.
131. Sommer, *Description of Denmark*, p. 2.
132. Sommer, *Description of Denmark*, pp. 6–7, 2.
133. Sommer, *Description of Denmark*, p. 8.
134. Sommer, *Description of Denmark*, p. 14.
135. Sommer, *Description of Denmark*, p. 15.
136. Sommer, *Description of Denmark*, p. 15.
137. Sommer, *Description of Denmark*, p. 15.
138. Sommer, *Description*, p. 25.
139. Sommer, *Description of Denmark*, p. 19.
140. Sommer, *Description of Denmark*, p. 31.
141. Sommer, *Description of Denmark*, p. 28. This detail was picked up in the 'Song on the New Affair in Copenhagen (not Lord Nelson's)' published in the *Morning Chronicle* on 15 February 1808, which lamented that, while Britain might have had Denmark as an ally against Napoleonic France, 'we only slew, / Little children a few, / And killed a blind man as he lay in his bed' (lines 14–16). The text is also available, with commentary, in Betty T. Bennett and Orianne Smith (eds), *British War Poetry in the Age of Romanticism*, at: https://www.rc.umd.edu/editions/warpoetry/index.html (last accessed April 2021).
142. Sommer, *Description of Denmark*, p. 31.
143. Sommer, *Description of Denmark*, p. 33.
144. Sommer, *Description of Denmark*, p. 31.
145. 'A Danish Tale (A la Southey)', lines 51–8; quoted from Pollin, 'A Whig Attack', p. 508.
146. Percy Bysshe Shelley, 'Fragment of a Poem, the Original Idea of which was suggested by the cowardly and infamous bombardment of Copenhagen', lines 22, 26–8.
147. Sommer, *Description of Denmark*, p. 33.
148. Sommer, *Description of Denmark*, p. 34.
149. Sommer, *Description of Denmark*, p. 39.
150. Sommer, *Description of Denmark*, p. 41.
151. Crookes, *Particulars of the Expedition*, p. 4.
152. Crookes, *Particulars of the Expedition*, p. 6; emphasis added. Both the general image and the specific phrase 'monuments of British valour' are taken from Sommer's *Account*.
153. Crookes, *Particulars of the Expedition*, pp. 19, 13.
154. Crookes, *Particulars of the Expedition*, p. 7.
155. Crookes, *Particulars of the Expedition*, p. 16.
156. Crookes, *Particulars of the Expedition*, p. 20.
157. Walter Scott, *Marmion; a Tale of Flodden Field* (Edinburgh, 1808), III xxiv lines 480–7. Burton Pollin, who also notes this reference, points out that John Gibson Lockhart (1794–1854), Scott's biographer, incorrectly

read these lines as a reference to the Battle of Copenhagen in April 1801; see Pollin, 'Southey's "Battle of Blenheim" Parodied in the *Morning Chronicle*', p. 512.
158. Crookes, *Particulars of the Expedition*, p. 19.
159. Crookes, *Particulars of the Expedition*, p. 24.
160. George Gordon, Lord Byron, *English Bards and Scotch Reviewers* (London, 1809), lines 320–2.
161. In his notes to the poem, Grahame attributes much of the information which he relates about civilian casualties in particular to a source which he names as *Extracts from a Letter from a Merchant at Copenhagen during the Siege*. I have not been able to identify any published source bearing this or a comparable title. It could be, of course, that Grahame refers to private correspondence. However, since all the incidents which he mentions are also recorded in Sommer's *Account*, my suspicion is either that the *Extracts* themselves drew heavily on Sommer's *Account* or, more likely, that the *Extracts* is simply one of the many formats in which Sommer's *Account* appeared in Britain.
162. Review of James Grahame, *The Siege of Copenhagen*, in *Anti-Jacobin Review*, 31 (September–December 1808), pp. 183–5 (183).
163. James Grahame, *The Siege of Copenhagen. A Poem; With Notes* (London, 1808), lines 1–4.
164. Grahame, *Siege of Copenhagen*, lines 9–10.
165. Grahame, *Siege of Copenhagen*, lines 11–12.
166. Grahame, *Siege of Copenhagen*, line 22.
167. Grahame, *Siege of Copenhagen*, lines 22, 25.
168. Grahame, *Siege of Copenhagen*, lines 41–2.
169. Grahame, *Siege of Copenhagen*, lines 55–60.
170. Grahame, *Siege of Copenhagen*, lines 64, 115, 120–5.
171. Grahame, *Siege of Copenhagen*, lines 87–92.
172. Sevaldsen, '1807 i Storbitannien', p. 209.
173. Grahame, *Siege of Copenhagen*, 'Note VIII', pp. 15–16.
174. Sevaldsen, '1807 i Storbritannien', p. 209.
175. Grahame, *Siege of Copenhagen*, lines 100–1, 103.
176. Grahame, *Siege of Copenhagen*, ll. 136–7, 142–7.
177. Grahame, *The Siege of Copenhagen*, lines 160–9.
178. Grahame, *The Siege of Copenhagen*, lines 172–3.

Chapter 2: 'The dwelling-place of a mighty people': Travellers beyond Copenhagen

1. John Murray (ed.), *A Hand-Book for Travellers in Denmark, Norway, Sweden, and Russia* (London, 1839), p. 7.
2. F. L. Sommer, *A Description of Denmark and a Narrative of the Siege [. . .] of Copenhagen*, second edition (Colchester, 1808), p. 2.
3. A number of accounts had also appeared in German, as well as some few in French. It must be said that Nugent's account of Denmark, given in the second volume of his *Grand Tour*, is sufficiently factual and impersonal in

tone as to raise doubts about whether he had actually been there himself or merely gleaned his information from other sources.
4. Andrew Swinton (pseudonym of William Thomson), *Travels into Norway, Denmark, and Russia, in the Years 1788, 1789, 1790 and 1791* (London, 1792), p. 21.
5. Jens Baggesen, *Labyrinten; eller Reise giennem Tydskland, Schweiz og Frankerig*, 2 vols (Copenhagen, 1792–3), vol. 1, p. 150.
6. The sole exception in anglophone scholarship is Jørgen Erik Nielsen. In addition to much valuable work, in both English and Danish, on the influence of British Romantic-period writing in Denmark (which I consider in Chapter 3), Nielsen has published, in English, an excellent overview of Feldborg's life and work, based, in part, on an some autobiographical notes in Danish, which survive in manuscript in the Royal Library at Copenhagen: 'Andreas Andersen Feldborg: In Denmark English, in England Danish', in *Angles on the English-Speaking World*, vol.1 (Autumn 1986), pp. 51–63. I am much indebted, throughout this book, to Nielsen's studies of Anglo-Danish literary exchanges in the early nineteenth century.
7. See Andreas Andersen Feldborg, *A Tour in Zealand, in the Year 1802* (London, 1805), p. ix; and *Denmark Delineated* (Edinburgh, 1824), p. i.
8. Anon., review of *Denmark Delineated*, in *Blackwood's Edinburgh Magazine*, vol. 10 (August–December 1821), pp. 172–80 (180). The review, which opens with an apostrophe to 'Feldberg [sic] the Dane' was presumably written by one of his circle in Edinburgh (172). I discuss Feldborg's acquaintance with Hogg below.
9. In his excellent *Northern Arcadia: Foreign Travellers in Scandinavia, 1765–1815* (Carbondale, IL: Southern Illinois University Press), for example, Hildor Arnold Barton has comparatively little to say about the Danish sections of the travel books which he describes. Equally, the collection of essays *Northbound: Travels, Encounters & Constructions, 1700–1830* (Aarhus: Aarhus University Press, 2007), edited by Karen Klitgaard Povlsen, has relatively little to say about travel to or within Denmark.
10. As Barton puts it: 'Denmark, although a civilized European country, was not yet "civilized" enough to meet the same rational, utilitarian criteria [by which the northern parts of Germany were evaluated], yet to the preromantic mind it was too civilized, too close to the corrupted continental European pattern [. . .] Denmark thus largely failed to appeal to either camp' (*Northern Arcadia*, p. 173).
11. Feldborg, *Tour*, pp. viii–ix.
12. Feldborg, *Denmark Delineated*, 'Advertisement'; 'Preface', p. i. Feldborg has dated the 'Advertisement' at Edinburgh on 7 July 1821.
13. Feldborg, *Denmark Delineated*, 'Preface', p. i.
14. Feldborg, *Denmark Delineated*, 'Preface', pp. i–ii.
15. Anon., review of Andreas Andersen Feldborg, *A Tour in Zealand*, in *The Annual Review and History of Literature*, 4 (1806), p. 63.
16. Just Mathias Thiele, *Af mit Livs Aarboger. I. 1795–1838* (Copenhagen: C. A. Reitzel, 1917), pp. 157–8; my translation.
17. Feldborg, *Denmark Delineated*, 'Preface', p. iv.
18. Feldborg, *Denmark Delineated*, 'Preface', p. iv.
19. Feldborg, *Denmark Delineated*, 'Preface', p. iii; original emphasis.

20. Robert Molesworth, *An Account of Denmark, As it was in the Year 1692* (Glasgow, 1694), pp. 7, 8.
21. Barton, *Northern Arcadia*, pp. 172–3. See Karen Klitgaard Povlsen, 'Travelling Mythologies of the North around 1760: Molesworth, Mallet, Gerstenberg and several others in Copenhagen', in Povlsen (ed.), *Northbound*, pp. 129–51 (131–2).
22. Anon., *Narrative of the Expedition to the Baltic [. . .] by an Officer Employed in the Expedition* (London, 1808), p. 218.
23. Joseph Marshall, *Travels through Holland, Flanders, Germany, Denmark, Sweden, Lapland, Russia, The Ukraine, and Poland, in the Years 1768, 1769, 1770*, 8 vols (London, 1772), vol. 2, p. 291.
24. Murray (ed.), *Hand-Book*, p. 41; original emphasis. The *Hand-Book* goes on to quote at length the account of two such tumuli near Jaegerspris given by Feldborg in *Denmark Delineated*, Part 2, pp. 75–9, 83.
25. As has been recently documented in, for example: Robert Rix, '"In darkness they grope": Ancient Remains and Romanticism in Denmark', in Robert Rix (ed.), *Romanticism in Scandinavia*, special, themed number of *European Romantic Review*, 26/4 (July 2015), pp. 435–51; and Robert Rix, 'Visiting the Nordic Past: Domestic Travels in Early Nineteenth-Century Denmark', *Scandinavian Studies*, 90/2 (Summer 2018), pp. 211–36.
26. As noted in Chapter 1, a number of subsequent British travel accounts note the damage caused by the 'deplorable bombardment', as Richard Jones describes it in *Copenhagen and its Environs* (Copenhagen, 1829), p. 113. Nyerup's collection of Nordic antiquities, which first became accessible to the general public in 1819, eventually provided the basis for the Danish National Museum. A number of British travellers comment approvingly on the collection in this 'Museum of Northern Antiquities', which is recommended to visitors by Jones in *Copenhagen and Its Environs* (pp. 111–13).
27. William Rae Wilson, *Travels in Norway, Sweden, Denmark, Hanover, Germany, Netherlands, &c.* (London, 1826), pp. 395–6.
28. For a thorough account of the place of Danish antiquity in the work of Oehlenschläger, and its relationship to the wider development of antiquarianism in Denmark, see Rix, 'Visiting the Nordic Past', pp. 215–23.
29. Various versions of this scene exist, including one in the Hirschsprung Collection in Copenhagen, entitled *Efterårs landskab* [Autumn Landscape], where the clouds above the tomb are given much more explicitly anthropomorphic features.
30. See, for example, Robert Rix, 'Visiting the Nordic Past'; Robert Rix, '"In darkness they grope": Ancient Remains and Romanticism in Denmark', in Robert Rix (ed.), *Romanticism in Scandinavia*, special, themed number of *European Romantic Review* 26/4 (July 2015), pp. 435–51; and Karin Sanders, '"Upon the bedrock of material things": The Journey to the Past in Danish Archaeological Imagination', in Povlsen (ed.), *Northbound*, pp. 151–70.
31. Nathaniel Wraxall, *A Tour through Some of the Northern Parts of Europe*, third edition (London, 1776), p. 65.
32. Wraxall, *Tour*, pp. 73, 6–7.
33. Wraxall, *Tour*, p. 74.
34. Wraxall, *Tour*, p. 74.
35. Wraxall, *Tour*, p. 74.
36. Wraxall, *Tour*, p. 74.

37. Wraxall, *Tour*, pp. 74–5.
38. William Stukeley, *Stonehenge: A Temple Restor'd to the British Druids* (London, 1740), preface, p. 4.
39. Wraxall, *Tour*, p. 74; emphasis added.
40. William Coxe, *Travels into Poland, Russia, Sweden, and Denmark*, 2 vols (London, 1784), vol. 2, p. 595.
41. Coxe, *Travels*, vol. 2, p. 597.
42. Coxe, *Travels*, vol. 2, p. 597.
43. Coxe, *Travels*, vol. 2, p. 598 and n.
44. Coxe, *Travels*, vol. 2, p. 599.
45. Coxe, *Travels*, vol. 2, pp. 597, 595.
46. Coxe, *Travels*, vol. 2, p. 598.
47. Coxe, *Travels*, vol. 2, pp. 598–9.
48. Coxe, *Travels*, vol. 2, p. 598n.
49. James MacDonald, *Travels through Denmark, and Part of Sweden, during the Winter and Spring of the Year 1809* (London, 1810), p. 39.
50. MacDonald, *Travels*, p. 9. For a detailed biographical account of MacDonald and his captivity in Denmark, see Harry Watson, 'The Reverend James MacDonald: An Opinionated Traveller in Denmark and Sweden', in *Northern Studies: Journal of the Scottish Society for Northern Studies*, 25 (1988), pp. 121–62; available online at: https://ssns.org.uk/resources/Documents/NorthernStudies/Vol25/Watson_1988_Vol_25_pp_121_162.pdf (last accessed April 2021).
51. MacDonald, *Travels*, p. 9.
52. MacDonald, *Travels*, p. 39.
53. MacDonald, *Travels*, p. 39.
54. Watson, 'An Opinionated Traveller', p. 121.
55. MacDonald, *Travels*, p. 39.
56. Wilson, *Travels*, p. 473.
57. Edward Daniel Clarke, *Travels in Various Countries in Europe, Asia and Africa*, fourth edition, 11 vols (London, 1816–24), pt 3, Scandinavia, vol. 9 (1824), p. 59.
58. Clarke, *Travels*, vol. 9, p. 8; original emphasis.
59. See Patricia James (ed.), *The Travel Diaries of Thomas Robert Malthus* (Cambridge: Cambridge University Press, 1966).
60. See Frederick L. Jones (ed.), *Maria Gisborne and Edward E. Williams: Shelley's Friends: Their Journals and Letters* (Norman, OK: University of Oklahoma Press, 1951), p. 113.
61. Clarke, *Travels*, vol. 9, p. 56; original emphasis.
62. Clarke, *Travels*, vol. 9, p. 59; original emphasis.
63. Clarke, *Travels*, vol. 9, p. 59; original emphasis. Clarke is evidently describing here the kind of megalithic tomb now usually described as a dolmen. In the late eighteenth and early nineteenth centuries, the term 'cyclopéan', applied to architecture, generally signalled (as it still does) a style of building in which large stones were fitted together according to shape, but not actually bound together by any adhesive material; but it often also and appropriately signalled 'enormous', that is (figuratively), the work of the giants of Greek myth known as Cyclops.
64. Clarke, *Travels*, vol. 9, p. 59 and n.5.
65. Clarke, *Travels*, vol. 9, pp. 59–60.

66. Clarke, *Travels*, vol. 9, p. 60; original emphasis.
67. For a recent account of this myth and its role in late eighteenth- and early nineteenth-century British antiquarianism and literary history, see Robert Rix, '"The North" and "the East": The Odin Migration Theory', in Cian Duffy (ed.), *Romantic Norths: Anglo Nordic-Exchanges, 1770–1842* (London: Palgrave, 2017), pp. 153–79.
68. Clarke, *Travels*, vol. 9, p. 61; original emphasis.
69. Clarke, *Travels*, vol. 9, pp. 64–5; original emphasis.
70. Clarke, *Travels*, vol. 9, p. 61.
71. Clarke, *Travels*, vol. 9, p. 64; original emphasis.
72. Clarke, *Travels*, vol. 9, p. 64; original emphasis.
73. Clarke, *Travels*, vol. 9, p. 64; original emphasis.
74. Clarke, *Travels*, vol. 9, p. 64; original emphasis.
75. Clarke, *Travels*, vol. 9, p. 64; original emphasis.
76. Clarke, *Travels*, vol. 9, p. 71.
77. Murray, *Hand-Book*, p. 41; Feldborg, *Denmark Delineated*, Part 2, p. 78.
78. Feldborg, *Denmark Delineated*, Part 2, p. 83.
79. Feldborg, *Denmark Delineated*, Part 2, p. 84n., quoting Robert Jamieson, *Illustrations of Northern Antiquities* (Edinburgh, 1814), p. 278.
80. Feldborg, *Denmark Delineated*, Part 1, p. 12. The concept of 'classic ground' – of a landscape familiar in advance to travellers because of its cultural associations – which is frequently invoked in late eighteenth- and early nineteenth-century travel writing can be traced back to Joseph Addison's *Letter from Italy* (1704). For a study of the influence of this concept in late eighteenth-century and Romantic-period writing about landscape, across a range of genres and areas of enquiry, see Cian Duffy, *The Landscapes of the Sublime, 1700–1830: 'Classic Ground'* (London: Palgrave, 2013).
81. Feldborg, *Denmark Delineated*, Part 1, p. 7.
82. Feldborg, *Denmark Delineated*, Part 1, p. 7.
83. Feldborg, *Denmark Delineated*, Part 1, p. 11.
84. Feldborg, *Denmark Delineated*, Part 1, p. 7. In his *Tour in Zealand* (London, 1805), Feldborg had already observed of Helsingør that 'it needs little penetration to discover to whom this town chiefly owes its prosperity; for, if the flag on the castle did not inform you it was Denmark, you would fancy yourself in England [. . .] Many of the inhabitants are Britons born [. . .] and those who are not, take peculiar delight in wishing to appear like Englishmen' (p. 32).
85. In his *Excursions in the North of Europe* (London, 1834), John Barrow junior – the son of Sir John Barrow (1764–1848), the celebrated traveller and second secretary of the British admiralty – drew a similar, though explicitly unflattering, comparison, describing Elsinore as 'a little sea-port of the lowest class, with one tolerable street in it, such as one might see in the neighbourhood of Wapping, or it might be compared with that which leads to the Point at Portsmouth; full of gin-shops from one end to the other' (p. 177).
86. For detailed discussion of the response of British writers to the fate of Caroline Matilda, see Chapter 5.
87. Murray, *Hand-Book*, p. 42. In his 1829 guide to *Copenhagen and its Environs*, Richard Jones points similarly to 'the spot from which *Shakespeare* has taken his beautiful tragedy of *Hamlet*' (p. 146; original emphasis).
88. Murray, *Hand-Book*, p. 42; original emphasis.

89. For the contemporary rise in Danish interest in Shakespeare, and for discussions by British travellers to Denmark of the historical basis of the play, see Chapter 3.
90. Wraxall, *Tour*, pp. 6, 7.
91. Wraxall, *Tour*, p. 9.
92. Matthew Consett, *A Tour through Sweden, Swedish-Lapland, Finland and Denmark* (London, 1789), p. 135.
93. Mary Wollstonecraft, *Letters Written during a Short Residence in Sweden, Norway, and Denmark* (London, 1796), p. 203.
94. J. F. H. de Drevon, *A Journey through Sweden*, trans. William Radcliffe (Dublin, 1790), p. 165.
95. De Drevon, *Journey*, p. 165.
96. John Carr, *A Northern Summer* (London, 1805), p. 89.
97. Carr, *Northern Summer*, p. 89.
98. Carr, *Northern Summer*, p. 89.
99. Carr, *Northern Summer*, p. 89.
100. Carr, *Northern Summer*, p. 89.
101. Carr, *Northern Summer*, p. 89.
102. Carr, *Northern Summer*, p. 89.
103. Carr, *Northern Summer*, p. 89.
104. Robert Ker Porter, *Travelling Sketches in Russia and Sweden, during the Years 1805, 1806, 1807, 1808* (Philadelphia, 1809), p. 4.
105. Porter, *Travelling Sketches*, pp. 1–2.
106. Porter, *Travelling Sketches*, p. 2.
107. Porter, *Travelling Sketches*, p. 2.
108. Porter, *Travelling Sketches*, p. 2.
109. Porter, *Travelling Sketches*, p. 2.
110. Porter, *Travelling Sketches*, p. 2.
111. Porter, *Travelling Sketches*, p. 3.
112. Porter, *Travelling Sketches*, p. 3.
113. Feldborg, *Denmark Delineated*, Part 1, p. 13.
114. Feldborg, *Denmark Delineated*, Part 1, p. 13.
115. Feldborg, *Denmark Delineated*, Part 1, p. 13.
116. Feldborg, *Denmark Delineated*, Part 1, p. 13.
117. Feldborg, *Denmark Delineated*, Part 1, p. 13.
118. Feldborg was a friend of Foersom, and shortly before the latter's death in 1817, the two had recited together in Copenhagen extracts from Feldborg's *Poems from the Danish*.
119. Nielsen, 'Andreas Andersen Feldborg', p. 60.
120. Feldborg, *Denmark Delineated*, Part 1, p. 7.
121. Feldborg, *Denmark Delineated*, Part 1, pp. 50, 56.
122. Feldborg, *Tour in Zealand*, pp. 55, 56.
123. Carr, *Northern Summer*, p. 65.
124. Letters IV–VII are dated there, in September–October 1785; the rest are dated from Copenhagen.
125. De Drevon, *Journey*, p. 26.
126. De Drevon, *Journey*, p. 26. In his *Encyclopedia of Gardening*, third edition (London, 1825), J. C. Loudon mentions 'Dronningaard as one of the best examples of the English style in Denmark' (p. 212).
127. Pauelsen also decorated a room at de Coninck's townhouse in Copenhagen.
128. Carr, *Northern Summer*, p. 65.

129. Carr, *Northern Summer*, p. 65.
130. Carr, *Northern Summer*, pp. 66–7.
131. De Drevon, who was an equerry of William V of Orange ('his prince', presumably, in Carr's account), did in fact leave Dronninggaard in 1786 – but not, apparently, to answer an urgent call to arms which led to his death, since he published his *Voyage en Suede* at The Hague in 1789 (although the journey it recalls took place, as we have seen, in 1785–6) and did not die until 1797. The exact circumstances of his death I have not been able to determine. However, both the year of his death and his age at death (63) make it unlikely that he was killed in any action connected with the formation of the Batavian Republic (which is presumably what Carr intends by his reference to 'the revolution of Holland'), during which William V fled to England. But Carr might, of course, have been told otherwise during his visit.
132. Margrethe Floryan, 'Eremittens virke, vink, og venner: Scener og stemninger i Dronninggaards 1700-tals have', in Peter Wager, Claus M. Smidt and Margrethe Floryan (eds), *En Verden i Harmoni: To Parker i 1700-Tallet* (Søllerød: GL Holtegaard, 1996), pp. 30–44 (33); my translation. Only a few stones of the hermitage remain today.
133. Jean Frédéric Henry de Drevon, *Description de Dronning-gaard, terre situeé dans l'isle de Zelande en Dannemark* (Copenhagen, 1786), p. 23 ('ou l'art a parfaittement su imiter la nature'); Feldborg, *Tour*, p. 56.
134. John Carr, *Poems* (London, 1809), pp. 153–4n.
135. I first drew attention to the existence of these poems, and published both them and their French sources, in Cian Duffy, '"The story of this retired spot": Dronninggaard, John Carr, and Forgotten Works by William Hayley and Leigh Hunt', *e-romantikstudier* 1 (November 2015), http://www.romantikstudier.dk/media/44673/Cian,%20combined.pdf. See also Cian Duffy, 'Les Adieux de l'Hermite de Dronning-Gaard', *Rêve: The Virtual Exhibition*, 26 November 2018, www.euromanticism.org/les-adieux-de-lhermite-de-dronning-gaard/ (last accessed April 2021).
136. Carr, *Northern Summer*, p. 66.
137. De Drevon, *Description*, p. 25.
138. Carr, *Northern Summer*, p. 67.
139. Carr, *Poems*, p. 154n.
140. John Carr, *The Stranger in France* (London, 1803), p. iii.
141. Quoted from the facsimile available at the University of Iowa Digital Libraries Leigh Hunt Collection http://digital.lib.uiowa.edu/edm/compoundobject/collection/leighhunt/id/3403/rec/1 (last accessed April 2021); Leigh Hunt, *Juvenilia*, second edition (London: 1801), p. xvi.
142. Carr, *Northern Summer*, p. 67.
143. For detailed consideration of the form and content of Hunt's 'translation' and additions, see Duffy, '"The story of this place"', pp. 10–12.
144. The notice in *The Monthly Mirror* for July 1805.
145. Andreas Andersen Feldborg, *A Danes Excursions in Britain*, 2 vols (London, 1809), vol. 2, pp. 22, 24.
146. Feldborg's lengthy *Appeal*, dated 12 July 1814, was published in *The Pamphleteer*, vol. 4 (1814), pp. 233–85.
147. Anon., 'Review of *Denmark Delineated*', p. 172.

148. Robert Southey to John Murray, letter of 19 October 1814, quoted from Ian Packer and Linda Pratt (eds), *The Collected Letters of Robert Southey*, Romantic Circles Electronic Edition (https://www.rc.umd.edu/editions/southey_letters); last accessed April 2021. See also a letter from Southey of 24 December 1812, in which he says of his research into Nelson's naval engagements that 'For that of Copenhagen there is luckily a Dane's account to help me, written in English; it supplies me with a few fine circumstances not to be found elsewhere' (quoted from Packer and Pratt (eds)).
149. James Hogg, *Queen Hynde. A Poem, in Six Books* (London, 1824), VI, pp. 312–23. Hogg's affectionately humorous portrait of Feldborg in these lines very much recalls the tone of the review of *Denmark Delineated* in *Blackwood's Edinburgh Magazine* for September 1821, suggesting that it, too, was the work of Hogg.
150. The '&c. &c.' on the title page presumably refers to Feldborg's translation of Malling's *Great Deeds*, which is identified as by the author of *A Tour in Zealand*.
151. Feldborg, *Excursions*, vol. 1, p. 189.
152. Feldborg, *Excursions*, vol 1., p. 206.
153. Feldborg, *Excursions*, vol. 1, pp. 206–7.
154. Feldborg, *Excursions*, vol. 1, p. 207.
155. Feldborg, *Excursions*, vol. 1, p. 212.
156. Feldborg, *Excursions*, vol. 1, p. 212.
157. Feldborg, *Excursions*, vol. 1, pp. 211–12.
158. Feldborg, *Excursions*, vol. 2, p. 71.
159. Feldborg, *Excursions*, vol. 1, pp. 158, 159.
160. Feldborg, *Excursions*, vol 1, pp. 144, 145.
161. Feldborg, *Excursions*, vol. 2, pp. 71, 81, 86.
162. Feldborg, *Excursions*, vol. 1, p. 65.
163. Feldborg, *Excursions*, vol. 1, pp. 5, 6.
164. Feldborg, *Excursions*, vol. 1, p. 6; Feldborg quotes *Othello* 3.3.369.
165. Feldborg, *Excursions*, vol. 1, p. 6.
166. The ship was first renamed *Holstein* and then *Nassau* by the British and saw service again in the Gunboat War between Britain and Denmark–Norway in 1814, where she was used against her former owners.
167. Feldborg, *Excursions*, vol. 1, p. 35.
168. Feldborg, *Excursions*, vol. 1, p. 35.
169. Feldborg, *Excursions*, vol. 1, p. 35.
170. Feldborg, *Excursions*, vol. 1, p. 35.
171. Feldborg, *Excursions*, vol. 1, p. 35.

Chapter 3: 'A mine yet to be explored': Romanticism and Anglo-Danish Literary Exchanges

1. Anon., 'Notices of Danish Literature', in *The New Monthly Magazine*, vol. 11, no. 61 (July 1819), pp. 487–92 (487, 492). Høst's *Litterärgeschichte Dänemarks in den letzten Jahren der Regierung Christian VII* was published at Copenhagen in 1816.

2. Anon., 'Notices of Danish Literature', p. 492. The article is signed 'INCOGNITO' and dated '*Yarmouth*, May 2, 1819' – which was one of the main ports of call, in early nineteenth-century England, of ships from Denmark. 'Notices' was certainly not written by the Danish traveller, writer and Anglophile Andreas Andersen Feldborg (1782–1838), nor by his friend and co-editor, William Sidney Walker (1795–1846), to whose collaboration in popularising Danish poetry in Britain I return later in this chapter. It is possible, however, that 'Notices' was written by another key figure in the transmission of contemporary Danish literature to Britain, to whose work I also return later in this chapter: the editor and translator Robert Pearse Gillies (1788–1858).
3. Anon., 'Notices of Danish Literature', p. 492.
4. Anon., 'Notices of Danish Literature', p. 492.
5. Mary Wollstonecraft, *Letters Written during a Short Residence in Sweden, Norway, and Denmark* (London, 1796), p. 225.
6. Lis Møller, 'British and Danish Romantic-Period Adaptations of Two Danish "Elf Ballads"', in Cian Duffy (ed.), *Romantic Norths: Anglo-Nordic Exchanges, 1770–1842* (London: Palgrave, 2017), pp. 129–52 (129).
7. In addition to Møller, 'British and Danish Romantic-Period Adaptations', see Cian Duffy, 'Comparing the Literature of "the North": William Wordsworth and Jens Baggesen' (in *Romantic Norths*, pp. 251–8); see also Lis Møller, 'The Dissemination of Danish Medieval Ballads in Germany and Britain, 1760s to 1830s', in Dan Ringgaard and Mads Rosendahl Thomsen (eds), *Danish Literature as World Literature* (London: Bloomsbury, 2017), pp. 31–51.
8. Kristian Smidt, 'The Discovery of Shakespeare in Scandinavia', in Dirk Delabastita and Lieven D'hulst (eds), *European Shakespeares: Translating Shakespeare in the Romantic Age* (Amsterdam: John Benjamins, 1993), pp. 91–103 (92).
9. See, for example, Robert Rix, *Norse Romanticism: Themes in British Literature, 1760–1830*, Romantic Circles Digital Editions (2012), available at https://www.rc.umd.edu/editions/norse/index.html (last accessed April 2021); and Møller, 'The Dissemination of Danish Medieval Ballads'.
10. As I argue in the Introduction to *British Romanticism and Denmark*, the seminal instances of such cultural geography during the Romantic period can be found in Germaine de Staël's (1766–1817) *De la littérature considérée dans ses rapports avec les institutions sociales* (1799; translated into English in 1812 as *The Influence of Literature upon Society*) and *De l'Allemagne* (1813; translated into English that same year as *Of Germany*). For more on de Staël's mapping of the 'two distinct kinds of literature still extant, one derived from the east, the other from the north', see Introduction and Coda (Germaine de Staël, *The Influence of Literature upon Society*, second edition, 2 vols (London, 1812), vol. 1, p. 269.
11. The Ossian poems by James Macpherson are only the most obvious example of the new directions taken by British poetry in response to these classical Scandinavian texts; Rix lists many more in *Norse Romanticism*.
12. For eighteenth-century speculation about the Asiatic origins of classical Scandinavian culture, see Robert Rix, '"The North" and "the East": The Odin Migration Theory', in Duffy (ed.), *Romantic Norths*, pp. 153–79.

13. British literary responses to the physical artefacts of the classical Scandinavian past have yet to receive the same level of scholarly attention as the legacy of ancient Nordic texts. In Chapter 2 of *British Romanticism and Denmark*, I examine the engagement with the prehistoric monuments of Denmark in a range of British travel writing. On a somewhat smaller scale, and just by way of example of how widespread the appeal of such physical artefacts might have been, one could mention Walter Scott's passing reference, in Chapter 23 of *The Antiquary* (1816), to the Oldenburg Horn, 'still in the Museum at Copenhagen', which is often described in contemporary British travel writing about the Danish capital (Walter Scott, *The Antiquary*, ed. Nicola Watson (Oxford: Oxford World's Classics, 2009), p. 229).
14. Rasmus Rask, *A Grammar of the Danish Language for the Use of Englishmen, Together with Extracts in Prose and Verse* (Copenhagen, 1830), p. vii.
15. See Jørgen Erik Nielsen, *Den Samtidige Engeleske Litteratur og Danmark, 1800–1840*, 2 vols, Publications of the Department of English, University of Copenhagen (Nova: Copenhagen, 1976); 'English Literature in Denmark in the First Half of the Nineteenth Century', in Jørgen Sevaldsen (ed.), *Britain and Denmark: Political, Economic and Cultural Relations in the 19th and 20th Centuries* (Copenhagen: Museum Tusculanum Press, 2003), pp. 357–72; '"His pirates had foray'd on Scottish hill": The Danish Reception of Scott with an Outline of his Reception in Norway and Sweden', in Murray Pittock (ed.), *The Reception of Sir Walter Scott in Europe* (London: Bloomsbury, 2007), pp. 251–67; and '"Look to the Baltic": Byron between Romanticism and Radicalism in Denmark', in Richard Cadwell (ed.), *The Reception of Byron in Europe* (London: Bloomsbury, 2014), pp. 365–74.
16. Nielsen, 'English Literature in Denmark', p. 357.
17. Nielsen, 'English Literature in Denmark', p. 357.
18. Pierre Marie Louis de Boisgelin de Kerdu, *Travels in Denmark*, in *Travels through Denmark and Sweden, To Which is Prefixed a Journal of a Voyage down the Elbe*, trans. Anon., 2 vols (London, 1810), vol. 1, p. 202; Andreas Andersen Feldborg, *A Tour in Zealand, in the Year 1802* (London, 1805), p. 90n.
19. Nielsen, 'Byron between Romanticism and Radicalism in Denmark', p. 366.
20. See Gertrud Oelsner, 'Inventing Jutland for the "Golden Age": Danish Artists Guided by Sir Walter Scott', in Duffy (ed.), *Romantic Norths*, pp. 101–27.
21. Karsten Engelberg, 'Shelley in the Nordic Countries: Would They Be Seeking Him If He Had Not Been Found?', in Michael Rossington and Susanne Schmid (eds), *The Reception of P.B. Shelley in Europe* (London: Bloomsbury, 2008), pp. 156–68 (156).
22. John Murray (ed.), *A Hand-Book for Travellers in Denmark, Norway, Sweden, and Russia* (London, 1839), p. 12.
23. Edward Daniel Clarke, *Travels in Various Countries of Europe, Asia and Africa*, fourth edition, 11 vols (London 1816–24), Part 3, Scandinavia, vol. 9 (1824), pp. 86, 88; original emphasis.
24. James MacDonald, *Travels through Denmark, and Part of Sweden, during the Winter and Spring of the Year 1809* (London, 1810), p. 69.
25. Macdonald, *Travels*, p. 69.
26. Macdonald, *Travels*, p. 69.

27. Macdonald, *Travels*, p. 69. 'Four' is perhaps a typesetter's error for 'other'; or perhaps Macdonald means Britain, France, Germany and Italy?
28. De Kerdu, *Travels in Denmark*, vol. 1, pp. 189–90. As we saw in Chapter 1, the English traveller Nathaniel Wraxall (1751–1831) suggests, in his *Tour through Some of the Northern Parts of Europe* (1775), that spring 'is pretty much unknown to Danish poets' (Nathaniel Wraxall, *A Tour through Some of the Northern Parts of Europe, Particularly Copenhagen, Stockholm, and Petersburgh*, third edition (London, 1776), p. 21).
29. Robert Stevens, 'Account of Copenhagen', in *The New Monthly Magazine*, vol. 73 (1 June 1801), pp. 381–5 (383). Stevens informs us that he 'resided some months in the Capital of Denmark' in 1796 and dates his 'Account' from Hackney. For a recent account of his observations about Danish beer, see Gary Gillman, 'Draughts of Danish and the Ghost of London Porter', available at: http://www.beeretseq.com/draughts-of-danish-and-the-ghost-of-london-porter/ (last accessed April 2021).
30. Matthew Consett, *A Tour through Sweden, Swedish-Lapland, Finland, and Denmark* (London, 1789), pp. 142, 139–40.
31. John Barrow, *Excursions in the North of Europe* (London, 1834), p. 182.
32. Clarke, *Travels*, vol. 9, p. 97.
33. John Carr, *A Northern Summer; or Travels round the Baltic* (London, 1805), p. 41.
34. Richard Jones, *Copenhagen and its Environs* (Copenhagen, 1829), pp. 60–1.
35. Murray (ed.), *Hand-Book for Travellers*, p. 38.
36. William Coxe, *Travels into Poland, Russia, Sweden, and Denmark*, 2 vols (London, 1784), vol. 2, pp. 556–7.
37. Clarke, *Travels*, vol. 9, p. 98; original emphasis.
38. Macdonald, *Travels*, p. 67.
39. Mary Wollstonecraft, *Letters Written during a Short Residence in Sweden, Norway, and Denmark* (London, 1796), p. 223.
40. Thomas De Quincey, 'Letters to a Young Man whose Education has been Neglected', quoted from *The Works of Thomas De Quincey*, gen. ed. Grevel Lindop, 21 vols (London: Pickering & Chatto, 2000–3), vol. 3, p. 82 and n.
41. Thomas De Quincey, 'My Brother', quoted from *The Works of Thomas De Quincey*, gen. ed. Grevel Lindop, 21 vols (London: Pickering and Chatto, 2000–3), vol. 19, p. 204.
42. De Quincey, 'My Brother', quoted from *Works*, vol. 19, p. 205.
43. See Grevel Lindop, *The Opium-Eater: A Life of Thomas De Quincey* (London: Weidenfeld, 1993), pp. 182–3. Richard was fortunate enough to have been released so relatively early, given that Britain and Denmark remained at war until 1814. That a good number of Danes were still held captive in Britain in 1813 is evident from Feldborg's proposed volume of *Particulars Relevant to the Danish Prisoners of War in England*, advertised in September of that year. Feldborg was active in attempting to negotiate prisoner exchanges, and he attempted to raise a subscription for those held in England, but whether or not he had any role in Richard De Quincey's release, it is impossible, now, to tell. For more information about Feldborg's work with Danish prisoners in England, see Jørgen Erik Nielsen, 'Andreas Andersen Feldborg: In Denmark English, in England Danish', in *Angles on the English-Speaking World*, vol. 1 (Autumn 1986), pp. 51–63 (55–6).
44. De Quincey, 'My Brother', quoted from *Works*, vol. 19, p. 205.

45. De Quincey, 'My Brother', quoted from *Works*, vol. 19, p. 205.
46. As Daniel Sanjiv Roberts notes, De Quincey himself had only recently stepped down from the editorship. See Daniel Sanjiv Roberts, 'Thomas De Quincey's "Danish Origin of the Lake Country Dialect"', in *Transactions of the Cumberland and Westmorland Antiquarian and Archaeological Society* 99 (1999), pp. 257–66 (257).
47. Thomas De Quincey, 'To the Editor of the *Westmorland Gazette*, 13 November 1819', quoted from *The Works of Thomas De Quincey*, 21 vols, gen. ed. Grevel Lindop (London: Pickering & Chatto, 2000–3), vol. 1, p. 292.
48. De Quincey, *Works*, vol. 1, p. 292; original emphasis. As Roberts and others have observed, while De Quincey's hypothesis has an element of truth to it, the strong version of his claim is overstated and inaccurate (Roberts, 'De Quincey's "Danish Origin of the Lake Country Dialect"', p. 264n.5).
49. De Quincey, 'To the Editor of the *Westmorland Gazette*, 4 December 1819', quoted from *Works*, vol. 1, p. 299.
50. De Quincey, 'To the Editor of the *Westmorland Gazette*, 8 January 1820', quoted from *Works*, vol. 1, pp. 304–5.
51. De Quincey, 'To the Editor of the *Westmorland Gazette*, 13 November 1819', quoted from *Works*, vol. 1, p. 294.
52. De Quincey, 'To the Editor of the *Westmorland Gazette*, 13 November 1819', quoted from *Works*, vol. 1, pp. 294, 295.
53. De Quincey, 'To the Editor of the *Westmorland Gazette*, 13 November 1819', quoted from *Works*, vol. 1, pp. 295, 296. For more on the eighteenth-century hypothesis concerning the eastern origin of the Northern European languages, see Rix, 'The Odin Migration Theory'.
54. De Quincey, 'To the Editor of the *Westmorland Gazette*, 8 January 1820', quoted from *Works*, vol. 1 p. 306.
55. De Quincey, 'Letters to a Young Man', quoted from *Works*, vol. 3, p. 82n.
56. See De Quincey, *Works*, vol. 1, p. 293; and Roberts, 'De Quincey's "Danish Origin of the Lake Country Dialect"', p. 257.
57. See Roberts, 'De Quincey's "Danish Origin of the Lake Country Dialect"', pp. 260–1.
58. De Quincey, 'To the Editor of the *Westmorland Gazette*, 4 December 1819', quoted from *Works*, vol. 1, p. 300.
59. Sydney Musgrove, 'Niels Klim, being an incomplete translation by Thomas De Quincey from the Danish of Ludvig Holberg, now edited from the manuscript by S. Musgrove', *Bulletin of Auckland University College* 42/5 (1953), pp. 1–37 (3–4).
60. Musgrove (ed.), 'Niels Klim', p. 8.
61. Musgrove (ed.), 'Niels Klim', pp. 11, 5. I discuss Gillies's *Horae Danicae* series later in this chapter.
62. David Groves, 'De Quincey and Danish Poetry', *Notes and Queries* 35 (September 1988), pp. 313–15.
63. Anon., 'Review of *Dansk Bibliothek*', in *Edinburgh Literary Gazette* for 23 May 1829 (no. 2; p. 24); quoted from Groves, 'De Quincey and Danish Poetry', p. 314.
64. Thomas De Quincey, 'Klopstock, from the Danish', quoted from *The Works of Thomas De Quincey*, gen. ed. Grevel Lindop, 21 vols (London: Pickering & Chatto, 2000–3), vol. 5, p. 20. Coleridge's 'memorandum' was published in *The Friend* on 21 December 1809 (no. 18).
65. De Quincey, 'Klopstock', quoted from *Works*, vol. 5, pp. 20–1.

66. De Quincey, 'Klopstock', quoted from *Works*, vol. 5, p. 21.
67. De Quincey, 'Klopstock', quoted from *Works*, vol. 5, p. 21.
68. De Quincey, 'Klopstock', quoted from *Works*, vol. 5, p. 21. Nor does De Quincey agree 'with the preposterous estimation of Klopstock's merit, set up by most Germans and Danes' (vol. 5, p. 21).
69. See Cian Duffy, '"There was a time": William Wordsworth and Jens Baggesen Recollecting Childhood', *ANQ* 28 (May 2016), pp. 170–3; and 'Comparing the Literature of "the North" – William Wordsworth and Jens Baggesen', in Duffy (ed.), *Anglo-Nordic Exchanges*, pp 251–8.
70. See, for example, Duncan Wu, *Wordsworth's Reading*, 2 vols (Cambridge: Cambridge University Press, 1993, 1995), vol. 1, p. 81.
71. Musgrove (ed.), 'Niels Klim', p. 5. In fairness to Musgrove, at least in relation to contemporary Danish literature, that honour properly falls, as we shall see later in this chapter, to Andreas Andersen Feldborg – whose work was still essentially unknown to anglophone scholarship while Musgrove wrote.
72. For a recent account of the inception, contents and significance of the 'Horae Germanicae', see Saglia, *European Literatures in Britain*, pp. 48–54.
73. In his *Denmark Delineated* (1824), Feldborg praises the work done by his friend Gillies as translator of Oehlenschläger and Ingemann, and affirms that were the Danish poet Johannes Ewald (1743–81) to be so fortunate in this respect, he would also 'be acknowledged in this country [i.e. England] as a writer of very superior merit'. See Andreas Andersen Feldborg, *Denmark Delineated; or, Sketches of the Present State of that Country* (Edinburgh, 1824), p. 33.
74. Robert Pearse Gillies, 'Horae Danicae I', in *Blackwood's Edinburgh Magazine*, 7 (April 1820), pp. 73–89 (73).
75. Gillies, 'Horae Danicae I', p. 74. Sigurdsson helped defend Denmark against the Holy Roman Empire, and struggled against the coming of Christianity; after a thirty-year reign in Norway, he was overthrown by a rival faction and murdered by a former friend for the bounty on his head.
76. Gillies, 'Horae Danicae I', p. 73.
77. Gillies, 'Horae Danicae I', p. 73.
78. Gillies, 'Horae Danicae I', pp. 73–4.
79. Robert Pearse Gillies, 'Horae Danicae II', in *Blackwood's Edinburgh Magazine*, 8 (December 1820), pp. 290–305 (290).
80. Gillies, 'Horae Danicae II', p. 290.
81. Gillies, 'Horae Danicae II', pp. 290–1.
82. Gillies, 'Horae Danicae II', p. 291.
83. Gillies, 'Horae Danicae II', p. 291.
84. Gillies, 'Horae Danicae II', p. 291.
85. Robert Pearse Gillies, 'Horae Danicae IV [for III]', in *Blackwood's Edinburgh Magazine*, 8 (March 1821), pp. 646–60 (646).
86. Gillies, 'Horae Danicae IV [for III]', p. 646.
87. Gillies, 'Horae Danicae IV [for III]', p. 646.
88. Gillies, 'Horae Danicae IV [for III]', p. 646.
89. Gillies, 'Horae Danicae IV [for III]', p. 646.
90. Gillies, 'Horae Danicae IV [for III]', p. 646; original emphasis.
91. Robert Pearse Gillies, 'Horae Danicae V', in *Blackwood's Edinburgh Magazine*, 9 (April 1821), pp. 43–59 (43).
92. Gillies, 'Horae Danicae V', p. 43.
93. Gillies, 'Horae Danicae V', p. 43.

94. Gillies, 'Horae Danicae V', p. 59.
95. William Herbert, *The Wierd Wanderer of Jutland. A Tragedy* (London, 1822), p. 165.
96. Herbert, *Wierd Wanderer*, p. 165.
97. William Herbert, *Select Icelandic Poetry, Translated from the Originals; With Notes*, Part First (London, 1804), Dedication (n.p.).
98. Anon., 'Review of *The Wierd Wanderer of Jutland*', in *The Monthly Repertory of English Literature* (July 1822); reprinted in *Galignani's Literary Gazette*, 15 (1822), pp. 163–5 (163).
99. George Borrow, *Romantic Ballads, Translated from the Danish; and Miscellaneous Pieces* (Norwich, 1826), p. vii.
100. The identity of the composer of the music to accompany Evald's words is still a matter of controversy among Danish scholars and historians, and various names have been proposed. Today, 'Kong Christian' is used mostly as the royal anthem of Denmark. The text of the other national anthem of Denmark, also still in use today, entitled 'Der er et yndig land' [There is a lovely country] was composed by Oehlenschläger in 1819, and set to music by Hans Ernst Krøyer (1798–1879) in 1835.
101. The American poet Henry Wadsworth Longfellow (1807–82) made another translation during his tour of Scandinavia in 1835.
102. Borrow, *Romantic Ballads*, pp. vii–viii.
103. Gillies, 'Horae Danicae I', p. 89.
104. Gillies, 'Horae Danicae I', p. 89.
105. Rask, *Grammar*, pp. vii–viii. Rask is referring to Knud Lyne Rahbek, *Dansk Læsebog og Exempelsamling til de forandrede lærde Skolers Brug*, 2 vols (Copenhagen, 1799, 1804).
106. Anon., 'On Feldberg's Denmark', in *Blackwood's Edinburgh Magazine*, 10 (September 1821), pp. 172–80 (172).
107. Anon., 'On Feldberg's Denmark', p. 172; original emphasis.
108. Andreas Andersen Feldborg and William Sidney Walker, *Poems from the Danish* (London, 1815), p. vi.
109. Feldborg and Walker, *Poems*, pp. v–vi.
110. Feldborg and Walker, *Poems*, p. vii.
111. Feldborg explains in his 'Advertisement' that some texts contained in *Poems from the Danish* were omitted from *Danish and Norwegian Melodies*, and others included in shortened versions, on account of their length. He directs the reader interested in the complete texts to consult *Poems from the Danish*. Andreas Andersen Feldborg, C. Stokes and William Sidney Walker, *Danish and Norwegian Melodies* (London, 1815), 'Advertisement', n.p.
112. Feldborg, Stokes and Walker, *Danish and Norwegian Melodies*, 'Dedication', n.p.
113. Feldborg and Walker, *Poems from the Danish*, p. ix.
114. See Nielsen, 'Feldborg', p. 57. The MS letter is held in the Royal Library at Copenhagen (NKS 2336 b).
115. Feldborg and Walker, *Poems from the Danish*, p. x.
116. Feldborg and Walker, *Poems*, p. 1.
117. Interestingly, in this respect, Borrow's translation in *Romantic Ballads* is less faithful to the tone and content of Evald's original, suppressing the more violent imagery and all explicit references to Sweden, which was in 1826 still an ally of Britain.

118. I discuss these works and their relationship to Danish abolitionism in Chapter 5.
119. Anon., 'On Feldberg's Denmark', p. 173. Curiously, the reviewer says this 'admirable' volume was published in 1808 and that 'who the translator is, we know not' – but the reference must be to *Poems from the Danish*, both on account of the context and of the more salient fact that no such volume was published, so far as I can tell, in 1808 (p. 173).
120. For more of Feldborg's account of landscapes and historical sites in *Denmark Delineated*, see Chapter 2.
121. Anon., 'On Feldberg's Denmark', p. 172.
122. Anon., 'On Feldberg's Denmark', p. 172.
123. Anon., 'On Feldberg's Denmark', p. 172.
124. Feldborg, *Denmark Delineated*, 'Advertisement', n.p.
125. Sydney Smith, 'Review of Jean-Pierre Catteau-Calleville, *Tableau des états danois*', in *The Edinburgh Review*, 2 (July 1803), pp. 287–308 (307). Cp. Feldborg, *Denmark Delineated*, 'Introduction', p. 3: 'It has been remarked by some critics, "That the fine arts hardly exist in Denmark"'.
126. Feldborg, *Denmark Delineated*, 'Introduction', p. 3.
127. Feldborg, *Denmark Delineated*, Part 3, p. 14. For a more thorough discussion of the time which Feldborg and Belzoni spent together, and of Feldborg's use of Belzoni to support his arguments about Danish culture in *Denmark Delineated*, see Chapter 4.
128. Feldborg, *Denmark Delineated*, Part 3, p. 36.
129. Feldborg, *Denmark Delineated*, Part 3, p. 42.
130. Feldborg, *Denmark Delineated*, Part 3, p. 42.
131. Feldborg, *Denmark Delineated*, Part 1, pp. 34–5, 55–6, 58–9.
132. Anon., 'On Feldberg's Denmark', p. 175.
133. Anon., 'On Feldberg's Denmark', p. 173.
134. For more on Molesworth's *Account* and its continued influence on British late eighteenth-century and Romantic-period engagements with Denmark, and of Feldborg's responses to it, see Introduction and Chapters 4 and 5.
135. Feldborg, *Denmark Delineated*, Appendix, pp. 1, 2.
136. Feldborg, *Denmark Delineated*, Appendix, p. 41.
137. Feldborg, *Denmark Delineated*, Appendix, pp. 55–6, quoting Smith, 'Review of Jean-Pierre Catteau-Calleville, *Tableau des états danois*', p. 292.
138. Feldborg, *Denmark Delineated*, Appendix, p. 56, quoting Smith, 'Review of Jean-Pierre Catteau-Calleville, *Tableau des états danois*', p. 292.
139. Feldborg, *Denmark Delineated*, Appendix, pp. 47, 48, 51, 57–8, 68.
140. Feldborg, *Denmark Delineated*, Appendix, p. 69, quoting Macdonald, *Travels*, p. 73.
141. For more on this rhetoric, see Chapter 1.
142. Feldborg, *Denmark Delineated*, Appendix, pp. 49–50.
143. As we have seen, the manuscript of the first translation of *Beowulf* which Thorkelín had prepared for publication in 1807 was destroyed during the British bombardment of Copenhagen in September of that year. It was finally published in 1815, after Thorkelín had returned to his original, surviving transcriptions.
144. Feldborg, *Denmark Delineated*, Appendix, p. 50.
145. Feldborg, *Denmark Delineated*, Appendix, p. 71.
146. Feldborg, *Denmark Delineated*, Appendix, p. 71.
147. Feldborg, *Denmark Delineated*, Appendix, pp. 71, 72.

148. Feldborg, *Denmark Delineated*, Appendix, p. 72.
149. Feldborg, *Denmark Delineated*, Appendix, p. 72.
150. Feldborg, *Denmark Delineated*, Appendix, pp. 72, 73.
151. Feldborg, *Denmark Delineated*, Appendix, p. 73.
152. Feldborg, *Denmark Delineated*, Appendix, p. 73.
153. Nielsen, 'Feldborg', pp. 56, 58.
154. Feldborg, *Denmark Delineated*, Appendix, p. 74.
155. Feldborg, *Denmark Delineated*, Appendix, p. 74, quoting John Russell, *A Tour in Germany*, 2 vols (Edinburgh, 1824), vol. 1, p. 298.
156. Feldborg, *Denmark Delineated*, Appendix, p. 74.
157. The lines which Feldborg quotes are taken, not entirely in order, from a poem entitled 'An Ode on Nelson's Battle of the Baltic', which was first printed in *The Living Age* in 1858. It is presented, there, as received from an anonymous correspondent who claims that poem was written by Campbell for Feldborg and inscribed in one of the Dane's notebooks (see *The Living Age*, 57 (1858), p. 419). The editor of *The Living Age* doubts the authorship. The full poem, as given in *The Living Age*, reads:

> *To Professor Andersen Feldborg*
> On presenting him with a Copy of my Poems
>
> 'An Ode on Nelson's Battle of the Baltic'
> Think me not, Danish stranger, a hard-hearted Pagan,
> If you find midst my War Songs one called 'Copenhagen',
> For I thought when your State joined the Emperor Paul,
> We'd a right to play with you the devil and all.
> But the next time our fleet went your city to batter,
> That attack, I allow, was a scandalous matter,
> And I gave it my curse – and I wrote on't a satire.
> To be-praise such an action of sin, shame, and sorrow,
> I'll be d——d if I would be the Laureate tomorrow!
> There is not (take my word) a true Englishman glories
> In that deed – 'twas a deed of our merciless Tories,
> Whom we hate, though they rule us – and I can assure ye
> They had swung for't if England had sat their jury.
> But a truce to remembrance blacken'd with pain,
> Here's a health to yourself, and your country, dear Dane,
> As our nations are kindred in language and kind,
> May the ties of our blood by the ties of our mind,
> And perdition on him who our peace would unbind!
> May we struggle not who shall in fight be foremost,
> But boldest in sense – in humanity warmest.
> May you leave us with something like love for our nation,
> Tho' we're still curst with Castlereagh's Administration.
> But what ever you think, or wherever you ramble,
> Think there's one who has lov'd you in England.
>
> Tom Campbell,
> London, 30 Foley Place,
> Great Portland Street, July 11th 1822.

As far as I have been able to determine, the poem has not since been published and is not part of the known canon of Campbell's work.
158. Feldborg, *Denmark Delineated*, Appendix, p. 74.
159. 'Hamlet's Garden' was found in what is today known as Kongens Have [The King's Garden], in the grounds of Marienlyst Castle, just outside Helsingør. For Feldborg's 'intimacy' with Foersom, beginning in 1810, see *Denmark Delineated*, Part 1, pp. 23–4.
160. Foersom, 'Dedicatory Lines', lines 2, 3; quoted from Feldborg and Walker, *Poems*, p. 64. For Louise Auguste as the daughter of Caroline Matilda, see Feldborg and Walker, *Poems*, p. 149n.
161. Smidt, 'Discovery of Shakespeare', pp. 94–5.
162. As also recognised by Smidt ('Discovery of Shakespeare', p. 96).
163. Feldborg and Walker, *Poems*, p. 149.
164. Foersom records in his 'Preface' that he used as source texts 'a pocket edition, published at London in 1798, from the text of Steevens'; see Foersom, 'Preface', trans. Feldborg and Walker, in *Poems*, p. 151. The work by George Steevens (1736–1800) to which Foersom refers is the ten-volume *Works of Shakespeare with the Corrections and Illustrations of Various Commentators* (1773), to the editing of which Samuel Johnson (1709–84) also made a small contribution.
165. Foersom, 'Preface', trans. Feldborg and Walker, in *Poems from the Danish*, p. 152.
166. Smidt, 'Discovery of Shakespeare', p. 96.
167. Smidt, 'Discovery of Shakespeare', p. 96.
168. See Alf Henriques, *Shakespeare og Danmark indtil 1840* [Shakespeare and Denmark until 1840] (Copenhagen: Einar Munksgaard, 1941), pp. 94–5; Smidt also notes these interventions ('Discovery of Shakespeare', p. 97).
169. Feldborg and Walker, *Poems*, pp. 170–1.
170. Holger Scheibel, 'Shakespeare's Sonnets in Danish Translation: A Phenomenon for Only the Few', in Manfred Pfister and Jürgen Gutsch (eds), *William Shakespeare's Sonnets for the First Time Globally Reprinted. A Quatercentenary Anthology, 1609–2009* (Dozwil, Switzerland: Edition Signathur, 2009), pp. 161–9 (161).
171. Feldborg, *Denmark Delineated*, Part 1, p. 14, quoting John Milton (1608–74), 'L'Allegro' (1645) on 'Sweetest Shakespeare' (lines 133–4).
172. As noted earlier, Feldborg's 'Introduction' to Part the First of *Denmark Delineated* consists, in effect, of an extended account of Thorvaldsen and his work, in which Feldborg notes, among various Anglo-Danish connections, Thorvaldsen's bust of Byron and his friendship with the novelist and art collector Thomas Hope (1769–1831). In Feldborg's account, Thorvaldsen, too, is presented as the product of Anglo-Danish cultural exchange. 'It fell to the lot of Denmark to give birth to his transcendent genius', we are told, 'but England fanned the heavenly spark into flame'; Feldborg identifies one aim of his account of Thorvaldsen as being to 'obviate some erroneous accounts which have appeared in some British publications'. See Feldborg, *Denmark Delineated*, 'Introduction', pp. 30, 22.
173. Feldborg, *Denmark Delineated*, Part 1, p. 16.
174. Feldborg, *Denmark Delineated*, Part 1, p. 16.

175. Feldborg, *Denmark Delineated*, Part 1, p. 17.
176. Feldborg, *Denmark Delineated*, Part 1, p. 17. For Thomas Gray's (1716–71) engagement with classical Scandinavian culture in poems like 'The Fatal Sisters' (1768) and 'The Descent of Odin', see Rix, *Norse Romanticism*.
177. Feldborg, *Denmark Delineated*, Part 1, p. 18.
178. Feldborg, *Denmark Delineated*, Part 1, p. 19.
179. Feldborg, *Denmark Delineated*, Part 1, p. 20.
180. Feldborg, *Denmark Delineated*, Part 1, p. 24.
181. Feldborg, *Denmark Delineated*, Part 1, p. 29.
182. Feldborg, *Denmark Delineated*, Part 1, p. 25.
183. Feldborg, *Denmark Delineated*, Part 1, p. 25. Feldborg adds a note suggesting that 'the use of the word *though* instead of *as* [in line 4] must have been an oversight'.
184. Feldborg, *Denmark Delineated*, Part 1, p. 25.
185. Anon., 'On Feldberg's Denmark', p. 173.
186. Anon., 'On Feldberg's Denmark', p. 173.
187. Anon., 'On Feldberg's Denmark', p. 174; original emphasis.
188. Anon., 'On Feldberg's Denmark', p. 174.
189. Anon., 'On Feldberg's Denmark', p. 180.

Chapter 4: 'The brothers of Englishmen': British Reflections on the Danish National Character

1. Matthew Lewis, *The Monk*, ed. Howard Anderson and Nick Groom (Oxford: Oxford University Press, 2016), p. 222.
2. Lewis, *The Monk*, p. 222.
3. Lewis, *The Monk*, p. 222.
4. On Lewis's familiarity with Danish literature, see Lis Møller, '"They dance all under the greenwood tree": British and Danish Romantic-Period Adaptations of Two Danish "Elf Ballads"', in Cian Duffy (ed.), *Romantic Norths: Anglo-Nordic Exchanges, 1770–1842* (London: Palgrave, 2017), pp. 129–52.
5. William Thomson, *Letters from Scandinavia, On the Past and Present State of the Northern Nations of Europe*, 2 vols (London, 1796), vol. 2, pp. 444–5.
6. David Hume, 'Of National Characters', in *Essays and Treatises on Several Subjects*, a new edition, 2 vols (London, 1784), vol. 1, p. 213.
7. In 2019 and 2020, Denmark was ranked second in the world by the World Happiness Report (http://worldhappiness.report/) and has held the top spot three times since 2012.
8. Mary Wollstonecraft, *Letters Written during a Short Residence in Sweden, Norway, and Denmark* (London, 1796), p. 202.
9. Anon., *Candide, ou, l'Optimisme. Traduit de l'Allemand de Mr. le Docteur Ralph, Seconde Partie* (1761, n.p.), p. 98: 'Tout n'est pas aussi bien que dans El Dorado; mais tout ne va pas mal.'
10. For more on Nelson's address, see Introduction and Chapter 1.
11. John Hayman, 'Notions on National Character in the Eighteenth Century', *Huntington Library Quarterly* 35/1 (November 1971), pp. 1–17. As we shall

see later, British accounts of the Danish national character often advance in support of their arguments, in addition to the ostensible first-hand testimony of the author, remarks from locals, actual or imagined.
12. Hayman, 'Notions on National Character', p. 1.
13. Thomas Ahnert and Susan Manning (eds), *Character, Self, and Sociability in the Scottish Enlightenment* (London: Palgrave, 2011), pp. 3–4, 25, 21.
14. Silvia Sebastiani, 'National Characters and Race: A Scottish Enlightenment Debate', in Ahnert and Manning (eds), *Character, Self, and Sociability*, pp. 187–205 (187).
15. See Sebastiani, 'National Characters and Race', pp. 188, 191. That there *were* such recognisable characteristics was a moot point for most of the eighteenth-century debate.
16. For detailed consideration of Hume's ideas about national character as a response to those of Montesquieu, with whom he was in correspondence, see Silvia Sebastiani, 'Hume versus Montesquieu: Race against Climate', in Silvia Sebastiani, *The Scottish Enlightenment: Race, Gender, and the Limits of Progress* (London: Palgrave, 2013), pp. 22–43. For an examination of the role of 'climate theory', including Hume's response to Montesquieu, in British Romantic-period configurations of Scotland and 'the North', see Penny Fielding, *Scotland and the Fictions of Geography* (Cambridge: Cambridge University Press, 2008), pp. 50–9.
17. Hume, 'National Characters', p. 213.
18. Hume, 'National Characters', p. 213.
19. Hume, 'National Characters', p. 213. In point of fact, the celebrated astronomer Tycho Brahe (1546–1601) was born in Scania, in south-west Sweden, then a territorial possession of Denmark.
20. Hume, 'National Characters', p. 213.
21. Hume, 'National Character', p. 214.
22. Hume, 'National Character', p. 216.
23. Hume, 'National Character', p. 214; original emphasis.
24. Hume, 'Of National Character', p. 214.
25. Sebastiani, 'National Characters and Race', pp. 191–2, 195.
26. Hume, 'Of National Character', p. 222. For assessments of the ostensible racism of Hume's essay, see Aaron Garrett and Silvia Sebastiani, 'David Hume on Race', in Naomi Zack (ed.), *The Oxford Handbook of Philosophy and Race* (Oxford: Oxford University Press, 2017), pp. 31–43.
27. Hume, 'Of National Character', p. 222; original emphasis.
28. Benedict Anderson, *Imagined Communities: Reflections on the Origin and Spread of Nationalism* (London: Verso, 1983), pp. 13–15; Joep Leerssen, 'Notes towards a Definition of Romantic Nationalism', *Romantik: Journal for the Study of Romanticisms* 2 (2013), pp. 9–35 (28).
29. Joep Leerssen, *National Thought in Europe: A Cultural History* (Amsterdam: Amsterdam University Press, 2006), p. 21.
30. Leerssen, *National Thought*, p. 21.
31. Leerssen, 'Notes towards a Definition', p. 27.
32. Ove Malling, *Great and Good Deeds of Danes, Norwegians, and Holsteinians*, trans. Andreas Andersen Feldborg (London, 1807); reviewed in *The Anti-Jacobin Review and Magazine*, 28, September–December 1807 (1808), pp. 53–62 (54).

33. *Anti-Jacobin Review* 28 (1808), p. 55.
34. Marilyn Butler, *Mapping Mythologies: Countercurrents in Eighteenth-Century British Poetry and Cultural History* (Cambridge: Cambridge University Press, 2015), p. 15.
35. Butler, *Mapping Mythologies*, p. 15.
36. Katie Trumpener, *Bardic Nationalism: The Romantic Novel and the British Empire* (Princeton, NJ: Princeton University Press, 1997), pp. 23, 27.
37. Trumpener, *Bardic Nationalism*, pp. 27, 29.
38. Trumpener, *Bardic Nationalism*, p. 29.
39. Jonathan Sachs, *The Poetics of Decline in British Romanticism* (Cambridge: Cambridge University Press, 2018), p. 7.
40. Laurence Goldstein, *Ruins and Empire: The Evolution of a Theme in Augustan and Romantic Literature* (Pittsburgh: University of Pittsburgh Press, 1997), p. 3.
41. Anne Janowitz, *England's Ruins: Poetic Purpose and the National Landscape* (London: Blackwell, 1990), p. 2.
42. Janowitz, *England's Ruins*, p. 4.
43. Sachs, *Poetics of Decline*, p. 4; emphasis added.
44. Sachs, *Poetics of Decline*, p. 6.
45. Edward Gibbon, *The History of the Decline and Fall of the Roman Empire*, 6 vols (London, 1776–89), vol. 3 (1781), p. 631; original emphasis.
46. Sachs, *Poetics of Decline*, pp. 34, 35–44 passim.
47. Wollstonecraft, *Short Residence*, p. 221.
48. Wollstonecraft, *Short Residence*, p. 221.
49. Wollstonecraft, *Short Residence*, p. 222.
50. Sachs, *Poetics of Decline*, p. 27.
51. Nelson's note is preserved in the National Archives of Britain (catalogue reference: ADM 1/4 (Ha 54)) and a facsimile can be seen here: http://www.nationalarchives.gov.uk/nelson/gallery6/copenhagen.htm (last accessed April 2021).
52. Robert Southey, *Life of Nelson*, 2 vols (London, 1813) vol. 2, p. 138.
53. Southey, *Life of Nelson*, vol. 2, p. 143.
54. The term 'Danelaw' dates from the eleventh century.
55. Robert Molesworth, *An Account of Denmark, as it was in the Year 1692*, sixth edition (Glasgow, 1752), p. 52.
56. Molesworth, *Account of Denmark*, p. 59.
57. Molesworth, *Account of Denmark*, pp. 7–8. As evidence of the longevity of Molesworth's book, we might note that this passage was paraphrased, without acknowledgement, by the anonymous author of *Narrative of an Expedition to the Baltic* (London, 1808), pp. 218–19.
58. Molesworth, *Account of Denmark*, p. 52.
59. Molesworth, *Account of Denmark*, p. 52.
60. Wollstonecraft, *Short Residence*, p. 133.
61. Molesworth, *Account of Denmark*, pp. 54, 52.
62. Molesworth, *Account of Denmark*, pp. 54, 58.
63. Molesworth, *Account of Denmark*, pp. 58, 65.
64. Molesworth, *Account of Denmark*, p. 64.
65. Molesworth, *Account of Denmark*, p. 65.
66. Molesworth, *Account of Denmark*, p. 67.

67. Molesworth, *Account of Denmark*, p. 68.
68. Molesworth, *Account of Denmark*, p. 61.
69. Molesworth, *Account of Denmark*, pp. 61, 65.
70. Jodocus Crull, *Denmark Vindicated: Being an Answer to a late Treatise called An Account of Denmark* (London, 1694), p. 108.
71. Crull, *Denmark Vindicated*, p. 110. For a discussion of the wider argument made in response to Molesworth by *Denmark Vindicated*, see Introduction and Chapter 5.
72. John Carr, *A Northern Summer* (London, 1805), p. 33.
73. Carr, *Northern Summer*, p. 16.
74. Molesworth, *Account of Denmark*, pp. 54, 58.
75. Nathaniel Wraxall, *A Tour through some of the Northern Parts of Europe*, third edition, corrected (London: 1776), p. 55.
76. Edward Daniel Clarke, *Travels in Various Countries of Europe, Asia and Africa*, fourth edition, 11 vols (London, 1816–24), Part 3, Scandinavia, vol. 9 (1824), p. 82; original emphasis. To add insult to injury, Clarke appends a footnote observing that the Danes 'are even said to be behind the *Germans*', and citing another work of travel writing in support of this claim (82n.)
77. Clarke, *Travels*, vol. 9, p. 82.
78. Clarke, *Travels*, vol. 9, p. 82.
79. Jean Frédéric Henry de Drevon, *A Journey through Sweden*, trans. William Radcliffe (Dublin, 1790), p. 187. I have not been able to identify the 'historian' whom de Drevon quotes.
80. The notable exception to this tendency, of course, is the almost universal praise in Britain for the heroic conduct of the Danes during the Battle of Copenhagen in 1801, which, as I have argued in Chapter 1, was routinely marshalled as evidence that Britons and Danes shared a common, 'Northern' heritage of valour.
81. Wollstonecraft, *Short Residence*, p. 168; Wollstonecraft misquotes John Milton, *L'Allegro* (1645), line 36.
82. William Herbert, *Hedin; or, The Spectre of the Tomb. A Tale. From the Danish History* (London, 1820), lines 1–8.
83. Herbert, *Hedin*, lines 17–18, 11, 14.
84. Wollstonecraft, *Short Residence*, p. 168.
85. William Rae Wilson, *Travels in Norway, Sweden, Denmark, Hanover, Germany, Netherlands, &c.* (London, 1826), pp. 480, 453, 437. Wilson further notes of Frederik VI, with whom he had an audience during his visit to Copenhagen, that 'the cast of his features appeared to me to be not unlike those of the royal family of Great Britain' (463).
86. Anon., *Narrative of the Expedition to the Baltic: With an Account of the Siege and Capitulation of Copenhagen [. . .] By an Officer Employed in the Expedition* (London, 1808), p. 28
87. Anon., *Observations on the Present State of Denmark, Russia, and Switzerland* (London, 1784), p. 46. The island of St Thomas, now one of the US Virgin Islands, was part of the Danish West Indies until 1917. For more on British responses to the Danish West and East Indies in the late eighteenth and early nineteenth centuries, see Chapter 5.
88. Anon., *Observations*, p. 55.
89. Anon., *Observations*, pp. 55–6.

90. Anon., *Observations*, p. 70.
91. Anon., *Observations*, pp. 70–1.
92. Andrew Swinton (pseudonym of William Thomson), *Travels into Norway, Denmark, and Russia, in the Years 1788, 1789, 1790, and 1791* (London, 1792), p. 69.
93. Swinton, *Travels*, p. 69.
94. Swinton, *Travels*, pp. 69, 73–4.
95. Swinton, *Travels*, p. 74.
96. Swinton, *Travels*, p. 74.
97. Swinton, *Travels*, pp. 77, 78, 76.
98. Swinton, *Travels*, p. 75.
99. Swinton, *Travels*, p. 76.
100. James MacDonald, *Travels through Denmark, and a Part of Sweden, During the Winter and Spring of 1809* (London, 1810), pp. 24, 27.
101. MacDonald, *Travels*, pp. 79, 86, 46.
102. MacDonald, *Travels*, p. 43.
103. MacDonald, *Travels*, p. 73.
104. MacDonald, *Travels*, p. 24.
105. MacDonald, *Travels*, p. 34.
106. MacDonald, *Travels*, p. 34.
107. MacDonald, *Travels*, p. 76.
108. MacDonald, *Travels*, p. 73.
109. MacDonald, *Travels*, p. 52.
110. MacDonald, *Travels*, p. 52.
111. MacDonald, *Travels*, p. 75.
112. MacDonald, *Travels*, p. 75.
113. MacDonald, *Travels*, pp. 75–6.
114. MacDonald, *Travels*, p. 76.
115. Anon., *Observations*, pp. 71, 78.
116. Anon, *Observations*, p. 30.
117. Wollstonecraft, *Short Residence*, pp. 215, 210, 214.
118. Wollstonecraft, *Short Residence*, p. 239.
119. De Drevon, *Journey*, p. 178.
120. Carr, *Northern Summer*, p. 16.
121. Anon., *Narrative of the Expedition*, p. 50.
122. Hume, 'Of National Character', p. 222; emphasis added.
123. Charles-Louis de Secondat, Baron de La Brède et de Montesquieu, *The Spirit of the Laws*, trans. Thomas Nugent, 2 vols (Dublin, 1751), vol. 1, pp. 273–4; Jean-Jacques Rousseau, *An Inquiry into the Nature of the Social Contract*, trans. Anon. (Dublin, 1791), p. 174.
124. Adam Ferguson, *An Essay on the History of Civil Society*, fifth edition (London, 1782), p. 198.
125. Rousseau, *Social Contract*, p. 174.
126. See review article in *The Monthly Review; or, Literary Journal*, 55 (July–December 1776), pp. 430–1. The review goes on to acknowledge some biographical evidence in favour of Marshall's actual existence under that name.
127. Joseph Marshall, *Travels through Holland, Flanders, Germany, Denmark, Sweden, Lapland, Russia, The Ukraine, and Poland, in the Years 1768, 1769, and 1770*, 8 vols (London, 1772), vol. 2, p. 149. I have not

been able to identify 'Count Roncellen'. As was the case with the supposed student writer of letters to the anonymous author of *Observations on the Present State of Denmark*, then, we cannot be sure whether the encounter Marshall describes ever actually occurred.
128. Marshall, *Travels*, vol. 2, pp. 148, 149–50.
129. Marshall, *Travels*, vol. 2, pp. 150, 165.
130. Marshall, *Travels*, vol. 2, pp. 152, 188.
131. Marshall, *Travels*, vol. 2, p. 154.
132. Marshall, *Travels*, vol. 2, p. 156.
133. Marshall, *Travels*, vol. 2, p. 184.
134. Marshall, *Travels*, vol. 2, p. 185.
135. Marshall, *Travels*, vol. 2, p. 277.
136. Marshall, *Travels*, vol. 2, p. 277.
137. Marshall, *Travels*, vol. 2, p. 277.
138. Marshall, *Travels*, vol. 2, p. 285.
139. Marshall, *Travels*, vol. 2, p. 285.
140. Marshall, *Travels*, vol. 2, p. 285.
141. Marshall, *Travels*, vol. 2, p. 277.
142. Marshall, *Travels*, vol. 2, pp. 277–8.
143. Marshall, *Travels*, vol. 2, p. 279.
144. Marshall, *Travels*, vol. 2, pp. 279–80.
145. Marshall, *Travels*, vol. 2, p. 280.
146. MacDonald, *Travels*, p. 35; John Murray (ed.), *A Hand-Book for Travellers in Denmark, Norway, Sweden, and Russia* (London, 1839), p. 10.
147. Some material from this section has already been published in Cian Duffy, '"The happiest country in the world": Mary Wollstonecraft in Denmark', https://wordsworth.org.uk/blog/2015/09/14/the-happiest-country-in-the-world-mary-wollstonecraft-in-denmark/ (last accessed April 2021). It is reproduced here by kind permission of The Wordsworth Trust.
148. For a recent overview of the extensive scholarship on the biographical backdrop to Wollstonecraft's *Short Residence*, see Christoph Bode, '"Imaginary circles round the human mind": Bias and Openness in Mary Wollstonecraft's *Letters Written during a Short Residence in Sweden, Norway, and Denmark* (1796)', in Duffy (ed.), *Romantic Norths*, pp. 29–51 (29–31).
149. Wollstonecraft, *Short Residence*, p. 227.
150. Wollstonecraft, *Short Residence*, p. 215.
151. Wollstonecraft, *Short Residence*, p. 213.
152. Wollstonecraft, *Short Residence*, pp. 211, 213, 227, 225.
153. Wollstonecraft, *Short Residence*, pp. 230–1.
154. Wollstonecraft, *Short Residence*, pp. 83–4, 202, 219.
155. Wollstonecraft, *Short Residence*, p. 202.
156. Wollstonecraft, *Short Residence*, p. 212.
157. Wollstonecraft, *Short Residence*, p. 202.
158. Wollstonecraft, *Short Residence*, p. 201.
159. The 'law of Jante', a strictly anti-individualist set of rules often thought either implicitly or explicitly to regulate individual and social conduct in Denmark, are formulated in the novel *En flyktning krysser sitt spor* [A Fugitive Crosses His Tracks] (1933), by the Danish-Norwegian author Aksel Sandemose (1899–1965), which is set in the fictional small town of Jante, in rural Denmark.

160. Andreas Andersen Feldborg, *Denmark Delineated; or, Sketches of the Present State of that Country* (Edinburgh, 1824), Part 3, pp. 13, 14.
161. Feldborg, *Denmark Delineated*, Part 3, p. 14.
162. See Stanley Mayes, *The Great Belzoni* (New York: Walker, 1961), p. 273. The factual details of Mayes's account of Belzoni's stay in the Danish capital (pp. 273–4) are based primarily on *Denmark Delineated*.
163. Feldborg, *Denmark Delineated*, Part 3, p. 15.
164. Feldborg, *Denmark Delineated*, Part 3, p. 42.
165. Feldborg, *Denmark Delineated*, Part 3, p. 42.
166. Feldborg, *Denmark Delineated*, p. i.
167. Feldborg, *Denmark Delineated*, Part 3, p. 35.
168. Feldborg, *Denmark Delineated*, Part 3, p. 35.
169. Feldborg, *Denmark Delineated*, Part 3, p. 35.
170. Feldborg, *Denmark Delineated*, Part 3, p. 40.
171. Feldborg, *Denmark Delineated*, Part 3, p. 52.
172. Feldborg, *Denmark Delineated*, Part 1, p. 4.
173. Feldborg, *Denmark Delineated*, Part 3, p. 54.
174. Feldborg, *Denmark Delineated*, Part 3, p. 56.
175. Feldborg, *Denmark Delineated*, Part 3, p. 56 and n.
176. Feldborg, *Denmark Delineated*, Part 3, p. 47.
177. Feldborg, *Denmark Delineated*, Part 3, p. 50.
178. Feldborg, *Denmark Delineated*, Part 3, pp. 48, 50.
179. Feldborg, *Denmark Delineated*, Part 3, p. 56.
180. Feldborg, *Denmark Delineated*, Part 3, p. 57.

Chapter 5: 'No trifling kingdom': Anglo-Danish Politics beyond the Revolutionary and Napoleonic Wars

1. John Murray (ed.), *A Hand-Book for Travellers in Denmark, Norway, Sweden, and Russia* (London, 1839), p. 28.
2. James MacDonald, *Travels through Denmark and Part of Sweden* (London, 1810), p. 73.
3. Murray (ed.), *Hand-Book*, p. 29.
4. Joseph Marshall, *Travels through Holland, Flanders, Germany, Denmark, Sweden, Lapland, Russia, the Ukraine, and Poland, in the Years 1768, 1769, 1770*, 8 vols (London, 1772), vol. 2, p. 291.
5. Mary Wollstonecraft, *Letters Written during a Short Residence in Sweden, Norway, and Denmark* (London, 1796), p. 148.
6. Wollstonecraft, *Short Residence*, p. 74.
7. Wollstonecraft, *Short Residence*, pp. 148–9.
8. Wollstonecraft, *Short Residence*, Appendix, n.p.
9. The first edition of Molesworth's *Account* was anonymous.
10. Andreas Andersen Feldborg, *Denmark Delineated; or, Sketches of the Present State of that Country* (Edinburgh, 1824), 'Appendix', p. 58 (quoting Molesworth, *Account of Denmark*, p. 244).
11. Robert Molesworth, *An Account of Denmark, as it was in the year 1692*, sixth edition (Glasgow, 1752), p. 52.
12. Molesworth, *Account*, p. 52.

13. MacDonald, *Travels*, p. 52.
14. MacDonald, *Travels*, p. 52.
15. Molesworth, *Account*, pp. xxi, 32.
16. Molesworth, *Account*, p. 29.
17. Molesworth, *Account*, p. xxxi.
18. Molesworth, *Account*, pp. 50, 183, 59.
19. Molesworth, *Account*, p. 183.
20. Molesworth, *Account*, p. xxxviii.
21. Molesworth, *Account*, pp. 79–80.
22. Jodocus Crull, *Denmark Vindicated: Being an Answer to a Late Treatise called An Account of Denmark* (London, 1694), p. xxiii.
23. Crull, *Denmark Vindicated*, p. xxiii.
24. Crull, *Denmark Vindicated*, p. xxii.
25. Crull, *Denmark Vindicated*, pp. 216, xxii.
26. Crull, *Denmark Vindicated*, pp. 109, 111.
27. Crull, *Denmark Vindicated*, pp. 216, xxi.
28. Nathaniel Wraxall, *A Tour through Some of the Northern Parts of Europe, particularly Copenhagen, Stockholm, and Petersburgh. In a Series of Letters*, third edition (London, 1776), p. 29.
29. Anon., *Observations on the Present State of Denmark, Russia, and Switzerland. In a Series of Letters* (London, 1784), pp. 24n., 67. As noted in Chapter 1, it is possible *Observations* was the work of the Oxford Divine and anti-slavery campaigner Francis Randolph (1714–97).
30. Anon., *Observations*, pp. 56, 5, 39.
31. Anon., *Observations*, pp. 44, 34–5, 42–3.
32. William Coxe, *Travels into Poland, Russia, Sweden, and Denmark*, 2 vols (London, 1784), vol. 2, pp. 528–43 (528).
33. Marshall, *Travels*, p. 291.
34. Marshall, *Travels*, p. 277.
35. Marshall, *Travels*, pp. 127, 145, 241, 242–3, 288.
36. Marshall, *Travels*, p. 149.
37. Marshall, *Travels*, pp. 148, 150.
38. Marshall, *Travels*, p. 156.
39. Marshall, *Travels*, p. 167.
40. Marshall, *Travels*, p. 285.
41. John Carr, *A Northern Summer: or Travels round the Baltic* (London, 1805), pp. 33, 65.
42. Richard Jones, *Copenhagen and its Environs* (Copenhagen, 1829), pp. 72, 1, 73.
43. William Rae Wilson, *Travels in Norway, Sweden, Denmark, Hanover, Germany, Netherlands* (London 1826), pp. iii–iv.
44. Wilson, *Travels*, pp. 468, 463.
45. Wilson, *Travels*, p. 466.
46. Wilson, *Travels*, p. 465.
47. Feldborg, *Denmark Delineated*, Part 3, pp. 52–3.
48. Feldborg, *Denmark Delineated*, Appendix, p. 55.
49. Sydney Smith, Review of Jean-Pierre Catteau-Calleville's (1759–1819) *Tableaux des états danois* (1802), in *The Edinburgh Review*, 4 (July 1803), pp. 287–308 (287, 288).
50. Smith, Review of *Tableaux des états danois*, p. 292.

51. Anon., 'On Feldberg's Denmark', in *Blackwood's Edinburgh Magazine*, 10 (August–December 1821), pp. 172–80 (176).
52. Wollstonecraft, *Short Residence*, p. 203.
53. Wollstonecraft, *Short Residence*, p. 206.
54. Wollstonecraft, *Short Residence*, pp. 204–5.
55. Wollstonecraft, *Short Residence*, pp. 203–4.
56. Wollstonecraft, *Short Residence*, p. 204.
57. Wollstonecraft, *Short Residence*, p. 204.
58. Wollstonecraft, *Short Residence*, p. 214.
59. Wraxall, *Tour*, pp. 37, 49.
60. Wraxall, *Tour*, pp. 7–8.
61. Coxe, *Travels*, vol. 2, pp. 516–17.
62. Coxe, *Travels*, vol. 2, p. 517.
63. Coxe, *Travels*, vol. 2, p. 517.
64. Carr, *Northern Summer*, p. 91.
65. Carr, *Northern Summer*, p. 93.
66. Carr, *Northern Summer*, pp. 97, 100.
67. Feldborg, *Denmark Delineated*, Part 1, p. 10. For the concept of 'classic ground' in British eighteenth-century and Romantic-period travel writing, see Cian Duffy, *The Landscapes of the Sublime, 1700–1830: 'Classic Ground'* (London: Palgrave, 2013).
68. Feldborg, *Denmark Delineated*, Part 1, p. 7.
69. Feldborg, *Denmark Delineated*, Part 1, p. 11.
70. Feldborg, *Denmark Delineated*, Part 1, p. 11 (quoting Southey, *Life of Nelson*, 2 vols (London, 1813), vol. 2, p. 108). In point of fact, this passage of *Denmark Delineated* is more deeply indebted to Southey's phrasing in his *Life* than Feldborg's footnote allows. Southey describes Kronborg as 'inseparably associated with Hamlet, and one of the noblest works of human genius [i.e. the play *Hamlet*]' and also affirms that it was 'the scene of a deeper tragedy' – exact precedents for Feldborg's account (*Life of Nelson*, vol. 2, pp. 107–8).
71. Nor were such sites limited to Kronborg. In his account of Frederiksborg Castle in Part 1 of *Denmark Delineated*, for example, Feldborg recalls having had 'eagerly pointed out to me by the person who conducts strangers over the castle' a pane of glass removed from one of the windows on which Caroline Matilda had ostensibly engraved her initials (p. 90).
72. Wilson, *Travels*, p. 374.
73. Wilson, *Travels*, p. 427.
74. Wilson, *Travels*, p. 428.
75. For an English-language account of the expedition and its achievements, see Lawrence Baack, *Undying Curiosity: Carsten Niebuhr and the Royal Danish Expedition to Arabia, 1761–1767* (Stockholm: Franz Steiner, 2014). For an assessment of how Niebuhr's account of Istanbul draws on the emerging aesthetics of the sublime, see Cian Duffy, '"Nothing in the world can equal such a scene": Istanbul and the "Romantic" Sublime', in Jens Martin Gurr and Berit Michel (eds), *Romantic Cityscapes* (Trier: WVT, 2013), pp. 249–56 (249–50).
76. Coxe, *Travels*, vol. 2, pp. 568–9.
77. Wraxall, *Tour*, p. 24.
78. Carr, *Northern Summer*, p. 70; Andrew Swinton, *Travels into Norway, Denmark, and Russia* (London, 1792), p. 29.

79. James MacDonald, *Travels*, p. 71; Swinton, *Travels*, p. 30.
80. Carr, *Northern Summer*, p. 52. Cp. Wilson, *Travels* on this 'noble equestrian statue . . .[. . .] erected by the liberality of the Danish East India Company' (p. 383). Jones, *Copenhagen and its Environs*, confirms the price of '80,000 Pounds Sterling' for the 'truly magnificent' statue, paid 'at the sole expense of the Danish East India Company' (p. 42).
81. Molesworth, *Account*, p. 28. Characteristically, Molesworth then allows himself to wonder aloud 'whether the lading of those ships I mentioned were the lawful product of trade, or acquired by some other means' (p. 28).
82. There is, of course, a great deal of Danish-language scholarship on Denmark's colonies and their economic and cultural significance, including Mikkel Venborg Pedersen's excellent *Luksus: forbrug og kolonier i Danmark in det 18. Århundrede* [Luxury: Consumption and Colonialism in Eighteenth-Century Denmark] (Copenhagen: Museum Tusculanum, 2013). Useful anglophone histories include Ole Feldbaek, 'The Danish Trading Companies of the Seventeenth and Eighteenth Centuries', *Scandinavian Economic History Review*, 34/3 (September 1986), pp. 204–18; and *Indian Trade under the Danish Flag, 1772–1808* (Copenhagen: Reitzel, 1969). On the trade in slaves in the Danish West Indies, see Erik Gøbel, *The Danish Slave Trade and its Abolition* (Leiden: Brill, 2016); Neville Hall, *Slave Society in the Danish West Indies* (Jamaica: University of the West Indies Press, 1992); and Thorkild Hansen, *Slavernes Oer* (Copenhagen: Gyldendal 1972; English translation by Kari Dako as *Islands of Slaves* (2004)).
83. Pierre Marie Louis de Boisgelin de Kerdu, *Travels through Denmark and Sweden*, 2 vols (London, 1810), vol. 1, pp. 144–5.
84. De Kerdu, *Travels*, vol. 1, pp. 140–1.
85. MacDonald, *Travels*, p 71.
86. Wilson, *Travels*, p. 460. The price agreed, on 15 June 1733, was 750,000 French livres.
87. Anon., *Observations*, p. 49.
88. De Kerdu, *Travels*, vol. 1, pp. 142–3.
89. Molesworth, *Account*, p. 28.
90. Marshall, *Travels*, pp. 125, 247–8, 263. For eighteenth-century speculation about the so-called *terra australis incognita*, an undiscovered supercontinent in the southern hemisphere of whose existence Marshall affirms there is 'no doubt' (266), see Duffy, *Landscapes of the sublime*, pp. 109–12, 116–19.
91. Marshall, *Travels*, pp. 264–5.
92. Carr, *Northern Summer*, p. 70.
93. Anon., *Observations*, p. 50n.
94. Andreas Andersen Feldborg, *A Dane's Excursions in Britain*, 2 vols (London, 1809), vol. 1, p. 23.
95. Andreas Andersen Feldorg, *A Tour in Zealand, in the Year 1802* (London, 1805), p. iv; Andreas Andersen Feldborg, *Denmark Delineated* (Edinburgh, 1824), 'Preface', p. iv.
96. Andreas Andersen Feldborg and William Sydney Walker (eds), *Poems from the Danish* (London, 1815), pp. iii–iv, vii.
97. Text from Feldborg and Walker (eds), *Poems from the Danish*, pp. 42–3.
98. Feldborg and Walker, *Poems from the Danish*, pp. 140–1.
99. Feldborg and Walker, *Poems from the Danish*, p. 141.

100. Feldborg and Walker, *Poems from the Danish*, p. 141.
101. For more on Malling's work and its reception in early nineteenth-century Britain, see Chapter 4.
102. Feldborg and Walker, *Poems from the Danish*, p. 141; quoting Andreas Andersen Feldborg, *Great and Good Deeds of Danes, Norwegians, and Holsteinians* (London, 1807), pp. 22–3.
103. Feldborg and Walker, *Poems from the Danish*, pp. 141–2; quoting Feldborg, *Great and Good Deeds*, p. 23.
104. Feldborg and Walker, *Poems from the Danish*, p. 142; quoting Feldborg, *Great and Good Deeds*, p. 23.
105. Feldborg and Walker, *Poems from the Danish*, pp. 142, 143, 144; quoting Feldborg, *Great and Good Deeds*, pp. 23, 24, 25.

Coda: The 'German' Oehlenschläger

1. Julius Charles Hare, 'The German Drama. No. 1. Oehlenschlaeger', in Charles Ollier, *Literary Miscellany, in Prose and Verse, by Several Hands*, vol. 1 (1820), pp. 90–153 (104). Hare in fact quotes from Shelley's play *The Cenci* (1819) and describes the author, whom he does not name, as 'a great modern poet' (Hare, 'German Drama', p. 149). The reference caught Shelley's attention, and Hare's essay may have influenced Shelley's revisions to his essay 'On the Devil, and Devils' (1819–20) as well as some key passages of 'A Defence of Poetry'. See G. F. McFarland, 'Shelley and Julius Hare: A Review and a Response', *Bulletin of the John Rylands Library*, 52/2 (1975), pp. 406–29.
2. Hare, 'German Drama', p. 90.
3. Hare, 'German Drama', p. 90.
4. Hare, 'German Drama', p. 94.
5. Hare, 'German Drama', p. 92.
6. Hare, 'German Drama', p. 107.
7. Hare, 'German Drama', p. 107.
8. Hare, 'German Drama', p. 107.
9. Hare, 'German Drama', p. 107.
10. Hare, 'German Drama', p. 108.
11. Germaine de Staël, *The Influence of Literature upon Society*, 2 vols (London, 1812), vol. 1, p. 269.
12. See Elisabeth Oxfeldt, *Nordic Orientalism* (Copenhagen: Museum Tusculanum, 2005), esp. Chapter 1: 'The Incorporation of Aladdin into the Image of Danish National Identity' (pp. 21–53).
13. Oehlenschläger's poem 'Fædrelands-Sang' [Homeland Song] was composed in 1819.
14. Hare, 'German Drama', p. 109.
15. Specifically, Hare quotes from Henrik Steffens, *Die gegenwärtige Zeit und wie sie geworden mit besonderer Rücksichte auf Deutschland*, 2 vols (Berlin, 1817), vol. 1, pp. 400–3.
16. Steffens's lectures were published in Copenhagen in 1803 as *Inledning til Philosophiske Forlæsninger* [Introduction to Philosophical Lectures].
17. Hare, 'German Drama', p. 109.

18. Hare, 'German Drama', p. 110.
19. Hare, 'German Drama', p. 110.
20. Hare, 'German Drama', p. 111; emphasis added.
21. Hare, 'German Drama', p. 110.
22. Hare, 'German Drama', p. 110.
23. Hare, 'German Drama', p. 110.
24. Hare, 'German Drama', p. 153; the emphasis is Hare's own.
25. Christoph Bode, 'Europe', in Nicholas Roe (ed.), *Romanticism: An Oxford Guide* (Oxford: Oxford University Press, 2005), pp. 126–36 (126); original emphasis.
26. Bode, 'Europe', p. 126.

Bibliography

Primary Sources

Anon., 'Review of *The Wierd Wanderer of Jutland*', *The Monthly Repertory of English Literature* (July 1822); reprinted in *Galignani's Literary Gazette* 15 (1822), pp. 163–5.
Anon., 'On Feldberg's Denmark', *Blackwood's Edinburgh Magazine*, vol. 10 (September 1821), pp. 172–80.
Anon., 'Notices of Danish Literature', *The New Monthly Magazine*, vol. 11 (July 1819), pp. 487–92.
Anon., *Narrative of the Expedition to the Baltic: With an Account of the Siege and Capitulation of Copenhagen [. . .] By an Officer Employed in the Expedition* (London, 1808).
Anon., Review of James Grahame, *The Siege of Copenhagen, Anti-Jacobin Review* 31 (September–December 1808), pp. 183–5.
Anon., *An Authentic Account of the Siege of Copenhagen by the British, in the Year 1807. Containing the Danish Description of the Attack [. . .] And The Whole of the Official Dispatches Relating to the Expedition, as Published in the London Gazette* (London, 1807).
Anon., *Observations on the Present State of Denmark, Russia, and Switzerland. In a Series of Letters* (London, 1784).
Anon., *Candide, ou, l'Optimisme. Traduit de l'Allemand de Mr. le Docteur Ralph, Seconde Partie* (n.p., 1761).
Baggesen, Jens, *Labyrinten; eller Reise giennem Tydskland, Schweiz og Frankerig*, 2 vols (Copenhagen, 1792–3).
Barrow, John, *Excursions in the North of Europe* (London, 1834).
Borrow, George, *Romantic Ballads, Translated from the Danish; and Miscellaneous Pieces* (Norwich, 1826).
Burke, Edmund, *Reflections on the Revolution in France* (London, 1790).
Byron, George Gordon, Lord, *The Curse of Minerva* (London, 1813).
Campbell, Thomas, *The Poetical Works of Thomas Campbell* (Edinburgh, 1837).
Carr, John, *A Northern Summer* (London, 1805).
Carr, John, *The Stranger in France* (London, 1803).
Clarke, Edward Daniel, *Travels in Various Countries of Europe, Asia and Africa*, 4th edn, 11 vols (London, 1816–24).
Consett, Matthew, *A Tour through Sweden, Swedish-Lapland, Finland and Denmark. In a Series of Letters* (London, 1789).

Coxe, William, *Travels into Poland, Russia, Sweden, and Denmark*, 2 vols (London, 1784).
Crookes, Septimus, *Particulars of the Expedition to Copenhagen* (Sheffield, 1808).
Crull, Jodocus, *Denmark Vindicated: Being an Answer to a Late Treatise called An Account of Denmark* (London, 1694).
De Kerdu, Pierre Marie Louis de Boisgelin, *Travels through Denmark and Sweden*, 2 vols (London, 1810).
De Quincey, Thomas, *The Works of Thomas De Quincey*, gen. ed. Grevel Lindop, 21 vols (London: Pickering & Chatto, 2000–3).
De Quincey, Thomas, *New Essays by Thomas De Quincey*, ed. Stuart M. Tave (Princeton: Princeton University Press, 1966).
Staël, Germaine de, *Germany*, 3 vols (London, 1813).
Staël, Germaine de, *The Influence of Literature Upon Society*, 2 vols (London, 1812).
Drevon, Jean Frédéric Henry de, *Description of Dronning-gaard, terre située dans l'isle de Zelande en Dannemark* (Copenhagen, 1786).
Drevon, Jean Frédéric Henry de, *A Journey through Sweden*, trans. William Radcliffe (Dublin, 1790).
Fairburn, John, *Authentic Account of the Bombardment of Copenhagen, and the Surrender of the Danish Fleet* (London, 1808).
Feldborg, Andreas Andersen, *Denmark Delineated; or, Sketches of the Present State of that Country* (Edinburgh, 1824).
Feldborg, Andreas Andersen, 'An Appeal to the English Nation in behalf of Norway', in *The Pamphleteer* 4 (July 1814), pp. 233–85.
Feldborg, Andreas Andersen, *A Dane's Excursions in Britain*, 2 vols (London, 1809).
Feldborg, Andreas Andersen, *Great and Good Deeds of Danes, Norwegians, and Holsteinians*, trans. Ove Malling (London, 1807).
Feldborg, Andreas Andersen, *A Tour in Zealand, in the Year 1802* (London, 1805).
Feldborg, Andreas Andersen, C. Stokes and William Sidney Walker, *Danish and Norwegian Melodies* (London, 1815).
Feldborg, Andreas Andersen, and William Sydney Walker (eds), *Poems from the Danish* (London, 1815).
Ferguson, Adam, *An Essay on the History of Civil Society*, fifth edition (London, 1782).
Gibbon, Edward, *The History of the Decline and Fall of the Roman Empire*, 6 vols (London, 1776–89).
Gillies, Robert Pearse, 'Horae Danicae I', *Blackwood's Edinburgh Magazine*, 7 (April 1820), pp. 73–89.
Gillies, Robert Pearse, 'Horae Danicae II', *Blackwood's Edinburgh Magazine*, 8 (December 1820), pp. 290–305.
Gillies, Robert Pearse, 'Horae Danicae IV [for III]', *Blackwood's Edinburgh Magazine*, 8 (March 1821), pp. 646–60.
Gillies, Robert Pearse, 'Horae Danicae V [for IV]', in *Blackwood's Edinburgh Magazine*, 9 (April 1821), pp. 43–59.
Godwin, William, *Memoirs of the Author of A Vindication of the Rights of Woman* (London, 1798).
Grahame, James, *The Siege of Copenhagen. A Poem; With Notes* (London, 1808).

Hare, Julius Charles, 'The German Drama. No. 1. Oehlenschlaeger', in *Ollier's Literary Miscellany*, 1 (1820), pp. 90–153.
Herbert, William, *Hedin; or, The Spectre of the Tomb. A Tale. From the Danish History* (London, 1820).
Herbert, William, *Select Icelandic Poetry, Translated from the Originals: with Notes* (London, 1804).
Herbert, William, *The Wierd Wanderer of Jutland. A Tragedy* (London, 1822).
Hogg, James, *Queen Hynde. A Poem, in Six Books* (London, 1824).
Hume, David, *Essays and Treatises on Several Subjects*, a new edition, 2 vols (London, 1784).
Jamieson, Robert, *Illustrations of Northern Antiquities* (Edinburgh, 1814).
Jamieson, Robert, *Popular Ballads and Songs from Tradition, Manuscripts and Scarce Editions with Translations of Similar Pieces from the Ancient Danish Language* (Edinburgh, 1806).
Jamieson, Robert, Walter Scott, and Henry William Weber (eds), *Illustrations of Northern Antiquities from the earlier Teutonic and Scandinavian Romances* (Edinburgh, 1814).
Jones, Richard, *Copenhagen and its Environs* (Copenhagen, 1829).
Lewis, Matthew, *The Monk*, ed. Howard Anderson and Nick Groom (Oxford: Oxford University Press, 2016).
Loudon, J. C., *Encyclopedia of Gardening*, third edition (London, 1825).
MacDonald, James, *Travels through Denmark and Part of Sweden* (London, 1810).
Macpherson, James, *Introduction to the History of Great Britain and Ireland* (London, 1770).
Mallet, Paul Henri, *Introduction à L'histoire du Danemarch où l'on traite de la religion, des moeurs, des lois, et des usages des anciens Danois*, 3 vols (Copenhagen, 1758–77).
Mallet, Paul Henri, *Monuments de la mythologie et de la poesie des Celtes, et particulierement des anciens Scandinaves* (1756).
Malling, Ove, *Great and Good Deeds of Danes, Norwegians, and Holsteinians*, trans. Andreas Andersen Feldborg (London, 1807).
Malthus, Robert, *The Travel Diaries of Thomas Robert Malthus*, ed. Patricia James (Cambridge: Cambridge University Press, 1966).
Marshall, Joseph, *Travels through Holland, Flanders, Germany, Denmark, Sweden, Lapland, Russia, the Ukraine, and Poland, in the Years 1768, 1769, and 1770*, 8 vols (London, 1772).
Molesworth, Robert, *An Account of Denmark, as it was in the Year 1692*, sixth edition (Glasgow, 1752).
Montesquieu, Charles-Louis de Secondat, Baron de La Brède et de, *The Spirit of the Laws*, trans. Thomas Nugent, 2 vols (Dublin, 1751).
Murray, John (ed.), *Hand-Book for Travellers in Denmark, Norway, Sweden, and Russia* (London, 1829).
Percy, Thomas, *Northern Antiquities: or, A Description of the Manners, Customs, Religion and Laws of the Ancient Danes*, 2 vols (London, 1770).
Percy, Thomas, *Reliques of Ancient English Poetry* (London, 1765).
Porter, Robert Ker, *Travelling Sketches in Russia and Sweden, during the Years 1805, 1806, 1807, 1808* (Philadelphia, 1809).
Rask, Rasmus, *A Grammar of the Danish Language for the Use of Englishmen, Together with Extracts in Prose and Verse* (Copenhagen, 1830).

Rodd, Thomas, *The Battle of Copenhagen; A Poem, with Notes* (London, 1806).
Rousseau, Jean-Jacques, *An Inquiry into the Nature of the Social Contract*, trans. anon. (Dublin, 1791).
Scott, Walter, *The Antiquary*, ed. Nicola Watson (Oxford: Oxford World's Classics, 2009).
Scott, Walter, *Marmion; a Tale of Flodden Field* (Edinburgh, 1808).
Shelley, Percy Bysshe, *Selected Poetry and Prose*, ed. Jack Donovan and Cian Duffy (London: Penguin, 2017).
Smith, Sydney, Review of Jean-Pierre Catteau-Calleville's (1759–1819) *Tableaux des états danois* (1802), in *The Edinburgh Review*, 4 (July 1803), pp. 287–308.
Sommer, F. L., *A Description of Denmark; And a Narrative of the Siege, Bombardment, and Capture of Copenhagen [. . .] From the Danish Account of F. L. Sommer*, trans. Anon., second edition (Colchester, 1808).
Southey, Robert, *Life of Nelson*, 2 vols (London, 1813).
Southey, Robert, *The Collected Letters of Robert Southey*, ed. Ian Packer and Linda Pratt, Romantic Circles (2009); https://www.rc.umd.edu/editions/southey_letters.
Steffens, Henrik, *Die gegenwärtige Zeit und wie sie geworden mit besonderer Rücksichte auf Deutschland*, 2 vols (Berlin, 1817).
Steffens, Henrik, *Inledning til Philosophiske Forlæsninger* [Introduction to Philosophical Lectures] (Copenhagen, 1803).
Stevens, Robert, 'Account of Copenhagen', in *The New Monthly Magazine*, 73 (1 June 1801), pp. 381–5.
Stukeley, William, *Stonehenge: A Temple Restor'd to the British Druids* (London, 1740).
Swinton, Andrew [pseudonym of William Thomson], *Travels into Norway, Denmark, and Russia, in the years 1788, 1789, 1790, and 1791* (London, 1792).
Thiele, Just Mathias, *Af mit Livs Aarboger. I. 1795–1838* (Copenhagen: C. A. Reitzel, 1917).
Thomson, William, *Letters from Scandinavia, On the Past and Present State of the Northern Nations of Europe*, 2 vols (London, 1796).
Wilson, William Rae, *Travels in Norway, Sweden, Denmark, Hanover, Germany, Netherlands &c.* (London, 1826).
Wollstonecraft, Mary, *The Collected Letters of Mary Wollstonecraft*, ed. Janet Todd (London: Allen Lane, 2003).
Wollstonecraft, Mary, *Letters Written during a Short Residence in Sweden, Norway, and Denmark* (London, 1796).
Wordsworth, William, *The Major Works*, ed. Stephen Gill (Oxford: Oxford University Press, 2011).
Wraxall, Nathaniel, *A Tour through Some of the Northern Parts of Europe, particularly Copenhagen, Stockholm, and Petersburgh. In a Series of Letters*, third edition (London, 1776).

Secondary Sources

Ahnert, Thomas, and Manning, Susan (eds), *Character, Self, and Sociability in the Scottish Enlightenment* (London: Palgrave, 2011).

Anderson, Benedict, *Imagined Communities: Reflections on the Origin and Spread of Nationalism* (London: Verso, 1983).
Baack, Lawrence, *Undying Curiosity: Carsten Niebuhr and the Royal Danish Expedition to Arabia, 1761–1767* (Stockholm: Franz Steiner, 2014).
Barton, Hildor Arnold, *Northern Arcadia: Foreign Travellers in Scandinavia, 1765–1815* (Carbondale, IL: Southern Illinois University Press, 1998).
Bennett, Betty T., and Smith, Orianne (eds), *British War Poetry in the Age of Romanticism*, Romantic Circles (2004); https://www.rc.umd.edu/editions/warpoetry/index.html.
Bode, Christoph, '"Imaginary circles round the human mind": Bias and Openness in Mary Wollstonecraft's *Letters Written during a Short Residence in Sweden, Norway, and Denmark* (1796), in Cian Duffy (ed.), *Romantic Norths: Anglo-Nordic Exchanges, 1770–1842* (London: Palgrave, 2017), pp. 29–51.
Bode, Christoph, 'Europe', in Nicholas Roe (ed.), *Romanticism: An Oxford Guide* (Oxford: Oxford University Press, 2005), pp. 126–36.
Bordoni, Silvia, 'From Madame de Staël to Lord Byron: The Dialectics of European Romanticism', *Literature Compass* 4/1 (2007), pp. 134–49.
Briens, Sylvain, 'Boréalisme: Le Nord comme espace discursif', *Études germaniques* 71 (2016), pp. 179–88.
Butler, Marilyn, *Mapping Mythologies: Countercurrents in Eighteenth-Century British Poetry and Cultural History* (Cambridge: Cambridge University Press, 2015).
Carruthers, Gerald, and Rawe, Anthony (eds), *English Romanticism and the Celtic World* (Cambridge: Cambridge University Press, 2003).
Colley, Linda, *Britons: Forging the Nation, 1707–1837* (New Haven: Yale University Press, 1992; revised 2009).
Davies, Mark, *A Perambulating Paradox: British Travel Literature and the Image of Sweden, c. 1770–1865* (Lund: Lunds Universitet, 2000).
Day, Aidan, *Romanticism* (New York: Routledge, 1996).
Domsch, Sebastian, Reinfandt, Christoph, and Rennhak, Katharina (eds), *Romantic Ambiguities: Abodes of the Modern* (Trier: WVT, 2017).
Duff, David, and Jones, Catherine (eds), *Scotland, Ireland, and the Romantic Aesthetic* (Lewisburg: Bucknell University Press, 2007).
Duffy, Cian, '"The happiest country in the world": Mary Wollstonecraft in Denmark', The Wordsworth Trust (2015) (https://wordsworth.org.uk/blog/2015/09/14/the-happiest-country-in-the-world-mary-wollstonecraft-in-denmark/).
Duffy, Cian, *The Landscapes of the Sublime, 1700–1830* (London: Palgrave, 2013).
Duffy, Cian, '"Nothing in the world can equal such a scene": Istanbul and the "Romantic" Sublime', in Jens Martin Gurr and Berit Michel (eds), *Romantic Cityscapes* (Trier: WVT, 2013), pp. 249–56.
Duffy, Cian (ed.), *Romantic Norths: Anglo-Nordic Exchanges, 1770–1842* (London: Palgrave, 2017).
Duffy, Cian, '"The story of this retired spot": Dronninggaard, John Carr, and Forgotten Works by William Hayley and Leigh Hunt', *e-romantikstudier* 1 (November 2015), http://www.romantikstudier.dk/media/44673/Cian,%20combined.pdf.
Duffy, Cian, '"There was a time": William Wordsworth and Jens Baggesen Recollecting Childhood', *ANQ* 28 (May 2016), pp. 170–3.

Engelberg, Karsten, 'Shelley in the Nordic Countries: Would They Be Seeking Him If He Had Not Been Found?', in Michael Rossington and Susanne Schmid (eds), *The Reception of P.B. Shelley in Europe* (London: Bloomsbury, 2008), pp. 156–68.

Erdman, David, 'Blake's Transcript of Bisset's "Lines Written on hearing the surrender of Copenhagen"', in *Bulletin of the New York Public Library* 72 (1968), pp. 518–21.

Feldbaek, Ole, *The Battle of Copenhagen 1801: Nelson and the Danes*, trans. Tony Wedgwood (Copenhagen: Politikens Forlag, 2002 [1985]).

Feldbaek, Ole, 'The Danish Trading Companies of the Seventeenth and Eighteenth Centuries', *Scandinavian Economic History Review* 34/3 (September 1986), pp. 204–18.

Feldbaek, Ole, *Indian Trade under the Danish Flag, 1772–1808* (Copenhagen: Reitzel, 1969).

Ferber, Michael (ed.), *A Companion to European Romanticism* (Malden, MA: Blackwell, 2005).

Fielding, Penny, *Scotland and the Fictions of Geography* (Cambridge: Cambridge University Press, 2008).

Fjågesund, Peter, *The Dream of the North: A Cultural History to 1920* (Amsterdam: Rodopi, 2014).

Fjågesund Peter, and Symes, Ruth, *The Northern Utopia: British Perceptions of Norway in the Nineteenth Century* (Amsterdam: Rodopi, 2003).

Floryan, Margrethe, 'Eremittens virke, vink, og venner: Scener og stemninger i Dronninggaards 1700-tals have', in Peter Wager, Claus M. Smidt and Margrethe Floryan (eds), *En Verden i Harmoni: To Parker i 1700–Tallet* (Søllerød: GL Holtegaard, 1996), pp. 30–44.

Garrett, Aaron, and Sebastiani, Silvia, 'David Hume on Race', in Naomi Zack (ed.), *The Oxford Handbook of Philosophy and Race* (Oxford: Oxford University Press, 2017), pp. 31–43.

Gaskill, Howard (ed.), *The Reception of Ossian in Europe* (London: Continuum, 2004).

Glenthøj, Rasmus, and Rasmussen, Jens Rahbek (eds), *Det venskabelige bombardement* (Copenhagen: Museum Tusculanum, 2007).

Goldstein, Laurence, *Ruins and Empire: The Evolution of a Theme in Augustan and Romantic Literature* (Pittsburgh: University of Pittsburgh Press, 1997).

Groves, David, 'De Quincey and Danish Poetry', *Notes and Queries* 35 (September 1988), pp. 313–15.

Gøbel, Erik, *The Danish Slave Trade and Its Abolition* (Leiden: Brill, 2016).

Hall, Neville, *Slave Society in the Danish West Indies* (Kingston, Jamaica: University of the West Indies Press, 1992).

Hamilton, Paul (ed.), *The Oxford Handbook of European Romanticism* (Oxford: Oxford University Press, 2016).

Hansen, Thorkild, *Slavernes Oer* (Copenhagen: Gyldendal 1972).

Hayman, John, 'Notions on National Character in the Eighteenth Century', *Huntington Library Quarterly* 35/1 (November 1971) pp. 1–17.

Henriques, Alf, *Shakespeare og Danmark indtil 1840* [Shakespeare and Denmark until 1840] (Copenhagen: Einar Munksgaard, 1941).

Hustvedt, Sigurd, *Ballad Criticism in Scandinavia and Great Britain during the Eighteenth-Century* (New York: American Scandinavian Foundation, 1916).

Janowitz, Anne, *England's Ruins: Poetic Purpose and the National Landscape* (London: Blackwell, 1990).
Jones, Frederick L. (ed.), *Maria Gisborne and Edward E. Williams: Shelley's Friends: Their Journals and Letters* (Norman, OK: University of Oklahoma Press, 1951).
Kidd, Colin, *British Identities Before Nationalism: Ethnicity and Nationhood in the Atlantic World, 1600–1800* (Cambridge: Cambridge University Press, 1999).
Kliemann-Geisinger, Hendriette, 'Mapping the North – Spatial Dimensions and Geographical Conceptions of Northern Europe', in Karen Klitgaard Povlsen (ed.), *Northbound: Travels, Encounters, and Constructions, 1700–1830* (Aarhus: Aarhus University Press, 2007), pp. 69–88.
Leerssen, Joep, *National Thought in Europe* (Chicago: University of Chicago Press, 2007).
Leerssen, Joep, 'Notes towards a Definition of Romantic Nationalism', *Romantik* 2 (2013), pp. 9–35.
Lindop, Grevel, *The Opium-Eater: A Life of Thomas De Quincey* (London: Weidenfeld, 1993).
Lovejoy, Arthur O., 'On the Discrimination of Romanticisms', *PMLA* 39/2 (June 1924), pp. 229–53.
Mayes, Stanley, *The Great Belzoni* (New York: Walker, 1961).
McFarland, G. F., 'Shelley and Julius Hare: A Review and a Response', *Bulletin of the John Rylands Library* 52/2 (1975), pp. 406–29.
Mortensen, Peter, *British Romanticism and Continental Influences* (London: Palgrave, 2004).
Musgrove, S., 'Niels Klim, being an incomplete translation by Thomas De Quincey from the Danish of Ludvig Holberg, now edited from the manuscript by S. Musgrove', *Bulletin of Auckland University College* 42/5 (1953), pp. 1–37.
Møller, Lis, 'British and Danish Romantic-Period Adaptations of Two Danish "Elf Ballads"', in Cian Duffy (ed.), *Romantic Norths: Anglo-Nordic Exchanges, 1770–1842* (London: Palgrave, 2017), pp. 129–52.
Møller, Lis, 'The Dissemination of Danish Medieval Ballads in Germany and Britain, 1760s to 1830s', in Dan Ringgaard and Mads Rosendahl Thomsen (eds), *Danish Literature as World Literature* (London: Bloomsbury, 2017), pp. 31–51.
Nielsen, Jørgen Erik, '"Look to the Baltic": Byron between Romanticism and Radicalism in Denmark', in Richard Cadwell (ed.), *The Reception of Byron in Europe* (London: Bloomsbury, 2014), pp. 365–74.
Nielsen, Jørgen Erik, *Den Samtidige Engeleske Litteratur og Danmark, 1800–1840*, 2 vols, Publications of the Department of English, University of Copenhagen (Copenhagen: Nova, 1976).
Nielsen, Jørgen Erik, '"His pirates had foray'd on Scottish hill": The Danish Reception of Scott with an Outline of his Reception in Norway and Sweden', in Murray Pittock (ed.), *The Reception of Sir Walter Scott in Europe* (London: Bloomsbury, 2007), pp. 251–67.
Nielsen, Jørgen Erik, 'English Literature in Denmark in the First Half of the Nineteenth Century', in Jørgen Sevaldsen (ed.), *Britain and Denmark: Political, Economic and Cultural Relations in the 19th and 20th Centuries* (Copenhagen: Museum Tusculanum Press, 2003), pp. 357–72.

Nielsen, Jørgen Erik, 'Andreas Andersen Feldborg: In Denmark English, in England Danish', in *Angles on the English-Speaking World* 1 (Autumn 1986), pp. 51–63.

Oelsner, Gertrud, 'Inventing Jutland for the "Golden Age": Danish Artists Guided by Sir Walter Scott', in Cian Duffy (ed.), *Romantic Norths: Anglo-Nordic Exchanges, 1770–1842* (London: Palgrave, 2017), pp. 101–28.

Oxfeldt, Elisabeth, *Nordic Orientalism* (Copenhagen: Museum Tusculanum, 2005).

Pedersen, Mikkel Venborg, *Luksus: forbrug og kolonier i Danmark in det 18. Århundrede* (Copenhagen: Museum Tusculanum, 2013).

Pollin, Burton R., 'Southey's "Battle of Blenheim" Parodied in the *Morning Chronicle*: A Whig Attack on the Battle of Copenhagen', *Bulletin of the New York Public Library* 72 (1968), pp. 507–17.

Povlsen, Karen Klitgaard (ed.), *Northbound: Travels, Encounters, and Constructions, 1700–1830* (Aarhus: Aarhus University Press, 2007).

Pittock, Murray *Scottish and Irish Romanticism* (Oxford: Oxford University Press, 2008).

Prickett, Stephen (ed.), *European Romanticism: A Reader* (London: Continuum, 2010).

Rix, Robert, 'Visiting the Nordic Past: Domestic Travels in Early Nineteenth-Century Denmark', *Scandinavian Studies* 90/2 (Summer 2018), pp. 211–36.

Rix, Robert, '"In darkness they grope": Ancient Remains and Romanticism in Denmark', *European Romantic Review* 26/4 (July 2015), pp. 435–51.

Rix, Robert, 'Introduction: Romanticism in Scandinavia', *European Romantic Review* 26/4 (July 2015), pp. 395–400.

Rix, Robert, (ed.), *Norse Romanticism: Themes in British Literature, 1760–1830*, Romantic Circles (2012); https://romantic-circles.org/editions/norse/index.html.

Rix, Robert, '"The North" and "the East": The Odin Migration Theory', in Cian Duffy (ed.), *Romantic Norths: Anglo-Nordic Exchanges, 1770–1842* (London: Palgrave, 2017), pp. 153–79.

Roberts, Daniel Sanjiv, 'Thomas De Quincey's "Danish Origin of the Lake Country Dialect"', in *Transactions of the Cumberland and Westmorland Antiquarian and Archaeological Society* 99 (1999), pp. 257–66.

Roberts, Michael, *The Age of Liberty: Sweden 1719–22* (Cambridge: Cambridge University Press, 2003).

Sachs, Jonathan, *The Poetics of Decline in British Romanticism* (Cambridge: Cambridge University Press, 2018).

Saglia, Diego, *European Literatures in Britain, 1815–1832* (Cambridge: Cambridge University Press, 2019).

Sanders, Karen, '"On the bedrock of material things": The Journey to the Past in Danish Archaeological Imagination', in Karen Klitgaard Povlsen (ed.), *Northbound: Travels, Encounters, and Constructions, 1700–1830* (Aarhus: Aarhus University Press, 2007), pp. 151–70.

Scavenius, Bente, *The Golden Age in Denmark: Art and Culture, 1800–1850* (Copenhagen: Gyldendal, 1994).

Scheibel, Holger, 'Shakespeare's Sonnets in Danish Translation: A Phenomenon for Only the Few', in Manfred Pfister and Jürgen Gutsch (eds), *William Shakespeare's Sonnets for the First Time Globally Reprinted. A Quartercentenary Anthology, 1609–2009* (Dozwil, Switzerland: Edition Signathur, 2009), pp. 161–9.

Silvia Sebastiani, Silvia, 'National Characters and Race: A Scottish Enlightenment Debate', in Thomas Ahnert and Susan Manning (eds.), *Character, Self, and Sociability in the Scottish Enlightenment* (London: Palgrave, 2011), pp. 187–205.
Silvia Sebastiani, Silvia, *The Scottish Enlightenment: Race, Gender, and the Limits of Progress* (London: Palgrave, 2013).
Smidt, Kristian, 'The Discovery of Shakespeare in Scandinavia', in Dirk Delabastita and Lieven D'hulst (eds), *European Shakespeares: Translating Shakespeare in the Romantic Age* (Amsterdam: John Benjamins, 1993), pp. 91–103.
Sweet, Rosemary, *Antiquaries: The Discovery of the Past in Eighteenth-Century Britain* (London: Hambledon & London, 2004).
Sørensen, Øystein, and Stråth, Bo (eds), *The Cultural Construction of Norden* (Oslo: Scandinavian University Press, 1997).
Trumpener, Katie, *Bardic Nationalism* (Princeton: Princeton University Press, 1997).
Watson, Harry, 'The Reverend James MacDonald: An Opinionated Traveller in Denmark and Sweden', in *Northern Studies: Journal of the Scottish Society for Northern Studie* 25 (1988), pp. 121–62.
Wellek, René, 'The Concept of "Romanticism" in Literary History II: The Unity of European Romanticism', *Comparative Literature* 1/2 (Spring 1949), pp. 147–72.
Wu, Duncan, *Wordsworth's Reading*, 2 vols (Cambridge: Cambridge University Press, 1995).
Ziolkowski, Theodore, *Stages of European Romanticism* (New York: Camden House, 2018).

Index

Ahnert, Thomas, 129
Anderson, Benedict, 131
Anker, Carsten, 18
Anti-Jacobin, The, 59, 85, 132–3
antiquarianism, 1, 2, 12, 21, 26, 57, 63, 67–75, 93–5, 98–9, 101, 116, 126, 133, 192n.6, 213n.13
Arctic, the, 12, 26, 33, 47, 58
Armed Neutrality, League of, 38–9, 42, 51, 174
Arrebo, Anders, 116

Baggesen, Jens, 62, 97, 102, 103, 104, 111, 113, 114, 116, 118, 184, 189–90
Barrow, John, 98, 208n.85
Barton, Hildor Arnold, 2, 14, 18, 63, 66, 205n.10
Beethoven, Ludwig van, 4
Belzoni, Giovanni Battista, 23, 115, 154–8
Bennett, Betty T., 202n.123, 202n.141
Beowulf, 31, 57, 118
Bernstorff, Johann, 103
Bille, Steen Andersen, 39
Bisset, James, 48
Blackwood's Magazine, 2, 19, 62, 102, 109, 114–15, 116, 118, 124, 125–6, 167
'Horae Danicae', 21, 104–7, 109, 119
'Horae Germanicae', 21, 104
Blake, William, 48

Bode, Christoph, 6–7, 34–5, 185, 199n.57
Bordoni, Silvia, 5
Borrow, George, 21, 108–10, 112, 217n.117
Brahe, Tycho, 27, 116, 130
Brandt, Enevold, 169, 170
Brun, Friederike, 97
Buffon, Georges-Louis Leclerc, Comte de, 130, 131, 143, 145
Burke, Edmund, 46, 170
Burns, Robert, 123
Butler, Marilyn, 133
Byrne, Angela, 12
Byron, Lord, 2, 4, 18–19, 49, 55, 95, 96, 119, 122, 220n.172

Campbell, Thomas, 40–1, 96, 119, 219–20n.157
Canning, George, 48, 121
Caroline Matilda, 2, 23, 27, 41, 61, 75–8, 80, 140, 160, 167, 168–72, 229n.70, 229n.71
Carr, John, 20, 37, 78, 82–5, 98, 139, 147, 166, 170–1, 173, 175, 186, 195n.67, 210n.131
Catteau-Calleville, Jean-Pierre, 115, 117, 167
Christian IV of Denmark, 27, 37, 113, 140
Christian VII of Denmark, 2, 36, 75, 109, 117, 168
Christian VIII of Denmark, 160, 167
Clarke, Kenneth, 6

Clarke, Edward Daniel, 20, 62, 72–4, 87, 98, 140–1, 154, 207n.63
climate, 11, 129, 130, 137, 143, 145, 147–8
Coleridge, Samuel Taylor, 49, 103, 104
Colley, Linda, 8
Coninck, Frédéric de, 82
Consett, Matthew, 31, 32, 77, 97
Copenhagen, 2, 15, 18, 20, 22, 23, 25–60, 61, 66, 92, 93, 115, 124, 128, 140, 145, 154–7, 169, 177, 184, 185, 186
  Battle of (1801), 2, 3, 18, 19, 22, 23, 26, 38–46, 51, 53, 56, 59, 64, 65, 78, 80, 86, 89, 90, 95, 96, 98, 99, 102, 108, 111, 112, 113, 117, 120, 121, 128, 136, 148, 159, 174, 176, 201n.113
  Bombardment of (1807), 2, 18, 19, 23, 25–6, 46–60, 64, 71, 86, 87, 88, 95, 100, 111, 113, 118, 121, 124, 137, 147, 151, 159, 167, 174, 176, 201n.113, 224n.80
  Fire of (1728), 29
  Fire of (1795), 34, 35, 135
  university of, 1, 29, 31, 45, 57, 146
Cowper, William, 84
Coxe, William, 6, 18, 20, 25, 29–31, 32, 34, 50, 61, 62, 70–1, 170, 172
Crookes, Septimus, 46, 54–5
Crull, Jodocus, 16, 139, 163–4

Danelaw, the, 136, 137
Danes,
  as 'brothers of Englishmen', 19, 22, 40–4, 49, 53, 80, 89, 117, 120, 128, 136–40, 146, 148, 149
  'national character' of, 15, 19, 22–3, 27, 32, 36, 39, 42–3, 87, 100, 127–58, 195n.67
  modern, compared with the Vikings, 23, 129, 135, 140–6, 175
Danish language, the, 15, 99–103, 138
Danish literature, 2, 9, 21, 27, 31, 81, 92–126
Davies, Mark, 14

Denmark,
  absolutism in, 15–17, 18, 23, 27–8, 36, 38, 59, 66–7, 97, 116, 117, 137, 138, 145, 148, 150, 153, 154, 160–8, 179–80
  as 'classic ground', 75, 80, 171, 208n.80
  as happiest country in the world, 22, 128, 151–4
  as 'Oriental', 28–9, 33, 67, 162–3, 167
  climate and environment of, 15, 27, 50, 61, 66, 129, 137
  East and West India territories, 2, 23, 111, 160, 172–80, 224n.87, 230n.80, 230n.82
  freedom of the press in, 117, 153
  national anthem of, 109, 113, 188–9, 217n.100, 217n.117
  slave trade and, 113, 137, 160, 173, 175–80
  state bankruptcy of (1813), 2, 19, 118, 145, 159, 172, 189
  trade with Britain, 2
  travel writing about, 2, 20, 23, 25, 26–38, 59, 61–91, 93–9, 136
De Quincey, Richard, 2, 49, 100, 214n.43
De Quincey, Thomas, 2, 9–10, 11, 21, 49, 87, 99–103, 104, 124, 155, 214n.43
De Staël, Germaine, 3, 10–12, 13, 183
De Windt, James, 111, 176
Drevon, Jean Frédéric Henry de, 77, 82–5, 141, 147, 210n.131
Dryer, Dankvart, 68

Edda, the, 98
Elsinore, 21, 41, 61, 63, 75–81, 120, 122, 208n.84
  Kronborg, 75–6, 78, 79, 167, 169, 170, 171–2, 229n.70, 229n.71
Engelberg, Karsten, 96
Engelstoft, Laurids, 45
Equiano, Olaudah, 177
Evald, Johannes, 21, 108, 109, 113, 116, 123, 184, 188–9, 216n.73, 217n.100, 217n.117

Fairburn, John, 41–2, 50
Feldbæk, Ole, 200n.84, 230n.82
Feldborg, Andreas Andersen, 16, 19, 20, 21, 23, 44–6, 50, 62, 63, 64–6, 75–6, 80–1, 85–91, 95, 110–26, 131, 136, 139, 154–8, 161, 164, 167, 171, 175–80, 188, 214n.43
Ferber, Michael, 12
Ferguson, Adam, 130, 131, 147–8
Fielding, Penny, 14, 222n.16
Fischer, Johan Olfert, 39
Fjågesund, Peter, 13, 14
Flora Danica, 30, 198n.31
Floryan, Margrethe, 83, 210n.132
Foersom, Peter, 81, 114, 120–5, 190–1, 220n.159
Frederik III of Denmark, 15, 66, 160
Frederik V of Denmark, 3, 30, 31, 102, 117, 173
Frederik VI of Denmark, 22, 36, 39, 40, 53, 55, 89, 98, 117, 136, 166, 168, 224n.85

Garrick, David, 80
George III of England, 47–8, 160
Gibbon, Edward, 134, 135, 138
Gillies, Robert Pearse, 20, 21, 102, 104–7, 110, 216n.73
Gillray, James, 48
Glenthøj, Rasmus, 201n.113
Godwin, William, 35
Goethe, Johann Wolfgang von, 9, 122
Goldstein, Laurence, 134
Grahame, James, 55–9, 204n.161
Gray, Thomas, 123
Greece, classical, 11, 23, 73, 94, 129, 183, 207n.63
Greenland, 12, 19
Grundtvig, Nikolaj Frederik Severin, 85

Hagerup, Hans, 102
Hamilton, Paul, 4, 5, 7
Hare, Charles Julius, 24, 182–5
Hayley, William, 20, 84, 186
Hayman, John, 129
Hegel, Georg Wilhelm Friedrich, 131
Henriques, Alf, 121
Herbert, William, 17, 107–8, 119, 141–2

Hogg, James, 62, 86, 211n.149
Hogg, Thomas Jefferson, 25
Holberg, Ludwig, 102, 116, 123, 184
Holmes, Richard, 199n.64
Holsteen, the (Danish ship), 90
Homer, 10
Hope, Thomas, 220n.172
Hume, David, 128, 130–1, 137, 147
Hunt, Leigh, 20, 82, 84–5, 186, 187
Hustvedt, Sigurd, 192n.6
Høst, Jens Kragh, 92
Høyen, Niels Lauritz, 68

Ingemann, Bernhard Severin, 21, 104, 106–8, 116, 216n.73

Jamieson, Robert, 65, 75, 86, 94
Janowitz, Anne, 134
Janteloven, 154, 226n.159
Jones, Inigo, 70
Jones, Richard, 25, 29, 59, 65, 98, 166
Jutland, 1, 17, 20, 49, 54, 62, 72–4, 87, 100, 123, 144, 148

Kames, Henry Home, Lord, 131
Keats, John, 181
Kemble, John Richard, 80
Kerdu, Pierre-Marie Louis de Boisgelin, 95, 97, 173, 174
Kidd, Colin, 8
Kiel, Treaty of (1814), 19, 47, 59, 86, 111, 113, 118, 121, 142, 159, 172
Kliemann-Geisinger, Hendriette, 13
Klopstock, Gottlieb Friedrich, 40, 102, 103, 104
Købke, Christen, 62
Kronborg *see* Elsinore

Laing, David, 65, 86
Leersen, Joep, 7–8, 131, 194n.31
Lewis, Matthew Gregory, 22, 127
Lockhart, John Gibson, 20, 104, 110, 203–4n.157
Longfellow, Henry Wadsworth, 217n.101
Loudon, J. C., 209n.126
Lovejoy, Arthur O., 5
Lundbye, Johan Thomas, 68

Macdonald, James, 71–2, 96–7, 98–9, 117, 144–6, 151, 159, 161–2, 172
McFarland, G. F., 231n.1
Macpherson, James, Ossian, 10, 11, 72, 94, 123, 195n.47, 212n.11
Mallet, Paul Henri, 1, 93, 94
Malling, Ove, 86, 113, 132–3, 178–9
Malthus, Thomas, 61, 73
Manning, Susan, 129
Marshall, Joseph, 16–17, 23, 66, 148–51, 155, 157, 159, 164–6, 175
Mayes, Stanley, 227n.162
Molbech, Christian, 112, 119
Molden, Gunnar, 35
Molesworth, Robert, 14–16, 17, 28, 59, 66–7, 69, 116, 117, 137, 138, 139, 143, 148, 149, 150, 151, 161–3, 164, 166, 173, 174–5, 179, 230n.81
Møller, Lis, 93, 94, 96, 118, 192n.6
Mølsted, Christian, 39
Montsequieu, 130, 137, 143, 145, 147
Mortensen, Peter, 3, 8, 9
Musgrove, Sydney, 102, 216n.71

'national character', 22, 129–36
Nelson, Horatio, 2, 3, 19, 22, 25, 39, 40, 41, 42, 43, 45, 46, 47, 56, 86, 89, 128, 136
Niebuhr, Carsten, 31, 172
Nielsen, Jørgen Erik, 81, 95, 96, 112, 119, 205n.6
'North', the, 2, 10–14, 18, 20, 22, 23, 25–6, 28, 30, 33, 34, 38, 39, 49, 53, 58, 63, 68, 72, 77, 90, 94, 99, 107, 108, 110, 117, 126, 128, 136, 137, 140, 141, 146, 148, 149, 154, 164, 183–5, 224n.80
Norway, 13, 18, 19, 20, 31, 38, 85, 86, 90, 111, 113, 118, 142, 146, 159, 160, 164, 172
Nugent, Thomas, 61, 130, 204–5n.3
Nyerup, Rasmus, 67, 75, 156, 206n.26
Nyström, Per, 35

Oeder, Georg-Christian, 30
Oehlenschläger, Adam, 21, 24, 68, 104–7, 108, 109, 111, 113, 115, 116, 118, 155, 181–5, 216n.73
Oelsner, Gertrud, 96, 193n.17
Ollier, Charles, 181
Orwell, George, 184
Ossian see Macpherson, James
Oxfeldt, Elisabeth, 183, 196n.75

Paulesen, Erik, 82
Peacock, Thomas Love, 181
Pennant, Thomas, 73
Percy, Thomas, 1, 94
Pittock, Murray, 8
Pollen, Burton, 48, 203–4n.157
Pontoppidan, Eric, 116
Porter, Robert Ker, 78–9
Povlsen, Karen Klitgaard, 13, 66
Prickett, Stephen, 4, 5, 8

Rahbek, Karen Margrethe ('Kamma'), 19, 65, 91
Rahbek, Knud Lyne, 46, 95, 110, 113, 117, 118, 121, 122, 124
Rask, Rasmus, 95, 110
Rasmussen, Jens Rahbek, 201n.113
Reid, Thomas, 40
Riber, Hans Wilhelm, 103
Rix, Robert, 12, 13, 94, 99, 192n.6
Roberts, Daniel Sanjiv, 101
Rodd, Thomas, 42–3
Roe, Nicholas, 6
Romantic nationalism, 3, 4, 7–10, 12, 13, 14, 18, 20, 22, 24, 39, 44, 46, 68, 93, 101, 122, 129, 131–2, 133, 134, 136, 159, 178, 179, 181–5
Romanticism, European, 3–12, 24, 181–5
Roskilde, 69, 72, 157
Rousseau, Jean-Jacques, 83, 84, 147, 148, 169

Sachs, Jonathan, 133, 134, 135, 140
Saglia, Diego, 4, 5, 8, 9, 12, 96, 193n.13, 216n.72
Sandemose, Axel, 226n.159
Sanders, Karen, 192–3n.6

Savigny, Friedrich Carl von, 131
Scheibel, Holger, 121–2
Scott, Walter, 2, 55, 94, 95, 96, 102, 104, 107, 119, 122, 203n.157, 213n.13
Sebastiani, Silvia, 131, 222n.16
Sevaldsen, Jørgen, 57, 58, 201–2n.114, 202n.116
Shakespeare, William, 21, 41, 61, 75, 76, 77, 78, 79–81, 95, 111, 171, 220n.159, 229n.70
  first Danish translations of, 81, 93, 114, 120–5, 190–1
Shelley, Mary, 73
Shelley, Percy Bysshe, 5–6, 25–6, 47, 53, 54, 58, 73, 96, 155, 181, 231n.1
Smidt, Kristian, 21, 93, 120
Smith, Adam, 131, 135
Smith, Orianne, 202n.123, 202n.141
Smith, Sydney, 115, 167
Sommer, F. L., 46, 50–3, 58, 61
Sørensen, Øystein, 13
Southey, Robert, 19, 22, 25, 32, 43, 48, 86, 136, 137, 171, 211n.148, 229n.70
Stanley, Carl Frederik, 82
Steffens, Henrik, 183–4
Stevens, Robert, 214n.29
Stonehenge, 69–71, 73–4
Stråth, Bo, 13
Struensee, Johann Friedrich, 27, 131, 168–9, 170
Stukeley, William, 69–70, 71, 75
Sweden, 8, 13, 18, 19, 20, 31, 33, 38, 62, 77, 85, 86, 111, 113, 159, 217n.117
Swift, Jonathan, 102
Swinton, Andrew (pseudonym of William Thomson), 1, 20, 22, 50, 62, 172–3
Symes, Ruth, 14
Symonds, Barry, 101
Syv, Peter, 116

Thaarup, Christen, 102
Thaarup, Thomas, 113, 176–7
Thomson, James, 121, 172
Thomson, William, 31–4, 127, 143–4
Thorkelín, Grímur Jónsson, 57, 118
Thorvaldsen, Bertel, 2, 62, 105, 111, 114, 115, 122, 155, 220n.159
Tieck, Johann Ludwig, 18
Tordenskiold, Peter, 113
Trumpener, Katie, 8, 133

Vincent, Patrick, 4
Voltaire, 22, 90, 128, 153

Walker, William Sidney, 21, 112, 176, 188, 212n.2
Watson, Harry, 207n.50
Weber, Henry William, 94, 102
Wedgwood, Josiah, 177
Wellek, René, 4, 5
Wellington, 1st Duke of, 46, 121
Wessel, Johan Herman, 184
Wiedewelt, Johannes, 85
Willemoes, Peter, 39
Wilson, William Rae, 2, 68, 72, 142, 166–7, 171–2, 174, 224n.85, 230n.80
Wollstonecraft, Mary, 2, 16, 18, 25, 32, 34–8, 51, 54, 59, 61, 77, 92, 96, 99, 127, 128, 135, 138, 140, 141–2, 144, 146, 152–4, 160, 166, 168, 169
Wordsworth, William, 4, 8, 9, 10, 49, 78, 79, 96, 101, 103, 104, 106, 114, 135
Worm, Ole, 71, 116
Wraxall, Nathaniel, 26–9, 31, 32, 33, 34, 36, 55, 66, 67, 69–70, 71, 72, 75, 77, 137, 140, 143, 148, 149, 161, 164, 170, 172, 197n.17

Zealand, 61, 66, 69–71, 75–85, 137, 157, 171
Ziolkowski, Theodore, 4, 6

EU representative:
Easy Access System Europe
Mustamäe tee 50, 10621 Tallinn, Estonia
Gpsr.requests@easproject.com